T0315019

THE EVOLUTION OF THE CHINESE INTERNET

THE
EVOLUTION
OF THE
CHINESE
INTERNET

Creative Visibility in the Digital Public

SHAOHUA GUO

STANFORD UNIVERSITY PRESS

Stanford, California

STANFORD UNIVERSITY PRESS
Stanford, California

Printed in the United States of America on acid-free, archival-quality paper

Library of Congress Cataloging-in-Publication Data

Names: Guo, Shaohua (Professor of Chinese), author.

Title: The evolution of the Chinese Internet : creative visibility in the digital public / Shaohua Guo.

Description: Stanford, California : Stanford University Press, 2020. | Includes bibliographical references and index.

Identifiers: LCCN 2020025602 (print) | LCCN 2020025603 (ebook) | ISBN 9781503613775 (cloth) | ISBN 9781503614437 (paperback) | ISBN 9781503614444 (epub)

Subjects: LCSH: Internet—Social aspects—China. | Internet—Political aspects—China.

Classification: LCC HN740.Z9 I5674327 2020 (print) | LCC HN740.Z9 (ebook) | DDC 302.23/10951—dc23

LC record available at https://lccn.loc.gov/2020025602

LC ebook record available at https://lccn.loc.gov/2020025603

Cover design: Derek Thornton | Notch Design

Text design: Kevin Barrett Kane

Typeset at Stanford University Press in 10.5/15 Minion Pro

Dedicated to my grandparents
GUO CHUNHUAN *and* ZHANG YUMO
with love

CONTENTS

ACKNOWLEDGMENTS

During the 2003 outbreak of Severe Acute Respiratory Syndrome (SARS) in China, I was segregated from the outside world for several months. To avoid possible contagion of the disease, all activities on university campuses like mine were called off. For the first time, surfing the web became a "full-time job" for students. Confined in my dorm, I worked remotely as a part-time translator for Sina, the then dominant news portal in China, while frequenting bulletin board systems to gather information about life in the US. As was later acknowledged in the Chinese media, SARS cultivated a special emotional attachment to the Internet for a large number of Chinese. This is not only because online media challenged the state's initial cover-up of SARS, but also because this moment of national crisis fostered a strong sense of community among early netizens. I am one of them.

Nine years later, I developed my emotional ties to the Chinese Internet into a research project. For her support throughout this project, I am deeply indebted to my advisor, Sung-Sheng Yvonne Chang. Her unflagging enthusiasm for this project, commitment to the highest standards, and guidance during different stages of my writing have continuously inspired me. I also benefited immensely from the wisdom of Janet Staiger, Kirsten Cather, Madhavi Mallapragada, and Huaiyin Li. Their words of encouragement and invaluable insights throughout the development of this project were sincerely appreciated.

The process of writing a book marks the beginning of another intellectual journey. Over the years, I have gained much from conversations with mentors, colleagues, and friends at various venues, including conferences, symposiums, workshops, invited talks, and informal gatherings. I thank Guobin Yang and Zixue Tai for their groundbreaking work on digital media studies, as well as their genuine support and unswerving belief in the value of this project. I owe earnest thanks to colleagues and friends who I have formed conference panels with, who have expressed their excitement about this book, and who have extended support to me. Among them are Chiu-Mi Lai, Wen-Hua Teng, Jie Zhang, Wu Yuesu, Liu Hongtao, Xin Yang, Weiyu Zhang, Jack Linchuan Qiu, Min Jiang, Rongbin Han, Ashley Esarey, Jonathan Sullivan, Yong Hu, Shuyu Kong, Ruoyun Bai, Marcella Szablewicz, Haili Kong, John Crespi, Jin Feng, Jing Jiang, Elaine Yuan, Lin Zhang, Kristina Sakamoto Vassil, Yuliya Ilchuk, Lei Guang, Belinda Kong, Gloria Bien, Jia Liu, Xuefeng Feng, Zheng Guoqing, Haomin Gong, Yipeng Shen, Hongmei Sun, and Lydia B. Tang.

Carleton College, my home institution, offers me a most congenial and supportive environment. I am deeply indebted to Mark Hansell, Kathleen Ryor, Mariko Kaga, and Noboru Tomonari for bearing witness to my professional growth. They all have played instrumental roles during this process, and continually enlighten and humble me with their critical acumen, generous spirits, and senses of humor. I also thank Asuka Sango, Jay Beck, and Palmar Avatar for providing unreserved advice and inspiration whenever needed. I am grateful for the support of Cathy Yandell, Stacy Beckwith, Carol Donelan, Éva Pósfay, Chérif Keïta, Stephanie Cox, Christine Lac, Adriana Estill, Anita Chikkatur, and Jean Sherwin. I owe an eternal debt to the institutional support of Beverly Nagel, Gretchen Hofmeister, Christopher Tassava, and Dee Menning.

If writing is a lonesome journey, then friends are the ones who make this journey cheerful. I thank the long-term intellectual companionship of Yuki Xueying Guan, Li Yang, Haiyi Liu, and Jun Lei. They carefully read draft chapters and thoroughly discussed them with me over phone, instant messaging, and Skype calls. I am particularly grateful to Yingru Li, Zhongwei Liu, Ying Zhou, Enning Zhang, Kwangjin Lee, and Tianyang Wang for lending me their unequivocal support through all of the ups and downs. I express my appreciation toward friends and colleagues Gu Haihui, Li Weidong, Zhou Peiyao, Zheng Tingying, Fu Yanyan, Peng Kun, Zhang Lei, Duan Ran, Guo Yun, Wei Shouhua, Hao Lei, Fan Xinzheng, Zhao Ruiqi, and Liu Xinchuan, for introducing to me industry contacts and making my fieldwork in China a lot more fun and productive. Naturally, I also owe my deepest gratitude to all the interviewees who spent enormous amounts of time offering their observations on Internet culture in China.

The publication of this book could not have been possible without the generous funding support from the Henry Luce Foundation/ACLS Program in China Studies Postdoctoral Fellowship. I am also indebted to Carleton College for its provision of the following grants to support this work: Large Faculty Development Fellowship Award, Small Faculty Development Endowment Award, Faculty Research and Assistance Fund, Humanities Center Student Research Assistant Grant, and Research Assistantship Class of '55. A sabbatical leave from Carleton College in the 2017–18 academic year allowed me the time to complete the book. I also gratefully acknowledge the wonderful research assistance of four brilliant Carls: Marianne Gunnarsson '22, Harry Wolff Landau '21, Madeline Geitz '17, and Sawyer Middleleer '16. I have learned so much from them.

At Stanford University Press, I appreciate the support of Sunna Juhn, Susan Karani, and Marcela Cristina Maxfield, a strong advocate of this project since our first meeting. I could not possibly imagine a smoother way to get a book published. I also wish to extend my sincere thanks to my copyeditor, Lisa Wehrle, and my editor, Rachel Evan Webb, a critical reader of earlier drafts. I have benefited so much from their insightful comments.

The book incorporates materials from three earlier publications, with deletions, additions, and revisions: "The Appeal of Style: Han Han and Microcultural Contention in Digital China," *Modern Chinese Literature and Culture* 28, no. 2 (2016): 90–138; "'Occupying' the Internet: State Media and the Reinvention of Official Culture Online," *Communication and the Public* 3, no. 1 (2018): 19–33; "Ruled by Attention: A Case Study of Professional Digital Attention Agents at Sina.com and the Chinese Blogosphere," *International Journal of Cultural Studies* 19, no. 4 (2016): 407–23. I thank the Ohio State University and SAGE Publishing for granting me the permission to use these materials.

Last, but by no means least, I convey my gratitude to my family, near and far, for their unreserved love and support over the years. I am deeply indebted to my grandparents and parents who have always encouraged me to go my own way. My grandfather passed away when I was wrapping up my dissertation and preparing for defense. Although he did not get to see this book come to fruition, I know he would be proud of me. My parents, each in their own distinctive way, have taught me about commitment and integrity. My uncles, aunts, and cousins always take such good care of me whenever I get back to China. I am also particularly thankful to my husband, Jianping Song, who always is interested to listen to all my observations on current events and shares with me his insights. While he completely fits the stereotype of a science major, I consider myself a true beneficiary in this regard. Without his patience, constant encouragement, and positive feedback, I would never have been able to come this far.

As I neared the completion of this book in March 2020, the global coronavirus pandemic was posing severe challenges to all walks of life, on a much broader scale than did SARS. Since the SARS outbreak in 2003, the digital ecosystems in China have changed drastically, due in part to the proliferation of social media platforms, the dominance of mobile applications, and ever-changing user demographics. Started in the mid-1990s as an alternative space, the Chinese Internet today showcases the enhanced corporate management of user-generated content, the prominent visibility of state actors online, and the development of a full-fledged model of e-commerce. Internet users researching COVID-19 find themselves embroiled in endless battles to access relevant information and discern truth from rumor. Pandemic-inspired measures such as border controls, suspended flights, and lockdowns further impede the essential ideas of mobility and utopianism promised by technological modernization. However, despite all the chaos and political strife, the world is more closely connected than ever before. An endorsement of global solidarity and human dignity is perhaps the only way to get out of these predicaments and future ones. Digital technologies contribute to this process in no small way.

THE EVOLUTION OF THE CHINESE INTERNET

A CULTURAL REVOLUTION IN CHINA'S DIGITAL AGE

THE HISTORY OF MODERN CHINA is a history of *revolution*—or the potential to bring about drastic societal change.[1] The opening up of China to the global Internet in 1994 immediately stirred excitement among social elites, entrepreneurs, China observers, and policymakers worldwide regarding the new possibilities created by digital technologies. Among these possibilities, the prospect of China's radical transition into a democratic country has been the most alluring.

Early studies of the Internet in China demonstrate the placement of these high hopes on digital technologies, along with the sense of disillusionment that arose when they seemed to fail to deliver such promises. These studies fall under one of two categories: "narratives of revolution" and "narratives of closure." Narratives of revolution address the extent to which digital technologies may drive the democratization of political systems in authoritarian regimes. Scholars have discussed, for instance, how dissident groups use the Internet to promote their political agendas and resist governmental control.[2] By highlighting individual agency, this body of literature envisions the rejuvenation of a revolutionary spirit from the nascent online space that, ultimately, may facilitate the progress of democratization. In contrast, narratives of closure foreground the omnipotence of the Chinese state in its power to enforce strict control over media and society, thereby closing the space for free expression.[3] In these narratives, digital technologies primarily serve the interests of the state, allowing the suffocation of free speech and the violation of human rights.

While addressing different subject matters, both narratives of revolution and narratives of closure assume that technological breakthroughs will either induce a radical break away from existing sociopolitical structures or contribute to sustaining authoritarian rule. Nevertheless, as the history of electronic inventions has shown, technological breakthrough is never a single event isolated from social needs, economic and political factors, and the technological imaginary.[4] Moreover, both narratives apply the "repressive hypothesis"[5] that characterizes the Chinese government and Internet users as antagonistic, the former being a monolithic force that suppresses the latter.

In her insightful study of sexuality in China, Elaine Jeffreys reveals how a prevalent interpretation of the "repressive hypothesis" conceptualizes sexual expressions as "perceived sites of resistance to official discourses."[6] However, this approach dismisses the positive role that state-affiliated actors—including administrators, media representatives, and university professors—play in creating new forms of sexual culture.[7] Xiaobing Tang points out how the "dissidence hypothesis," a popular view that "presupposes any expression of criticism voiced in China to be an act of political dissidence against a repressive regime,"[8] offers a reductive interpretation of Chinese visual culture. Internet studies and popular commentaries on the subject of digital media in China frequently reiterate this rhetoric, which tends to reinforce the prevalent ideological demarcations between democracy and autocracy, between freedom of speech and governmental control. The binary opposition between the state and its citizens not only ignores the reality of a more sophisticated interplay between the two, but also results in a narrowly defined, politicized study of the Chinese Internet that neglects the daily experiences of netizens.

As China has moved away from totalitarianism toward hegemonic rule, the state has prioritized using a system of "bargaining and reciprocity"[9] over the adoption of coercive measures to reach a consensus with multiple parties. Under the ruling logic of "responsive authoritarianism,"[10] the Chinese state dynamically makes adjustments to cope with the changing socioeconomic environment. Media have not only played a pivotal role in the process of "manufactur[ing] consent,"[11] they have also gained a considerable amount of bargaining power and autonomy from the Party-state. This dynamic process of negotiation opens up opportunities for the emergence of new narratives and social norms that may align with state interests at some times, while at other times they may be oppositional to official discourses.[12]

Chinese Internet studies in recent years have strived to move beyond the aforementioned binary narratives and investigate how the intricate dynamics between the state, semi-official forces, and nonstate actors have jointly catalyzed China's technological modernization process. Scholarly works have addressed the reinvented modes of state governance online,[13] the political economy of new media sectors,[14] and the complexity of state-society relations.[15] Literary and communications scholars have studied the ways in which the online space constitutes a crucial site for civic engagement, leisure activities, and the rejuvenation of creative writing.[16] Delving into various forms of digital literary experiments, including narrative poetry, microfiction, and erotic fiction, Michel Hockx analyzes how the transgressive dimension of online literature challenges publishing norms and pushes the limits of individual expression.[17] Heather Inwood addresses how China's media spaces revive the production, circulation, and consumption of poetry, a conventionally high-brow genre.[18] In contrast, Jin Feng examines the enormous popularity of Internet romance fiction, and analyzes how romance readers and writers construct their identities, sometimes by challenging the patriarchal system and other times by aligning with it.[19] The collaborative work of Haomin Gong and Xin Yang covers a wide range of Internet phenomena, from online spoofing to Internet literature and its adaptation to visual formats.[20]

Despite these insightful works, little critical attention has been devoted to how and why an ingenious Internet culture has flourished in China, under a seemingly repressive authoritarian regime that straddles socialist legacies and a global capitalist economy. In this respect, this book addresses the ambivalence, nuances, and paradoxes surrounding the Chinese Internet. I define the Chinese Internet as a product of the ways in which Chinese-language users navigate digital spaces and make sense of their everyday lives. Indeed, "netizen" (*wangmin*, "net citizen"), the term by which Internet users in China refer to themselves, already denotes the strong sense of entitlement to the online space that has emerged since 1994. These netizens' active engagement with the Internet, as both a technology and cultural form, constitutes the primary driving force behind the vitality of Chinese popular culture. As such, this book investigates the cultural dimension of Internet use through the four most dynamic discursive spaces to emerge over the past two decades in China (1994–2019): the bulletin board system, the blog, the microblog (Weibo), and WeChat (Weixin). The creation of these digital platforms not only showcases the local appropriation of global technologies in China but also exemplifies how Internet users' mundane activities hold significant potential for forging politically minded citizens at a micro level. As these four applications constitute the main veins of the developmental history of China's Internet, a systematic investigation of digital cultural formation deriving from these platforms will cover the major trends, controversies, and idiosyncrasies of the Chinese Internet.

Central to this book's inquiry are the ways in which culture has been redefined, reappropriated, and reshaped in China's digital era, and how developments in technological features have changed the function of culture accordingly. As Raymond Williams writes, culture is "a particular way of life which expresses certain meanings and values not only in art and learning, but also in institutions and ordinary behaviour."[21] Everyday life is not only "the site in which the popular meanings and uses of new media are negotiated and played out,"[22] but is itself constantly transformed by new technologies. In detailing Internet users' daily experiences, I foreground the interconnections of these four platforms as well as their roles in promoting user-generated content, configuring new modes of publicity, and shaping emerging forms of public culture in contemporary society. I argue that the vitality of Chinese digital culture is rooted in the dynamic process of negotiation, collaboration, and contestation enacted by the interplay of diverse agents, including the state, cultural institutions, commercial entities, and Internet users. These actors compete for discursive legitimacy—defined by their deployment of discursive strategies, mobilization tactics, and established institutional or cultural authority. Their competition constitutes the primary driving force of digital innovation in China. By delineating this process of competition for discursive power among multifarious players, this book highlights the pivotal roles that cultural history, technological platforms, and individual agency have played in shaping the sociopolitical meanings of the Chinese Internet.

Next, I provide a historical backdrop for this study by giving an overview of the state's role in engineering the transformation of Chinese media and society.

Censoring Culture, Engineering Culture

Since the founding of the Chinese Communist Party (CCP) in 1921, literature and the arts have been essential components of the CCP's "mass line" policy, and have played a vital role in mobilizing and educating the masses. In 1942, Mao Zedong's famous "Talks at the Conference on Literature and Art" in Yan'an reinforced the importance of mass line policy, which constituted a turning point in modern Chinese literature and culture. Mao emphasized that literature and the arts should serve the revolution and the people, as represented by workers, peasants, soldiers, and the urban petty bourgeoisie. The political stance of literary and artistic works matters more than their intrinsic qualities. The "Talks" were subsequently canonized and treated as the ultimate guideline for literary and artistic policies since the founding of the People's Republic of China (PRC) in 1949.[23] Taking the Soviet cultural system as its model, the state eliminated private ownership and established cultural institutions to exert political control over the production of art. The founding in 1949 of the Film Bureau and the All-China Federation of Literary and Art Workers (renamed the Chinese Writers' Association in 1953) illustrates these endeavors to control at the central and provincial levels.[24] From 1949 to 1976, amidst political upheaval, the state owned, controlled, and financed all media organizations, including newspapers, journals, publishing houses, radio stations, movie studios, and TV stations. Cultural works were used primarily as ideological tools. The severe decline in the production of artistic and literary works reached its height during the Great Proletarian Cultural Revolution (1966–76). Notably, even during this chaotic historical period, authorities demonstrated their ambition to "invent a new mass culture" by reforming Peking operas and encouraging amateur participation in the process of cultural production.[25]

Mao's death in 1976 and the subsequent change of political leadership ushered in a new era in modern Chinese history. Since 1978, China has launched a series of economic reforms. Media commercialization has been an integral part of this process. The watershed moment was the removal of the restrictions on media advertising in 1978, followed by the appearance of the first TV advertising on the Shanghai-based Dragon TV in the same year. This officially marked the recognition of media space as a tradable commodity. Subsequently, the state-led economic reforms have fostered a fundamental change from perceiving cultural products as enlightening and ideological tools to viewing them as consumable goods. With the exception of a few central Communist Party organs, the state began to cut back on its subsidization of media organizations and required them to gain financial independence. The Chinese state also launched a series of campaigns to promote the cultivation and consumption of popular culture, after realizing that popular culture was conducive to furthering economic reforms.[26] Then, following China's entry into the World Trade Organization in 2001, Jiang Zemin, the then–secretary general of the CCP, distinguished "cultural undertakings" (*wenhua shiye*) from "cultural industry" (*wenhua chanye*) in his report to the Sixteenth National Party Congress. The notion of "cultural industry" marked the official recognition of cultural production as a commercial activity and enterprise.[27] In July 2003, the Party-state started a reform program that aimed to shift "the culture sector, including the media, from the periphery of policy-making to the core."[28] Since 2004, the culture industry has experienced an annual growth of 15 to 20 percent.[29] In the twelfth Five-Year Plan (2011–15), the state envisioned the cultural sector to be China's "pillar industry," which "contributes five per cent or more of the mainland's annual gross domestic product."[30] China's thirteenth Five-Year Plan (2016–20) further emphasized the leading role that innovation plays in science and technology, and propagated the slogan "created in China" with an emphasis on "technological innovation and cultural creativity."[31]

This overview of China's strategic plan demonstrates the flexible means by which the state has defined culture and its functions at different times. Accordingly, the Chinese state has assumed a variety of roles in its efforts to capitalize on culture, acting not only as a censor and guardian of social norms and value systems or a tool for propagating official ideologies, but also as a facilitator during the entire transformative process. To echo Jing Wang's point, an investigation of "the mutually constitutive relationship between state policies and popular social discourses"[32] is fundamental to understanding the cultural dynamics of the contemporary era. The development of the field of popular culture, in which the Internet soon arose as a vital player, has become indispensable with the state's vision of culture as an industry.

Structural Transformation of the Cultural Field

Since the 1980s, the restructuring of the cultural field[33] has transformed media organizations from government mouthpieces into self-financed business enterprises at the central, provincial, and prefectural levels. In the field of cinematic production, film reform brought about a total institutional restructuring that started at the level of distribution and exhibition and later extended into production.[34] The ultimate goal was to decentralize the state-run film industry, grant local distributors more financial autonomy and responsibility, and define cinema as an industrial product. Many state-owned film studios carried significant debt and had to adopt reform measures to fix their dire financial situations, including seeking private funding and opportunities for coproduction with international players.[35] Meanwhile, Hollywood's reentry into the mainland market in 1994 sparked a nationalistic concern about the viability of the domestic movie industry. Both film critics and industry practitioners made a populist turn, and considered producing films for popular entertainment as the only solution to get the movie industry out of its financial trouble. Feng Xiaogang's New Year Pictures of the late 1990s, soon followed by the 2001 release of China's first blockbuster film, *Hero*, are some early examples of successful commercial movies. The prominence of commercial filmmaking increased in the 2010s, along with the popularization of such new concepts as "IP movies" and "fan movies" (*fensi dianying*). Both terms illustrate the alliance that arose between the Internet and the movie industry, and celebrate the phenomenal consuming power of fans, since the cinematic adaptation of existing online works—known as "IP" (intellectual property)—that already enjoyed a strong fan base was often found to be commercially successful. In this era, the artistic quality of movies became less relevant. In the meantime, propaganda movies exhibited a significant shift to incorporate commercial elements, such as star cameos and special effects, in an effort to create greater visual appeal.[36] Simply put, from the mid-1990s onward, the entertainment function of Chinese cinema was greatly enhanced.

The surge of the entertainment tide is even more evident in the television industry, which was formerly monopolized by the state-sponsored China Central Television (CCTV), the only national-level broadcaster in China. Under the rule of the market, all television stations at the provincial and municipal levels have gone through reforms to become financially self-reliant. Commercial advertising has come to constitute nearly 95 percent of television stations' revenues.[37] As news programs are still heavily controlled by the state, entertainment-oriented programs flourish on regional TV stations. Less restrained by propaganda aims, channels such as Hunan Satellite TV, Zhejiang Satellite TV, and Jiangsu Satellite TV have taken the lead and demonstrated a greater degree of ingenuity in creating entertainment shows, producing TV dramas, and attracting a global audience. Meanwhile, CCTV has transformed into a giant media conglomerate and possesses vast production and distribution resources. It owns multiple corporations in charge of producing TV dramas, documentaries, and science and educational films, in addition to its ownership of TV journals, newspapers, and an online network. To fulfill the dual needs of market demand and ideological control, CCTV has invested in and produced a large variety of prime-time dramas that have gained unprecedented popularity in both the domestic and overseas markets. CCTV's evolution illustrates the crucial transformation of a dominant mainstream culture that aims to consolidate the state's ideological control, to represent China on the global stage, and to have popular appeal all at the same time. Overall, the commercialization of Chinese television has also been a process of internationalization, as illustrated by the adoption of a coproduction model in producing television dramas, the consolidation of media groups, and the convergence of Chinese television outlets with online video platforms.[38]

In the arena of print media, institutional reform has transformed publishing houses and literary institutions into self-reliant entities that do not merely serve as ideological tools of the state. Under the socialist literary system, writing and publishing activities were fully sponsored by the state, with the Chinese Writers' Association at the national and local levels mediating the relationship between writers and the Communist Party's Department of Propaganda. Since the inauguration of reform in the 1980s, the state has significantly reduced funding to literary magazines and institutions, while the decentralization of distribution channels has enabled the rise of secondhand book agents and the private book distribution system.[39] While serious literature has been losing its appeal, the boom in popular reading has enhanced the entertainment function of literature, as represented by the popularity of women's writing, urban fiction, and teen literature.[40] On a broad scale, the emergence of leisure newspapers, magazines, and bestsellers exemplified the rapid growth of commercial print media from the mid-1990s until 2012, when the breathtakingly rapid development of digitalization and the comprehensive expansion of advertising to Internet-based media began to pose severe challenges to print outlets.

Since China's economic reforms, the cultural field has experienced a fundamental structural transformation. Amidst the accelerated pace of media commercialization in the 1990s—as traditional media struggled with the market logic because of their transition from propaganda organizations into business entities—the Internet industry took off at an unprecedented speed because of state support. Free from the legacy of the previously centralized institutional constraints that hamper news, television, and literature outlets, Internet media have enjoyed a greater degree of freedom when experimenting with commercial mechanisms. The declining appeal of state media and propaganda organizations, the institutional reform of traditional media outlets, and massive state investment directed toward building up new media infrastructure have granted an unprecedented competitive advantage to China's Internet industry. As the fastest-growing commercial medium, the Internet not only shaped the developmental trajectory of China's entertainment culture, but it also opened up a discursive space for civic engagement, political deliberation, and creative practices. From the mid-1990s onward, the intricate dynamics between new and "old" media in transition—with each striving for recognition, visibility, content authority, and market share—have contributed to an unprecedented level of cultural productivity in the contemporary era.

The Network of Visibility

The "eyes" of the Internet in China—the gaze that the state directs onto Internet users and industry practitioners—have drawn much research interest. In contrast to the flourishing of research findings on what is made *invisible* online, such as monitored, censored, and removed content, we know little about the driving mechanisms that grant *visibility* to particular kinds or instances of user-generated content. On occasions of social controversy, the terms "stir fry" (*chaozuo*) and "pushing hands" (*tuishou*) often indicate the manipulation of commercial media to promote sensational issues. These general terms hint at a politics of visibility at work on the Chinese Internet, but they do not elucidate the operational logic of the Internet as a business and how it differs from the way traditional media operate. What strategies do Internet corporations adopt to enhance their visibility? How do they decide when to promote certain issues, and when not to? How exactly do network media differ from traditional media when reporting on sensitive issues? A crucial intermediary in shaping what is visible online, the operational logic of Internet media deserves scrutiny.

In addition to the role of Internet corporations, other mechanisms that shape visibility online involve the dominant official media and traditional media outlets. While state media largely manage discursive parameters, the marketized news media have emerged as powerful players in pushing for the opening up of discursive spaces since the 1990s. In the meantime, traditional media outlets have actively experimented with digital publishing and engaged in fierce competition with emerging Internet portals for user attention, content authority, and market share.

I propose "the network of visibility" as an analytical lens to examine the mechanisms behind the vibrancy of online culture in China. I analyze the network of visibility through the process of competition for (1) user attention, and (2) content authority among Internet corporations, media outlets, and individual players in the cultural realm. Competition for user attention refers to how the desire of corporations and individuals to seek, retain, and exchange attention underscores the significance of attention in a click-driven Internet industry. Competition for content authority refers to the constantly evolving process by which media institutions—new and old, official, semi-official, and commercial—and individual players strive to restore, sustain, or challenge discursive legitimacy. These two dimensions of competition, one emphasizing the economic rule of monetizing user attention and the other focusing on the possession and acquisition of authoritative voices, weave the network of visibility that shapes what is seen online, by whom, and in what way. In turn, the myriad ways of seeing, ranging from surveillance and censorship to consuming online content to digital witnessing that bears political implications, indicate different degrees of viewer involvement with the subject matter being attended to, and thereby contribute significantly to the vibrancy of the online sphere.

The Rule of Attention

Although the study of human attention has had a long tradition in the fields of psychology, physiology, and education,[41] the emphasis on attention as a scarce commodity did not emerge until the rise of postindustrial economies. In 1971, Herbert Simon, a Nobel Prize–winning economist, first pinpointed the prominent role attention plays against the backdrop of an information explosion.[42] Given the definite nature of attention as "focused mental engagement on a particular item of information,"[43] it is no longer the seeking of information but the competition for attention, created by an information explosion, that primarily drives the economy. The attention economy, therefore, not only transforms the old economy based "on money, on the market, and on the industrialized exchange, distribution and production of standardized material goods," it also redefines the role information plays in a postindustrial economy.[44] This counterbalancing dynamic of information and attention, which is "de-materializ[ed] and virtualiz[ed]," consolidates the central role of attention in the digital economy.[45] Georg Franck conceptualizes attention as "capital" that is involved in a myriad of business activities, such as investment, circulation, transaction, and more capital generation. The practical need of Internet businesses to monetize user attention, the technological features of new media, and the individual's desire for self-expression and reciprocating attention on the web foreground the significance of attention in the digital age.

While vying for user attention has always been important for the cultural industry, the idiosyncrasies of the web leverage the importance of attention for online businesses. The core elements of the web—hyperlinks, hypertext, permalinks, and the search function—make it extremely easy for new media users to control what they attend to. Attention and diversion of attention are nearly concurrent in the online space. When Internet users engage in specific activities (browsing, writing, playing games, watching videos, etc.), they also are continuously distracted by other "attractions," such as links to related items, pop-up and inline text ads, instant messaging applications, and so on. Consequently, attention online is fickle, transient, and easily transferable. Internet companies that succeed in capturing public attention can quickly reap substantial rewards by selling advertising space, launching an initial public offering, and setting up new business models. Conversely, websites that suffer from attention deficit can fail to attract advertising agencies and quickly encounter dire financial situations. The dynamic between attention and capital pressures websites to employ multifaceted strategies to capture and keep a user's attention. In addition, web technologies enable a more precise manner of analyzing attention-related data than traditional media outlets, and position Internet users under 24/7 surveillance. Commonly used measurement data range from page rank in search and the number of page views, click-throughs, and subscribers of a website, to viewer preferences and activities recorded in excruciating detail. These hard data serve both as quantifiable indicators of the attention a website generates and a barometer of user preferences, which in turn may shape the offerings of Internet content providers. Moreover, these data may function as major evaluation standards for venture capitalists, investors, and advertising agencies to aid in making business decisions.

While Internet companies attend to customer needs by analyzing user behaviors and soliciting feedback, the flourishing of self-expression online foregrounds the importance of reciprocating attention among individual users. From it has emerged a specific netiquette and online sociality. Owing to the flourishing of personal media channels and the high level of interactivity facilitated by Web 2.0 technologies, an explosion of self-expression now lives in symbiosis with a yearning for others' attention. Internet users not only exert a large amount of control over what they browse, but they also contribute actively to content. Thus online attention is both calculated using hard data and reified in such forms as blogs, instant messaging, Wikis, and forum posts. Reciprocating attention is a crucial part of any web dynamic and is vital to establishing and maintaining the bonds between Internet users. It is represented by such things as an exchange of messages, a reply to others' posts, a click on the "like" button on Facebook, or a visit and link to others' blogs. As reciprocating attentive behavior shapes new social norms online, attention management programs reinforce this norm by constantly notifying users about their visitors and urging them to pay a return visit. Moreover, individuals capable of gathering more attention possess a great degree of symbolic prestige, which may be converted into upward career opportunities.

This dominant rule of attention and its role in shaping the emerging code of netiquette has given rise to new forms of visibility, alongside "new forms of action and interaction" in the digital sphere.[46] As John B. Thompson argues, online media play an unprecedentedly prominent role in mediating the relationship between power and visibility.[47] The old surveillance model, in which the few in positions of power monitor the powerless majority, takes a reverse turn since the powerful few may be subject to grassroots surveillance by the many.[48] The gaze that Internet users project on authorities, commercial portals, trivial daily matters, and each other brings forth a variety of connotations that can be found in the act of looking. The gaze of Internet users may take myriad forms, ranging from witnessing and spectating to surveillance to paying attention (*guanzhu*). While some forms of looking are more active than others, the collective attention that netizens projected onto societal issues constitutes the primary driving force of web-based incidents. These incidents range from the frivolous celebration of play, like the birth of China's first Internet celebrity Furong Jiejie (Sister Lotus), to more serious political pursuits that aim at defending social justice, fighting against corruption, and pushing for free expression. Oftentimes, the eruption of these incidents links to commercial portals' interest in whipping up public sentiment to increase web traffic. Driven by the rule of attention, the prominence of particular user-generated content online embodies the symbiotic relationship between the flourishing of citizen activism and the boom in entertainment culture in China's digital age.

Competition for Content Authority

In addition to the role the rule of attention plays in influencing content, dominant official media and traditional media outlets are important gate-keepers that define content authority. While official media remains authoritative, commercial print media have experienced a golden period of growth from the late 1990s until around 2012. This transition is best represented by commercial newspapers. Despite being primarily driven by market forces, commercial newspapers have allowed greater space for journalistic reporting and helped investigative journalism to flourish.[49] Consequently, these newspapers, and their investigative journalists, have gained a much greater degree of credibility and prestige among urban audiences than official newspapers.[50] This golden period of growth for commercial print media occurred concurrently with the rapid takeoff of the Internet industry. As Internet media are not officially authorized to conduct interviews and release news, except in less-sensitive areas such as entertainment and sports, portal news websites often plagiarized news content from traditional media outlets. From 1998 to 2000, a growing tension formed between Internet media and traditional media outlets. On April 16, 1999, twenty-three traditional news media organizations gathered in Beijing and called for increased societal attention to online copyright infringement. These organizations issued the "Network Media of Chinese Press Convention" (*Zhongguo xinwenjie wangluo meiti gongyue*), requesting that Internet news media portals obtain authorization and compensate the traditional news organizations before quoting and publishing their news content.[51] The impasse between the new and traditional media organizations lasted until the end of 1999, when major commercial portals, represented by Sina, signed contracts with the traditional media organizations and began to build strategic alliances with them.[52] On November 6, 2000, the government issued the first stipulation regarding

Internet news media. The stipulation prohibits web portal companies from using unauthorized press sources, instead requiring web portals to comply with strict sanctions when dealing with both internal and external news reports.[53]

The resolution of these conflicts fostered more than ten years of strategic alliance between Internet news media and traditional media outlets. Up until 2012, the newspaper industry as a whole exhibited a steady growth in advertising revenue and audience reception. From 1990 to 2003, the gross advertising revenue of newspapers increased from 677 million RMB to 24.301 billion RMB, second only to the advertising revenue of the television industry.[54] The number of magazines in publication increased from 5,751 in 1990, to 9,029 in 2002, and magazine advertising revenue increased from 87 million RMB to 1.521 billion RMB in the same time period.[55] Constituting an important content feeder for online portals, traditional media outlets have significantly enhanced their influence via the Internet.[56] Reciprocally, given the prestige and credibility that traditional news media have established, their coverage of online content offers symbolic recognition to Internet media portals. On occasions of social controversies, while the Internet constitutes the primary site of discussion accessible to every Internet user, the participation of official and traditional media outlets significantly steers the discussion. My investigation of web-based incidents in this book demonstrates how traditional media and dominant official media enhance the legitimacy of Internet media in some cases, while in other instances they suppress voices that emerge online, the dynamic between these media thus constantly shaping the ecology of the online space.

In response to the state's policies pertaining to news coverage, Internet portals have invented alternative practices that focus on timeliness and interactivity of editorial news content to cultivate their market appeal. The strategies of Sina, the leading news portal in China, represent such practices. In addition to sending out reporters to cover events, at its peak Sina had signed contracts with 1,500 media organizations to carry their reports and provide comprehensive coverage of major events.[57] Sina was the first domestic online media portal to implement twenty-four-hour rolling news updates. They also pioneered different methods of user interaction through VIP chat rooms, enabling comment boxes for each news item, and setting up a rating system based on the popularity of a news item and its comments. This emphasis on user experience and interactivity has encouraged a fundamental change in the function of editors in the dotcom era. For instance, editors of all Sina channels regularly analyze general trends of user preferences, based on the quantitative statistics of page views, web traffic during different time periods, and ranking lists of real-time news feeds and user comments.[58] In addition to screening and cross-posting news items, editors process netizens' comments, conduct online surveys, compile special issues, and invite Internet users to join online chats with special guests.[59]

These features of commercial portals make traditional media's experimentation with online editions pale in comparison. News media and governmental agencies took the lead among traditional media outlets in developing dedicated websites. As of mid-1999, 14.6 percent of newspapers in China had established an online presence.[60] In February 2000, the state began to develop central media organizations online, including Xinhua News Agency, *China Daily*, *People's Daily*, and China Radio International.[61] While aiming at increasing the influence of traditional and dominant media, these websites mostly reposted content already available in print, thereby falling far behind commercial portals in terms of popularity, economic gain, and timeliness in responding to user inquiries.[62] Nevertheless, although traditional news media and government websites were less popular, they possessed greater control over the authorial voice, dictating what was said and how it was said.

From the 2010s onward, the media ecology of China has exhibited another radical shift compared to twenty years prior. The rapid development of digitalization, the prevalence of smartphone use, and the sweeping expansion of advertising into Internet-based media posed new challenges to print outlets. In 2012, the golden period of growth for commercial print media officially came to an end. Back in 2003, Internet advertising revenue took sixth place among revenue figures for all media outlets, falling far behind television, newspapers, radio broadcasts, and magazines.[63] However, the compound growth rate of Internet advertising was 129.27 percent from 1999 to 2003, far exceeding that of all other media types.[64] In 2012, the advertising revenue of newspapers dropped for the first time, by 19.2 percent,[65] a trend that only worsened with time. In 2013, newspapers reported an 81 percent decline in print advertising. The drop rate reached 183 percent and 354 percent in 2014 and 2015 respectively.[66] Relatedly, from 2011 to 2016, the distribution numbers of newspapers decreased steadily, from 46.743 billion in 2011, to 39.007 billion in 2016.[67]

The rise and fall of metro newspapers (*dushi bao*) is a microcosm of this overall trend in print media. A result of economic reforms, metro newspapers first emerged in the capital cities of most provinces in China in 1993. These newspapers offer lively coverage of stories pertaining to urban residents' daily lives[68] and are distinguished from Party-sponsored newspapers by their funding source, style of writing, and flexibility of reportage.[69] Some of the most influential metro newspapers include the *Southern Metropolis Daily* (*Nanfang dushibao*), *Western China Metropolis Daily* (*Huaxi dushibao*), and *Chengdu Business News* (*Chengdu shangbao*). In 2012, metro newspapers commanded more than 70 percent of the market share of the newspaper industry.[70] Since then, metro newspapers have witnessed a drastic decline. In 2017, more than forty newspapers announced permanent shutdowns, including the influential *Beijing Times* (*Jinghua shidao*), *Morning Express* (*Jinri zaobao*), and *Oriental Morning Post* (*Dongfang zaobao*).[71] Alternatively, some media groups merged existing newspapers, published at longer intervals to reduce costs, transfered some of their content to online portals, and experimented with newly launched news platforms online.[72]

In contrast to this sharp decline in commercial print media, the 2010s onward have witnessed the enhanced visibility and viability of official media. Catalyzed by the new political climate, politically oriented newspapers have secured more funding and increased readership.[73] More important, alongside the implementation of new regulatory measures,[74] the formerly sporadic experimentation with e-governance via blogging and microblogging has developed into a full-scale practice since President Xi Jinping took office in 2012.[75] Several governmental agencies, as represented by *People's Daily* and the Communist Youth League of China, have begun to appropriate fan culture to make emotional appeals to the public, reinventing propaganda as they do so.

Since the mid-1990s, the intricate dynamics between the new and "old" media have been constantly shifting. The tension, cooperation, and competition among these major actors, including commercial print media and their online portals, state media, and commercial websites, have jointly shaped the nature of authoritative content at different stages of China's Internet development. Consequently, what defines content authority is not static but subject to fluid configuration throughout the process of competing for discursive legitimacy and market share that occurs among these players. The credibility and authority that media institutions have accumulated, the prestige and connections individuals have established, and the technological affordances of digital media all factor into shaping content authority online. Together, the economic rule of attention and the sociocultural process of contestation involved in the acquisition of content authority weave the web of visibility, which foregrounds creative practices, individual aspirations, and vibrant cultural formation on major digital platforms.

Digital Cultural Formation through Technological Platforms

An emerging area of research, platform studies draw insights from the fields of political economy, management literature, software studies, and labor studies.[76] Broadly speaking, digital platforms refer to "mixtures of software, hardware, operations, and networks. . . . [T]hey provide a set of shared techniques, technologies, and interfaces to a broad set of users who can build what they want on a stable substrate."[77] Studies of digital platforms have addressed issues ranging from labor relations to corporate responsibilities to governance.[78] For instance, Tarleton Gillespie argues that commercial companies employ the term "platform" to highlight their role as intermediaries, thereby neutralizing corporations' acts of commodifying user data to avoid getting involved with potential disputes regarding platform use.[79] Researchers also analyze platforms' role in arranging the division of labor,[80] as well as the ways in which "platformativity," defined as "performativity via platforms,"[81] remediates the relations between users and platforms, individualism and collectivity. Similarly, scholarship on Chinese platforms has focused on such issues as business strategies of Internet corporations, digital labor, and gender relations that emerge from the E-commerce platform Alibaba,[82] app-based transportation service Didi,[83] and live streaming platforms.[84]

In contrast to the proliferation of scholarly writings on platforms from the economic, legal, and infrastructural perspectives,[85] little critical attention is devoted to the role that platforms play in promoting, censoring, and fostering the creation of user-generated content online. With few notable exceptions,[86] the ways in which cultural tradition, media ecosystems, and content creators have significantly shaped the substance and dynamics of content production, manners of content management, and channels of content delivery remain understudied. Moreover, the types of platforms that are conducive to generate creative content, which might not be converted into material interests, tend to receive far less attention.

In addressing these questions, this book joins an emerging body of scholarship that calls for studying platforms from a relational perspective.[87] To borrow Marc Steinberg's words, platforms are perceived as "structures of relation, or the formalization of relations in varying degree of techno-logical means."[88] I contextualize the study of platforms by delving into the cross-fertilization of user-generated content and platforms, as well as the interconnections between diverse platforms over a long time span. In this sense, I historicize the study of four dominant platforms—BBS, the blog, the microblog, and WeChat—since the early days of the Chinese Internet. My investigation of digital platforms focuses on the ways in which user-generated content has been promoted, debated, censored, and commodi-fied at different stages of China's Internet development, as well as how the interaction among Internet corporations, cultural institutions, netizens, and traditional and official media have jointly increased the visibility of certain user-generated content. This user-generated content ranges from BBS posts and blog entries to tweets and videos to Internet fiction and WeChat essays. Contributors of original content include anonymous netizens, celebrities, cultural authorities, journalists, writers, and digital influencers. I chart the conditions for the emergence of these creative content within their particular sociocultural circumstances, and detail the ways in which digital contents traverse from one platform to another. In so doing, I pay particular attention to the technological affordances of each platform and their interconnections, as well as their role in reinvigorating the practices of writing, promoting content with attentive value, and commodifying original content.

The developmental trajectory of these four digital platforms exemplifies the cultural history of Chinese Internet over the past two decades. The age of BBS and blogs highlights a sense of idealism shared among elite netizens, who genuinely believed that information transparency and free expression would create a better, more egalitarian world. This vision of digital technologies and their functions shifted to a glamorized celebration of entrepreneurship in the era of the microblog and WeChat, against a backdrop of the enhanced corporate management of online content, the prominent visibility of state actors, and a full-fledged model of e-commerce. Despite the different technological affordances embedded in these four platforms, they all exemplify new modes of producing, promoting, and disseminating user-generated content. In this sense, the evolving trajectory of the four digital platforms exemplifies how existing technological features are constantly reinvented and incorporated into innovations. It also illustrates the process by which Chinese tech companies and attention entrepreneurs have transitioned from being copycats of global business models to digital creators. Throughout this process, digital culture has evolved from marginalized genres, practices, and forms to become a mainstay of contemporary Chinese popular culture.

Methodology and Chapter Outline

This project is based on long-term study of the online space, as well as extensive work in the field in China from June 2007 to July 2019. To understand the perspective of the Internet industry, I spent on average one to two months conducting fieldwork in China every year, mostly during summer and winter academic breaks. I have consulted web editors, IT professionals, and managers at major Internet content providers in China, including the state-sponsored CNTV.cn (the online portal of CCTV), the new media department of the state-affiliated radio program *Voice of China* (*Zhongguo zhisheng*), and the newspaper *People's Daily*, as well as major commercial sites such as Sina, Tencent, Tianya, Sohu, Ifeng, and Baidu. Due in large part to the dominant status of Sina as an Internet news media corporation, as well as its role in popularizing blogging and microblogging services in China, I have paid particular attention to the promotional strategies of Sina and its interaction with other major players in the cultural realm. In addition to working in the field, I held personal accounts on all these applications and published posts. I also logged into all major sites online on a daily basis. During these visits, I observed online traffic without participating in discussion in order to not disrupt the existing dynamics.

As an interdisciplinary attempt, my qualitative methodological approach synthesizes various humanistic research methods, including textual reading, discourse analysis, interviews, and participant observation. I have integrated online postings, including messages, images, hyperlinks, and videos, into an analysis of state policies, official documents, statistical reports of commercial portals, and media coverage of influential cases. In so doing, I elucidate the connection between texts and the sociopolitical contexts that shaped the emergence of these texts, as well as their cultural ramifications. I highlight the role of the state as an agent that not only steers China's technological modernization process, but also proactively adjusts its modes of governance and reinvents its propaganda culture via digital media. My study also emphasizes the importance of creative ideas, the tech-savvy generation, and the simultaneous alliance between, and competition among, various cultural institutions in the push for cultural pluralism in a Chinese society that has undergone radical transformation over the past two decades.

Aside from the introductory chapter (chapter 1) and concluding chapter (chapter 8), the main body of this book contains six chapters. Chapter 2 delineates the developmental history of the Internet in China through the four predominant platforms already introduced: the bulletin board system, the blog, the microblog, and WeChat. I address how the defining features of these platforms and competition among major players in the field have contributed to shaping public culture and publicity strategies emerging in the technology-mediated sphere. The following five chapters analyze the digital cultural formation that has emerged from these technological platforms. Chapter 3 expands our current understanding of the predominant fun-seeking mode of the Chinese Internet and its symbiotic relationship with a culture of contention. Chapter 4 focuses on the intersection of the entertainment industry, entrepreneurial culture, and the golden age of blogging in China. I probe the rise of cultural entrepreneurs, who quickly aligned themselves with enterprises seeking to develop culture-related business and, in doing so, transformed the ways that cultural works are produced and publicized. Chapter 5 explores celebrity blogging through the lens of microcultural contention. Taking the blogs of Mu Zimei and Han Han as case studies, I investigate how an entertainment-oriented blogosphere has catalyzed the rise of opinion leaders who tactically disrupt preset parameters of social, moral, and political norms. Chapter 6 delves into six microblog-based incidents that involve media scandal, state mobilization, and civic issues, and examines the multifaceted role digital witnessing plays in transforming apathetic spectators into active agents. Chapter 7 addresses the rise of segmented publics on WeChat, the most phenomenal mobile application to date. I elucidate how WeChat public accounts have revolutionized the ways in which original content is distributed and commodified. The concluding chapter discusses the implications of these findings and pinpoints areas for future research.

Essentially, the chapters together map out the "being" and "becoming"[89] of the Chinese Internet. As China's Internet population continues to grow, so does the urgency of examining how online space constitutes a key site for understanding the convergence between contested ideologies and diverse Internet generations. In detailing how various players negotiate for agency and compete for visibility, the book highlights the formative and transformative moments in the development of China's digital culture. I argue that the liberating power of new media does not lie in their potential to provoke democratic revolutions at the structural level. Rather, this liberating effect is rooted in how digital media opens up symbolic spaces to expressive differences. Ultimately, exploring the sociocultural meaning of the Chinese Internet not only deepens the scholarly understanding of China's digital revolution by adopting a new angle, but it also illuminates how the interplay between the authoritarian state, cultural institutions, emerging technologies, and Internet users has collaboratively catalyzed the crucial transformation of dominant and mainstream culture in China.

2 A HISTORICAL OVERVIEW THROUGH TECHNOLOGICAL PLATFORMS

THE INTERNET INDUSTRY in China got a considerably later start than in the US, yet the speed of its development has been remarkable. In 1994, there were approximately 1,600 Internet users in China.[1] In 2008, China surpassed the US to become the country with the largest number of Internet users.[2] From 2002 to 2017, the compound growth rate of China's Internet population was 25 percent, taking the lead globally.[3] As of March 15, 2020, China had 904 million Internet users and 897 million mobile Internet users.[4] The Internet penetration rate is 64.5 percent,[5] much higher than the global average rate of 4.1 percent and the Asian average rate of 9.1 percent.[6] Meanwhile, China's Internet economy has constituted an important component of GDP growth. In 2018, digital economy in China constituted 34.8 percent of GDP.[7] It is estimated that by the end of 2025 the contribution of the Internet to China's total GDP increase will reach 7–22 percent, while the Internet's contribution to China's productivity growth will reach 22 percent.[8]

The scale and scope of Internet development in China could not have been achieved without the joint efforts of the state and commercial sectors. The major phases of Internet development in China map onto four dominant platforms: the bulletin board system (BBS), the blog, the microblog, and WeChat. This chapter examines the role that the Chinese government and commercial portals play in building research and education networks, creating business models, and continuously expanding into new markets. Proceeding chronologically, the analysis begins with BBS, the first Internet application encountered by Chinese netizens, and addresses the rise of China's first cohort digital publics who enjoyed "living" online for the first time.

From Intranet to Internet

Since its inception, the development of the Internet in China has essentially been global, as represented by the frequent cooperation between Chinese and Western academic institutions, the rush of international venture capital, the return of IT entrepreneurs from overseas, and the innovative adaptation of global technologies and business models. Internet development in China began with the efforts of researchers, scientists, faculty, and students in leading academic institutions in the late 1980s. With help from European and North American universities, intranets were set up on university campuses. In 1986, the Beijing Applied Computing Institute and Karlsruhe University in Germany agreed to cooperatively develop the Chinese Academic Network (CANET). CANET supports research in computer science and enables data sharing and email exchange among researchers.[9] On September 20, 1987, Professor Qian Tianbai sent out China's first email, which read that it was time to "cross the Great Wall to connect with the world."[10] In 1988, the networks of the Institute of High Energy Physics (IHEP) and the China Education and Research Network (CERNET) were established, to enable email exchanges with North America and Europe. Another milestone occurred in April 1994, when the National Computing Facilities of China (NCFC), with the help of the American National Science Foundation Network (NSFNET), became the first network to connect to the emerging World Wide Web. China set up the first ".cn" domain name server on April 20, 1994, along with a backbone router to connect to the Internet officially.[11] In the same year, IHEP introduced the first "www" servers and opened the first home page in China.[12] In 1995, the nationwide network China Public Computer Internet (CHINANET) was founded; commercial Internet service was opened to the public in 1996.[13] The China Internet Network Information Center (CNNIC), directed by the Ministry of Information Industry and operated by the Chinese Academy of Sciences (CAS), was established in 1997. CNNIC manages Chinese domain name registration, allocates IP addresses and Autonomous System Numbers (ASN), and crafts Internet policy proposals, among other duties.

The Chinese government has played an indispensable role in facilitating both the establishment of these networks and their associated international collaborations. Convinced that new technologies are vital to China's integration into the global economy, the state has invested substantially in the expansion and modernization of telecommunication infrastructure since the 1980s. Former state leaders, such as Deng Xiaoping and Jiang Zemin, considered information infrastructure development essential to China's achieving its goal of the "four modernizations" in agriculture, industry, national defense, and science and technology.[14] The Chinese government also noted US development of the Internet. In October 1993, the Clinton administration allowed the Internet to move from an exclusive US military project to commercial use, and web usage gained momentum throughout the late 1990s. Alarmed by the Clinton administration's support for building up the "Information Superhighway," the Chinese government conducted extensive research and made substantial investments to build a national information network infrastructure.[15] From 1994 to 1996, the four national backbones of China's Internet infrastructure were put into service in specific areas: the general public (CHINANET), sponsored by the Ministry of Posts and Telecommunications (now the Ministry of Industry and Information Technology); education (CERNET), hosted by the State Education Commission; research, China Science and Technology Network (CSTNET), hosted by the CAS; and commerce, China Golden Bridge Network (CHINAGBN), sponsored by the Ministry of Electronics Industry. These networks were linked with one another and, in 1996, were connected to the global Internet.[16] Since all Internet service providers must use the national infrastructure, and all international Internet traffic must go through these networks, state surveillance of the Internet is feasible. These massive infrastructure-building projects have also sped up the development of the Internet industry in China. With the State Planning Commission's funding, all Chinese university campuses were connected to the Internet within ten years (1994–2004).[17] In the years that followed, the State Council implemented comprehensive initiatives to improve the construction of Internet infrastructures, including those necessary to support "broadband, mobile internet, iCloud and new technologies."[18] In 2009, more than 95 percent of Chinese cities, towns, and villages had access to the Internet.[19] More recently, since the launch of the Belt and Road Initiative in 2013, the Chinese government has expanded the construction of Internet infrastructure to Belt and Road countries, as represented by Pakistan.[20]

In addition to propelling the construction of network infrastructure, the Chinese government has experimented with digital publishing and engaged in e-government applications. China's first electronic magazine appeared in January 1995; *China Scholars Abroad* (*Shenzhou xueren*) targeted overseas Chinese students and was published via CERNET, under the sponsorship of the State Education Commission. In the same year, two state-affiliated media organizations, *China Daily* and *China News Service*, pioneered the digitization of their content, as well as the setup of Internet portals for government mouthpieces, such as Xinhua News Agency, China Central Television Station (CCTV), China Radio International (CRI), and *Guangming Daily*.[21] By 2001, government-controlled news websites had been launched on a massive scale.[22] These measures precipitated the challenges that such propaganda organizations would encounter, in that they now needed to compete with the burgeoning commercial media outlets for user attention. For instance, the State Council of China launched the "Government Online Project" to promote the application of Internet-based technology at all levels of government. This three-stage initiative (1) put up government websites for the public to acquire information and procure services, (2) implemented office automation via these websites, and (3) facilitated collaboration between the government and IT enterprises in China.[23] The overarching goal was to enhance transparency and decentralize administration by adding new channels for propaganda, while monitoring information dissemination and economic activities.[24] Government officials also experimented with the newest offering of technologies for communicating with citizens, such as launching personal blogs and engaging in online conversations with Internet users. With a few notable exceptions,[25] most of these experiments were ineffective in the late 1990s and early 2000s, largely due to delay of government agencies' response to citizens' inquiries. Nevertheless, these early endeavors lay the groundwork for the reinvention of state propaganda and Internet governance in the administration under President Xi Jinping.

Government sponsorship of infrastructure building also paved the way for the rapid takeoff of China's Internet industry in the years since the mid-1990s. All of the influential commercial portals were founded between 1997 and 2000. These sites quickly captured a huge share of the market and established recognizable brand names through their specialized content services, for example, Sina's news aggregate, Sohu's search function, NetEase's online gaming and news commentary, and Tencent's instant messaging service. Capitalizing on the liberalization of the economy, these Internet startups have continuously expanded into new markets and secured their positions as dominant players in China's IT industry because of their size, breadth of offerings, and massive user base. These corporations' collaboration and negotiation with both state sectors and Internet users constitute the primary driving forces behind the vibrant online culture.

Braving the New World: The Bulletin Board System

The technology of the bulletin board system (BBS) was invented in the US in 1974.[26] Early BBS sites were accessed over phone lines through the terminal software Telnet. Users could send and receive local emails, upload and download files, and play online games with rudimentary graphics. The early 1990s witnessed a rapid increase in BBS sites in the US.[27] Yet very soon, the commercialization of the World Wide Web enabled users to access BBS sites via web browsers, leading to a sharp decline in the popularity of pure BBS sites from 1995 to 1997.[28] Since BBS preceded the World Wide Web by fifteen years in the US, it was commonly perceived as an antiquated technology.[29] In China, however, the Telnet-based BBS shifted to web-based interfaces within only a couple of years. Thus, despite the fact that BBS technically differs from online forums, these two terms are used interchangeably in the Chinese context.

Given that the development of the Internet in China began with a number of leading universities, the first cohort of Chinese netizens, in the late 1990s, consisted mainly of college students, researchers, and urban professionals. Free intranet service and File Transfer Protocol (FTP) first became available on university campuses, with Tsinghua University leading the way. CERNET, responsible for the operation and management of the CERNET backbone nationwide, is located at Tsinghua University. Pioneering the field of Internet research and development, CERNET connected more than 300 university networks in China in the late 1990s.[30] In August 1995, "ace," a student at Tsinghua University, set up SMTH BBS (*Shuimu shequ*), the first and foremost BBS in China, following the model of Palm BBS at the National Taiwan University. Shortly afterwards, three other influential BBS sites were launched: Unknown Space (*Weiming kongjian*) of Peking University, Little Lily (*Xiao baihe*) at Nanjing University, and the Space BBS (*Shenzhou wuhao*) at the Center for Space Science of the Chinese Academy of Sciences. Partly due to the scarcity of online content in 1995 and 1996, early netizens gathered around these first few student-run discussion forums. Consequently, university BBS fostered the birth of Chinese netizens, marking the formation of China's digital public for the first time. As the very first collaborative platform accessible to every Internet user, BBS in China catalyzed the emergence of a new kind of public culture that encouraged debates, challenged authorities, and endorsed users' contribution of original content.

The early features of BBS were mainly group discussion, news posts, and file sharing. Services such as chat rooms, blogs, online games, and search engines were later incorporated. The BBS's position as an open online forum determines the large variety of topics under discussion, including news, current events, and entertainment. Since BBS users are required to register to publish posts, users who frequent a number of similar forums may recognize each other's online names and avatars; thus the relative homogeneity of early BBS users facilitated on- and offline socialization and gave rise to the community-oriented nature of BBS. In addition to university BBS, commercial BBS sites gradually flourished and brought together massive audiences—the most well-known being Tianya Community, Xici Valley, Mop, and Srsnet (predecessor of Sina).

BBS has exerted a fundamental influence on the developmental trajectory of Internet culture in China. Among university BBS sites, Yita Hutu, an independent site launched by a Peking University student, Wu Tao, in 1999, is the most archetypal. The operation of this site embodied democratic practices, as all forum administrators and staff members were elected by Internet users. These administrators had fixed terms and were supervised by netizens, who were entitled to file complaints and impeach administrators at any time. In addition, the hot topics and articles recommended by the site were selected and promoted solely based on readers' rating of posted content.[31] As of September 13, 2004, Yita Hutu had 293,793 registered users and more than 800 discussion forums, on topics ranging from citizen life to anti-rumor campaigns to cross-Strait relations.[32] In the fond memories of early netizens, Yita Hutu stood out for its openness to a wide variety of debates.[33] Commercial sites, such as Tianya and Sina, adopted similar practices and encouraged Internet users to elect moderators and monitor their behaviors.[34] In 2003, the active role that BBS sites played in social activism earned the year the appellation "Year of Online Public Opinion," as collective actions by Internet users resulted in a change of governmental decisions over quite a few well-known incidents.[35]

Alerted by these cases, the state began to strengthen control over campus networks. In 2004, the Central Committee of the Chinese Communist Party and the State Council jointly issued a document that aimed at reinforcing ideological campaigns among college students.[36] Subsequently, the Ministry of Education organized a symposium and a conference to discuss the possible measures of regulating campus networks. The precursor to the massive regulation of university BBS was the sudden shutdown of Yita Hutu on September 13, 2004, with the charge of "disseminating political rumors."[37] Then, in March of the next year, the Ministry of Education issued a mandate. It stipulated that users unrelated to universities should be denied access to college BBS sites and required users to register with their real names. Some BBSs, such as those of Peking University, Nanjing University, Nankai University, and Fudan University, went through the transformation peacefully. Some of the commonly adopted measures were to deny access to users outside of campuses, restrict registration for new users, and set the posts as read-only to disable comments.[38] By contrast, SMTH BBS, with more than 500 discussion forums and 300,000 registered users in 2005, had several head-to-head confrontations with the authorities of Tsinghua University.[39] Students initially endeavored to convince the authorities to change their decision and contributed essays expressing their feelings. Then, they organized large-scale protests on- and offline, employing actions such as the deletion of data from the site, the collective resignation of forum hosts, and the pursuit of support from overseas alumni.[40] Despite these efforts, SMTH BBS was restricted to campus users on March 16, 2005, meaning that 82.3 percent of SMTH's users were suddenly denied access to the site.[41] The immediate consequence was the founding of NEW SMTH as a commercial site in May 2005, which provided a meeting place for former SMTH BBS users. The old SMTH BBS gradually lost its popularity among student users. While commercial BBS sites continue to thrive today, the year 2005 officially marked the end of the era of campus BBS, reflecting the shared sense of idealism, solidarity, and disillusionment that arose from BBS users' interactions with the authorities.

Ironically, the decline in influence of university BBS contributed to the boom of blogging that occurred around the same time. If the emergence of BBS in the late 1990s spearheaded the forming of a new public culture characterized by collectivism, egalitarianism, and autonomy, then the mounting number of bloggers in the new millennium demonstrates how individual expression, sociality, and commercialism have become increasingly integrated into Internet users' everyday lives.

Blogging in China: Free Discourse, Sensationalism, and Monopolization

Shortly after the blog emerged in the US in 1997, it was introduced to China by Sun Jianhua, a journalist who publishes observations of global technological trends on his personal website, New Media Review (*xinmeiti guancha*). In his essay "Discussion about the Blog" (*boke lun*), Sun elaborated on the emerging blogging revolution and introduced the US-based Drudge Report to Chinese technocrats. This news aggregation website is well known for disclosing the 1998 sex scandal between former US president Bill Clinton and twenty-two-year-old White House intern Monica Lewinsky, a story that later broke in the mainstream press. Another landmark event in the history of blogging in China was the visit of Dan Gillmor, an American technology writer and columnist, to Tsinghua University on November 20, 2001. In his invited talk, Gillmor showed his blog to the audience and discussed the rise of citizen journalism via blogging in the US, as well as the declining influence of traditional journalists. This was most likely the first time that the blog was discussed publicly in China.[42]

Born in 2002, the Chinese blog seemed to pursue the lofty mission of advocating free speech, which correlates with the essence of the blog as a flexible publishing platform with a potential to boost grassroots journalism. Fang Xingdong, a web entrepreneur, renowned Internet industry commentator, and the "godfather of the blog" in China, stated that he promoted blogging to fight for free speech. Interestingly, during that time, Fang's target was not the authoritarian regime but the complicity in censorship between transnational and domestic commercial corporations. In July 2002, Fang published two essays, "Surrender to Microsoft" and "Microsoft, Why?," both critical of the marketplace monopoly of multinational corporation. Within two hours of their publication, they were removed from several websites, including the influential portal websites Sina and Sohu. Fang attributed the removal of these posts to commercial pressure from Microsoft. This was not the first time Fang had encountered difficulties in publishing his work. Disillusioned by the manipulation of commercial forces, he decided to build a personal website. Following Sun Jianhua's suggestion, Fang registered for an account at blogspot.com (now Blogger) and became convinced that blogs could empower netizens and revolutionize cyberspace.[43]

In August 2002, Fang established China's first blog-hosting site, Blogchina (now bokee), and, with web entrepreneur Wang Junxiu, coined the Chinese term *"boke"* (literally, "knowledgeable guest") to refer to blogs.[44] Just as the Chinese translation of the word "blog" accentuates the importance of knowledge in the digital age, Fang and Wang believed that blog culture could "lead China's transition into a knowledge-based society, and herald a new era of responsibility."[45] For them, information inundation represented the negative effect of the first stage of the dotcom economy. They envisioned that the new Web 2.0 era would stress the conversion of information into knowledge. Blogchina invited the pioneers of China's Internet industry to contribute to its special columns and aimed to provide high-quality content that would inspire critical thinking. The target audience was defined as "knowledge workers" (*zhishi gongzuo zhe*), including those working in academia, finance, and media. In terms of appearances, the website was designed to minimize the distractions of commercials and special effects.[46]

This elite-centered approach took effect at first. In 2002 to 2005, Blogchina played a leading role in China's blogging scene. Additional coverage in various print media significantly enhanced the site's visibility. After Fang released the beta version of Blogchina, *Southern Weekly*, the influential liberal-leaning newspaper, published four introductory articles on blogs in a full-page spread on September 5, 2002.[47] On the same day, the state-sponsored newspaper *China Youth Daily* published an article introducing Blogchina to its readers.[48] This coverage by the mainstream media proved significant. As Fang later acknowledged, it was only after the publication of these articles that the number of visits to Blogchina increased exponentially.[49] Moreover, the antipornography movement that Blogchina launched in June 2003 enhanced the site's media exposure and political legitimacy, winning accolades from such state-affiliated media organizations as Xinhua and Qianlong. Fang interpreted the antipornography campaign as emblematic of a nonmainstream website's challenge toward the dominance of commercial forces in cyberspace, in particular, commercial websites such as Sina, NetEase, and Sohu, all of which provided short message services (SMS) with explicit sexual content. Ironically, this movement soon took a dramatic turn when Mu Zimei's "sex diary," made available on Blogchina, became a nationwide sensation.

A journalist at *City Pictorial* (*Chengshi huabao*) in Guangzhou, Mu Zimei wrote a semimonthly sex column for the magazine. On June 19, 2003, Mu Zimei started publishing her "sex diary," which chronicled everything from her penchant for sexual intercourse and Internet dating to her skepticism toward marriage. One August 2003 entry documented her sexual experience with Wang Lei, a famous rock star in Guangzhou, which attracted thousands of visitors, momentarily paralyzing the web server. For Fang Xingdong, his past efforts to advocate for the blog form faded in the face of the sensational effect brought on by Mu Zimei's writing, as the following quote shows:

> In the morning of November 11, 2003, it suddenly became very difficult to load web pages from Blogchina. Loading an article took an extremely long time, and it was impossible to upload any articles. . . . At first I thought

the system had crashed. Later, I found out that it was because traffic to the site had increased tenfold! The three major portal websites [Sina, Sohu, and NetEase] all recommended Mu Zimei's articles in the news feed section of their home pages, simply because Mu Zimei's blog was reported by *Newsweek* in the United States. Under such circumstances, the number of visitors [to Blogchina] on that day reached 110,000. Before that, the highest number of visits per day was 19,000 on average. The page views were four times as high as before. . . . It is through me that the elite learned about blogs, but the general audience learned about blogs from Mu Zimei.[50]

Fang's recollection was representative of the media sensation that surrounded the Chinese blogosphere. Almost all websites related to blogs witnessed a sharp increase in visits at that time, in particular Blogcn and Blogchina.

The high-profile campaigns that Fang launched to target commercial websites, alongside the Mu Zimei incident, helped to carve out a niche in the marketplace for Blogchina. Capitalizing on the touching rhetoric of "free speech," Fang picked on safe targets—whether it was the multinational conglomerate Microsoft or sexually explicit content provided by commercial portals—to legitimize his cause. Nevertheless, Fang's rhetoric also exemplifies the sense of idealism that early IT entrepreneurs and netizens shared and the genuine belief that the Internet could create a more egalitarian world. With the backing of mainstream and official media, Blogchina created a sensation in 2005 when it received 10 million USD of venture capital investments, turned itself into a blog service provider (BSP), and changed its name to Bokee. At that time, Fang ambitiously vowed to build the largest knowledge-based portal website and envisioned that it would surpass Sina within two years.[51] However, his elite-centered strategy led to the gradual downfall of Blogchina after 2005, when the major portal websites entered the blogging scene.

In these early years, Blogchina was far from the only player in the field. In October 2002, CNBlog, China's first online discussion forum about blogging technology and culture, was cofounded by Isaac Xianghui Mao and Zheng Yunsheng. If Blogchina favored highly selective knowledge by inviting technology enthusiasts to post original content, then CNBlog aimed to foster an egalitarian exchange of ideas on blog applications and e-learning among ordinary users. Consequently, the website functioned on an autonomous basis: there were no administrators to monitor and control discussion; all tech enthusiasts were welcome to join discussions.[52] In November 2002, the first free BSP in China, Blogcn, was established by three college students in Hangzhou. Two other BSPs quickly followed: Blogdriver and Blogbus.[53] In addition, a blog feature was incorporated as a service on BBS at leading universities in China, starting with the University of Science and Technology of China and Nankai University.

From 2002 to 2005, professional blogging sites introduced blogs to China, offered exclusive blogging services, and mostly attracted tech-savvy users. The year 2005 was a landmark year for the blogging industry in China in several important respects. The 2005 governmental crackdown on university BBS and the advancement of blogging technology, such as the ability to incorporate visuals and podcasts, offered opportunities for the rapid growth of the blogging industry. All major commercial portals joined the blogging trend beginning in 2005 and quickly dominated the market, including Hexun, Sohu, and Sina.[54] However, when blogs moved in from the margins to the mainstream space, BSPs gradually lost their popularity. In 2005, 20 percent of the top 100 BSPs in China terminated their services,[55] a trend that has only increased with time. A major difference in the blogging services offered by BSP and commercial portals is that the latter had already dominated the market for their signature products, such as Sina's news aggregation service and Tencent's SMS. For these portals, blogs were only a supplementary product to be added to their current signature service. These companies could divert some of their already extensive resources to promote their blogging services. Thus, the participation of commercial portals in the blogging industry has drastically changed the ecology of the blogosphere, and Sina represents this most clearly.

Sina: A Case Study

With 948 million registered users averaging 412 million page views daily,[56] Sina is "a leading online media company serving China and the global Chinese communities."[57] Sina's business model mainly consists of three segments: "SINA.com (portal), SINA mobile (mobile portal and mobile apps) and Weibo (social media)."[58] According to the statistics of Alexa.com, an Internet information provider specializing in web traffic reporting and ranking, Sina.com.cn and Weibo ranked nineteenth and twentieth among the top 500 sites in the world. Meanwhile, these two websites took seventh and eighth place in China, preceded only by China's domestic search engine Baidu, the communication and information-sharing website QQ, Sina's longtime competitor Sohu, and the e-commerce sites Taobao, Tmall, and Jingdong.[59] Sina's flagship products range from news, online forums, and email service, to the blogging and microblogging platforms. The blogging and microblogging services that Sina provides have not only enacted profound changes in the media landscape, but have also reshaped sociocultural norms and writing conventions.

The birth of Sina's celebrated blogging model emerged from the chief executive officer's concerns that Sina might lose its market share in the blogosphere. By 2005, three years after blogging services became available in China, all of Sina's main competitors, including NetEase, Hexun, and Tencent, were offering blogging services to their users. In hopes of addressing the competition, Sina organized a seminar and invited media experts to discuss the current state of blogging in China. Wang Xiaofeng, a famous blogger and journalist, recalled his experience at the meeting: "My impression was that [staff at Sina] were anxious and their mentality was this: 'I did not take the lead in offering blogging services, as others have now done. I have to catch up. How can I catch the public's attention?'" At the seminar, Wang offhandedly proposed that maybe Sina could consider inviting famous people to write on the blogs hosted by the website. He did not expect his words to be taken seriously by those in charge.[60] Sina soon coined the term "*mingren boke*" (celebrity blog), put up a blog channel (the first one among portal websites in China), and initiated a comprehensive campaign to promote blogging. In September 2005, Sina organized a team to lobby famous people to use their blogging service. Chen Tong, the then editor-in-chief of Sina, emailed 300 invitations to IT specialists. The scope of this recruitment quickly extended to well-established figures from all walks of life, including actors, sports stars, cultural critics, writers, professors, TV anchors, and the like.[61] Sina's well-established fame as an online news source, the potential for publicity it promised to celebrities, and the underdeveloped star-making mechanisms in China enabled the site to gather more than 2,500 celebrity bloggers in three short months. This number has been increasing exponentially since then. In the years that followed, Sina continually improved and expanded its blogging service, maximizing its breadth and depth in an effort to reach the largest possible audience. In addition to Sina's administrative structure and the incorporation of sophisticated recommendation and ranking systems, web editors as "professional digital attention agents" are essential to maintaining the corporation's position as the dominant trendsetter in the blogging industry.

The Professionalization of Digital Attention Agents

"Professional digital attention agents" are hired by Internet portals to boost online traffic via both promotional strategies and technological means. These professionals typically include web editors, forum hosts, public relations personnel, and publicists. Their main objective is to attract and sustain user attention. As with agents in other professions, professional digital attention agents' job performance is evaluated by how many transactions they facilitate. In this case, the transaction is reified in such symbolic forms as web traffic statistics and the number of visits generated by specific content. For instance, all web editors of commercial portals are expected to regularly analyze general trends of user preferences, based on the quantitative statistics of page views, web traffic during different time periods, and ranking lists of real-time news feeds and user comments.[62] If web editors fail to fulfill their monthly quota of network traffic, such penalties as salary deduction are imposed.[63] In addition, these agents function as intermediaries who evaluate and balance the needs of various parties, most notably new media users and state authorities, in order to strike a balance between generating profits at full capacity and complying with state censors.

The rapid professionalization of digital attention agents in China took place almost immediately after the launching of major dotcom corporations such as Sina, Sohu, and NetEase in the late 1990s. Early examples of digital attention agents are the few "well-known IDs" (*zhiming ID*, meaning "online names") who first gained fame and symbolic prestige on BBS. The length of time spent online, level of technical prowess, specialties displayed (good writing style, humor, critical analysis skills, etc.), and online social skills all contributed to the recognition and symbolic power of posters. Posts by these well-known IDs quickly generated numerous follow-up posts, and, in a way, these contributors functioned as opinion leaders since any of their proposals could easily be translated into action by other online users. In this way, the attention-getting capacity and online sociality demonstrated by early web enthusiasts were regarded as possessing great commercial value. This led Internet companies to hire them as professional digital attention agents. One example is Chen Tong, a volunteer Sports Salon forum host of Srsnet from 1996 to 1998, who demonstrated his attention-gathering capacity by mobilizing BBS users to participate in live broadcasting of sports events. Live broadcasting was groundbreaking in this early stage of the Chinese Internet.[64] Chen was soon hired as Srsnet's first professional editor and later became the editor-in-chief of Sina. Subsequently, the ranks of professional digital attention agents expanded from a few well-known Internet celebrities to ordinary individuals who formally joined this new profession. Within a few years, the number of web editors far exceeded those editors working for print media, and the job is still in high demand as new media further integrates into people's daily lives.[65]

The rapid professionalization process changed the connotations of attention-gathering capacity for individuals. During the pre-professionalization stage, as represented by early phases of BBS, the netizens who gained online recognition and symbolic prestige were primarily content generators. Most of them claimed an altruistic motive[66] for the "immaterial labor"[67] they contributed to the online space. However, after they formally joined the profession of web editors, their role shifted from generating to publicizing online content. These agents now capitalized on the immaterial labor of other Internet users and aimed at publicizing their user-generated content in an attractive manner. These professional digital attention agents fostered a fundamentally different perception of sociality, individual expression, technological advancement, and online culture. The ways in which web editors at Sina popularized blogging are characteristic of the common practices of such editors in all commercial portals.

Sina's administrative rules have long emphasized the multifaceted function of web editors. In addition to analyzing the overall trends of user preferences, web editors screen and cross-post news items, process netizens' comments, conduct online surveys, compile special issues, and invite Internet users to join in live chats with special guests.[68] Web editors also screen and select entries to publicize, update webpages, plan special issues, maintain connections with well-known bloggers, and network with potential bloggers.[69] Thus, web editors' sensitivity to the attractiveness of user-generated content, the innovative means by which they publicize online content, and their capacity to socialize with Internet users both on- and offline are essential for their success as professional digital attention agents. Web editors at Sina adopt three key strategies to maximize the possibility of attracting Internet users who will generate original content: (1) encouraging celebrities to blog via Sina, (2) "blogging on the scene," and (3) emphasizing the human dimension of technologies.

Celebrities as Vehicles of Public Attention

Well aware that celebrities intrinsically garner public attention, Sina launched an aggressive campaign to lobby famous people to use the company's blogging service. Given the nuanced difference between "*mingxing*" (celebrities or stars) and "*mingren*" (famous people), the coined term "*mingren boke*," although translated into "celebrity blogging," has a broader coverage. Sina aimed to demonstrate its function as a leading multimedia promotional platform for celebrities by means of its technical support, content rating system, and publicity plans. In turn, celebrity blogs significantly enhanced the Internet traffic on Sina by offering insider information that easily generated millions of visits by fans, general readers, and journalists. This newly conceived business plan effectively increased the web traffic on Sina's Blog Channel by 30–40 percent.[70] Consequently, the success of celebrity blogs catalyzed a new profit model for Sina in which it shared with the most popular bloggers the advertising revenue generated from their personal blogs. In this way, celebrity blogs integrated the interests of celebrity bloggers (boost reputation), readers (voyeurism and star appeal), and the website (generate profits), and exemplified the trend of online media companies experimenting with new forms of communication.

Behind the media sensation revolving around celebrity bloggers were professional digital attention agents who optimized the content generated by "attention-haves" like celebrities. The everyday tasks of web editors included assisting in managing celebrity accounts, publicizing celebrity updates, and networking with influential figures. To encourage celebrities who were less tech-savvy, web editors assigned special personnel to assist with the publishing process, to include suggesting possible topics, setting up typesetting and fonts, and addressing technical issues. Celebrity bloggers seeking technical support could call web editors at any time. Celebrity bloggers' feedback regarding the technological features of the blog was rapidly accommodated. In publicizing celebrity updates, web editors followed a hierarchy linked to the celebrities' level of popularity. Thus, the celebrities' "class status" largely determined the ways in which their updates were monitored and publicized. For instance, Sina staff members monitored blogs written by renowned figures on a 24/7 basis, posting recent status changes immediately in prominent positions on webpages. Web editors' effective promotion of blog entries contributed to enhancing these celebrities' cultural capital. In contrast, less-famous bloggers needed to notify web editors themselves about updates to get them publicized in a timely fashion.[71]

In addition to determining how to promote celebrity entries, web editors tracked the status of celebrity updates and cultivated close relationships with celebrities. If a celebrity normally updated every other day but failed to post for a week or two, the web editor would remind the celebrity via email or instant messaging.[72] According to web editors, those celebrities who agreed to write on Sina's blog had already developed a strong bond with the website. Therefore, they were not required to sign exclusive agreements with the website, nor were they "penalized" for updating infrequently or terminating their blog. Celebrities also considered it paramount to maintain a good relationship with the web editors. Celebrities usually would notify editors if they changed their mind about blogging, as one of my interviewees at Sina stated:

> Celebrities won't neglect web editors' messages [about the need to update]. . . .
> [W]hether they are going to write on our blog or not, they definitely will
> explain. If a celebrity decides not to work with Sina anymore, she or he will

list specific reasons. Or if she or he will be busy, for an out-of-town film shoot or something, she or he will let us know. Celebrities definitely won't dismiss [the message].[73]

In this way, celebrity bloggers and web editors maintain a peer-like relationship, even on occasions of disagreement. The ways in which web editors and celebrity bloggers collaboratively addressed the rules of the censorship game best exemplify this point. In the case of blogging, censorship not only included the removal of content and blocking of user accounts deemed subversive or improper by web editors, but more important, it encompassed the dialectic logic of deletion and recommendation that helps boost web traffic. During many occasions of social controversy, web editors informed celebrities when their entries were either recommended or removed; oftentimes controversial content was first recommended and then deleted shortly after, further arousing public curiosity about the removed content. Likewise, celebrity bloggers played with the notion of "being censored" to evoke public sympathy. While the celebrity blogger might have decried the "censorship," with few exceptions, the celebrity and the web editor would have reached a consensus regarding the censored content. In short, web editors tried all means available to them to sustain celebrities' enthusiasm for blogging, while the sensational success of celebrity blogs attracted a large number of devoted fans who enjoyed the virtual sense of intimacy by accessing the personal space of their idols.

"Blogging on the Scene": The Rise of Citizen Journalism

The cultural ramifications of celebrity blogs were not limited to the entertainment realm. Because of the extensive publicity measures employed by web editors, cultural elites' critiques on current affairs not only directed netizens' attention to a myriad of controversial issues, but also reinvigorated societal interest in discussing the role of public intellectuals in an authoritarian regime. Professional digital attention agents further promoted this trend by mobilizing ordinary netizens to publish original blog entries on various topics, including current events, overseas experiences, and leisure activities. The rise of citizen journalism and the flourishing of user-generated content challenged the dominance of the heavily censored traditional media and enriched the broader narratives of traditional news reports by providing a more personalized perspective. Since online news media are not authorized to distribute their own reports—except in the areas of entertainment and sports—and have had to purchase news items from traditional media outlets,[74] the blog as a form of alternative journalism carried a great weight of cultural significance.

Professional digital attention agents at Sina adopted two strategies to promote citizen journalism. First, attention agents capitalized on Sina's position as a comprehensive news portal and promoted "blogging on the scene" to enhance the website's news value. When important events occurred, web editors made a great effort to contact eyewitnesses and invite them to blog about their experiences, as one of my interviewees at Sina explained:

> In essence, Sina is a news media outlet, and our blogs all have a similar touch, more or less. We stress that the eyewitnesses of news events report on the blogs in real time. After all, for readers, it makes a huge difference between the media coverage of an event and reports from eyewitnesses. . . . Readers especially hope that eyewitnesses will step forward and speak up. I do not need to explain why—the number of hits [these blogs create] is self-explanatory. Sometimes when the articles we recommend and post in the highlights section only receive tens of thousands, or hundreds of thousands, of hits, we know it is very likely that netizens are not interested in that topic. But when eyewitnesses offer their perspective, an article can easily generate millions of hits. . . . The blogs of witnesses have a much higher level of credibility and news value.[75]

During the 2010 Haiti earthquake, staff members at Sina invited Chinese witnesses of various backgrounds to post their experiences online. These eyewitness bloggers included survivors, the captains in charge of transporting corpses from Haiti, peacekeeping police, and the families of victims. These personal accounts of disaster supplemented the available information from other media outlets and generated much discussion. In addition, blog editors ran keyword searches on Sina's database to retrieve any related blog articles and compiled them into special issues highlighting various perspectives.[76]

The call for public participation in reporting and commenting on current events has developed more fully since Sina incorporated a microblogging service into its blogging platforms in 2010. The nature of the microblog as a highly interactive platform, the initiatives launched by blog editors to promote time-sensitive topics, and Sina's reputation as a well-established online news media have jointly catalyzed this rejuvenation of public interest in broadcasting and commenting on current affairs since the age of BBS.

The second strategy adopted by attention agents was to emphasize the nature of the blog as a remediated genre of the traditional diary, designed to chronicle personal experiences. On September 26, 2005, Sina announced the First Nationwide Blog Contest, and enhanced the credibility of the contest by inviting renowned writers, scholars, editors, and cultural critics to serve as judges. The First Nationwide Blog Contest recruited more than 5,000 participants and awarded prizes in eight categories of blogs, such as personal life, movies, pictures, design, and so on. Within the first two months of the competition, Sina reached 1 million registered users; the number of daily posts reached 30,000 to 40,000, on average.[77] In subsequent years, Sina continuously revised the rules of the blog contest based on current user interests and new technological offerings. In response to the soaring number of microbloggers, web editors launched the inaugural "micro-novel" (*wei xiaoshuo*) competition in 2010, which required participants to submit a mini-novel within the 140-character limit of the microblog. These series of contests not only offered new career opportunities to bloggers but also altered the landscape of the publishing industry. Many award winners became professional writers, columnists, and photographers. Blog publishing became one of the newest trends in the publishing industry, with editors of traditional publishing houses routinely keeping track of blogs to spot talented writers.[78] These Sina-sponsored contests bore witness to an appropriation of the enduring appeal of literature in its most extensive definition, demonstrated an innovative engagement in cultivating new genres of writing, and initiated a nationwide blogging movement. In the years that followed, web editors have continued to cultivate connections with grassroots bloggers by organizing offline get-togethers. Most grassroots bloggers also have developed strong bonds with web editors. These bloggers voluntarily partake in screening and recommending quality articles, and help test new applications developed by Sina, such as its microblogging service.[79] In so doing, web editors foster the flourishing of individual expression and civic engagement activities while strengthening Sina's user base.

Determining Popularity through Ranking and Recommendation Systems

If ordinary bloggers enjoy the freedom of linking and recommending sources, then professional digital attention agents play an even greater role in fashioning what is popular. Web editors employ a sophisticated ranking and recommendation system to structure content and direct readers' attention to the blog channel. Ranking systems largely depend on the quantitative data gathered from attention management software, while the evaluation standards of web editors are essential to the implementation of recommendation mechanisms. Evaluation standards vary depending on the time-sensitiveness of blog entries, topicality of content, and the disposition and background of editors, as well as quality and style of the content. For time-sensitive topics such as current affairs and foreseeable future events, web editors retrieve any related blog articles from the blog channel, contact eyewitnesses, and invite them to contribute new articles. Then, web editors assess the news value of the article and decide on the follow-up actions, such as whether to recommend the article and, if so, where it should be placed—on the home page of Sina, the front page of the blog channel, or a subsection of a column. Placement is of the utmost importance as it affects how quickly the content may capture the audience's attention. If the entry is of particular significance, attention agents will advertise the same article in different sections of the website and tailor the title to better attract an audience. For less time-sensitive topics, such as personal lives, culture, and entertainment, editors evaluate articles for their quality, news value, and potential interests to readers, and then decide on whether and how to recommend these articles.[80] In addition to regularly screening blog entries and propagating those with high attention value, editors encourage users to adopt a self-recommendation system. A blogger can recommend his or her own article or others' articles to web editors. The total number of recommendations a blog receives is displayed on the sidebar of the blog entitled "recommended articles." This sidebar offers detailed lists of articles that have been recommended by web editors, as well as showing the section to which the article has been recommended, thereby granting symbolic prestige to bloggers. By implementing a well-developed recommendation and ranking system, attention agents put effort into promoting blog entries that are deemed to possess a high attention value, while encouraging user participation by awarding ordinary bloggers with intangible benefits.

From Celebrity Blog to Chinese-Language Blogosphere

Although a latecomer to the blogging industry, Sina quickly dominated the Chinese-language blogosphere after 2005. Its rich media and social resources, advanced technical support, and large user base accumulated since the late 1990s ensured the rapid development and enhancement of its blog channel within a fairly short period of time. Sina's blog model as outlined in the preceding pages exemplifies how the public attention and user engagement was implemented at all levels. Web editors at Sina remained highly sensitive to user preferences and the attention value of online materials, extended the breadth and depth of blog content, spared no effort in cultivating promising bloggers, and nurtured the relationship between individual users and the website. Although these web editors remained mostly invisible online, their function as professional digital attention agents exerted tremendous influence on the developmental path of the Chinese blogosphere.

The success of Sina's model spawned the emulation of many websites. Overnight, inviting famous people to set up blog accounts became an important selling point for Internet content providers. Major online portals either embroiled themselves in the battle of fighting for celebrity resources or went in the opposite direction to develop alternative markets. CNTV and Ifeng capitalized on the resources of their sister organizations—CCTV and Phoenix Satellite Television—and invited TV hosts from within the same corporation to create blog accounts. The CNTV's "*mingren*" (famous people) channel and Ifeng's "*mingbo tuijian*" (recommendations of famous blogs) channel both focused on promoting their own TV anchors. By contrast, Sohu,

Sina's major competitor, devoted much attention to carving out markets for grassroots blogging (*caogen boke*) to gain a competitive advantage, in addition to launching a "*mingbo*" (famous blog) section.

Despite its enormous success, however, Sina's celebrity blogging model was not without controversy. One such controversy arose from the URLs assigned to celebrity blogs. While ordinary bloggers were assigned unique numbers, celebrity bloggers had the privilege of keeping their names in their URLs. This privilege caused quite a stir, as netizens argued that Sina violated the essence of blogging—equality.[81] Journalists, represented by Wang Xiaofeng, expressed their contempt at Sina's desperate pursuit of profit, which was satirized in Wang's first blog movie, *A Hard Day's Night* (*Xiaoqiang lixian ji*, 2006). Dissatisfied with the quality of blog entries on Sina, Luo Yonghao and Huang Bin founded Bullog (*Niubo wang*) in 2006. From 2006 to 2009, Bullog gathered more than 100 liberal-leaning intellectuals to comment on current affairs, including Fang Zhouzi, Wang Xiaofeng, Chai Jing, and Huang Zhangjin.[82] To avoid direct competition with Sina, smaller websites such as Blshe and Blogchina defined their audiences more narrowly by targeting intellectuals and technocrats, and they were more selective about their offerings.

Despite the disagreement Sina sparked among Internet users, the fierce competition for attention among dotcom businesses constituted the driving force of the vibrant blogosphere. Web editors at all sites emphasized updating operational models, fighting for consumers, and diversifying blog content to attract new users. In the fierce competition for user attention, browsing competitors' websites to understand their recommendation and ranking systems, methods of publicity, and other new features became a daily routine for all editors at major commercial portals.[83] Any business models, recommendation methods, and promotional strategies deemed effective by attention agents were quickly emulated. Consequently, commercial portals played a crucial role in popularizing blogging as a new form of writing. From 2005 onward, the Chinese blogosphere has constituted one of the most productive discursive spaces, not only reinvigorating writing practices but also playing a prominent role in encouraging individual expression, promoting citizen journalism, and boosting China's entertainment culture. These cultural trends heightened with the advent of the microblog.

From Blog to Microblog

The developmental trajectory of the microblog in China resembles that of the blog. The story began with startup entrepreneurs who were eager to imitate US technological trends and business models. In May 2007, one year after Twitter was founded, Wang Xing, a technology entrepreneur, launched Fanfou, the first microblogging site in China. The participation of cultural celebrities such as Chen Danqing, Liang Wendao, and Lian Yue, from June 2007 onward, helped bring in a large number of followers to Fanfou.[84] Shortly after Fanfou was launched, technological entrepreneur Li Zhuohuan launched Jiwai, another stand-alone microblogging service provider. During the years 2008 and 2009, small microblogging service providers grew rapidly. More than thirty microblogging websites were launched, including Zuosha, Mangfou, Digu, Leihou, 9911, and Tongxue-wang.[85] Fanfou continued to take the lead in the industry, with the number of users reaching 1 million in June 2009.

Following the model of Twitter, early microblogging service providers in China encouraged Internet users to instantaneously share information on time-sensitive events. An example of such an event is the Uygur riots that occurred in western Xinjiang province on July 5, 2009, and resulted in almost 200 dead and 1,700 injured.[86] Due to the sensitive nature of this incident, influential commercial portals such as Sina and Sohu posted only the information provided by official media outlets. Distrustful of what was reported by state media outlets, Internet users logged into microblogging sites to retrieve alternative information. Consequently, major microblogging service providers, including Fanfou, Jiwai, and Digu, were all forced to shut down due to their failure to censor information in a timely manner. Fanfou remained inaccessible until November 25, 2010, while Twitter, YouTube, and Facebook have been blocked in China ever since the riots.

The setbacks suffered by small microblogging service providers in 2009 provided opportunities for larger commercial portals to catch up. One month after the Xinjiang riots, Sina launched a beta version of its microblog. Sina managed to convince the state authorities that rather than posing a threat to the government, their proffering of microblogging services would help sustain authoritarian rule. Other major commercial websites, including Tencent,

Sohu, Hexun, Baidu, Ifeng, and NetEase, soon began to offer microblogging services as well. From 2010 to 2011, microblogs led the way as the web application with the greatest increase in popularity (208.9 percent).[87] The level of user engagement was unprecedented. In July 2010, 3 million messages were produced, on average, every day; forty tweets were posted per second.[88] In September 2010, the microblogging market share of Sina Weibo reached 60.9 percent, followed by NetEase, Tencent, Sohu, and other smaller companies.[89] Building on its well-developed model of celebrity blogging, Sina Weibo soon dominated the microblogging marketplace and expanded its user base to Hong Kong, Taiwan, and the overseas market.

The early phase of Weibo illustrates the competition for celebrity resources between Sina and other major commercial portals, like Tencent, in particular. In the initial stage, editors at Sina invited grassroots users to test Weibo and offer feedback. Editors observed that ordinary users were more excited about checking out new products, while celebrities tended to be more conservative due to concerns about their public image.[90] However, it was soon determined that grassroots users had a rather limited influence on the larger community. Under the direction of editor-in-chief Chen Tong, Sina initiated a massive campaign to invite well-established figures to participate in microblogging. Editors from each channel first submitted a recommendation list of well-known figures in their field of specialty, including education, news, entertainment, travel, and photography. After the Weibo channel approved the list, staff members invited those people on the list to test the beta version. Sina then opened up registration to everyone and encouraged existing users to invite their friends to set up accounts. As it had during its promotion of blogging, Sina implemented a strict reward and punishment system for its staff members to expand Weibo's user base. Every editor was expected to invite one celebrity and two journalists to register microblogging accounts per week. These new users were expected to post original content on a regular basis, such as contributing seven tweets each week. Staff members who failed to fill the quota were criticized in the corporation's public announcements. Later on, the penalty for failure changed to a fine of 200 RMB (approximately 32 USD). At the same time, those who succeeded in inviting extremely well-known figures were awarded monetary incentives.[91]

This massive mobilization campaign, along with Sina's well-established celebrity blogging model, contributed to an exponential growth of microbloggers. Within six months of launching its microblogging service, Sina's user base surpassed that of Fanfou.[92] In 2010, Sina released the official version of Weibo and gradually transitioned from an imitator of Twitter and Facebook into a multifunctional platform that included blogging, video sharing, live broadcasting, networking, advertising, and gaming.

Due to the swinging stance Tencent held toward microblogging,[93] the formal launch of Tencent Weibo took place in May 2010, ten months after Sina's move. To convince celebrities and opinion leaders to use Tencent's service, the corporation paid for their contribution of tweets.[94] In February 2011, Tencent announced that its Weibo users had reached 100 million. By December 31, 2011, registered users at Sina and Tencent had reached 373 million and 300 million respectively.[95] In the third quarter of 2012, there were 507 million microbloggers on Tencent, while the number of Sina's microbloggers reached 536 million in the first quarter of 2013.[96] As in the case of celebrity blogging, when dominant portals engaged in fierce competition for resources, stand-alone microblogging service providers quickly lost their market share. Although Fanfou was reopened to Internet users in 2010, it had already missed the golden opportunity of growth. To this day Fanfou remains popular only among niche user groups who oppose the excessive commercialization of Sina's service.

In addition to individual microbloggers, institutional accounts grew steadily. As of August 2010, one year after Sina launched its Weibo channel, 466 mainstream media outlets had set up their accounts on Sina, including 118 newspapers, 243 magazines, 36 television stations, and 69 radio stations.[97] In addition, 41 governmental organizations and 60 public security bureaus established their accounts. The microblogging accounts of dominant and mainstream media continued to grow in the years that followed. As of September 30, 2017, the number of official microblogging accounts on Sina Weibo had increased from 60,064 in October 2012 to 171,000.[98]

The year 2014 officially marked the consolidation of Sina's dominant position in the marketplace, when Sina's major competitors, Tencent and NetEase, both closed down their microblogging sectors. Tencent, meanwhile, had shifted its strategic focus to the full-scale development of WeChat, a mobile messaging application that evolved into a multimedia platform. The enormous popularity of WeChat, in turn, diverted a large number of users from Sina Weibo by 2013. In response, Sina constantly adjusted its strategies to cope with fluctuations in market dynamics, user demographics, and state policies. Because of the tremendous influence of Sina Weibo, my analysis of microblogging in China focuses on Sina's interplay with major social actors, particularly the state, and with Sina's competitors and Internet users.

Sina Weibo: Major Phases and Strategies

The early stage of Weibo (2009–13) furthered the two mutually constituting trends that first became phenomenal in the age of blogging: the boom of the entertainment culture and increased activities of political engagement. Technical features of Weibo, particularly the accelerated pace of information dissemination and its networking function, reinforced both trends. In addition to adopting new features, commercial portals incorporated all previously available functions into their microblogging platforms, including features of BBSs and blogs. Like Twitter, Sina adopted the 140-character limit for each tweet and allowed users to retweet (*zhuanfa*). Sina also added a feature that encourages users to comment on others' posts or add a comment when sharing a message. To sustain the appeal of the traditional blog, Sina invented the "long tweets" (*chang weibo*) feature, incorporating the function of blogging into the microblogging platform.

As in the case of celebrity blogs, a hierarchical rule of attention applies to the Chinese microblogosphere. Sina introduced the designation "V," meaning verification, to distinguish well-known figures from ordinary users. The phrase "big V" (*da v*) came to refer to users who had millions of followers, while "middle V" (*zhong v*) and "small V" (*xiao v*) were used to describe those who had comparatively smaller numbers of followers. The color of "V" also bore different connotations: institutions carried a blue "V," while individuals carried an orange "V." As of July 2010, more than 20,000 celebrities had registered on Sina Weibo. The ten microbloggers who attracted the most attention were mostly entertainment stars and cultural celebrities, including Yao Chen, Xiao S, Zhao Wei, and Guo Jingming.[99] Tencent, Sohu,

Ifeng, and NetEase soon joined the competition to invite renowned figures to create microblogging accounts. By the end of 2013, the number of big Vs who had more than 10 million followers had reached 200, while 3,300 big Vs had more than 1 million followers.[100]

The flourishing of celebrity accounts on Weibo opened new avenues for fans to interact instantaneously with their idols. More important, given the large number of followers celebrities attracted, these accounts easily functioned as "network nodes" that directed fans' attention to societal issues, thereby catalyzing "the flow of information, sentiment, and emotion" in the Chinese microblogosphere.[101] Celebrity opinion leaders on Weibo played a crucial role in promoting civic engagement activities. As with the operational logic of the blog, behind the vibrant microblogging scene was the invisible workforce of Weibo's editorial team. Writing about the capabilities of Sina in 2014, Marina Svensson stated that the corporation "launches special topics (by setting up hashtags), organizes public events and takes up specific causes, including organizing online debates with famous people on hot topics. Sina Weibo is also engaged in public welfare work, and it teams up with and provides platforms for organizations and individuals engaged in such activities."[102] From 2009 to 2013, Weibo carried on Sina's function as a news media outlet and played a pivotal role in stimulating public discussion of societal issues. The participation of other web portals and mainstream media outlets reinforced these trends. In addition to maintaining the accounts of well-known figures, Sina constantly adjusted its strategies to carve out new market niches, in particular among Internet users in third- and fourth-tier cities. When the market for celebrity microbloggers was almost saturated, editors traveled to provinces in China to recruit local users. Each editor at Sina's Weibo channel recruited users in a single designated province, often the home province of that particular editor. For three months, editors assisted local radio stations and television stations to promote their programs concerning Weibo. The objective was to enhance Sina's collaboration with traditional media outlets and, at the same time, increase the overall number of microbloggers.[103] Another important new measure adopted by Sina was to invest in deep analytics to sell advertisements in a more targeted manner. When new users registered on Weibo, they were required to classify their fields of interest. Weibo then recommended the top twenty microbloggers in these fields. Weibo also recommended celebrity figures and advertisements based on a user's browsing history. These strategies partially ameliorated a number of crisis situations that Sina encountered around 2012 to 2014, due to the change in China's political leadership, factional struggles from within the Sina Corporation, and the rapid rise of WeChat.

In the aftermath of the 2012 transition in political leadership, the new administration under President Xi Jinping implemented institutional measures to tighten ideological control over the online space and rejuvenate propaganda work. Following Xi's speech at a national propaganda conference in July 2013, the state launched massive campaigns that detained influential Weibo celebrities, human rights activists, journalists, and Internet publicity personnel, under charges of "rumour-mongering," "disturbing public order," "tax evasion," and morality issues.[104] Some of the well-known figures included the online opinion leader Xue Manzi, journalist Liu Hu, human rights advocates Yang Maodong and Xu Zhiyong, and Qin Huohuo, an Internet publicity figure at Beijing Erma Interactive Marketing and Planning. Meanwhile, the state began to take a proactive approach to enhancing e-governance and disseminating ideological messages in a more persuasive manner. Official institutions, representatively *People's Daily*, the Communist Youth League of China, and the radio station *Voice of China* innovatively experimented with new forms of propaganda via their Weibo accounts. The enhanced visibility of dominant official media, along with strengthened censorship control, significantly factored into a changing ecology of Sina Weibo.

In the midst of this sensitive political atmosphere, factional struggles within the leadership of Sina led to further inconsistency regarding the strategic planning for Weibo. The disagreement between Sina Corporation and its Weibo division resulted in policy and personnel changes. Chen Tong, Sina's chief editor and executive vice president, was demoted and became less engaged in developing Weibo; he left the company in November 2014. Given Chen's seventeen years of experience at Sina, his resignation exerted a negative influence on the company's staff. As to the strategic development of Weibo, the executives constantly debated between two models: advancing Weibo as a social networking site or developing Weibo into a multifunctional platform that incorporated all possible elements, including video sharing, e-commerce, and blogging. This conflict of focus led to several rounds of unsuccessful upgrades to Weibo.[105] In early 2014, for the first time Weibo witnessed a decline of users, by 28 million or 9 percent of the entire Weibo population.[106]

To remain competitive in the marketplace, Sina took a series of measures to revive its microblogophere. In 2013, Alibaba, the largest e-commerce company in China, paid 586 million USD to acquire an 18 percent stake in Sina Weibo. The collaboration between these two corporations enhanced Weibo's e-commerce capabilities, as retailers on Tmall, one of the most popular online shopping sites owned by Alibaba, began to actively use Weibo for personal branding and publicity. Subsequently, Sina Weibo was renamed Weibo, separating it from its parent company. Weibo was listed on NASDAQ on April 17, 2014. In addition, mobile Internet, an area in which Sina had fallen behind, began receiving a greater level of attention from the leadership. In December 2012, Wang Gaofei, general manager of Sina's Wireless Industry Department, assumed the position of Weibo's general manager. Aside from these changes in personnel and partnership, Sina adopted three strategies to revive Weibo.

First, in response to the massive government crackdowns on opinion leaders, Sina toned down its focus on celebrity opinion leaders and enforced stricter measures for governing content to comply with state censors. In an effort to retain users, Sina shifted its content emphasis to civic issues pertaining to everyday life and focused on helping small Vs and middle Vs to increase their number of followers. In addition, Weibo promoted several initiatives to encourage the contribution of original content. Sina invited experts in specialized areas such as health care, finance, and technology to contribute original content to Weibo and arranged micro-interviews (*wei fangtan*) to allow them to interact with users. Sina also incorporated two popular models into the microblogosphere that originated from literary websites—paying virtual rewards (*dashang*) and pay-per-read. Both models offered monetary incentives to contributors of original content. Q&A on Weibo, a feature that was invented by Zhihu—a question-and-answer-based website—encouraged users to pay a fairly small amount (0.15 USD) to read the answers to questions posed to celebrity microbloggers by fans. On June 15, 2015, Sina announced its plan to invest 150 million RMB (23 million USD) to compensate selected microbloggers for their original content. Sina's contracted writers included film critics, academics, and freelancers. These moves exhibited Sina's tendency to value and commodify knowledge production in flexible forms, ranging from long essays and shorter answers to live streaming and short-form videos.

Second, Weibo collaborated more closely with traditional media outlets, in particular television stations and print media. Weibo positioned itself as an interactive platform for communication and helped publicize the programs that television stations were broadcasting.[107] User interaction on Weibo that revolved around these television programs contributed to increased web traffic, which encouraged sponsors of television programs to sell advertisements on Weibo. In 2014, more than 20 satellite stations and over 100 television programs collaborated with Weibo.[108] In this respect, Weibo pushed the entertainment industry to a new stage of development. If celebrity blogs highlighted the efforts of individuals to construct a star persona, then Weibo's collaboration with legacy media outlets enabled comprehensive coverage of entertainment-related activities, connecting media institutions, followers of programs, celebrities and their fans, and ordinary users.

Last, Weibo integrated emerging cultural and technological trends into the microblogging platform. Live streaming and short-form videos (*duan shipin*) are two of the most popular applications on Weibo. Starting in 2014, Weibo collaborated with several tech companies, such as Miaopai, Xiaokaxiu, and Yizhibo, to develop these features. In the following year, Sina introduced live broadcasts as a new feature and encouraged both well-established figures and Internet users who aspired to become social influencers to broadcast their everyday lives. These moves catered to the current audience tastes that favored visuals, live broadcasts, and webinars. As of May 2016, short videos on Weibo created 1.7 billion views per day on average, while the number of daily views for Xiaokaxiu was close to 100 million.[109]

Sina's three strategic approaches to reviving its microblogosphere produced results. Weibo showed signs of recovery in the fourth quarter of 2014. By June 30, 2016, Weibo had turned a profit for seven quarters in a row and exhibited a continuous growth in advertising revenue.[110] Surviving through several crises, the developmental trajectory of Sina Weibo showcases how this medium has shifted from an emphasis on celebrity politics and citizen journalism to a multifunctional platform that celebrates the knowledge economy and e-commerce, cultivates Internet stars, and enhances collaboration with mainstream and official media outlets. While Weibo retains some of its earlier characteristic features, such as its role in promoting citizen journalism and aggregating information, the platform has transitioned into a mainstream media channel. This changing ecology of Weibo is jointly shaped by corporate responses to the fierce market competition, new technological offerings, the changing demographics of Internet users, and ever-changing sociopolitical circumstances.

WeChat, "a Lifestyle"

Tencent's advertising slogan, "WeChat, a lifestyle," accurately summarizes the full-scale integration of this single mobile app into users' everyday lives. In the course of competing with Sina for a share in the microblogging market, Ma Huateng, the founder, chairman, and chief executive officer of Tencent, concluded that only an entirely different product could possibly compete with Weibo. Launched in January 2011, WeChat evolved from a mobile messaging app into a multifunctional platform that includes text messaging, voice messages, video and audio calls, mobile payments, gaming, photo and video sharing, mini programs, personal status updates ("moments"), and public accounts (*gongzhong hao*). In 2015, the app became available for tablets and desktops. To date, WeChat supports twenty languages, including English, Indonesian, Spanish, Thai, Hindi, and Russian. Since its release, WeChat has gone through many upgrades and adjustments to meet market demands.[111]

Despite its enormous popularity, WeChat is by no means the sole mobile application that provides such services. In November 2010, Interactive Technology launched iGexin; Xiaomi Technology developed Mi Chat (Miliao) one month later. MoMo, another location-based instant messaging application that focuses on dating, was launched in 2011. The telecommunications sector gave rise to similar products, such as Yiliao by China Telecom, Feiliao by China Mobile, and Woyou by China Unicom.[112] However, WeChat soon stood out from these products because of the large user base that its predecessor,

QQ, had accumulated since 1999, as well as the variety of functions offered by WeChat's single platform. Fifteen months after the initial release of We-Chat, its registered users surpassed 100 million, making it the fastest-growing online communication tool at that time. QQ had taken almost ten years to reach 100 million users, while Facebook and Twitter took five-and-a-half and four years, respectively, to reach the same level of popularity.[113] In March 2018, registered users of WeChat reached 1 billion globally.[114]

WeChat exemplifies several major breakthroughs in the Internet history of China. WeChat is the first mobile application that reaches the same level of popularity as desktop applications like BBSs, blogs, and microblogs. All of these earlier platforms had limited appeal for the senior generation in China, some of whom are illiterate and less technologically oriented. However, WeChat's easy-to-use features—such as voice messaging, video calls, and the conversion of voice messages into text—do not require language or technical literacy, which largely accounts for its popularity among seniors. As of November 2017, 50 million active WeChat users were aged between 55 and 70.[115] More important, WeChat merges functions such as telecommunication, social networking, information dissemination, and e-commerce.[116] As an integrated platform, WeChat enables users to perform a variety of daily activities, from paying bills to meeting potential dinner dates to establishing professional networks. WeChat makes up 34 percent of mobile traffic in China, while Facebook accounts for only 14.1 percent of mobile traffic in North America.[117] These designing features drive users' reliance on WeChat as a must-have app.

Moreover, the three prominent features of WeChat—the "friends' circle" (*pengyou quan*), "group" (*qun*), and "public accounts" (*gongzhong hao*)—have reshaped the conception of public culture, the public, and the publicity methods embodied in BBSs, blogs, and microblogs. The openness of these early platforms enabled the eruption of web-based incidents on a massive scale, while the anonymity of online interactions was also conducive to debate. By comparison, the design of WeChat prioritizes private connections that are based on individuals' existing social networks. The highlighting of inter-personal relations reinforces a sense of trust among users who are already connected through personal acquaintances, friends' recommendations, or professional relationships. In this sense, WeChat strengthens ties among users' existing contacts, classified into groups such as colleagues, family, classmates, interest groups, and so on, thereby forging segmented publics and new publicity channels.

Specifically, the friends' circle, also known as "moments," resembles a Facebook page, and an individual may add up to 5,000 friends to his or her contact list through multiple means, including phone numbers, friends' recommendation, scanning a QR code, and location-based searches. By clicking on "moments," an individual can access friends' updates or post personal updates via text, images, and short-form videos. Unlike Facebook, where responses to an individual's post are open to all friends of the user, published content on WeChat features selective openness. Follow-up comments on a WeChat post are not visible to everyone, unless the commenter and viewer of the post are also friends. Since each individual's friends' circle varies, this feature reduces the chance that a post may incite a public incident or raise public sentiment. Meanwhile, this function also creates a sense of intimacy among these who have access to the same content. Relatedly, while the feature of sharing is common among social networking sites like Facebook, Twitter, and Weibo, shared content on WeChat is limited to texts and visuals openly published on public accounts and websites. In addition, when publishing a post in "moments," the content creator has several privacy options. The user may set the post to be visible to selected groups and users or make it accessible to all friends. Thus, the visibility of content on one's "moments" page is contingent on the decision of the poster.

If the friends' circle is a semipublic space, then groups on WeChat are more open, available to members yet restricted to outsiders. Individual users may establish various groups based on their social relations and interests, with categories such as classmates, news, sports, conferences, family, special occasions, and so on. Each group can accommodate 3 to 500 users, and administrators of each group are responsible for the content posted. Group members may invite others to join the group; individual users also have the liberty of withdrawing from a group. Although each group excludes outsiders, a shared sense of openness exists among group members. Nevertheless, the extent to which group members interact with one another and engage in

in-depth discussion depends on the group's cohesiveness. The group function of WeChat also greatly advances "local-based interests."[118] Residents of a
specific region may easily form interest groups to make announcements and
organize social activities for interests ranging from parenting and property
management to hobbies and charity work. Thus, the sense of publicness
formed in "groups" and the "friends' circle" is conditional, contingent on a
user's social relations and personal interests.

In contrast to the semipublic nature of "friends' circles" and "groups,"
content published on WeChat's public accounts is accessible to all users of
smartphones and tablets. Nevertheless, content on WeChat's public accounts
differs from the openness of BBS forums, blogs, and microblogs. Readers'
comments are selectively published by account holders, while users may
interact with only the account holder in the comments section, not directly
with other users. While this design enhances the central role of the account
operator, it limits the opportunities for readers to socialize in these spaces.

Launched on August 23, 2012, WeChat public accounts allow users to
publish essays, audios, videos, and images. Individuals with more than 500
followers were qualified to register public accounts. In May 2014, public account holders were allowed to host online stores within the app. This policy
attracted the participation of major brands, retailers, small business owners,
and startup entrepreneurs. The exponential growth of public accounts following the introduction of these initiatives has been phenomenal. In November
2013, there were 2 million registered public accounts.[119] Between 2014 and
2016, the number of official WeChat accounts nearly doubled, from 6.86 million to 12.1 million. As of September 2017, there were 20 million registered
WeChat official accounts.[120]

Within a short span of time, WeChat public accounts have risen as the
premium platform for well-established figures, social media influencers,
enterprising journalists, and enterprises to promote their content offerings.
Public accounts allow enterprises and businesses to rapidly disseminate
information, at the lowest cost, to their target audiences. For these original
content contributors, public accounts further the trend that Weibo initiated several years earlier—the cultivation and dissemination of specialized
knowledge in every aspect of a user's life. At this time, the well-developed

model of e-commerce is ready to offer a myriad of ways to monetize content. Renowned public account writers may generate profits by displaying advertisements or sponsored content on their media space. They may also write advertorial content for brands or sell products by embedding a click-to-buy button in their articles, while readers may make direct deposits to authors they like. These flexible models of garnering revenue, taken together with the decline in print media and the prevalence of smartphones, have acted as a large incentive for contributors of original content to flock to WeChat. As a result, WeChat public accounts have furthered the nationwide enthusiasm for self-publishing that began in the age of BBSs and have once again revolutionized the production, dissemination, and consumption of original content.

Simply put, the services of these four platforms have largely contributed to the vibrancy of the Chinese Internet. As the following chapters will demonstrate, the trajectory of the Internet in China reflects how the age of innocence, which embodied the collective spirit of egalitarianism, gradually developed into the age of commerce, and how the age of idealism evolved into the era of pragmatism. It is during this process that a *cultural* revolution reached into every corner of Chinese society.

3 TRACKING PLAYFULNESS

THE YEAR 2014 MARKED the twentieth anniversary of the premiere screening of Stephen Chow's cult film *A Chinese Odyssey* (*Dahua xiyou*, dir. Jeffrey Lau). Voted in 1995 as one of the ten worst movies imported to mainland China,[1] *A Chinese Odyssey* miraculously turned into a timeless classic. When *A Chinese Odyssey* was reshown in Chinese theatres in 2014, countless fans competed with one another to purchase movie tickets. These fans claimed that they owed Chow a movie ticket because, twenty years prior, they had first accessed *A Chinese Odyssey* through illegal distribution channels, particularly pirated VCDs and DVDs. Chow's devoted fan base in mainland China paved the way for the phenomenal box office success of two sequels that were loosely based on the same story. *Journey to the West: Conquering the Demons* (*Dahua xiyou xiangmo pian*, 2013), codirected by Chow and Derek Kwok, garnered a total of 215 million USD worldwide and held the record for the highest-grossing Chinese-language film until 2015.[2] This movie's sequel, *Journey to the West: The Demons Strike Back* (*Xiyou fuyao pian*, dir. Tsui Hark, 2017), produced by Chow, was the highest-grossing film among the various adaptations of *Journey to the West*.

Chow's cult status in the mainland market, as evidenced by fans' nickname for him, "*Xingye*" (Master Xing), would not have been possible without the frenetic reception of *A Chinese Odyssey* by the first cohort of Chinese netizens. They thoroughly dissected the movie through creative discussion, innovative performance, and reappropriation of the text via the university bulletin board systems (BBSs). Indeed, the ways in which Internet users imitated the film's style in their everyday lives exemplify the rise of a Chinese Internet culture that accentuated playfulness and sentimentalism. Existing scholarly literature has addressed the predominance of online playfulness through the lens of netizens' political and cultural resistance.[3] While these studies deepen our understanding of the ingenuity of Chinese netizens in appropriating parody and creating memes, the particular sociopolitical conditions that fostered the rise of the fun-seeking nature of the Chinese Internet need more study.

This chapter addresses this gap in the literature and investigates a number of the early idiosyncrasies of the Chinese Internet through a close examination of the shared stance among the first cohort of netizens in the late 1990s. My examination focuses on the enormous popularity of three foundational texts among early Internet users: *A Chinese Odyssey* (*Dahua xiyou*, 1994), *The First Intimate Contact* (*Diyici de qinmi jiechu*, 1998), and *Night Talks at Tsinghua* (*Tsinghua yehua*, 2001). I argue that early netizens' emphasis on absurdity, comic sensibility, and excessive sentimentality in everyday life lays the groundwork for the predominant mode of playfulness online, which then paved the way for the sensational rise of Furong Jiejie, the first Internet celebrity in China. In this regard, the BBSs constituted the primary affective platform where Furong Jiejie's followers sought pleasure by contributing original content, sharing fanatical sentiments, and staging virtual fights. The formation of mock fandom on these BBS sites cultivated the symbiotic relationship between frivolity and serious political engagement among early Internet users. It also nurtured the rise of attention agents who converted instant popularity into upward career opportunities. Furong Jiejie's miraculous transformation from a public laughingstock into a role model is just one example, for which she inspired quite a few emulators.

If the accidental rise of Furong Jiejie, and the controversies she generated, illustrates the historical juncture at which elite netizens first embraced populism in the age of declining idealism, the rapid development of the online star-making industry that followed commodifies online parody and entertainment. In the 2010s, the creation and maintenance of Internet celebrities (*wanghong*) became a streamlined industry that attracted the participation of creative talents, public relations personnel, e-commerce sectors, and the visual industry. The final section of this chapter addresses these new developments, and investigates the foremost Internet celebrity of 2016, Papi Jiang. In contrast to the crudeness embodied in Furong Jiejie's self-presentation, the clownishness projected in Papi Jiang's self-made videos is a calculated production that, despite its unpolished appearance, resulted from a careful consideration of her audience's tastes. In this respect, the journey of Internet celebrities in China reflects how buffoonery in public entertainment has been rapidly institutionalized. Moreover, the flourishing of web-based genres in the 2010s, ranging from parodies and dramas to reality shows, demonstrates how the predominant fun-seeking mode among early netizens has exerted a profound impact on the Internet industry's continuous experiments with comedic mechanisms.

The First Cohort of Chinese Netizens

The late 1990s marked a crucial turning point in Chinese society. Amid the high tide of state-led commercialization and privatization campaigns, the function of culture as a tool of both enlightenment and propaganda largely declined. Institutional restructuring took place in all areas of cultural production, including film, TV, and print media. These groups began to learn how to cope with market laws, fostering the surge of entertainment trends in the cultural realm. The golden age of "high culture fever"[4] in the 1980s, represented by the revived status of intellectuals as social elites, the burgeoning of serious artistic pursuits, and the massive introduction of Western cultural works, was eclipsed by the rise of popular culture in the 1990s. Accompanying the decline in idealism and high culture was the rise of popular entertainment outlets, including commercial cinema, fashion magazines, paparazzi journalism, bestsellers, and entertainment television, as well as a fascination with and aspiration for the urban middle-class lifestyle. The takeoff of the Internet industry in the late 1990s soon enhanced this entertainment surge and established the Internet as the major competitor of traditional media.

The banal turn of Chinese society and the opening up of online space in the late 1990s prepared the collective debut of the first generation of Chinese netizens and shaped their "structures of feeling."[5] As "a trend that is developing but is not yet clearly emergent,"[6] "structures of feeling" refer to a "particular quality of social experience and relationship . . . which gives the sense of a generation or of a period."[7] This social experience is a process in formation and conveys "meanings and values as they are actively lived and felt."[8] Given that Internet development in China started with elite research institutions and leading universities, this first cohort consisted mainly of college students, researchers, and urban professionals. In response to the radically changing sociocultural circumstances around them, this nascent Internet generation used a new language to define their experience. The Internet as a new technology, BBS as a novel content platform, and the particular sociocultural conditions of the late 1990s nurtured the rise of new structures of feeling among these young netizens. Their concern for mundane issues rather than an obsession with grandeur, their lack of deference to authority online, and their playful subversion of the orthodox constituted some of the most important factors that accounted for the predominant mode of playfulness online.

"Life in Jiujing": The Birth of Chinese Netizens

I have had my true love before, but I did not treasure her. When I lost her, I felt true regret. It was the most painful matter in this world. If God gave me another chance, I would say three words to her, "I love you." If you have to give a time limit to this love, I hope it is 10,000 years! (*A Chinese Odyssey*, 1994)

If I had only one day left to live, I would want to be your girlfriend that day. Do I have one day to live? No. Therefore, too bad, I can't be your girlfriend in this life. If I had wings, I would fly down from Heaven to see you. Do I have wings? No. Therefore, too bad, I will never be able to see you from this moment on. Even if all the water in my bathtub could be poured out, my love for you would never be extinguished. Can I pour out all the water? Yes. So, it's true that . . . I love you. (*The First Intimate Contact*, 1998)

There are three kinds of men in Beijing. The first kind are men in *Jianguomenwai* [commercial districts], handsome, rich, and fun. The second kind are men in *Zhongguancun* [China's Silicon Valley], handsome, rich, but fucking boring. The problem is that they do not have time for fun. Alas, as for the third kind, they are men in *Sanlitun* [bar areas], handsome, fun, but poor! So it's of the utmost uselessness for a man to be handsome, because you are handsome as long as you are a man! . . . A year-long fellowship [you receive to study in the US] is 20,000 USD. How many words are there in GRE? More than 20,000. So, a dollar a word! (*Night Talks at Tsinghua*, 2001)

"*Jiujing*," written as 9#, refers to both the physical dorms inhabited by undergraduates of the Computer Science Department at Tsinghua University and the name of the building's intranet under the SMTH BBS. "[Living] in *jiujing*" thus carries a dual meaning that describes the college students' life online as well as the physical location in which they reside.[9] For the first time, surfing online constituted an integral component of the everyday life experience of college students. The forging of their collective identity as netizens was marked by the popularity of three foundational texts: a Hong Kong film, *Dahua xiyou* (*A Chinese Odyssey*, dir. Jeffrey Lau, 1994); an Internet novel, *Diyici de qinmi jiechu* (*The First Intimate Contact*, 1998), by Taiwanese writer Tsai Jhi-hsin; and an amateur video, *Tsinghua yehua* (*Night Talks at Tsinghua*, 2001), produced by undergraduate students at Tsinghua University. These three texts were of different genres and had different distribution channels and release quality, yet the reception of all three was inextricably linked to the net culture boom that began in the mid-1990s in China. Chinese netizens' frenetic celebration of these works illuminates a number of generational traits, as manifested by their particular way of interpreting, reiterating, parodying, and performing lines from these texts. Consequently, the formulation of a collective taste for excessive sentimentality, comic sensibility, and absurdity set the tone of the budding Internet culture in China.

A Chinese Odyssey

Originally shot as a three-hour movie, *A Chinese Odyssey* was later divided into two films: *A Chinese Odyssey Part One: Pandora's Box* (*Dahua xiyou zhi yueguang baohe*) and *A Chinese Odyssey Part Two: Cinderella* (*Dahua xiyou zhi xianlü qiyuan*). The films' Chinese title, *Dahua xiyou*, identifies them as fabricated accounts of traditional tales. *Dahua* (literally, "to talk big") carries the negative connotation of bragging or making things up. *Xiyou* refers to one of the four classic novels of Chinese literature, *Journey to the West* (*Xiyou ji*), on which *A Chinese Odyssey* is loosely based. The novel fictionalizes the adventures of the Buddhist monk Tang Seng (Xuanzang), who travels to India to bring Buddhist scriptures back to Tang Dynasty China (618–907 AD). The Bodhisattva Guanyin, upon the Buddha's instruction, gives this task to Tang Seng and his three disciples, one of whom is the Monkey King (Sun Wukong). In the story, various monsters attempt to gain immortality by capturing Tang Seng, and the monk's disciples do everything possible to rescue him. Combining slapstick comedy with romance, *A Chinese Odyssey* complicates the original storyline and makes major changes to the portrayal of its characters. Thus, the film differs drastically from both the original novel and the 1986 TV drama adaptation of *Journey to the West* (1986, dir. Yang Jie), a classic in its own right. In one such difference, Tang Seng (known in the film, as Longevity Monk), who was originally portrayed as an upright figure known for his kindheartedness, is cast as an annoyingly garrulous monk:

> Monkey King, you are so naughty! I've told you not to throw things. Look! You've thrown away the stick. Pandora's Box is the treasure. [If you throw things away], you'll pollute the environment. You'll hurt kids. If there are no kids, it is bad to hurt plants. . . . Monkey King, do you like [Pandora's Box]? Tell me if you do. I'll give it to you if you like it. I won't give it to you if you don't tell me. I'm pretty sure that I will give it to you if you like it. I'm pretty sure that I won't give it to you if you don't like it. We're reasonable human beings. I'll count to three. Tell me if you like it or not.

In contrast, the Monkey King, traditionally a rebellious and mischievous but capable character, is portrayed as a clownish figure uncommitted to his mission, who even has romantic encounters with several women.

At the outset of *A Chinese Odyssey*, the Bodhisattva Guanyin kills the Monkey King because he was plotting with King Bull to eat Longevity Monk. To save the Monkey King, Longevity Monk takes his own life, and, moved by this selfless sacrifice, the Jade Emperor gives the Monkey King a second chance to help Longevity Monk, in a later reincarnation. Five hundred years later, Zhi Zunbao (Joker, played by Stephen Chow), a reincarnation of the Monkey King, is the leader of a gang of bandits. When monsters come to the bandits' place looking for Longevity Monk, Joker falls in love with one of them, Bai Jingjing (White-Skeleton Demon). Chunsanshi niang (Spider Demon), Bai Jingjing's sister, lies to Bai in an attempt to learn the whereabouts of Longevity Monk, telling her that she has had a son with Joker. Out of despair, Bai Jingjing commits suicide. Joker wants to use Pandora's Box to go back in time to bring Bai Jingjing back to life. However, he accidentally travels 500 years back in time and meets Zixia (Purple Clouds), an immortal who has escaped from her place as the wick in Buddha's lamp. Zixia confiscates Pandora's Box, puts three marks on the bottom of Joker's left foot, and makes him her servant. However, she soon falls in love with Joker. In an attempt to get the Box back from Zixia to save Bai Jingjing, Joker promises Zixia that he will run away with her and love her for 10,000 years. The rest of the story focuses on how Joker finally comprehends the impermanence of life and death and is immediately incarnated into the Monkey King, who vows to serve Longevity Monk devotedly. Before the Monkey King sets out on his journey to the West, he tries to save Zixia from King Bull, who wants to force Zixia to marry him. It is only at that moment that Joker realizes he has fallen in love with Zixia, yet it is too late. At the end of the film, the current incarnations of Joker and Zixia get involved in an argument in front of a crowd. The Monkey King uses his power to make the incarnations of Joker and Zixia kiss and reconcile. The final scene shows the Monkey King looking back at the couple one final time before beginning his journey to the West.

A Chinese Odyssey boldly reinvents the classic tale. The film relentlessly pokes fun at positive figures in the original story, while adding many provocative elements, such as the Monkey King's affairs with demons. The movie's nonlinear narrative style, as well as its frequent use of travel in time and space, also differs significantly from the novel and TV series, both of which greatly influenced mainland audiences. All these factors ultimately resulted in the poor reception of A Chinese Odyssey. The film was a box office flop in Hong Kong and Taiwan,[10] and, in 1996, was regarded as a typical example of a release failure for garnering only 400,000 RMB (70,000 USD) in box office revenue in Beijing.[11]

The rekindled interest in *A Chinese Odyssey* and its sweeping influence on college students surprised many observers. Seemingly overnight, university students in Beijing considered it trendy to discuss and analyze the film from every angle, dissecting everything from its popular lines, shooting techniques, and character relations to the philosophical questions it raises about human existence and love. The film's influence on the younger generation imposed new meanings on the word *dahua* (talking big) and catalyzed the integration of *dahua* into popular discourse, represented by such terms as "*dahua* movement," "*dahua* revolution," and "*dahua* culture." *Dahua* narratives were integrated into the daily lives of college students and were spontaneously performed on various occasions. Students at Tsinghua University recited lines from the movie in their dorms at night and created their own shows based on *A Chinese Odyssey* at student festivals.[12] Simple expressions like "it's thundering; it's raining; it's pouring; put away your clothes" (a line from the film) would elicit uncontrollable laughter from fans; Longevity Monk's version of the song "Only You" became popular at sing-alongs. Consequently, *A Chinese Odyssey*, originally a de-canonizing film, was consecrated as a new classic work, to the extent that the first 20,000 copies of *Bible of A Chinese Odyssey* (*Dahua xiyou baodian*)—a special edition dedicated to the film, released in 2000—were immediately sold out in bookstores in Beijing.[13] On May 4, 2001, Stephen Chow was invited to speak at Peking University's historic auditorium, symbolically marking the film's cult status in China.

Dahua refers to a mix of two film styles in *A Chinese Odyssey*: nonsensical comedic style and excessive sentimentality. These two characteristics partly accounted for the film's failure in Hong Kong and Taiwan,[14] yet contributed to its phenomenal success in mainland China. Originally a Cantonese slang term, *wulitou* ("nonsense") is used to describe a way of doing things that is odd, irrational, and without sense. Chow's nonsensical films are known to "privilege local viewers with their wordplay, Cantonese slang, folk and burlesque humor, mischievous characters, and obsession with oral pleasures."[15] With the resurgence of *A Chinese Odyssey*, this exaggerated comic style suddenly won the favor of mainland audiences, who enthusiastically adopted the film's irreverent gestures to poke fun at authority. Meanwhile, Joker's love triangle with Bai Jingjing and Zixia turned out to be thought-provoking for college students. In their first encounter, Joker was being chased and beaten by Bai Jingjing. There is no hint as to why Joker might fall in love with her at first sight, yet Joker could never seem to forget Bai Jingjing. For Zixia, right after Joker pulled her sword out of her scabbard, she announced "let's start this affair immediately." In both cases, there are no explanations about exactly how love at first sight takes place. However, all three figures are persistent once they think they are in love. Such elements of sincerity and naivety, mixed with the story's absurdity and hilarity, struck a chord with the college-age viewers.

The time lag between the release of *A Chinese Odyssey* and its sudden popularity among college students was not a coincidence. The opening up of discursive spaces online in 1996 and 1997, and the diversification of screening channels in the years between the film's original release and its reintroduction, created the conditions under which a campus-wide *dahua* movement could take place. New technologies, especially university BBSs and technologies that enabled movie pirating, played an indispensable role in this process. Following its unsuccessful theatrical release, *A Chinese Odyssey* was screened at the prestigious Beijing Film Academy in 1996. College students began discussing it on SMTH BBS, which had been launched a year earlier and had attracted many student users. In 1997, the script of *A Chinese Odyssey* was posted on SMTH BBS;[16] a special forum was later set up to gather the most interesting discussion threads on the film. As a new discussion platform, BBS motivated students to collaboratively unearth intricate details about the film. More important, the unique position in the marketplace as the first BBS, SMTH BBS ensured the endurance of the *dahua* craze. In 1996 and 1997, SMTH BBS was the main source of online content for Internet users, due to a dearth of comparable competitors and Internet content providers. Traditional media's experiment with digital content was still in its infancy and thus exerted little influence on netizens,[17] while important portal websites like Sina and Sohu had yet to be launched. Under such circumstances, SMTH BBS attracted the most web traffic in China. Any topics that caused a stir on SMTH BBS tended to exert a profound influence on Internet users and society at large.

Furthermore, the richness of *A Chinese Odyssey* offered textual frameworks that could be infinitely parodied and appropriated, and they were played out to an extreme in the open space of the university BBS. Drawing on sentence patterns from the film, such as "I have had ____ before, but I did not ____. When I lost ____, I felt true regret. It was the most painful matter ____," students played a sort of "Mad Libs," creating scripts related to real-life scenarios. On a larger scale, by internalizing the *dahua* style of thinking, students produced creative works online, ranging from self-contained posts such as *A Chinese Odyssey: Exam Edition* (*Dahua xiyou zhi kaoshi ban*) and *A Chinese Odyssey: Dating Edition* (*Dahua xiyou zhi yuehui ban*) to influential works, like online fiction *The Story of the Monkey King* (*Wukong zhuan*) and *Diary of Pigsy* (*Bajie riji*), which were later published in print.[18] Thus, the emerging online space not only marked the reception of *A Chinese Odyssey* in mainland China as a unique cultural phenomenon, but it also functioned as a space for Internet users to engage in creative writing.

Outside of college campuses, the diversification of screening channels, facilitated by both old and new technologies, ensured the increasing visibility of *A Chinese Odyssey* across multiple media platforms. During the Lunar New Year in 1997, China Central Television (CCTV) began to repeatedly air *A Chinese Odyssey* on its film channel. Provincial television stations quickly followed suit. This timing was important as Hong Kong, a former British colony, was scheduled to be officially returned to China in July 1997, and the burlesque style of *A Chinese Odyssey*, a Hong Kong film, was thought to accord with the festive atmosphere.

The "golden age" of movie piracy in China also drove the popularity of *A Chinese Odyssey*. Pirated videocassettes of *A Chinese Odyssey* began circulating as early as 1995, though they had rather low sales.[19] At the end of 1996, pirated VCDs became available on the black market and attracted consumers because they offered better image quality than videocassettes. Soon afterwards, pirated VCDs of *A Chinese Odyssey* topped the sales charts for pirated films.[20] As technology advanced, the cost of VCD players and computers decreased, allowing audiences to view movies in private settings.

Additionally, film screenings on university campuses and in illegal movie theatres attracted viewers with their cheap prices. Through repeated viewings, audiences were better able to sort through the convoluted plot and enjoy the hybridity of a film that blended genres (legendary story, martial arts, comedy, etc.), emotional modes (comic sensibility, sentimentality, absurdity, genuineness, etc.), and time-space dislocation.

It seems incredible that a work based on the reinvention of an ancient story could evoke so many strong feelings among young viewers in China, but the boom of net culture stemming from campus networks, along with the diversification of screening channels, dramatically changed the reception of *A Chinese Odyssey*. A line from *A Chinese Odyssey* is analogous to the movie's journey in China: "I may conjecture about the beginning right, but I would never figure out the ending." No one, including actor Stephen Chow and director Jeffery Lau, had anticipated the advent of the *dahua* movement that swept through mainland China.[21] As a process in formation, this *dahua* movement not only proved to be a lived experience for early netizens, it also set the underlying tone for the Internet culture in China.

BBS Culture in the Making

The opening up of a novel discursive space on BBSs incubated two emerging cultural forms that dominated Internet applications in the years that followed: Internet literature and self-made videos. From the late 1990s onward, Internet literature quickly transformed from an individual artistic pursuit for aspiring writers and enthusiastic readers into a streamlined industry. Driving this trend were players such as web editors and literature websites, as well as the alliance of such cultural industries as film, television, and games. Their success was enormous: as of June 2017, 50 percent of China's Internet population—352 million users—read online literature through multiple platforms,[22] including literature websites, BBS forums, blogs, microblogs, and WeChat. By the same token, self-made videos gradually evolved into professional productions that further developed comedic mechanisms in the cultural realm. Some examples are the flourishing of web-based talk shows and television series, as well as the enormous popularity of short-form videos in the second decade of the new millennium. Both Internet literature and self-made videos have their roots in the early university BBSs and trace back to the popularity of two works: Internet fiction *The First Intimate Contact* and the self-made video *Night Talks at Tsinghua*. These texts pioneered new genres via digital technologies, while incorporating the comic and sentimental elements of the *dahua* convention.

The First Intimate Contact was first released in online installments from March 22, 1998 to May 29, 1998. Posted on the BBS of the National Cheung Kung University in Tainan, Taiwan, it was written by Tsai Jhi-hsin (pen name Pizi Cai, b. 1969), then a doctoral student majoring in hydraulic engineering. The novel's simple plot portrays the new social phenomenon of Internet dating. The male protagonist, who shares the same name as the author, Pizi Cai, is a bookish engineering graduate student who has never had any luck forming romantic relationships. However, he meets Qingwu feiyang (Fly in Dance) on the university BBS and falls in love. They meet offline and have a short-lived romance. Soon after, without telling Pizi Cai, Qingwu feiyang returns to Taipei to receive treatment for lupus, but tragically dies from the disease and does not get to see Pizi Cai before she passes away.

The First Intimate Contact marked the beginning of the Internet literature era. Despite its lack of structural complexity and character development, the novel gained exceptional popularity among BBS users, who cross-posted the story to other websites and brought Tsai Jhi-hsin numerous fans. Subsequently, *The First Intimate Contact* was adapted into a variety of forms in mainland China, Hong Kong, and Taiwan, including print, film, television, cartoons, computer games, spoken drama, and Yue opera.[23] From 1999 to 2001, *The First Intimate Contact* topped the ranking of Chinese Internet literature. By 2005, it had sold more than a million print copies in mainland China.[24] This novel also officially launched Tsai Jhi-hsin's literary career. He has published more than ten novels since 1998.

The sentimental and humorous description of online romance constitutes the major attraction of Tsai's novel.[25] *The First Intimate Contact*'s portrayal of youthful innocence and the tragic dimension of unfulfilled love draws on the middlebrow romance tradition of Chinese literature. Meanwhile, *The First Intimate Contact* tackles a new subject for its time, Internet dating, which riveted readers who were experimenting with meeting friends and potential

dates online. The considerable use of BBS lingo in the novel, including ac-
ronyms, web slang, and special symbols, accorded with the college students'
experience of living their (love) life on- and offline. Some examples of popular
Internet-based vocabulary include "*konglong*" (dinosaur, unattractive female),
"*qingwa*" (frog, unattractive male), "*jianguang si*" (die on the spot, indicating
disappointment of meeting online friends), and "*wangyou*" (net friend). The
mixture of BBS terms with other language styles—such as word play based
on classical literature, the English language, and scientific formulas—offered
a light-hearted and up-to-date reading experience for urban readers. Via the
medium of the Internet, *The First Intimate Contact* initiated a new wave of
romance fever in China. Not only did a slew of copycat novels titled "____
Intimate Contact" quickly appear, but the commercial success of *The First
Intimate Contact* also inspired new writers who adopted online publishing
as a new profession, including Anni Baobei, Jin Hezai, Ning Caishen, and
Murong Xuecun.[26] The recycling, reappropriation, and multiplication of romance tropes initiated by Tsia Jhi-hsin and furthered by fellow Internet writers
thereby enriched the motif of sentimentality and youthful innocence.

   Night Talks at Tsinghua was also a sensation among college students for
its realistic presentation of their life online. Originally titled *Nothing is More
Delicious than Dumplings; Nothing is More Comfortable than Lying Down*
(*Haochi buru jiaozi, shufu buru tangzhe*), *Night Talks at Tsinghua*[27] was a
thirty-minute video shown as act six in a three-hour student play, *The Girl
in a White Dress* (*Chuan baise lianyiqun de nühai*). This play was written and
performed by undergraduates in the Computer Science Department of Tsinghua University at the end of 2001. The unusual format of a video screened
in the middle of a stage play was a phenomenal success. Initially, the students
planned to arrange for four male actors and four female actors to perform a
skit on dorm life. They abandoned this plan due to the difficulty of creating a
night scene onstage and instead decided to shoot a video and project it onto
a large screen during the performance.[28] Subsequently, the video recording
of the live screening, which captured the applause, laughter, and praise from
the audience, was renamed *Night Talks at Tsinghua* and uploaded onto SMTH
BBS. Soon, this video was cross-posted to other websites and became one of
the most frequently downloaded files on campus networks.

Night Talks at Tsinghua revolves around the conversation between roommates in both a male and a female student dorm after lights out. Looking forward to life after graduation, four male and four female college students discuss their career plans, thoughts about youth and love, ideas about American life, and so on. Focusing on two popular options among Tsinghua graduates—pursuing postgraduate studies at Tsinghua University or studying abroad—the discussion in the male and female dorm rooms foregrounds two different outlooks. In the male dorm, getting rich and studying abroad are students' major concerns. The ultimate ideal is to live a superficial life—"possessing beautiful houses and luxury cars, and marrying a beautiful girl." These students convey their firm belief that without money they cannot obtain success in their careers or family lives. They express this sense of pragmatism through comedic mechanisms such as quasi-vulgar sex jokes, a play on regional accents, an exaggerated tone and acting style (mimicking that commonly seen in Stephen Chow movies), and comic long-windedness. The following passage, for example, imitates the lengthy linguistic style of *A Chinese Odyssey* and is delivered in a comically distinctive regional accent:

> Why the hell do men work so hard day in and day out? Isn't it for the sake of that girl or woman—whom he meets directly or indirectly, intentionally or unintentionally, dreams about but has yet to meet in reality, or who he has met in person but differs from the woman in his dreams, or whose whereabouts, appearance, or existence he is not even sure about—that she could eat better, dress nicer, sleep sounder, walk less, and live in more open spaces?

Such a wry tone dominates the conversation of the male students' pursuit of materialism. As for the chat among the female students, sentimentalism prevails. Covering similar topics, the female students discuss their uncertainty about the future, their love lives, feelings of nostalgia, and their imagination of American life. This mood is accentuated when the students begin to sing along to two popular love songs—*I Wish I Were the Sea* (*Wo xiang wo shi hai*, 1998) and *Who Else Can I Love* (*Chule ai ni haineng ai shei*, 1998). The final scene continues this thread by portraying students' handwritten reflections about their four years of college life and ending with a poetic interpretation of love.

Night Talks at Tsinghua internalizes the comic and sentimental modes of expression in *A Chinese Odyssey* but adds a realistic dimension.[29] In addition to addressing subjects familiar to audiences, *Night Talks at Tsinghua* faithfully represents the way in which college students integrate the Internet into their everyday lives. In the very first scene, we see the activities of students in their dorm before lights out. In the female dorm, a girl uses her computer to watch *Romance in the Rain* (*Qing shenshen yu mengmeng*, dir. Li Ping, 2001), a middlebrow drama adapted from Qiong Yao's novel. In the male dorm, two guys also use their computers, busily typing. When the lights suddenly go out, a female student delivers the first line of the video: "FT, why were the lights turned off so early today?" Standing for "faint," "FT" connotes surprise or disagreement, a shorthand that originated in online chat rooms. In this way, the opening scene shows how computer-related activities and Internet lingo integrate into the students' daily activities. Other BBS terms, or "secret" codes of the online world, and commonly used English expressions like "no problem," have also been assimilated into daily speech patterns. In addition, this video summarizes how life on the Net began for the class of 2002 at Tsinghua University: "In our second year of college, [we] began to live in *jiujing*, own computers, play online games, and browse the Internet." "[Living] in *jiujing*," with *jiujing* referring to both the physical building of the student dorm and the building's intranet name, thus symbolizes the beginning point at which college students' on- and off-line lives became inseparable.[30]

These three Internet-related texts illustrate how the first generation of Chinese netizens made their collective debut in the late 1990s. *A Chinese Odyssey* marked the beginning of a new kind of reception that tied closely to the emergence of the BBS as a culture platform and that established the film's cult status in popular culture. *The First Intimate Contact* and *Night Talks at Tsinghua* illustrated how college students across the Taiwan Strait engaged in the creative production of original content online, the former showing how romance fever could be rekindled by virtue of pouring new wine into old bottles—adopting the form of clichéd sentimental love stories, while adding Internet-related content—and the latter marking the beginning of a digital video era in China and proving the formation of a collective cultural taste. These students' unabashed embrace of mundanity and pragmatism revealed the beginnings of a banal turn in campus culture—a cultural system that had been the symbolic center of elitism in the 1980s. Consequently, this nascent Chinese digital public catalyzed the birth of China's first Internet star, Furong Jiejie.

The Rise of Furong Jiejie

My sexy appearance and ice-and-jade purity attract a lot of attention wherever I go. I'm always the center of everything. People never get sick of looking at my face, and my physique gives men nosebleeds. But I feel that I am misperceived. My appearances always make people think that I am fashionable and on the cutting edge. Nobody knows that underneath my physique I have many of the virtues of a traditional woman.[31]

Now a household name, Furong Jiejie was the nickname early Internet users gave Shi Hengxia (b. 1977) when she first became famous on the BBSs of Peking University and Tsinghua University, sometime between 2002 and 2005. Within nine years (2002–11), Furong Jiejie transitioned from a public laughingstock into an inspirational role model in contemporary society. In 2005, the state's Publicity Department requested that Blogchina, for which Furong Jiejie cohosted the discussion forum Super Girls, relocate any Furong-related content to a less prominent place on its webpage.[32] Six years later, however, the state-owned CCTV released an in-depth interview with Furong Jiejie, while her glamour shots appeared on the website of Xinhua News Agency.[33] In March 2018, Furong Jiejie said she hoped to be an "inspirational figure nationwide" during an interview posted to the portal site of state-affiliated *People's Daily*.[34] These examples indicate the dramatic change in the official attitude toward Furong Jiejie over the space of a decade. As for Internet users, their initial perception of Furong Jiejie as a clownish figure changed to genuine admiration, most notably manifested by the increasingly positive feedback posted on her blog, microblog, and official website.

Furong Jiejie's quasi-legendary transition makes her case one of the intriguing myths of the Chinese Internet. The Internet community has at times fanatically idolized, vehemently condemned, and obsessively attended to her; public opinion of her has changed drastically over the years. Using the special tie between Furong Jiejie and Chinese netizens as a starting point, I delve into the particular circumstances that laid the groundwork for Furong Jiejie's enduring fame. I also highlight the process by which the comic sensibility and excessive sentimentality adopted by Internet communities fostered the rise of Furong Jiejie.

Born in a small town in Shaanxi province, Shi Hengxia (Furong Jiejie) considered herself a talented beauty who was well versed in every genre of art. Shi's ambition remained unfulfilled as she failed several times to get the scores needed on the national college entrance exams to enroll at Peking University or Tsinghua University—the top two elite universities in China. In 1996, Shi was admitted to Shaanxi Technical College in Hanzhong, Shaanxi, where she majored in mechanical engineering. After graduation Shi Hengxia worked in a factory in Shaanxi for a year. Her ambition "summoned" her to quit this job and relocate to Beijing in 2002, where she prepared for and took the graduate entrance exams for Peking University and Tsinghua University three times between 2003 and 2005. Under online aliases such as Lin Ke, Shuimei yaoji, and Huobing ke'er, Shi started posting articles and pictures of herself on the two most renowned university BBSs: Peking University's Unknown Space BBS (*Weiming kongjian*) and Tsinghua University's SMTH BBS (*Shuimu shequ*). One of her earliest articles to catch users' attention was "Peking University, You Are the Most Traumatic and Beautiful Sadness of My Past Life," posted in the Graduate Forum of the Unknown Space BBS in September 2002. The article recorded Shi's frustrations with her continual failures during her pursuit of elite education, as well as her determination to succeed in spite of these failures.[35] This article was promoted as one of the top ten hottest topics of the day, and a great number of BBS users responded to Shi's article to extend their support.

However, BBS users' sympathy for Shi's aspirations quickly soured. While Shi's pursuit of elite education accorded with mainstream value systems in China, her constant boasting about her beauty and all-around talent diverged from cultural norms that encourage modesty. In the latter half of 2004, Shi began to upload her photos on the Picture forum of SMTH BBS. BBS users observed a significant gap between her self-description and their perceptions of her as below-average in appearance and with poor taste, an unfit body shape, and awkward dance skills. The contradiction made Shi an immediate campus sensation. Thousands of BBS users reportedly waited anxiously online for Shi's updates and competed with one another to leave messages for her, ranging from verbal abuse to playful mockery. Each and every one of Shi's posts was quickly circulated via email, instant messaging, and text messages. Students who bumped into her on campus rushed to their computers to publish their experiences, which never failed to immediately elicit numerous follow-up comments.[36]

What is most intriguing about the sensation surrounding Shi's emergence is the playful mood that prevailed among BBS users at the time. Spontaneously, students of these elite schools collectively celebrated the absurdity of this on- and offline sensation. While the students' curiosity about Shi resembled a crowd mentality, with everyone clamoring for a slice of the action, the newly available online space proffered exciting new opportunities for these students to experiment with community effects. BBS users imposed two labels on Shi—"S-shape" (*S xing*) and "Furong Jiejie" (Sister Lotus). Both nicknames have been so widely adopted that her real name is rarely mentioned these days. "S-shape" referred to a typical gesture Shi employed in her photos and dance videos, in which she arched her back and thrust out her chest. As for "Furong Jiejie," BBS users wrote mock essays to explain how they reached a consensus on this name. According to Shi's blog, her favorite flower was hibiscus (*furong*). Shi also frequently referred to herself as "ou," a homonymic pun on the Chinese words for "I" and "lotus," and the upper part of a lotus flower is called "*furong*." In addition, the name was also connected, in a somewhat elaborate way, to Shi's rise to fame through Tsinghua University's SMTH BBS. SMTH's full name is "the land of waters and woods" (*Shuimu qinghua*), and the image of water and the water lily together corresponds to a famous line from a classical Chinese poem by Li Bai: "Lotus comes out of crystal-clear water" (*Qingshui chu furong*), which describes the unpretentiousness of beautiful things.[37] Thus, the naming process played on the irony of the striking contrast between Shi's self-proclaimed beauty and netizens' perceptions of her.

In addition to appropriating the phenomenon of Furong Jiejie's rise, BBS users steadfastly defended their right to seek fun. In the latter half of 2004, each picture Furong posted on SMTH BBS's Picture forum caused quite a stir, eliciting mixed responses from viewers. Whenever Furong Jiejie made an online appearance, the Picture forum would become chaotic, since BBS users were not interested in reading or responding to others' posts at all. To resolve this problem, the forum hosts suspended three of Furong's online accounts on the charge of "disturbing the normal forum order." After Furong Jiejie made an online appeal, forum hosts changed their decision and set her posts as read-only to prevent users from publishing comments. Furong Jiejie's followers became furious and questioned the legitimacy of this decision. In November, forum hosts set up a Picboard forum for administrators and moderators to discuss management issues relating to this case, yet they did not enact any changes after the meeting. In early December, Internet users organized a flash mob in SMTH BBS's Joke Section. At a prearranged time, every user online posted a message that stated "fight for human rights, love Furong" (*pin renquan, ai furong*).[38] These BBS users were not seriously defending human rights or loving Furong Jiejie. Yet the protest that was designed purely for entertainment resulted in the revocation of the decisions made previously by the forum hosts and, thereby, the restoration of both Furong Jiejie's and her followers' right to speak up. In this sense, actions taken on the BBS symbolized the arrival of a new world order that users believed was egalitarian in nature and that connected the domains of entertainment and pan-political activities.

The dominant moods of playfulness prevalent among the first cohort of netizens explained why Furong Jiejie was able to attract the full attention of students. Her sensational rise from university BBSs had its share of the same irony, comic effects, and innocence that were shown in *A Chinese Odyssey*. On the one hand, the gap between Furong Jiejie's self-perception and the public opinion of her lent a sense of absurdity to her online activity. Her self-indulgent performance can be read as a sequence of freak shows, updated constantly and encouraging her audience to participate at any time. On the other hand, her beleaguered pursuit of an elite education conveyed a moral similar to that of *A Chinese Odyssey*: in the face of formidable external forces, an individual possesses limited powers. Just as the Monkey King could never escape from the Buddha's power, Furong Jiejie continuously failed to realize her dream. This message again struck a chord with college students who were no longer the most favored group in society and had to fight for their own futures.[39]

Where the Furong Jiejie phenomenon departs from the reception of *A Chinese Odyssey* is in its timing. While Internet discussions of *A Chinese Odyssey* were largely concentrated on SMTH BBS due to the scarcity of online materials in 1996, this situation had drastically changed by 2005. The flourishing of commercial websites, the advancement of digital technologies, and the exponential growth of Internet users constituted new conditions under which the case of Furong Jiejie was able to generate a much larger impact. Netizens' founding of the Furong Cult on Tianya Community (*Tianya shequ*), one of the earliest commercial BBS forums in China, illustrates the unprecedented productivity of BBS as a content platform conducive to elicit emotions.

Mock Fandom as a Virtual Carnival: The Furong Cult on Tianya

While for two years Furong Jiejie's online notoriety remained confined to the elite students who frequented SMTH BBS and Unknown Space BBS, it took only a month in 2005 for her fame to spread to a more general audience. The influence of Tianya Community, as well as the subsequent coverage of the Furong phenomenon by traditional media outlets, wove the network of visibility that contributed to Furong's nationwide fame. Founded in 1999, Tianya Community was known for its endeavor to promote original content since its early days, for which the website cultivated quite a few well-known Internet writers and commentators on current affairs, including Dangnian Mingyue and Murong Xuecun. Tianya's most popular forums include Entertainment and Gossip, History, and Creative Writing.

Furong Jiejie's fame on Tianya started with a post. On May 24, 2005, a BBS user named "dachy" posted a discussion thread titled "How come nobody gossips about Furong Jiejie" in the Entertainment and Gossip forum. Dachy's cross-posting of pictures and original comments about Furong Jiejie attracted the attention of Tianya users, many of whom were unfamiliar with her. On May 25, 2005, dachy published a follow-up post. This entry sorted through Furong Jiejie's writings and conjectured about Furong's romantic relations. Two days later, "Huanpei dingdang," another Tianya user, edited and published *Basic Literacy Manuals for the Disciples of the Furong Cult* (*Furong jiaozhong rumen chuji saomang shouce*; hereafter, *Furong Manual*). In *Furong Manual*, Huanpei dingdang innovatively interpreted Furong Jiejie's posts and photos. Jokingly, BBS users founded the Furong Cult (*Furong jiao*) on Tianya and worshipped Furong Jiejie as their founding mother (*jiaomu*). Given that the Chinese words for "founding mother" and "yeast" are homophonous, netizens began to use "yeast" to refer to Furong Jiejie. Moreover, inspired by dachy and Huanpei dingdang, other Tianya users took part in searching for and posting any Furong-related information, supplementing existing posts with newly found content, and interacting with one another in mock praise of Furong Jiejie. Representative works of mockery include *Ode to the Founder of the Furong Cult* (*Furong jiaozhu qu*) and *The Advanced Complete Manual of the Tianya Furong Cult: A Must Read for Junior Disciples* (*Tianya Furongjiao gaojie wanquan shouce: Xiaolianpeng bibei*).[40] Indulging in this imaginary world, Furong Jiejie's loyal "disciples" contributed essays and poems, circulated and paraphrased Furong's words and images, and paid virtual tribute to her, especially when she had online chat sessions with netizens on Tianya.[41] The virtual sensation surrounding Furong Jiejie grew on a daily basis. Any discussion threads related to Furong Jiejie would generate at least 10,000 page views within a short period of time, a scale of participation that was unprecedented in Tianya's history.

This virtual sensation surrounding Furong Jiejie can be understood through the analytical lens of carnival. As an integral component of medieval folk culture, carnival temporarily suspends existing social norms and subverts the seriousness of official culture.[42] The linguistic system employed during carnivals celebrates the use of profanity and vulgarity to subvert the sublime, while the boundary between spectators and actors is blurred: "Carnival is not a spectacle seen by the people; they live in it, and everyone participates because its very idea embraces all the people."[43] In the same way, the active participation and performance of Furong Jiejie and fellow Internet users mutually shaped one another's reactions. The open access to Tianya also removed the time-place constraints seen in medieval carnivals, making this spectacle even more inviting in nature. The frenzy of mock fandom and the virtual carnival on Tianya illustrated the forging of a "community of imagination," defined as "a community which . . . constitutes itself precisely through a common affective engagement, and thereby through a common respect for a popular cultural representational space."[44] For Matthew Hills, imagination should be conceptualized as an affective process, which is fundamental to the formation of the fan community.[45] This community of imagination is less interested in imagining itself as a community than in constantly refining the relationships between individual fans and the text. Hills's analysis of the importance of affective engagement in sustaining online fandoms sheds light on understanding the sensational effects created by Furong Jiejie on Tianya.

In the mock fandom of Furong Jiejie, netizens' affective engagement and imagination, revolving around a parodied *jianghu* world, sustained the formation of a community. If, by convention, the *jianghu* (literally, "rivers and lakes") world—an important concept in martial arts fiction—is read as a space of freedom, adventure, justice, and heroism,[46] then the bustling scene Furong evoked on Tianya illustrates how *jianghu* could be imagined differently. In this *jianghu* world, social justice and moral support were not as important as having fun. Fans reimagined three classical themes of the martial arts genre—speculation about the whereabouts of group leaders, factional strife, and the passing on of secret martial arts manuals—to great comedic effect. BBS users competed with one another to become the most loyal followers of Furong Jiejie and swore to defend the integrity of the Furong Cult to their death. They acted like historians and archaeologists, scouring Furong's writings to uncover unnoticed details. They wrote humorous analogies about her life and even set up a virtual graduate seminar class to figure out her real identity. By the time the Furong Cult was founded on Tianya, the site was already host to several other sects, including the Chrysanthemum Cult (*juhua jiao*) and Cool Beauty Cult (*lengyan jiao*), which netizens founded to ridicule the youth writer Guo Jingming and entertainment stars like actress Chen Hong and singer Cai Guoqing. Tianya users imagined these groups as rival martial arts sects and discussed whether it was against professional ethics for an individual to be affiliated with multiple sects. Members of other sects also contributed new threads that both extolled and mocked Furong Jiejie. In addition, there was a proliferation of the Furong Cult "bibles" that constituted markers of the mock fan community, including such secret "martial arts manuals" as *Furong's Family Background* (*Furong shenshi*), *A Textology of Furong's Life* (*Furong shengping kao*), and *Quotations from Furong* (*Furong yulu*).

Netizens' imagined experiences of living in this parodied *jianghu* world formed the basis of their group identity, as well as their relationship with the object of mock fandom. If Furong Jiejie was perceived as overly narcissistic, then BBS users were no less obsessive when they took pleasure in analyzing Furong Jiejie's deeds and writings. Their group identity strengthening, mock fans integrated parodies into their daily lives:

[Post 1]

Today, I join the Furong Cult and swear never to abandon it for the rest of my life.

[Post 2]

Before I log off, let me come back to Furong Jiejie's post again. I will bring the *Furong Manual* home and thoroughly study the principles of the Furong Cult. I will peruse Furong Jiejie's words, further develop the Furong Cult, and popularize the brilliant image of Furong Jiejie among the Chinese people.

[Post 3]

Thank you FR [Furong Jiejie]! She has revolutionized my views of aesthetics and the world over the years.

[Post 4]

I worship the Founding Mother three hundred times a day, so that I would not resist the temptation to live on Tianya forever! [*Ribai jiaomu sanbai ci, buci changzuo tianya ren*, a parody of a classical Chinese poem].[47]

In these posts, the juxtaposition of two seemingly irrelevant genres—popular martial arts literature and mass slogans propagated by the official discourse of the 1960s and 1970s—brought forth entertaining effects. Mock fans reappropriated earlier popular and state discourses and parodied almost all cultural genres, ranging from literature, film, painting, and photography to pop songs, cartoons, and reality shows. The mock fans' frequency of interaction legitimized the notion of community entertainment online, which had been under careful monitoring. Admittedly, quite apart from this virtual worshipping of Furong Jiejie, negative responses to the Furong phenomenon ranged from playful mockery to extreme hatred. The frequency and intensity of these carnival-like "flame wars" made Tianya one of the most appealing online attractions in 2005, since any Furong-related topics may generate an unusually high number of visits. Nonetheless, for mock fans, any responses that departed from the shared mood of hilarity were considered off topic, particularly those of the moral defenders. It is worth quoting at length BBS user dachy's comment:

> To be honest, I kind of regret introducing Furong Jiejie to Tianya. As an amateur, I was very proud of my contribution to China's gossip industry in 2005. But now the course of events has somehow deviated from the original track. . . . In the beginning, we all knew there was no need to treat Furong Jiejie seriously, apart from seeking fun. But some people are so paranoid. . . . Look at those who persistently interrogate and humiliate Furong on her blog every day. It seems that these people have become moral defenders overnight. Isn't this ridiculous? Why not defend social justice one or two years earlier [when Furong first became notorious on SMTH BBS]? Why wait till now?[48]

Likewise, another netizen called for the "protection" of Furong Jiejie to preserve her entertainment value.[49] Commentaries such as these revealed the urgency to police the boundary of mock fandom to distinguish mock fans from other groups.

The mock fandom of Furong Jiejie exemplifies how varying forms of audience responses—ranging from antagonism to different degrees of attachment—emerge during the process of affective engagement: "Hate or dislike of a text can be just as powerful as can a strong and admiring, affective relationship with a text, and they can produce just as much activity, identification, meaning, and 'effects' or serve just as powerfully to unite and sustain a community or subculture."[50] Along the same line of thinking, the affectivity of mock fans, albeit performed, faked, and manipulated, is significant for understanding the entertainment effects triggered by Furong Jiejie. The activities of mock fans, such as collecting and collaborating, both mirror and depart from conventional fandom. An important component of fan culture, collecting tends to emphasize "inclusivity" instead of "exclusivity."[51] The quantity of collected objects is more important than the uniqueness of these objects.[52] In the case of Furong Jiejie, the mock fans used technological know-how to search for and post the most comprehensive collection of Furong Jiejie's videos, images, and written posts. Furong Jiejie's mock fans offered humorous analogies, participated in bantering wordplay, and built on insider jokes as a group. Thus, collecting was largely a group activity instead of an individual one and thereby differed from conventional fandom. Through collecting and collaborating, these mock fans actively engaged with both texts (Furong-related words, images, etc.) and contexts (online discussions, media reports, etc.). Consequently, this community of imagination paved the way for Furong Jiejie's transformation into an inspiring role model, acknowledged by the dominant Party-state and mainstream society since 2010.[53]

The Digital Economy of Mock Fandom

The collective agency of Tianya users nurtured the rise of newly emergent attention agents. Well-known figures of the Furong Cult, represented by dachy, Chen Mo, Huanpei dingdang, Han Xiaoxie, and cherry66, are influential among Tianya users for various reasons: accumulated knowledge (Huanpei dingdang's *Furong Manual*, cherry66's *Advanced Manual*), distinctive humor (dachy, Han Xiaoxie, and Huanpei dingdang), special skills (Chen Mo's photography techniques), and in-depth analytical prowess (dachy). The role these agents played in popularizing Furong Jiejie also heralded the logic of emerging web publicity, where online popularity is quickly subject to the commercial appropriation of the media industry, old and new. In June 2005, Hu Xudong, a literature professor at Peking University, published an article about the crazy worship of Furong Jiejie by college students on *Beijing News* (*Xin jingbao*).[54] This is the first time that Furong phenomenon was reported in print media. Two weeks later, the first batch of Furong Jiejie's photos simultaneously debuted on Tianya and a Shanghai-based pictorial, *Shanghai Bund Pictorial* (*Waitan huabao*), based on an agreement between the website and the journal. Twelve hours after these pictures were published on Tianya, they were cross-posted to a number of websites. Tianya's server was paralyzed because of the high number of visits.[55] Subsequently, discussions and reports about Furong Jiejie flourished in all of China's major newspapers, magazines, academic journals, and websites.

Notably, the pictures of Furong Jiejie released online differed from those published by traditional print media outlets in their channels of presentation, circulation, and reception. Tianya released a total of forty pictures, while the *Shanghai Bund Pictorial* published only one picture of Furong Jiejie, complemented with one page of text to discuss the Furong phenomenon. Unlike the picture published in the *Shanghai Bund Pictorial*, these forty photos on Tianya were carefully edited, each picture accompanied by specially written text and music. Chen Mo invited Han Xiaoxie, a user known on Tianya for her sharp observations and witty posts, to compose the accompanying text. In these photos, Furong Jiejie's notorious "S-shape" and dance poses were unchanged; however, Han Xiaoxie's poetic writing style offered an alternative interpretation of the Furong phenomenon. Han's writing responded to the prevailing mockery of Furong Jiejie and sympathized with her struggle. One caption that accompanied a picture of Furong Jiejie's S-shaped pose read: "Many people say I am not pretty. I do not believe it. Why would I? So I keep going, despite my lonesome persistence."[56] Next to another picture of Furong Jiejie's dance pose was the line: "My dance only has a couple of postures. So does my life. It's always been like this: simple, enjoyable." Another two statements responded to Furong Jiejie's attackers: "I understand everything about you—your extreme comments and vicious attacks—in the hopes of making you understand my adamancy"; "The eyes on the left cannot see the eyes on the right. You do not understand me, because I am on the left, while you are on the right."[57] The light sentimentalism implied in Han Xiaoxie's commentary pointed out the somewhat pitiable dimension of the Furong phenomenon. The juxtaposition of visual, textual, and musical elements, suffused with a sentimental mood, made Furong Jiejie's photos an immediate hit. At this time, Furong Jiejie became one of the top ten search terms on Baidu, China's homegrown search engine.[58] Tianya also organized a virtual forum for Han Xiaoxie to chat with BBS users, in which she described her writing process and explained why she defended Furong Jiejie.[59]

Just as these photos illustrate the degree of flexibility and innovation offered by digital media, the diverging career paths taken by newly minted digital agents are also thought-provoking. As with the case of Furong commentators dachy, Huanpei dingdang, and cherry66, the wide circulation of these photos elevated the symbolic status, among BBS users, of Han Xiaoxie and Chen Mo. The esteem Han Xiaoxie gained among mock fans earned her the position of moderator for the Creative Writing forum on Tianya. However, this online prestige can hardly have brought her any real-life changes, as Han Xiaoxie remained anonymous and gradually faded from public sight. In contrast, Chen Mo and Furong Jiejie exemplify the coming of a new era in which online popularity or notoriety could be converted into career advancement. Chen Mo soon became the spokesperson for China's Internet star-making industry and started his own media company that specialized in Internet marketing. As for Furong Jiejie, her fame has ushered in a new age of Internet celebrity.

An Unexpected Celebrity Transformation

Media coverage of and existing scholarship on the Furong phenomenon have tended to focus on understanding such a seemingly ridiculous figure. Scholars, media professionals, psychologists, and anonymous netizens have all taken pains to make sense of Furong Jiejie's unconventional behavior. Diagnoses of narcissism or mental illness were made,[60] while the frenetic behavior of Furong's followers, particularly college students, was attributed to a failure in college-level education. In 2005, Li Yinhe, a renowned sociologist in China, predicted that Furong fever would be ephemeral and discouraged the public from paying too much attention to Furong Jiejie.[61] Li's opinion was representative of many at that time who considered the transient rise and fall of other contemporary overnight celebrities, such as Huang Xin, Tianxian Meimei, and Liumang Yan. What Li and most observers did not anticipate, however, was that Furong's online comedy series would turn out to have an inspirational sequel. As time passed, Furong Jiejie transitioned from the comedic center of the imaginary Furong Cult to a real celebrity, integrated into mainstream society and hailed as an "inspirational goddess" (*lizhi nüshen*) by netizens. This transition illustrates how Furong Jiejie successfully converted online notoriety into a career opportunity. Indeed, Furong Jiejie's journey to fame had a close bearing on the Internet industry's pioneering experiment with new genres and expressive modes. Here I discuss three factors that contributed to Furong Jiejie's upward mobility: (1) Furong Jiejie's strategic appropria-tion of uniqueness and grass-rootedness, (2) the dotcom industry's efforts to adopt comic sensibility for the marketplace, and (3) Furong Jiejie's beau-tification of her public image.

Strategies: Acceptance of Mockery and Capitalization on Social Class

Reading Furong Jiejie as a morbid figure who acts differently from the majority of Chinese does not pay enough attention to her role as a digital attention agent in the field of popular culture. Furong Jiejie's active partici-pation in her own public mockery, as well as her changing strategies of self-promotion over the years, demonstrate her constant adjustment to secure her position in the emerging Internet celebrity industry.

The comic effects of the Furong phenomenon in the early stage, origi-nating from the self-entertaining activities of netizens, were continuously intensified by Furong Jiejie's voluntary cooperation. Furong Jiejie, alongside her fans, anti-fans, and mock fans, played the dual role of actor and spectator in this virtual carnival. Furong Jiejie's timely responses to netizens' condem-nation, mock praise, and parodies boosted these users' interest in produc-ing more entries. Her replies adopted a style that was similar to the ways in which netizens made fun of her. In response to an oft-quoted commentary that Furong Jiejie was like a demon-spotting mirror, a metaphor employed to imply her unattractiveness, she wrote:

> Today I finally figured out why people think I am like a demon-spotting mirror. . . . I walked by a neighbor's house and heard a woman immersed in discussion about Furong Jiejie. That distorted face of hers is so ugly that I cannot help but take a perverse comfort in it. Indeed, Furong Jiejie is like a demon-spotting mirror, which makes monsters show their true color. Hence the mirror helps display their inner ugliness![62]

To those who persistently posted malicious messages about her, Furong Jiejie fired back:

If you feel like it, please come over here and attack me. Your censure [of me] will be even better than my blog entries. Given that my blog has a high number of visits, a new star specializing in verbal abuse would probably arise. I am a bit busy nowadays, so am unable to post new articles quickly enough for you to attack me. Nevertheless, you are more than welcome to keep working on the old posts. Please, I beg you, wait for me.[63]

These two examples show that Furong Jiejie either deliberately misinterpreted netizens' perception of her to enhance the absurdity of her statements or satirized these "Internet Red Guards" who constantly resorted to verbal violence. With posts that enthusiastically exalted her, she unabashedly concurred. In this way, Furong Jiejie's tailored responses to various comments about her motivated more people to join in the discussion and facilitated an open exchange of opinions and virtual fights among netizens.

The second quote from Furong Jiejie illustrates her awareness of the importance of attention in the online sphere, where a high volume of web traffic is proportional to the potential profits a website or individual may generate. In the years that followed, Furong Jiejie continued to create media hype by posting marriage ads with amusing prerequisites (a sexual virgin, well-rounded appearance, etc.), auctioning clothes and accessories that she had worn, offering to sell the rights to the content of her blog for an outrageously high price (1 million RMB, approximately 150,000 USD), and launching a Furong Hotline to provide mental counseling. Between 2006 and 2008, Furong Jiejie released a series of blog videos for the 2008 Beijing Olympics, emphasizing the benefits of daily exercise and expressing patriotic sentiments. By continuing to add new elements to her online presence, Furong Jiejie was able to remain in the public's view.

The amateurish self-promotion in Furong's video series, her exaggerated poses, and the poor-quality clothes and accessories she wore in her videos and photos all worked to convey her ordinariness. This paved the way for Furong Jiejie's subsequent self-positioning as an alternative comic star in the marketplace, in which the ordinariness of her public image constituted the most significant selling point that distinguished her from other celebrities:

I write all kinds of blog entries, in all types of formats. I present daily trivial issues in a humorous and lovely way. I want to help everyone let go of their stress, so I continue to write to encourage everybody through the power of words. No matter how great the difficulty you might encounter in life, smile, and embrace it.

I contribute to the diversification of social entertainment via the Internet. I help people understand that entertainment is not merely under the control of authorities, it also is in the hands of many talented netizens.[64]

As shown in these statements, Furong Jiejie's justification of her entertainment value is based on the extreme social polarization in China. Drawing a boundary between the privileged and the underprivileged in Chinese society, Furong Jiejie deems herself spokesperson of the marginalized class: "Furong is no longer all about me. She represents the marginalized groups as a whole, and she exemplifies the virtues of confidence, bravery, and perseverance!"[65] This argument evokes a prevalent public resentment against the dominant groups in contemporary society, where the growing gap between the rich and the poor has jeopardized the legitimacy of the ruling regime. Within this context, Furong Jiejie interprets the alternative entertainment type she represents as a challenge to the authorities and a comfort to her peers who also come from ordinary families. In essence, the "challenge" Furong Jiejie describes cannot be substantiated, but the rhetoric has become rather appealing to netizens who have idealized the kind of "Chinese Dream" she embodies. Ironically, this rhetoric is now favored by the dominant power, given that it encourages the cultivation of a positive attitude and down-to-earth work ethic in the face of social inequality.

Furong Jiejie's emphasis on her grassroots origins needs to be taken with a grain of salt, however. When she first became famous, Furong Jiejie never drew attention to her humble origin. Instead, she made a clear distinction between small towns and rural areas, and prided herself on her small town upbringing, which, she claimed, made her much more fashionable than her classmates from the countryside. Furong Jiejie stressed how she stood out from the masses ("In the vast sea of humans, my appearance will brighten your eyes") and expressed a genuine desire to become a member of the elite class: "This third-tier university [where I graduated] suffocated me," which also illustrated her internalization of the orthodox educational hierarchy and an idea that acquiring an elite education could change an individual's destiny.

Following her futile efforts to get admitted into prestigious schools and the unexpected notoriety she gained among the elite students of Peking University and Tsinghua University, Furong Jiejie began to label herself a representative of the marginalized class. However, even this claim was a bit of a reach, given that Furong Jiejie had the luxury of receiving a college-level education and therefore possessed more privilege than the majority of the Chinese population. In 2003, those with college degrees made up only 5.15 percent of the entire population, while the college enrollment rate in 2004 was just 19 percent.[66] Having entered college in 1997, when the competition was even harsher, Furong Jiejie belonged to the first generation of netizens who were exposed to digital technologies. At that time, the majority of the "marginalized class" Furong claimed to identify with was perhaps not even aware of the existence of computers. Therefore, Furong Jiejie's continual assertion of her humble origin should be read as a strategic move, based on a timely assessment of the status quo and a swift adjustment of her position. In taking up this new position, Furong Jiejie justified the alternative media type she represented.

New and Old Comic Genres

Furong Jiejie's involvement with web-based genres exemplified the Internet industry's continued experiment with the comic sensibility that marked her early reception. After Furong Jiejie made her name on Tianya, commercial online media outlets quickly sought to capitalize on her newly established notoriety. In addition to hosting the web talk show *Here Comes Furong*, in 2005 she starred in several blog movies (*boke dianying*)—a short-lived genre that refers to mini movies published on blogs—such as *Appreciation of Beauty* (*Shenmei*) and *Shih* (*Jing dian'er*). Both the talk show and the movies stressed Furong Jiejie's identity as an Internet celebrity. *Here Comes Furong* was produced and broadcast online by China.com (*zhonghua wang*). This show imitated the famous Taiwanese variety program *Here Comes Kang Xi*, in which hosts Hsu Hsi-ti and Tsai Kang-yung interviewed celebrities and disclosed little-known aspects of the celebrities' lives to audiences. *Here Comes Kang Xi* was most famous for its humorous bantering style, accompanied by hilarious sound effects, on-screen visuals, and animated text. *Here Comes Furong* applied irony in one sense: by treating Furong Jiejie—then a clownish figure—as a celebrity, the show proclaimed to present a true or serious (*zhengjing*) Furong to the audience. This show presented Furong Jiejie as a role model who educated the audience on varying topics such as aesthetics and success; engaged in mock dialogues with her attackers, fans, and journalists; and even acted as a fitness instructor. Interestingly, while *zhengjing* has several positive meanings, including true, serious, conventional, and sincere, it is the subtle unorthodox (*bu zhengjing*) aspects of Furong Jiejie—the awkward dance and unabashed confidence—that resulted in the controversy that surrounded her. Thus, the apparently "serious" show had no real intention of presenting a "real" Furong Jiejie, one that differed from her public image. As audiences watched Furong Jiejie teach fitness and share her life philosophy, they felt a sense of superiority that reinforced their previous perceptions of her. Through the lens of parody, *Here Comes Furong* celebrated the absurd aspects of the Furong phenomenon and resonated with popular sentiment via new cultural forms.

Similar to web-based shows, Furong Jiejie's roles in conventional genres had a close affinity with her real-life story. In director Ning Ying's film *The Double Life* (2009), Furong Jiejie plays Taohua, a sales assistant working at a Chinese herbal medicine store in a city. Taohua speaks a northwestern regional dialect, which indicates her identity as an outsider in the city. The dialect she speaks and her role as a migrant worker accords with Furong Jiejie's experience of relocating to the city for better opportunities. In the film, Taohua approaches store visitors by sticking out her chest and twisting her rear end, all typical gestures of Furong Jiejie. Although Furong Jiejie plays one of the few mentally healthy people in *The Double Life*, a movie on patients with mental disorders, her role constantly reminds the audience of the societal opinion that her mental status is problematic. Thus, the interconnection between Furong Jiejie's role in the film and her real-life experiences constitutes one of the entertaining aspects of watching *The Double Life*. In addition, Furong Jiejie took a leading role in the New Year comic stage play

Meteor Shower, shown between December 2009 and January 2010. The stage play made full use of the Internet lexicon and anecdotes related to Furong Jiejie, who starred as the five well-known beauties of ancient China and celebrated her S-shaped pose, awkward dance, and out-of-tune voice.

In short, Furong Jiejie's participation in both conventional genres and new media genres foregrounded the integration of her real-life experience into each respective storyline. The comedic effects played off the sense of irony created by her exaggerated body gestures and performance style. The lack of distinction between Furong Jiejie's real-life experience and her performance in these shows showcases a crude way of appropriating comic sensibility. In this sense, the case of Furong Jiejie represents the budding stage of China's entertainment industry that capitalized on online buffoonery as a form of public entertainment.

A Misfit Turned Celebrity

It was not just public opinion of Furong Jiejie that changed with her move into the mainstream entertainment industry; her outward appearance changed as well. Furong Jiejie's media appearances after 2009 demonstrate improved taste, as evidenced by the application of delicate makeup, a fashionable selection of dresses, and elegant poses. The funny S-curve gesture so prevalent in her earlier media coverage was replaced with professional poses that celebrities tend to employ. In a photo series released in November 2010, Furong's appearance provoked as much discussion on BBS forums as it did five years earlier. Furong Jiejie's slim figure, luxurious dress, star-like gaze, and conservative poses all indicated the birth of a real star. In these pictures, Furong Jiejie posed seductively, with her eyes open wide and staring into the camera, with lips slightly parted, creating an aesthetic distance between her as a star and the audience as voyeurs. Netizens on BBS forums, particularly Tianya, enthusiastically discussed the dramatic change in Furong Jiejie's public image. Two representative comments are as follows: "Even Furong Jiejie has become so skinny. Aren't you ashamed of your belly fat?" "Man, I miss her S-shape so much. From now on the 'godmother' has disappeared from earth, and a product called 'beauty' has debuted."[67]

With Furong Jiejie's transformation into a celebrity, the Internet community bemoaned the loss of their source of fun. And with this physical metamorphosis, Furong Jiejie changed the content and tone of her blog. In the past, she had expressed her unabashed self-confidence, which received much satire. However, accompanied by the change in her public image, she began to take a much humbler position. Her blog posts no longer boasted about her perfect body, glowing complexion, and talent in the arts. Instead, she shared with readers her worries about weight gain, workplace challenges, and a lack of confidence about her acting skills. Her former boldness transformed into a concern about public opinion and a constant expression of appreciation to the numerous netizens who promoted her in the first place.

Read in this light, both Furong Jiejie's body and mind needed to be disciplined for her to obtain upward mobility. Her significant weight loss, adoption of elegant poses, application of delicate makeup, and low-key stance all demonstrated a restraint imposed on excess: an excessive female body, her exaggerated tone of voice, and the immoderate behaviors that were exhibited previously. As a stigmatized word, "excess" is often associated with female instant celebrities who demonstrate an inability to cope with their fame in an appropriate manner.[68] Imogen Tyler and Bruce Bennett's study of instant celebrities, called "female celebrity chavs" in a British context, reveals the dilemma that they tend to encounter. Although these grassroots stars can gain fame overnight—mostly through reality shows—and even improve their financial situation by their display of vulgarity and inappropriate tastes, their lower-class identity is still essential in the construction of their public image in media coverage.[69] Thus, the emphasis on the vulgarity, low family origin, and poor taste that makes the "celebrity chavs" famous constitutes a major obstacle for these figures to receive recognition in mainstream society.[70] In the Chinese context, the mainstream and dominant forces, and the associated value systems, are constantly subject to change. Hence, social class is not the single decisive factor that either restrains or catalyzes a celebrity's upward mobility. For Furong Jiejie, the dominant and mainstream forces' changing opinions have helped to transform her story from that of a social anomaly into an inspiration.

Internet Stars in the Age of Selfies

The tremendous influence of the Furong phenomenon ushered in a new era of grassroots stars in China's digital age. A decade after Furong Jiejie initially rose to fame, the proliferation of social media platforms, enhancement of network infrastructure, and prevalence of mobile applications have contributed to fostering the emergence of Internet stars in all walks of life, ranging from e-commerce and content entrepreneurship, to mental counseling and health care, to the fashion industry. Against this backdrop, Papi Jiang, the online moniker of Jiang Yilei (b. 1987), rose to fame on Sina Weibo as the foremost Internet celebrity of 2016. A graduate of China's prestigious Central Academy of Drama, Papi Jiang created a short-form video series that offered pointed commentaries on everyday life, including entertainment news, social norms, holiday events, and family relationships. Boasting about 8 million followers on Weibo, Papi Jiang expanded her offerings into a self-media brand and launched her official channel, Papi Tube, on YouTube.

The case of Papi Jiang demonstrates the significance of content entrepreneurship in China's new era of Internet Plus. Papi Jiang's journey to fame heralds the emergence of a younger generation of Internet users who fully embrace the age of selfies to self-promote and are comfortable with consuming online. Prior to her nationwide fame on Weibo, Papi Jiang already had a small following on other social media platforms, including Tianya and Douban, a website for users interested in literature and the arts. Papi Jiang's initial posts on Tianya, in 2013 and 2014, featured her distinctive style of matching clothes and wearing light makeup. Her appearances in these pictures received repeated user comments that Papi Jiang looked exactly like a young Xu Jinglei,[71] a first-generation youth idol in China who achieved fame in the 1990s. In these photos, Papi Jiang's looks accorded with the mainstream standard of youthful femininity, making her appear docile, innocent, and sweet. Subsequently, her changing manner of self-presentation on social media sites and the changing style of her videos illustrated her continuous endeavor to test the market. In 2015, Papi Jiang and her college friend Huo Nifang began to publish short-form videos on Weibo, under the account "TCgirls Love to Complain" (*TCgirls ai tucao*). The video series, *The Baseline for Males*

(*Nanxing shengcun faze*), began to attract wider attention after it received more than 20,000 shares and 30,000 likes. Starting in October 2015, Papi Jiang began to upload her own videos that featured a computer-accelerated voice. She wrote the script, performed in the videos, and poked fun at common societal issues. Her background in directing and her work experience as a host for entertainment shows, assistant director, and actress contributed to the popularity of these videos. Within four months, Papi Jiang's fans increased to 2 million; by March 2016, that number was 7.6 million.[72]

Papi Jiang's videos are known for her satirical style and skillful parody of social phenomena. Her video series present Papi Jiang as an old, hysterical, and unattractive woman, a portrayal that differs drastically from her early images on Tianya. Her exaggerated manner of performance, the adoption of self-deprecating gestures, and her insightful observations about everyday life account for the entertaining quality of her videos. The topics she satirizes range from gender discrimination to Internet violence to social customs. On the eve of International Women's Day, Papi Jiang released a video titled *You Must Have Heard These Lines*. Using a computer-generated voice, Papi Jiang lists various examples of the stereotypical perception of gender norms, gender discrimination, and sexual harassment in daily life.[73] In another video, Papi Jiang satirizes the pretentiousness of white-collar workers who mix the Shanghai dialect, Mandarin, English, and Japanese to emphasize their status as global citizens.[74] As Jie Zhang has argued, the allure of Papi Jiang's videos lies in her adaptation of self-deprecation and self-mockery to create comedic effects: "Making a point is never the point here; rather, the ultimate point is the freedom for playfulness and the celebration of performativity."[75] For instance, Papi Jiang's most famous slogan goes: "I am Papi Jiang, the woman who possesses the qualities of both beauty and talent." Her videos, however, immediately sabotage this seemingly boastful self-definition, since Papi Jiang often performs the role of someone hysterical and lacking in feminine appeal. Papi Jiang's shrewd maneuvering of the comedic mechanisms of self-mockery creates a distance between the subject of parody and Papi Jiang herself. Her deliberate use of parody thereby distinguishes Papi Jiang from the cruder form of unintentional, audience-based parody exemplified by Furong Jiejie. Moreover, if traditional media outlets and BBS jointly contributed to Furong

Jiejie's nationwide fame, then Internet celebrity as represented by Papi Jiang illustrates the significance of visual content production and an elevated status of online media in the 2010s. In this sense, the journey of China's Internet stars, from Furong Jiejie to Papi Jiang, may be read as an analog of the gradual development of China's nascent entertainment industry alongside the rapid growth of the Internet sector.

Conclusion

More than a decade after Furong Jiejie rose to nationwide fame, the term "Internet celebrity" has come to constitute an essential component of China's vibrant web-based economy. The flourishing of the live streaming industry, social media platforms, and e-commerce sites has jointly incubated the mushrooming of grassroots stars across a wide range of career paths. In August 2015, Taobao, the largest online retail store in China, formally proposed the concept of the "Internet celebrity economy" (*wanghong jingji*). The key idea was to boost online sales by attracting the fans of Internet celebrities to visit their stores on Taobao. These store owners are adept at using selfies and video streaming to promote their products and cultivate close connections with fans.[76] Content entrepreneurship exemplifies another new development in the arena of Internet celebrity. WeChat public accounts and the proliferation of self-made programs online are just two examples of this kind of content-based enterprise. Internet celebrities now fully embrace self-promotion via social media platforms to publicize their business ventures, ranging from contracts with retailers to content entrepreneurship to cultural innovations.

This evolving trajectory of Internet stars in China illustrates how, over a span of two decades, the age of innocence, with its emphasis on youth and playfulness, has developed into the era of commerce. The age of selfies blatantly celebrates a pursuit of fame and the conversion of fame into material interests. In this new social media environment, none of Furong Jiejie's deeds would have become a sensation. Nevertheless, the Furong phenomenon deserves our scrutiny precisely because, while her rise in the online space seems to have been accidental, the sociocultural circumstances that laid the groundwork for her everlasting fame were not arbitrary. The rudimentary formation of netizen communities, which internalized the *dahua* convention and celebrated the mundane aspects of life, demonstrates the primary conditions under which a star like Furong Jiejie could rise from the online sphere. More important, the nine years during which Furong Jiejie made her name illustrates the profound influence that BBS exerts on the developmental trajectory of the Chinese Internet. Jing Wu and Guoqiang Yun have addressed the instrumental role that BBS plays "in constructing a new culture of activism, civic engagement, self-mobilization, and resistance to authority."[77] My discussion of BBS furthers this characterization and demonstrates how BBS users' rights consciousness went hand in hand with their collective spirit of seeking fun, for which they created their own entertainment stars, fussed about trivial matters of various kinds, and actively engaged in self-publishing. The proliferation of user-generated content on BBS, ranging from online debates to creative writing to web-based genres, paved the way for the booming Internet celebrity industry in the years to come. Celebrity blogs, the focus of the next two chapters, carry on the legacy of early BBS and foster the development of participatory culture and content production to a new stage.

4 NATIONAL BLOGGING AND CULTURAL ENTREPRENEURSHIP

China is not yet a country that excels in the art of writing (shuxie, *to express feelings and write), but the emergence of blogs . . .*

IN OCTOBER 2002, Isaac Xianghui Mao wrote this line on the homepage of CNBlog, China's first online discussion forum about blogging technology and culture. His nickname, "Chairman Mao of the Internet" (*wangluo maozhuxi*), due to his extensive blogging and research into social media, brings to mind the possibility of another wave of revolution fostered by digital technologies. What is most intriguing about Mao's statement is his use of an ellipsis, as it raises the unspoken question of how blogs may facilitate change of the status quo, which, according to Mao, is the comparative lack of good, emphatic writing in China, despite the country's long history.

This chapter unravels the mystery Isaac Mao alludes to in the above quote. Along with the prevalence of fun-seeking sentiments among the first-generation Chinese netizens, industry efforts to experiment with new technologies were in full swing. Major dotcom corporations, particularly Sina and Tencent, had effectively incorporated blogging into their business models by 2005, hoping to capture the attention of readers, increase web traffic, and encourage the creation of user-generated content. Consequently, the dominant portal websites of these corporations catalyzed the formation of an entertainment-oriented blogosphere full of mundane celebrity gossip and chaotic scenes of celebrity worship by fans. In contrast to the rise of digital agents such as Furong Jiejie and Chen Mo, who succeeded in converting online popularity into career opportunities, the class of "attention-haves," individuals who had already established their fame, exemplifies a different mode of implementing the attention rule online.

In this chapter, I discuss how cultural celebrities, as represented by Xu Jinglei, Yang Lan, Hong Huang, and Guo Jingming, have fully capitalized on their established connections, prestige, and economic capital to explore alternative modes of cultural production. Despite the difference in age and background among these celebrities, they are emblematic of a new generation of Chinese cultural entrepreneurs who have actively explored many roles—from those of directors, producers, writers, and TV hosts to editors, publishers, and bloggers—to cultivate the symbiotic relationship between culture and commerce. As trailblazers, these celebrities have implemented the rule of attention online and appropriated their cultural appeal to experiment with new business models. Through writings on blogs, these figures have enhanced the authenticity of their star personas, which have been integrated into publicity-related work.

In what follows, I first analyze how the career paths of all four celebrities have converged in the age of blogging, as well as how celebrities in general maximize publicity opportunities through interconnected, diverse media platforms. On these platforms, elements of old and new media (e.g. photography, audio clips, hypertext, videos, emoticons, and hyperlinks) refashion one another, while emergent marketing strategies both disrupt and complement previous distribution channels. Thus, emerging digital platforms supplement mainstream media outlets, through which these celebrities first achieved fame, to enhance the network of visibility for a wide variety of goals. Among them, celebrities utilize online interactivity not only to maintain close ties with fans but also to convert their audience's desire for interaction into cultural productivity. Consequently, although Internet users may get actively involved in the process of media production, this site of user empowerment is also the site of omnipresent surveillance. By interacting with their favorite stars, Internet users subject themselves to constant monitoring and exploitation by media producers. This hidden tension concerning online interactivity surfaces particularly when gender-related issues emerge. While these celebrities' embodiment of gender equality is inspiring to their supporters, they are subject to criticism for neglecting marginalized groups in their cultural endeavors. Thus, the construction of celebrities' public images through the selective sharing of their lives, the audience's interpretation of their images, and the self-positioning of these celebrities in the cultural marketplace speaks volumes about the contrast between netizens and celebrity values in contemporary society.

Cultural Entrepreneurs in Digital China

The rise of cultural entrepreneurs is not a new phenomenon. Christopher Rea and Nicolai Volland's coedited volume on the business dimension of culture, for instance, addresses how cultural entrepreneurship evolved during the late nineteenth and early twentieth centuries as modern technologies such as radio, cinema, and print media developed.[1] The new social conditions of the early 2000s in China, particularly the deepening of cultural reforms and the proliferation of digital technologies, redefined Chinese cultural entrepreneurship. In 2003, state planners initiated a sweeping "cultural system reform," in keeping with the accelerated commodification of communication and culture.[2] As a result of this reform, private sectors that tie closely to state forces have grown rapidly; the strategies needed to gain business success have become a popular topic of books, magazines, and television shows.[3] Relatedly, "a new entrepreneurial class of cultural elites"[4] has arisen in contemporary society. These elites differ drastically from the notorious upstarts who first rose to prominence in the late 1980s for their eagerness to show off wealth and their exhibition of poor taste. Adept at assuming multifaceted roles, this new generation of cultural entrepreneurs deftly maneuvers between a diverse range of positions, maximizing their opportunities to commodify culture. Yuezhi Zhao's study of Zhejiang-based industrial conglomerates reveals how these elite entrepreneurs form joint alliances with state media and transnational capital.[5] John Osburg's investigation of the new rich in Chengdu pinpoints the significant role that moral economies, membership of elite networks, and a close affinity with the state play in the success of these entrepreneurs.[6] Simply put, cultural entrepreneurship in China's new millennium celebrates the commercial value of culture, emphasizes the importance of transnational and domestic networks, and establishes close ties with the dominant Party-state.

In line with these scholarly findings, my discussion of cultural entrepreneurship foregrounds the essential role that digital media play in enabling these entrepreneurs to build their star personae, connect with fans, and enhance their corporate identities. As well-established figures in Chinese society, Xu Jinglei, Yang Lan, Hong Huang, and Guo Jingming had already built visibility networks before embarking on their new career paths. They focused on three distinct areas of cultural industry—film, television, and print media. With the advent of blogging, all four became pioneers in digital media, using their blogs to explore new modes of cultural production. Meanwhile, they took pains to maintain close ties with those in dominant and mainstream positions, such as state-sponsored organizations and elite institutions. The capacity of these cultural elites to maneuver between their positions in both alternative and mainstream media not only enabled them to mobilize all available resources to accomplish their goals, but also created their distinctive appeal that conforms to the Zeitgeist of neoliberalism, celebrating individual agency and the entrepreneurial spirit.

Xu Jinglei (b. 1974) and Yang Lan (b. 1968) began their careers in the film and television industry, catching the media's attention at an early age. Xu began her star-studded career in 1995, when she was a college student majoring in performance arts at the Beijing Film Academy. Dissatisfied with the restrictions placed on her as an actress, Xu became a director in 2003. Since then, she has released seven movies. Her experimentation with emergent publicity platforms such as blogs and microblogs has significantly enhanced her role as a cultural entrepreneur. Six months after starting her personal blog in October 2005, Xu's account made Technorati's list of top-ranking blogs worldwide.[7] On April 16, 2007, Xu launched an interactive electronic magazine titled *In Blossom* (*Kaila*), for which she wrote articles, conducted interviews, and took photographs. *In Blossom* could be downloaded from her blog and was subdivided into three different magazines—*In Blossom: A Must Read for Those Who Know* (*Kaila: Zhidao fenzi bidu*), *In Blossom: Street Scenes* (*Kaila jiepai*), and *In Blossom: Workplaces* (*Kaila zhichang*)—thereby targeting urban professionals. *In Blossom* released sixty-two issues in total before Xu stopped updating the magazine in 2011. Nevertheless, Xu continued to explore new channels of cultural production and distribution, as represented by her role as a producer of the 2017 web-based television drama *My 200-Million-Year-Old Classmate* (*Tongxue liangyi sui*, dir. Si Weiwei). Transitioning from a popular youth idol to a multifaceted career woman, Xu thus capitalized on the offerings of new technologies to remain competitive in the cultural marketplace.

Yang Lan started her career as a television host in the 1990s and subsequently embarked on new professional adventures, such as working as the creator, executive producer, and anchor of the *Yang Lan Studio* (*Yang Lan gongzuoshi*) at Hong Kong–based Phoenix Satellite Television. In 2000, Yang started her own media company, Sun Television Cybernetworks, in Hong Kong. Three years later, due to financial failures, Yang sold 70 percent of the company's shares to a media corporation. She also published three electronic magazines: *Ripple* (*Lan*), *Her Village* (*Tianxia nüren*), and *StarMook* (*Ta meng*). Currently, Yang Lan is an independent producer of two popular shows—*Yang Lan One on One* (*Yang Lan fangtanlu*) and *Her Village* (*Tianxia nüren*). One of the most highly regarded in-depth talk shows in China, *Yang Lan One on One* airs interviews of leading world figures from the fields of international politics, business, society, and culture. In contrast, *Her Village* focuses on issues related to urban women in China. In December 2005, Yang Lan started a personal blog on which she frequently reports on the progress of her projects. In March 2009, Yang launched Tiannv.com, a website that aims to build the largest hypermedia virtual community for urban professional women in China.

In contrast to Xu Jinglei's and Yang Lan's experience of working in China's visual industry, Hong Huang (b. 1961) and Guo Jingming (b. 1983) started in print media. After graduating college, attending school abroad, and later working as a CEO of an international company, Hong entered the Chinese media industry in 1996. She is currently the CEO and editor-in-chief of China Interactive Media Group, which publishes fashion magazines such as *Time Out* (Beijing), *Time Out* (Shanghai), and *World Metropolitan iLook*. On

February 14, 2006, Hong started a personal blog, "Hong Huang Looking for Fun," which received more than 4 million views in the first month.

Both Hong Huang and Guo Jingming have assumed active roles in China's publishing industry. While Hong Huang's magazines target upper-middle-class women, Guo Jingming has demonstrated his business acumen by filling a lacuna in China's youth literary market. Guo's background showcases how the Internet culture influenced the experience of growing up as part of the post-1980s generation in China. While a high school student, Guo Jingming published prose essays and short stories on the renowned literature website "Under the Banyan Tree" (*Rongshu xia*), under the penname "Disiwei" (the fourth dimension). Nicknamed "Little Four" (*Xiao si*) by his readers, in both 2001 and 2002 Guo Jingming won first place at the National New Concept Writing Competition, sponsored by the Shanghai-based literary magazine *Sprouts* (*Mengya*). *Sprouts* also serialized Guo Jingming's first novel, *City of Fantasy* (*Huan cheng*). The book version of *City of Fantasy* was released in 2003 and sold more than 1.5 million copies.[8] In 2002, Guo Jingming enrolled at Shanghai University, majoring in film art and technology. After a number of unpleasant experiences of wealth inequality and regional discrimination, Guo ended up quitting college, starting a writing studio, "Island" (*Dao*), with friends in 2004, and publishing the magazine series *i5land*. In 2006, Guo Jingming founded Ke Ai, which was expanded and renamed the Shanghai Zui Culture Development Company in 2010.

As a beneficiary of China's booming youth literature market, Guo Jingming's works consistently topped the ranks in terms of distribution.[9] Guo Jingming was also one of the first to streamline the production of literary works across media platforms. From 2007 to 2010, *Zui Novel* serialized Guo Jingming's *Tiny Times* (*Xiao shidai*) trilogy, which subsequently was published in book form from 2008 to 2011. During 2013 to 2015, Guo directed the film versions of *Tiny Times*, and the four movies generated 245 million USD total box office revenue.[10] In 2016, Guo directed the film version of the fantasy novel *The Mark of the Cavalier* (*Jue ji*, 2010), the first computer-generated film in China. In 2016 and 2017, televisual adaptations of Guo's novels *City of Fantasy* and *Rushing to the Dead Summer* (*Xiazhi wei zhi*) were aired by Hunan Satellite Television Station. The commercial success of these cross-media adaptations illustrates the effectiveness of Guo's model and foreshadows the increasingly prominent role played by the fan economy in China's cultural industry.[11]

In spite of Guo Jingming's status as a bestselling author and the popularity of the visual adaptations of his works, Guo's real ambition lies in fostering changes in China's publishing industry—perceived by some as a business in decline. Guo inaugurated a model of team collaboration, Zui Company, to jointly carve out a niche in the teen cultural market.[12] Zui Company has signed twenty comic creators and eighty writers, including Di An, Luo Luo, and An Dongni, and produces a large number of original stories and mangas.[13] In 2011, twenty-five of the top thirty bestsellers in the category of fiction were by contracted writers of Zui Company.[14] In 2013, the sales figures for magazines published by Zui Company alone exceeded the overall distribution numbers for literary journals nationwide.[15] The core product of Zui Company, *Zui Novel*, has consistently been ranked the most popular literary magazine since 2007, with a monthly sales record of more than 5 million copies.[16] *Zui Novel* offers many opportunities for writers to gain exposure and interact with readers, for instance, by encouraging readers' responses on forums regarding serial fiction. Writers may then decide on future plot development based on such feedback. For good measure, *Zui Novel* also regularly conducts surveys to monitor trends in readers' tastes.[17] Guo Jingming has also experimented with new modes of collaborative writing, such as inviting multiple authors to work on the same novel or screenplay, further accentuating his distinctive role in cultivating young talent and a teen literary market by means of his publishing empire.[19]

The professional trajectories of Xu Jinglei, Yang Lan, Hong Huang, and Guo Jingming started a decade before "mass entrepreneurship and mass innovation" (*dazhong chuangye wanzhong chuanxin*) became an integral component of the state's strategic plan. These celebrities epitomized a new generation of Chinese entrepreneurs who cultivated a diversified market of cultural products. All four figures played proactive roles in building their star personae and establishing connections with fans online, heralding the trend of growing personal brands via social media platforms that would flourish in the coming years.

Circulating Transmedia Stories

Celebrity blogs exemplify a mode of "transmedia storytelling,"[18] a term Henry Jenkins employs to discuss how corporations work together at a micro level. By means of *The Matrix*, Jenkins showcases how the products derived from the film (such as animated shorts, video games, and fandoms) have created a narrative extending beyond the stand-alone film medium. A single company can thus exert influence on, and dictate the flow of narratives across, a variety of media platforms.[19] In contrast to the materialistic desire of corporate conglomerates to generate spin-offs, the goal of transmedia storytelling in celebrity blogs is to maximize publicity opportunities.

As attention-haves, celebrities like Xu Jinglei, Yang Lan, Hong Huang, and Guo Jingming immediately recognized the blog as a convenient publicity tool and used it to explore a variety of modes of personal branding. The original content created by celebrities—mostly a narration of their personal lives and work—constitutes the most intriguing selling point of their blogs, attracting voyeuristic readers. An example of an individualized mode of transmedia storytelling on celebrity blogs is the use of gossip or insider information, as there inevitably exists a constant flow of rumors surrounding a star. In the past, press conferences and public announcements were the two means by which celebrities addressed such rumors, but the emergence of blogs offers a more convenient and credible channel for celebrities to do so. For instance, Yang Lan employs formal language on her blog to respond to negative news about her, issuing "clarifications" as blog titles. Likewise, Xu Jinglei and Hong Huang use their blogs to respond to tidbits that might harm their images, albeit in a less serious manner. Xu Jinglei typically comments on ongoing rumors while writing about other issues, while Hong Huang makes fun of the gossip about herself. In this way, celebrity blogs and microblogs have become a primary source to which audiences turn to verify ongoing rumors.

In addition to using their blogs to combat rumors, celebrities turn to blogging to disseminate insider information about themselves and others. By "selling" exclusive reports about the personal lives of celebrities and their family members and friends, celebrity blogs offer insider information that can generate millions of visits by fans, general readers, and journalists. Consequently, this more authentic, personalized mode of storytelling has impacted traditional journalism in that media professionals now turn to celebrity blogs for the most updated information. Despite the seemingly informal nature of blogging, these blogs feed mainstream media channels, particularly entertainment television and print media.

Notably, celebrities and their work teams strategically present and manipulate this transmedia storytelling, such as the way in which Yang Lan blogs about personal issues and those of other well-known people. As a public figure, Yang has been cautious about protecting her family, especially her two children, from the media spotlight. On the other hand, her blog has provided a space where Yang selectively shares stories about her family that rarely appear in mainstream media. The recording of details of her family life resonates so greatly with Yang's audience that many have expressed their gratitude for her portrayal of quotidian life. Nevertheless, Yang Lan's portrayal of her family life focuses more on her children than on her husband, a successful but controversial businessman who has been dogged by scandals, and her real-life struggles, failures, and frustrations are barely mentioned.

In addition to selectively presenting themselves on their blogs, celebrities amplify narratives about themselves that are already available in mainstream media. Most of these narratives are related to work and aim to promote their products. Xu Jinglei used her blog to innovatively publicize her low-budget independent film *Dreams May Come*, the very first Chinese film that was promoted primarily through a personal blog. Between December 18, 2005, and October 30, 2006, Xu wrote more than fifty blog entries about the film that she financed, directed, starred in, and produced. These articles covered a wide range of topics, including the beginning stages of brainstorming, problems encountered during the process of shooting and editing, detailed progress reports during production, postproduction reflections, and marketing plans. Xu also posted hyperlinks that connected her blog to her film production company's website. These hyperlinks included clips of the film, mini documentaries that chronicled the daily progress of filmmaking, and the screenplay of *Dreams May Come*. The theme song for *Dreams May Come* was also available for downloading from her blog. Thus, text, photos, video, and audio on Xu's blog all added to the popular, mainstream media narratives surrounding *Dreams May Come*. Just like Xu Jinglei, Yang Lan posts behind-the-scenes scoop on her blog, mainly related to the two weekly shows she hosts. In addition to routinely posting formal introductions to upcoming shows written by their directors, Yang enriches the narrative surrounding the shows with personal reflections on these television programs, as well as behind-the-scenes stories. When contributing to these blog entries, Yang Lan employs moderately sensational lines to motivate readers to read her blog entries and consume her media products.

In addition to telling transmedia stories by creating new content, celebrities frequently repost materials that have been published elsewhere on their blogs. In contrast to a film like *The Matrix*, where the original movie leads to derivative products such as comics and video games, celebrity blogs do not always generate spin-off products or narratives. The redistribution of similar media content across celebrity blogs creates an alternative model of transmedia storytelling, which ensures the multidirectional flow of media content to publicize each piece to the fullest extent. Furthermore, the sources of these blog entries illustrate the elasticity of cultural forms in the digital era. Roughly two-thirds of Yang Lan's essays are about her television programs. Yang regularly posts a brief introduction, along with pictures, video clips, trailers, broadcast times, behind-the-scenes stories, and her thoughts on the show. Once these shows have been broadcast, the content flows back into other online spaces in various forms. Parts of the shows are transcribed and published on Yang's blog, as well as in her e-magazines and on the Tiannv website, both of which link to her blog. Thus, the television program *Her Village*, the daily e-magazine *Her Village*, and the Tiannv website complement one another, with all three focusing on similar subjects and constantly advertising for one another to make Yang's shows a ubiquitous presence on the Internet.

Yang Lan's shows are also translated into print media. Both *Yang Lan One on One* and *Her Village* are transcribed and published in book form every one or two years. Yang posts prefaces to these books on her blog and announces upcoming book launch events to encourage readers to attend. A blog entry titled "Women's Liberation" was the preface for a book published under the same name in 2007. An article titled "Talk Less about Success, More about Difficulties" was the preface for a book series of *Yang Lan One on One*, also published in 2007. Thus, one type of media content—in this case, a television show—is repeatedly presented in multiple forms such as print media, videos, photographs, online text, e-magazines, and so on.

In a similar vein, Yang frequently recycles content that is readily available elsewhere on her blog, such as journal articles she has written for print media, interviews she has conducted, commercials she has made, and public speeches she has given, albeit all in slightly modified forms. Because blogs consist of relatively short entries, Yang's public speeches and interviews are serialized and given individual titles in her blog. One public speech she gave to college students at Peking University was serialized into six parts, each part published under separate dates and different titles. Similarly, to commemorate the death of Wang Guangmei, the wife of China's former Vice President Liu Shaoqi, Yang reposted an interview with Wang that had appeared several years earlier in a series on her blog. The modification of existing content to fit a new medium demonstrates Yang's endeavor to make full use of available content to tell transmedia stories, which "assume many different forms at the point of reception."[20]

Therefore, celebrities contribute blog entries to create or enrich the narratives about themselves or others, as well as to facilitate the flow of existing content across multiple platforms, enhancing their network of visibility by bridging digital and traditional media outlets. At the same time, while celebrities take the initiative in conversing with audiences, audiences also play active roles in online space. The attention that these audiences pay to celebrities online, reified in such forms as leaving comments, filling in questionnaires, or simply clicking on the "paying attention" button, indicates the productive value of attention as well as the importance of interactivity.

Negotiating Interactivity in Celebrity Blogs

The advent of Web 2.0 made the dream of online interactivity come true. As one of the derivatives of Web 2.0 technologies, the interface of a blog constitutes a convenient channel for Internet users to participate in online discussions, such as through blog entries, reader comments, and blogger responses. This dynamic disrupts the stability of the original texts and demonstrates the indispensable role of readers. Within the context of celebrity blogging, the act of "rushing to the sofa" (*qiang shafa*), a popular metaphor referring to the competition between readers to post messages on celebrity blogs, highlights the audience's passion for online interaction. The person who successfully leaves the first message on a message board usually writes "sofa" (*shafa*) to indicate their excitement, while those who take the second or third place post "stool" (*bandeng*) or "floor" (*diban*), indicating that they fall slightly behind.

Such enthusiasm for posting messages on Chinese celebrity blogs originates from an inclination toward voyeurism and exhibitionism, which is both amplified and facilitated by the ease of interactivity in the Internet age. As Joanne Jacobs discusses, a reader's drive to post online is "both exhibitionistic, and an exercise in self-discovery . . . where the disreputable aspects of voyeurism are regarded by both authors and readers of blogs as being 'overcome' by the mutually negotiated permission to engage with ideas implicit in the blog format."[21] Clearly, the readers' initiative to post messages on celebrity blogs is as much about the readers as it is about the celebrities. While readers are eager to learn about the lives of celebrities, their responses to celebrity posts are also an important means of exploring their own identities. A message one reader left for Yang Lan states:

> As a matter of fact, people visit celebrity blogs simply because they want to learn about a celebrity's inner thoughts and every aspect of their daily lives. Yet, you [celebrities] will definitely not show every aspect of your true selves to the public, and we can only see your positive sides. . . . What I want to read is the way you, a member of the upper class, view the world and your attitude toward big or small issues in your daily lives.[22]

According to this post, although readers are well aware of the performative dimension of self-representation on a celebrity's blog, they are nevertheless driven to learn about celebrities' "true" thoughts. The pleasure the audience receives from reading celebrity blogs also originates from a sense of equality facilitated by interactivity, as reflected in these two posts:

[Post 1]

Yang Lan, finally you are not so distant from us.

[Post 2]

The Internet is such a great product! In the past I could only see you on television, read about you in print media, and talk about you with other people. I would never have thought that I could communicate with you one day. Although you might not see my comments, I'm still thrilled.[23]

These two posts show how blogging, which was a new interface at the time, makes celebrities more approachable to ordinary people, thereby bridging the gap between the renowned and the anonymous. The second post also reveals that the motivation to post messages on celebrity blogs stems not so much from an expectation that the celebrity will read them or respond but from a desire for self-expression. For Rob Cover, the readers' desire for self-expression in online spaces reflects their eagerness to participate in the creation and transformation of the text, which has been denied by previous technologies of media production and distribution.[24] By constantly "writ[ing] back into the text . . . to add to the text by registering their own messages,"[25] readers feel empowered, as they are able to access the personal space of celebrities and to exert a certain amount of control over that space. More important, a reader's online productivity has a great potential to be converted into material interests for the celebrity. Xu Jinglei, Yang Lan, Hong Huang, and Guo Jingming all feel an urgent need to maintain close ties with their audiences via blogging. They closely observe audience comments and selectively reply to these messages. Xu Jinglei occasionally adds her response immediately following a commenter's initial post, using a couple of words or emoticons. She even responds to inflammatory messages that attempt to tarnish her star image: "I just read through the comments posted on my blog. Although I tried to take a middle ground on many issues, there are still people who want to attack me. Calm down. I won't delete your posts. I won't delete any of them. Since I can talk, so can everybody else."[26] Xu's stance on respecting everyone's freedom of speech has been well received among her readers. Similarly, Hong Huang expresses gratitude to readers who correct typographical errors in her online posts. Hong humorously writes in an entry, "Thanks to everybody who made corrections for me—an illiterate! I will post some pictures tomorrow to reward you."[27] Hong also set up a subsection in her blog entitled "Ask Me: Private Meeting Room" that she uses to respond to questions raised by her readers.

Celebrities all appear to consider it of paramount importance to reciprocate attention by responding to their readers' messages, emphasizing interaction not only to enhance their popularity among fans but also to get users involved in activities such as filling out online surveys, registering to attend shows, and offering feedback on entertainment products. Yang Lan frequently employs the titles "Advertising Time" and "Recruiting Audiences" to invite those interested in her shows to attend the recordings. These "search notices" also extend to the workplaces of Hong Huang and Xu Jinglei. Both have posted "wanted" ads on their blogs looking for professionals to work for their magazines. Unlike many "wanted" ads that formally list job descriptions and qualifications, the "wanted" ads on celebrity blogs are typically of an informal style. In a blog entry titled "Looking for Writers," Hong Huang starts with "it's driving me crazy." She complains about the low-quality content she has received and states her need for editors:

> I'd like to invite those who love to write to contact me. Shoot me some of your writing. If we're happy with each other, let's strike a deal. We need people who can tell good stories with details. . . . [I know] this might not be the best way to hire someone. It makes me look rather demanding. But, let it be.[28]

This post generated more than 900 responses from readers. Many expressed their gratitude for Hong's sincerity and claimed to have submitted writing samples to her. These personalized search notices complement the use of regular media for celebrities to reach out to readers.

In addition to seeking audience participation and placing job ads, all four celebrities solicit reader opinions on issues ranging from the trivialities of everyday life to serious questions about media production and reception. As new media users embrace the age of interactivity by actively contributing original content to the Internet—including original ideas, feedback, and personal information—their voluntary participation also suits the need of the media industry to conduct market surveys. As the case of Yang Lan demonstrates, the "collective intelligence"[29] and "free labor"[30] of Internet users has great potential to be converted into productive values.

While online interactivity empowers Internet users, it also contributes to a new means of surveillance in which producers can monitor audience activity at any time.

Playing Interactivity to an Extreme

Of the four celebrities profiled in this chapter, Yang Lan interacts online most actively. A media professional, Yang Lan is exploring new possibilities heralded by digital technologies. Anxious about the younger generation's turning away from television, she tries to "reach out to the same target community" via blogs and e-magazines.[31] Yang Lan solicits their feedback about potential improvements to her cultural products. The small rewards given to those who participate, as well as Yang's personalized acknowledgments in various forms (e.g., words, photographs, autographs), continually motivate readers to become more involved.

While Yang's television audience is asked to suggest questions and offer feedback to producers, Yang's electronic magazines offer Internet users a greater degree of agency. When Yang Lan first launched e-magazines at the end of 2005, she encouraged readers to post comments on her blog's message board. Readers' comments were also displayed on a special section in the e-magazines titled "From Readers," which included editors' responses. Issues discussed there ranged from the content and layout of the magazines to downloading problems, and from background music selections to sound quality problems. E-magazines seem to indicate the possibility of shared space and shared control, where media consumers and producers witness the development of a product from the beginning and share moments of difficulty and joy together as the product matures. All three of Yang Lan's e-magazines stress the role that "you"—readers, consumers, and participants—play in the process of consumption. The advertising slogan of *Lan* reads: "We listen to your voices all the time. We care about your feelings in each and every issue. Please allow us to try to change your way of reading." Likewise, the back page of *Her Village* summarizes the magazine's central tenet as "Let us hear your voices. Who are we? We are a group of people who love to dream and talk. This is a magazine that converses with you from deep inside." To implement these principles, Yang's e-magazines not only publish the audience's responses in hypertextual forms but also encourage readers to submit a recording of their voices in mp3 format. Therefore, the diversity of media forms, including voicemail, hypertext, text messages, videos, and audio clips, seems to empower audience members wishing to make their voices heard. The visibility of readers' opinions brings to the audience a sense of self-importance as media consumers, especially when their participation is reciprocated. This reciprocation, in turn, continues to prompt audiences to participate as desired by celebrities and sustains consumer loyalty to celebrity-endorsed products. Meanwhile, although consumers may enjoy freedom of expression in online spaces, their enthusiastic responses to the call of celebrities and their voluntary participation are subject to subtle, yet constant, exploitation by producers.

Mark Andrejevic addresses the flip side of online interactivity from the perspective of "value-enhancing labor."[32] The pleasure of television fans lies in the fact that networked media enable their formerly nonproductive activities to generate valuable information commodities.[33] In this process, media interactivity facilitates the "simultaneity of labor as something which is voluntarily given and exploited."[34] An important facet of digital culture, the "continuous production of value"[35] generated by the free labor of Internet users can make significant contributions to media producers. Audience participation across all available platforms—including voice mail, mp3, hyper-textual elements, text messages, and online questionnaires—constitutes an important means for Yang Lan and her team to research their audiences. In this way, media producers develop a better idea of who their audience is and what they desire. In other words, the space that allows for free expression and social interaction is simultaneously a space that enables surveillance. While new media users may enjoy spying on celebrities and expressing their opinions online, the very digital media platforms that provide them enjoyment constitute spaces where the watchers themselves are constantly watched.

Although many instances of such surveillance go unremarked, voluntary audience participation and its contribution to media production occasionally indicates a contentious collaboration between media consumers and producers. As an interface bringing these two parties together, celebrity blogs are sites filled with negotiation and tension, because users fight over issues ranging from blog content, the style of media products, and the overcommercialization of celebrity blogging, to details about the public image of celebrities. For example, while some of Yang Lan's fans are excited about the opportunity to interact with her, some are nonetheless offended when publicity-related content dominates her blog. A number of readers reacted strongly to one blog entry, in which Yang Lan posted the preface she wrote for a series of books on jewelry appreciation. In the last line of this essay, Yang Lan announced that she would collaborate with Celine Dion to launch a joint jewelry brand, HV Love. One reader wrote sarcastically, "We cannot help but wonder, is this commercial? Seeking profit for oneself in the name of culture!" Another post stated, "By posting commercials here, you let down those netizens who root for you. I really hate that you're doing this. It feels like you're fooling around with us."[36] These comments reflect audiences' resistance to manipulation by celebrities. Some readers suggested that Yang Lan should set up another section for advertisements, leaving her blog entries for personal reflections. A reader who held a relatively neutral stance concurred with the previous two posts: "Indeed, incorporating commercial endorsements into blogs makes publicity-related purposes too obvious. This makes celebrities easy targets."[37]

Such reader responses exemplify a common perception of the blog as a channel for genuine self-expression, instead of a publicity platform. As Yang Lan has gradually shifted the focus of her blogging from personal reflections to publicity, she has incurred more reader resentment. Not only are Yang Lan's excessive publicity campaigns on her personal blog vehemently criticized by netizens, but the neutral stance Yang takes toward societal issues has also been interpreted as lacking individuality:

[Post 1]

One time, I didn't visit your blog for over six months. It's mainly because you've pretty much transformed this place into a commercial section for *World Women* and *Lan*. It seems like your blog lacks your own life reflections, and this is the wrong strategy for blogging. . . . In terms of subject matter, you should write more on issues unrelated to work. It's not that we like gossip; but rather, it's to let fans know more about the real you.

[Post 2]
Sister Yang Lan, after reading your blog, I feel like your words are overly rational and lack emotion. This is similar to the style of your book. Indeed, as new women, we need to reflect on our lives and societal issues. However, for each and every individual, blogs should be a space where you can relax. If you carefully think about every sentence you write down, then your blog lacks personality.[38]

To a large degree, readers perceive the predominance of work- and publicity-related issues on celebrity blogs as a "contamination" of personalized space, which is ideally a space for self-expression. The strong reaction of readers against Yang Lan's ploy to "seek profit in the name of culture" reflects the lingering perception of culture as something sacred, instead of a mere commodity. These objecting readers perceive culture and commerce as two opposing entities. They hold the opinion that excessive self-promotion of commercial products on personal blogs is unacceptable. However, seeking a perfect convergence of culture and commerce exactly embodies the career aspirations of Yang Lan, who hopes to pursue her cultural idealism while generating profit. Yang's response to the commercial failure of Sun Television Cybernetworks reflects this rationale:

I define my professional career as belonging to the "cultural industry," which is different from the IT, business, finance, and industry. . . . I have a cultural ideal. I felt that China needed a TV platform that emphasized our culture and value system. I put that idea into practice. In 2000, I launched Sun Television Cybernetworks, which mainly produced and broadcast documentaries. . . . In retrospect, the impulse to realize my cultural ideal far exceeded my understanding of business management. As of today, I have never considered Sun Television Cybernetworks a cultural failure. It failed commercially, but its cultural value remains. After all, it was after the endeavors of Sun Television Cybernetworks that documentary and humanity-based channels began to appear on CCTV and local television stations.[39]

It was after Yang Lan sold 70 percent of the company's shares in 2003 that she began to attend to the Internet's potential for integrating old and new media platforms. She continues to experiment with new modes of cultural production and distribution online, and attempts to build personal brands based on her star image, cultural pursuits, and mainstream appeal. Ironically, while some readers felt Yang Lan's blog lacked a strong personal imprint, individuality—embodied in her personal branding—is what Yang has been promoting all along. The series of cultural products launched by Yang are all personal brands based on her public image as a successful career woman. These include her television show *Yang Lan One on One* and the jewelry brand Lan. The emphasis on individuality is also seen in several of Yang's e-magazine advertising slogans, such as "Yang Lan's electronic magazines: Just like Lan." Another example, "Live a life with serenity on the outside and ripples inside," the advertising slogan for *Lan*, is a poetic interpretation of both Yang's first name (literally meaning waves) and her personality. Usually, the cover page of *Lan* is a closeup of Yang Lan looking elegant, fashionable, and professional. This image, along with Yang Lan's assumption of challenging roles, like cultural producer and entrepreneur, continues to inspire urban audiences in China.

The gap between readers' understanding of individuality as the free expression of one's opinions and the individuality promoted by Yang Lan illustrates the multiple possibilities of interpreting her public image. Moreover, the neutral stance Yang takes toward controversial societal issues not only confirms readers' comments on her lack of personality when blogging, but it has also resulted in some criticism for her failure to address class differences when treating women's issues on her television shows and in her e-magazines. Online disputes about the definition of woman and femininity reflect how readers use the message board on Yang Lan's blog to convey their understanding of issues pertaining to gender and class divide in contemporary society.

"Intellectual Women" and Female Liberation in Question

The term "intellectual women" first appeared as part of a literary series launched by the Hundred Flowers Art and Literature Publishing House in Tianjin, in 1998. This series was a collection of prose works by female writers who focused on the experiences of urban women.[40] Amid the exponential growth of the urban consumer class, the notion of "intellectual women" stressed the perfect combination of intelligence and femininity embodied in the image of the modern woman. The star personas of Xu Jinglei, Yang Lan, and Hong Huang, portraying them as intelligent, successful, yet nonthreatening figures, inspire their audiences. All three women capitalize on this image to explore the dominant market logic of identifying consumers, envisioning new trends, and producing niche products. The cultural products they create include Yang Lan's *Her Village* and its sister website Tiannv.com, Hong Huang's fashion magazines and her fashion store that promotes local Chinese brands, and Xu Jinglei's films that guide urban women on how to succeed in the workplace.

In spite of these celebrities' claim that the rising middle class represents their primary target audience,[41] they are often criticized for neglecting other types of women, particularly the underprivileged. Among the three celebrities, Yang Lan has shared the most reflections on the role of the urban woman in society and the family. Two of her essays, titled "Women's Liberation" and "Three Ways to Balance Work and Life," offered the most detailed accounts of her viewpoint and generated a heated discussion among netizens. "Women's Liberation" looks back on the connotations of "liberation" over several generations of women in Yang Lan's family.[42] For Yang's grandmother, liberation meant escaping the painful foot-binding process; for her mother, liberation meant being able to attend college. By contrast, for Yang Lan, liberation refers to both new opportunities and uncertainty in life. She states that although her generation enjoys freedom of choice and no longer has to worry too much about poverty or so-called political correctness, new problems such as women's anxieties revolving around work-life balance have appeared along the way.[43] Yang Lan interprets "liberation" for the modern woman as taking on responsibility in life:

> When I graduated from college, my parents said to me, "Now that you have completed your college degree, you will be on your own from now on. As a girl, you need to count on yourself." I was nervous and helpless. Inevitably I grew up, and did not know what I would face. Today, when I look back, that was the best gift my parents ever gave me. My liberation started at that very moment.[44]

In her opinion, independence is the key to a woman's happiness, and her discussion about such female liberation sparked genuine reflections by netizens. One poster wrote: "My liberation started at the moment when I argued with my boss and left my boyfriend. The moment that I built up my self-confidence was the moment of my liberation." Some netizens questioned Yang's arguments concerning women's empowerment and gender relations in the contemporary era. One user wrote that "while we as women are liberated, society imposes on us more pressure and challenges." Another post expressed a similar opinion: "What about social problems? Our society does not treat women equally. You only tell your sisters about liberation, yet do not pinpoint the root cause of their anxiety. It might work better to tell men how to deal with women's liberation in the first place." Netizens also criticized Yang Lan for her neglect of the discrepancies between urban and rural women: "Do you know how women in rural areas will respond to your words?" "Better interview women from rural areas first; that is an entirely different story. They have a long way to go for their liberation." Alternatively, some netizens asked Yang Lan to clarify her stance regarding sexual liberation.[45]

Reflections on Yang Lan's perception of women's issues were furthered by audiences' active engagement in criticism of Yang Lan's shows. Yang's disregard of the underprivileged class in Chinese society, in particular, has repeatedly incurred criticism from readers: "Yang Lan, apparently now you're the spokesperson for white-collar women who live a good life. Why not pay more attention to ordinary women? You know, they're the majority! I hope that one day you may offer new perspectives in your shows." Another reader concurred, "I hope that your shows focus more on the conditions of ordinary people and their thoughts. . . . [T]here has been a lack of genuine concern for marginalized groups in this society, which I really don't understand."[46]

This sampling of netizens' responses showcases how Yang Lan's construction of femininity has evoked conflicting reactions in online spaces. As Christine Gledhill has argued, the production of meaning "arises out of a struggle or negotiation between competing frames of reference, motivation and experience."[47] The construction of femininity at both the "production" and "reception" end of celebrity blogs demonstrates how the online productivity enables readers to comment on celebrities' career choices and to publish their own interpretation of these celebrities' public images. The readers' diverging opinions about celebrity blogging and its function not only contribute to the dynamic of online spaces but also are conducive to the collective discussion of the role of celebrities in shouldering social responsibilities.

Entrepreneurial Masculinity in Contestation

The criticism raised by Internet users of these female entrepreneurs' reluctance to discuss societal issues applies equally to Guo Jingming, who generated controversy during his rise in the literary world. Prior to 2005, Guo remained somewhat mysterious in his role as editor-in-chief for *Zui Novel*, as he mainly connected with readers through conventional channels, such as book-signing events, interviews, and personal correspondence. The advent of blogging offered new opportunities for Guo's fans to interact with him. Many of Guo Jingming's devoted readers expressed excitement about finally being able to access his personal space, particularly when he first started blogging in late 2005. Meanwhile, Guo Jingming's representation of himself on his blog fueled more controversies.

At the age of twenty, Guo Jingming was embroiled in a scandal regarding his second novel, *Never Flowers in Never Dreams* (*Mengli hualuo zhi duoshao*), the bestselling book of 2003. Zhuang Yu, the author of *In and Out of the Circle* (*Quanli quanwai*, 2002), filed a lawsuit against Guo under allegations of plagiarism. In 2004, the Beijing No. 1 Intermediate People's Court ruled that Guo Jingming and his publisher, the Chunfeng Literature and Art Publishing House, could no longer publish *Never Flowers in Never Dreams*. Guo appealed this decision but lost in 2006. Guo paid a fine of 200,000 RMB (24,000 USD), yet he refused to issue an apology.[48] Lena Henningsen argues that Guo's work *Rushing to the Dead Summer*, published in 2005, reflects his response to this conviction. In the story, Guo distinguishes between plagiarism and imitation,[49] the latter a literary and artistic practice popular since ancient China. Guo also satirizes the media and those who try to gain fame by raising charges against the artist—an allusion to Zhuang Yu.[50] Since Guo Jingming never admits to the act of plagiarism, this gesture helps sustain the legitimacy of his writings among fans. Nevertheless, his past conviction, wrongful or otherwise, continues to haunt Guo's present. In the comments section of Guo Jingming's blog, fans express confusion as to why Guo was convicted of the charge. Guo Jingming's attackers, by comparison, celebrate the opportunity to openly criticize him.

The second controversy concerned Guo Jingming's blatant consumerism plus his lack of masculinity, at least as shown in his public persona. The cosmopolitan imaginary portrayed in Guo Jingming's works, including an obsession with luxury brands and other trappings of upper-class lifestyles, strongly appeals to the large sector of Guo's fans residing in third- and fourth-tier cities. At the same time, Guo's celebration of materialism inspires criticism against him for displaying an apathetic attitude toward public affairs. The controversy created by the film versions of the *Tiny Times* series is a case in point. The tremendous commercial success of the *Tiny Times* series exemplifies an effective model for the "intermedial"[51] promotion of cultural products across media platforms, including print media, digital media, cinema, and television. The marketing of the *Tiny Times* series was innovative in terms of integrating big data analysis into the films' production and promotion.[52] However, the films' celebration of hedonistic values and its obsession with materialism drew criticism from mainstream and official media outlets. Many of Guo Jingming's loyal fans fought back against these negative reviews of *Tiny Times*, and their efforts constituted one of the most sensational media spectacles of the time.

Criticism of Guo Jingming's espoused value system and the rabid enthusiasm of his fans tend to overlook the areas in which Guo Jingming demonstrates remarkable cultural sensitivity. The androgynous-looking male characters in the *Tiny Times* series accord with the emerging type of "pan–East Asian soft masculinity"[53] that portrays males as nonthreatening, beautiful-looking, and yet financially powerful. Digital media have further popularized these newly constructed masculine ideals, which have gained traction among female consumers in China.[54] Guo Jingming's self-representation on his blog from 2005 onward heralded this trend, while his personal branding strategy connects closely with the marketing agenda of Zui Company.

Guo Jingming's appearance, slight and short in stature, is commonly perceived as effeminate. This appearance accords with his melancholy style of writing that often expresses self-pity, narcissism, and the evasion of reality.[55] Meanwhile, Guo's expression of love and filial piety toward his parents resonates with China's first generation of only children, who were raised as the center of their parents' world. Nevertheless, both Guo's image and his writing are subject to criticism by attackers. For three years, Guo Jingming was voted China's most hated male celebrity on Tianya (2004–7). To ridicule Guo's effeminate qualities, Tianya users founded the Chrysanthemum Cult (*juhua jiao*) and worshipped Guo as the central figure. Guo also received nicknames like "the fourth girl" (*si guliang*), since Guo's fans call him "Little Four." Interestingly, Guo Jingming posted photos on his blog that reinforced these negative perceptions. Guo's selfies resembled glamorous celebrity shots, exhibiting luxury brands, spacious housing, and fashionable hairstyles. In addition to commenting on brand names, he frequently expressed pleasure about shopping with female friends and negotiating prices with sellers, having a close relationship with his mother, and cooking.[56] The effeminacy Guo Jingming embodies is complemented by an internalization of the hegemonic notion of masculinity that emphasizes aggressiveness and physical strength.[57] In some photos, Guo Jingming highlights this perception of male sexuality by exhibiting his upper body muscles. In terms of personality, Guo is known as a bossy figure at work, who enjoys being in control. Guo's self-representation on his blog parallels the increasingly popular social ideal of the metrosexual: gentle and caring, yet capable at work.

Guo Jingming's self-branding strategies align with his career ambitions. The operation model of Zui Company resembles that of a talent agency; each contracted writer is marketed as a glamorous celebrity. Given the underdeveloped teen literary market in the mid-2000s, this strategy fostered Guo's rapid transition from a writer to a literary agent and publisher.[58] The careful curation of content on his blog illustrates his shrewdness in business. Guo has acknowledged that since blog entries are free to readers, he is cautious about reserving content that may be published in print.[59] Consequently, Guo's blog posts focus on the trivial matters of daily life, such as illnesses, fashion, friendship, and pets. While the everyday content of his posts creates a sense of intimacy among his readers, Guo does not shy away from converting this virtual intimacy into productive value. In contrast to Yang Lan, Guo seldom launches publicity campaigns that offend his fans. Growing up in the age of consumerism, the post-1990s generation seems to feel comfortable with such sponsored content. Guo's readers even seem to appreciate the personalized approach Guo takes. In an entry that publicized the book version of *Tiny Times 1.0*, Guo frankly stated his purpose: "My readers seem to have already reached a consensus: as long as I am active on blog, it is advertising time. So there are no exceptions today."[60] Guo Jingming then offered a detailed description of the illness he suffered working to complete *Tiny Times 1.0*. At the end, he made an emotional appeal to his readers: "I suddenly realized that it has been more than a year since I published my last book, *The Sorrow Rivers*. After congratulating myself for topping the sales figures in 2007, I could not help but wonder if *Tiny Times* might make it to first place in 2008. That is to say, the sales figures of *Tiny Times* in November and December of 2008 would have to compete with books that had been released in January of this year."[61] This statement employed the rhetoric of market competition to stimulate the fans' passion to defend their idol, in the hopes of converting their emotional support to monetary gain. In return for readers' support of his latest endeavor, Guo Jingming constantly expressed his gratitude to them and posted updated sales figures. In addition, he took proactive measures to prevent potential copyright infringement. Upon the release of *Tiny Times* 3.0 in print, Guo pleaded with his readers not to disclose the storyline online: "Please do not deprive readers in remote areas the pleasure of reading. If you live in a big city, you might be able to access the book a few days earlier simply because you know someone who works in book distribution channels or in the retail industry. However, I hope you would allow other readers the equal opportunity to share the joy and surprise during the process of reading."[62] Although this statement appears to defend readers' interests, it was actually intended to protect the intellectual property of the *Tiny Times* series.

In summary, Guo Jingming actively uses the blog as a new publicity channel to promote cultural products, engage readers, and build his star persona. His personal branding strategies, along with the cultural products of Zui Company, promote the rise of soft masculinity that is sensitive to women's needs, meticulous about appearances, and successful at work. Reportedly a workaholic, Guo frequently mentions how packed his schedule is, to the extent that he does not even have time for dating.[63] Guo's commercial success and his work ethic could be read as a response to the early controversies he experienced. His transition from author to publisher, literary agent, and director exemplifies his embodiment of the entrepreneurial spirit in the age of neoliberalism. Read in this light, Guo's personal experience and brand-building strategies have contributed to a diversification of masculine ideals in contemporary society.

Conclusion

The career experiences of Xu Jinglei, Yang Lan, Hong Huang, and Guo Jingming began at a time when the idea of culture as an industry and cultural products as commodities was in its infancy. Fully recognizing the Internet's potential to encourage alternative cultural practices, these celebrities linked blogs and traditional media outlets. They blazed trails by engaging with China's nascent promotional culture based on personal branding, experimenting with multimedia platforms, and carving out niches within the emerging market.

The ways in which celebrities use personal blogs to achieve their varied goals illustrate how the rule of attention is implemented on a daily basis. By selectively presenting exclusive transmedia stories about themselves and others, celebrities endeavor to enhance their media visibility and foster a new participatory culture. New modes of collaboration, and new sources of tension, have emerged from this process. The pleasure of new media users originates from the visibility of user-generated content in all recordable forms and the enhanced sense of empowerment they experience in online spaces. Moreover, digital media usage can be converted into productive value, and as a result, celebrities frequently call for their audiences' physical, virtual, and symbolic participation in the process of media production, offering economic and symbolic rewards to reciprocate user participation. In this respect, Xu Jinglei, Yang Lan, Hong Huang, and Guo Jingming have all assumed pioneering roles in capitalizing on fans' feedback to identify market trends and cater to emerging tastes. The advent of big data analytics and the proliferation of social media platforms further this trend.

Celebrities' construction of their public images is also simultaneously embraced, contested, and negotiated by their audience on personal blogs. Highly acclaimed as "intellectual women," Xu Jinglei, Yang Lan, and Hong Huang inspire the younger generation of Chinese women. Nevertheless, their intellectual femininity is both hailed and questioned in celebrity blogs, as the three women are constantly criticized for failing to consider class differences when addressing gender-related issues. In the case of Guo Jingming, the ambivalent facets of the masculinity embodied in his star persona have contributed to the diversification of male images in contemporary society. However, he is also criticized for his political apathy and celebration of luxurious lifestyles, largely because of the traditional expectation that writers should shoulder social responsibilities.

The criticisms against these successful cultural entrepreneurs illustrate an inherent paradox of neoliberalism—one that exists "between the promised neoliberal fantasy/imaginary of emancipation and empowerment for all, on the one hand, and the market reality of a principle of competition and economized self-interest, on the other."[64] The chances for ordinary individuals, like many of these celebrities' readers, to celebrate freedom of choice and live aspirational lifestyles are becoming increasingly rare. In this respect, the taboo breakers, the focus of the next chapter, use blogging to engage more deeply with societal problems by challenging existing sociocultural hierarchies and norms. Thus, the vibrant Chinese blogosphere not only fosters the flourishing of individual expression and a booming celebrity culture, but it also catalyzes the rise of critical voices from a commercially dominant online space.

5 TABOO BREAKERS AND MICROCULTURAL CONTENTION

THE 2010 NOBEL PEACE PRIZE was awarded to Liu Xiaobo, a renowned literary critic and activist whose push for political reform in China led to his imprisonment. Immediately after this event, the widely read blogger Han Han published an entry entitled "October 8, 2010." Han Han's entry contained only a pair of white-colored quotation marks with some space left in between.[1] This mysterious entry generated 1,554,154 visits and 28,408 discussion threads in just over ten weeks. The pair of quotation marks raised a storm of conjecture among netizens, who returned repeatedly to respond to the post. Some Internet users were excited about Han Han's entry and yet puzzled by his message; some wondered whether the textless entry resulted from censorship, a common practice for websites seeking to comply with state authorities. Meanwhile, those who sought to decode the message turned to topics similar to those Han Han often detailed on his blog, such as the need to coin euphemisms to get around the great firewall. They also offered innovative interpretations of the cryptic blog post. One Internet user stated that the missing characters symbolized the state of speechlessness that arises when a government exerts control over free expression. Another reader commented that Han Han was alluding to Liu Xiaobo because there were exactly three spaces in between the quotation marks, for the three characters that make up Liu's name.

Then, a follow-up post identified the three missing characters as "peace prize" (*heping jiang*).

Why would a pair of quotation marks elicit so many responses among netizens? What exactly did Han Han want to articulate, and why had he chosen such an abstract form? How was Han Han connected to Liu Xiaobo, the former a popular youth idol and the latter a dissident intellectual whose "Cold War style of political dissent and confrontation"[2] against the Chinese state had witnessed declining influence in recent years? Or were these two figures linked at all?

This chapter addresses these questions through the lens of microcultural contention. The role that digital media have played in reinventing contentious activities in China has attracted much scholarly attention. Most research focuses on the conventional style of contention, represented by such activities as "slogan chanting, banner-hanging, and placard-waving"[3] in public protests. It also addresses how activists appropriate digital media technologies to reinvent mobilizing tactics and to organize social protests.[4] Little attention is paid, however, to the microcultural contention that takes place in netizens' everyday encounters with digital media. This aspect deserves critical investigation. Along with the consolidation of authoritarian rule, "reciprocity and consensus"[5] have been the most prioritized goals that all agents, including the state, media, and society, have endorsed. Consequently, grand-scale activism, as exemplified by the 1989 Tiananmen protest, has largely given way to the "prosaic"[6] style of digital contention, which is less confrontational. Scholarly research reveals, for instance, that activists in China broadly define politics and seek to resolve the "immediate social problems"[7] embedded in everyday life, instead of aiming to facilitate any change in political structures.[8] Moreover, popular contention in the online sphere, although often seemingly frivolous, catalyzes the microrupture from within the "hegemonic formation"[9] that exposes the underlying dissonance among participants, thereby bearing significant implications for democratic practices. Seen in this light, the ways in which cultural contention online opens up microruptures from within dominant mainstream formations are particularly pertinent to authoritarian regimes.

The microcultural contention embedded in so ordinary a genre as blog-ging testifies to how this discursive space fosters a generation of "new per-formance modes, [and] newer ways to make meaning"[10] in authoritarian China. Delving into the taboo-breaking activities of bloggers, this chap-ter examines how writers and journalists born in the late 1970s and early 1980s have questioned the status quo, engaged with controversial issues, and stretched the boundaries of individual expression. I argue that style constitutes an integral component of their strategies of contention, with the backing of Internet corporations, their fans and anti-fans, and China's liberal-leaning media.

I first examine how Mu Zimei's "sex diary," which boldly portrays sexual-ity and gender relations, both offended the nationwide audience and popu-larized blogging as a new mode of individual expression when it emerged in 2003. On the one hand, Mu Zimei contributed to cultural diversification by inspiring a group of women bloggers to publicize their thoughts about sexuality, femininity, and gender relations, thus overthrowing the stereotypi-cal definitions of women. On the other hand, while the commercial websites that host these blogs have played an important role in creating sensation and thereby promoting diversity in the online space, they also subject these female bloggers to the public's voyeuristic gaze. Paradoxically, the realistic style of Mu Zimei's writing, while cultivating diversity, also seems to have contributed to her stigmatization as a "sex blogger."

I next turn to Han Han, bestselling author, racecar driver, and well-known blogger. While Mu Zimei initiated the popular trend of blogging by depicting the alternative lifestyle of an urban, white-collar woman, Han Han gradu-ally expanded his blog until it became the influential public forum for social critique in China. The quotation marks that Han Han employed in his blog entry about Liu Xiaobo epitomize an ascendant trend of digital contention that foregrounds performativity and style over substantial political actions. Simultaneously entertaining and enlightening, Han Han's entries on current affairs account for his appeal as a media star, while providing a safe channel for him and his peers to expand discursive parameters through humor, satire, and parody. Moreover, the heated debates that Han Han's entries stimulate among Internet users highlight the indispensable role that commercial media play in generating and spreading contentious issues. They also illustrate the significance of microcultural contention in opening ruptures from within the preset parameters of social, political, and cultural norms in a transitional Chinese society.

Elastic Discursive Parameters in Context

Scholars of Chinese studies have long noted how prescribed discursive parameters impinge on individual expression in China. In the literary arena, Chinese writers from the mid-1950s onwards became keenly aware of the existence of a "permissible scope"[11] for artistic expression, but one that was constantly redrawn, forcing writers to make continuous adjustments to stay within the acceptable bounds. The process of expanding and contracting boundaries was contingent on manifold factors, including factional political struggles, changes in Chinese Communist Party policies, and the Party's assessment of intellectuals. Consequently, even though literature was subject to ideological control, the permissible scope of creative writing was nevertheless in flux. Since the economic reforms of 1978, the gradual consolidation of hegemonic rule has prioritized consensus among the state, media, and society over an adoption of coercive measures.[12] Although the Chinese state still acts as the hegemonic player, the process of constant interaction between diverse actors—the central and local governments, commercial media, nongovernment-affiliated institutions, global corporations, and individual agents—make the discursive boundary between what can and cannot be articulated increasingly elusive. A case in point is the growing journalistic practice of overstepping discursive boundaries (*da cabian qiu*) and releasing alternative reports, which is often the work of high-profile TV anchors and journalists working for mainstream and official media.[13]

The increasingly predominant role of digital media in everyday life furthers this trend and exemplifies how the elastic discursive parameters of individual expression characterize the online space. On the one hand, online space expands discursive parameters and offers ample opportunities for individuals to express opinions, opportunities largely unavailable in traditional media outlets. Needless to say, the active use of new media by multifarious parties, including commercial corporations, Internet users, and activists, is concomitant with the implementation of increasingly sophisticated censorship mechanisms. However, the fact that Internet censorship prioritizes the curbing of collective actions rather than critical words[14] leaves ample room for critical voices to flourish online. On the other hand, although the state sporadically tightens its grip on free discourse, such as on occasions of political events and social unrest, "the limits of the permissible"[15] are often ambiguous due to factional struggles. The essence of the online sphere as a fluid space, the government's priority of censoring political actions instead of verbal criticism, and the fragmented nature of authoritarian rule all account for the elasticity of discursive parameters on the Chinese Internet. This idiosyncrasy, in turn, has paved the way for the reinvented style of microcultural contention in postmillennial China.

Mu Zimei: Blogging to Fame

On June 19, [2003], I started my blog, *Ashes of Love* [*Yi qingshu*], on Blogcn because all my colleagues and friends were blogging at that time. It was just like how we all logged onto OICQ or MSN to chat in the past. I was just keeping up with the times and didn't have a clear goal. My understanding of a blog was rather simple: it's a private diary (later, I realized that a blog is different from a diary, as blogs may have many different themes and forms). So I wrote about daily life, including work, killing time in bars, and making love. . . . It was fun, entertaining, and gossipy to visit your acquaintances' blogs. Maybe it was because I hosted a sex column for a magazine and the subject matter of my diary was explicit, gradually it attracted more and more visitors. I was not aware of this until early August when an entry related to a musician evolved into a public event. *Ashes of Love* seemed to have lost its original personal attributes. All kinds of people have become curious and paid lots of attention to it, at the same time interfering with my life.[16]

Originally named Li Li (b. 1978), Mu Zimei was a sex advice columnist for the Guangzhou-based *City Pictorial* (*Chengshi huabao*), a magazine targeting urban middle-class women. Because of the many restrictions imposed on print media, Mu Zimei blogged about more trivial matters.[17] Her blog focused on bold depictions of sex and her unconventional attitudes toward gender relations, encompassing issues ranging from her penchant for sexual intercourse and Internet dating to her cynicism toward marriage. The explosive entry Mu Zimei alludes to centered around a sexual encounter with Wang Lei, a famous rockstar. Soon, this piece was cross-posted to Xici (Western Temple Alley), a BBS popular among urban professionals and college students. Following that event, Mu Zimei's blog received an unprecedented wave of collective condemnation of her explicit sexual expressions and alternative lifestyle. The Mu Zimei phenomenon also generated massive responses that ranged from free expression and sexual rights to social progress to community responsibilities.[18] The competing forms of interaction that resulted from these divergent views in particular allowed for women's sexual expression in particular, and civil discourse in general, also broadened as a result.[19]

The trajectory of the Mu Zimei controversy was shaped jointly by print media, the Internet, the state, and netizens. On the one hand, the Mu Zimei incident demonstrates the close affinity between Internet media and traditional journalism in China. The online sensation triggered by Mu Zimei's entries offered news feeds for print media outlets, which defined the discursive parameters of journalistic reports. On the other hand, while traditional journalism possessed greater authority over free discourse, commercial websites showed their incomparable advantage in disseminating information, creating media sensation, and sustaining discussions. In contrast to the homogeneous opinions rampant in print media, commercial Internet outlets constituted a more heterogeneous space for the public to contemplate the Mu Zimei controversy. The fact that both sides continuously adjusted their stances based on one another's reports enhanced the visibility of the Mu Zimei controversy in public.

Specifically, in mid-October 2003, Mu Zimei's blog became one of the few personal webpages to record the highest daily number of visits in China, which increased to more than 6,000 per day.[20] On November 11, 2003, the Guangzhou-based *New Express Daily* (*Xin kuaibao*) first reported on the Mu Zimei phenomenon. This article was immediately cross-posted by Sina, followed by Sohu and NetEase. Both Sina and Sohu placed the report in prominent positions on their news feed sections. Within twenty-four hours, all three websites had launched special issues on Mu Zimei. In the coverage that followed, Sina took the lead and serialized *Ashes of Love*, running Mu Zimei's photos and interviews on its front page. As a result, Sina's web traffic jumped from 20 million to 30 million hits per day, a record that lasted for ten days,[21] while Sohu reported that "Mu Zimei" was one of the most searched terms in its search engine.[22] Baiyan Tree (*Rongshu xia*), an influential litera-ture website in China, carried the serialization of Mu Zimei's blog entries and recommended them on its home page. In addition, discussion forums and special issues about Mu Zimei proliferated online and attracted the active participation of scholars, journalists, and ordinary netizens.

It was through the promotion of influential commercial websites that Mu Zimei became a household name. This aspect had important implications for China's incipient blogging industry. As discussed in chapter 2, the enthusi-astic endeavors of Internet entrepreneurs to promote blogging in China had initially been rather ineffective. It was not until Mu Zimei appeared, together with her "sex diary," that the whole nation's attention became directed toward (sex) blogs as a new medium of expression. Due to the sudden explosion of Internet traffic, Mu Zimei's blog was shut down intermittently in 2003, but in spite of this, her writings were widely available online.[23] Public attention to the blog as a new medium for individual expression went hand in hand with the heated exchange of opinions regarding the Mu Zimei phenomenon, whether they were opinions about her explicit portrayal of sex, her exces-sive sexual escapades, her derogatory attitude toward men, or her liberal political stance. Mu Zimei fueled a wide-ranging debate about gender norms and sexual expression in a transitional Chinese society, engendering not only much collective verbal abuse but also much support. An online survey conducted by Sina showed that 18 percent of the 37,747 survey participants considered her behavior to be shameful, 22 percent thought Mu Zimei was willing to pay any price to gain fame, and 8 percent felt her conduct infringed on others' privacy.[24] At the same time, 38 percent of the netizens surveyed considered her behavior to be an individual choice, while 23 percent of those polled hailed her for "being sincere and challenging the hypocrisy in people's lives."[25] In contrast with the diverse opinions held by netizens, the survey re-sults presented in state-affiliated media were more homogeneous: the official

China Youth Daily reported that only 10 percent of forum posts supported Mu Zimei, while 90 percent of the posts criticized her deeds.[26]

The Mu Zimei incident took another dramatic turn when mainstream media outlets initiated a campaign denouncing Internet media sites for their excessive pursuit of web traffic to increase commercial gain. The *Beijing Evening News* (*Beijing wanbao*) took the lead and attacked Sina for magnifying the negative effects of the Mu Zimei phenomenon due to a lack of "rational judgment" and "moral autonomy."[27] In the name of "countering to public interest," *China Youth Daily,* the online portal of *People's Daily*, *Jiefang Daily*, and *Beijing Morning Post* all carried articles criticizing Mu Zimei's blog and her behavior, advocating for the social responsibility of the media, and accusing commercial sites of wrongly promoting her for the sake of attracting visitors.[28] In response, major websites reduced their coverage and placed related reports in a less prominent position on their webpages; Blogchina removed links to Mu Zimei's blog from its home page. An edited version of Mu Zimei's online entries, *Ashes of Love: A Complete Diary* (*Yiqing shu: Riji quanbanben*), was banned shortly after being released. Officially, Mu Zimei was prohibited from publishing works under either her pen name or her real name.[29]

Ironically, "being banned" (*fengsha*) contributed to the sudden soar of Mu Zimei's global fame. While the growing "aura of scandal"[30] surrounding Mu Zimei cost her job as an editor, the fact that she was banned by the Chinese authorities brought forth new opportunities. She was featured in interviews with famous entities, in both the domestic and international press, including *Magazine: Famous Brand* (*Magazine, mingpai*), *Southern People Weekly* (*Nanfang renwu zhoukan*), the *New York Times*, and *Time* magazine. Mu Zimei was also the first Chinese blogger to win the Deutsche Welle Blog Awards (the Best of the Blogs, or BOBs), in Germany in 2004, and was invited to sit on the selection committee for the BOBs the following year. By the end of 2005, her work had been published in Taiwan, Hong Kong, and France; she had also signed contracts with publishers in Japan, Germany, and the Netherlands.[31] Mu Zimei relocated to Beijing and was hired as a senior manager to promote blogging by Blogchina (now Bokee), where she made podcasts and posted blog entries.[32] She recorded an audio clip of herself making love and uploaded it online. More than 50,000 people simultaneously tried to download the twenty-five-minute podcast, crashing the host server.[33] Mu Zimei also hosted a microcolumn (*wei zhuanlan*)—a remediated genre of Twitter that invites renowned figures to post brief comments—entitled "Mu has a say" (*Mu youhuashuo*) at NetEase, as well as a column in the print newspaper *Southern Metropolis Weekly* (*Nandu zhoukan*). While the microcolumn retained some of the characteristics of *Ashes of Love*, Mu Zimei's column at *Southern Metropolis Weekly* widened the scope of her writing from an exclusive emphasis on sexual pleasure to a critical reading of current affairs, particularly on issues related to gender discrimination in China. Despite her insightful analysis, this column attracted only a niche audience. On the message boards of both columns, abusive messages abounded, and few readers appreciated her role as a sharp social commentator. The strong reactions Mu Zimei's "sex diary" triggered were a microcosm of the clashes of value systems and gender norms in a Chinese society undergoing drastic changes.

The Mu Zimei Phenomenon: Truth Value, Moral Panic

The truth value in Mu Zimei's coverage of a once-taboo subject encouraged readers to interpret her work as if it were completely factual, which accounts for her readers' voyeuristic satisfaction and the formation of digital moral crusaders against her. The formal characteristics of blogging distinguish Mu Zimei from such "beauty writers" as Wei Hui, Mian Mian, and Jiu Dan, who, since the late 1990s, had risen to fame in the field of popular literature for their semi-autobiographical novels. As Shuyu Kong analyzes, the flourishing of these writings took place against the backdrop of the increasing tabloidization of the Chinese media, the emergence of the commercial publishing industry, and the rise of middle-class consumers.[34] Women's sexuality, privacy, and femininity constitute marketable labels that both the publishing industry and women writers capitalize on to gain financial rewards.[35] In essence, Mu Zimei's writing consists of elements similar to that of Wei Hui, Mian Mian, and Jiu Dan, such as eliciting the reader's satisfaction in imagining the culture of metropolitan living—decadent love, trendy bars, and the varying men with which women are involved. Nevertheless, the close affinity of Mu Zimei's writing and her real-life experiences,

the media hype generated via the Internet, the avalanche of national and international media coverage, and her particular style of blogging as a whole
have carved out a different niche for Mu Zimei.

Unlike these "beauty writers," Mu Zimei has failed to gain recognition
as a professional writer in the popular literary field. She regards the blog
as a public channel for recording one's personal life: "I would never have
anticipated that a presentation of real life experiences and a real life attitude
would have proven to be such a huge mistake in this country."[36] This recording of "real-life experiences" stirred up controversy, triggered extreme
conservative reactions online, and at the same time satisfied readers' voyeuristic desires. The truth value of Mu Zimei's blog is showcased by her bra-
zen portrayal of sexual love as a female's consumption of the male body—a
call for the separation of sex from emotional entanglements—as well as her
high-profile admission of having affairs with married men and men with
girlfriends. An unadulterated celebration of female desire is reflected in Mu
Zimei's half-joking statement: "If you want an interview, make love with me
first. The longer you can last in bed, the longer the interview will be."[37] The
pride Mu Zimei took in violating conventional codes of gender, romance,
and sexual expression stoked outrage and triggered moral panic in society.
Concerned parents, academics, and conservatives unanimously sided with
the state and mainstream media. Mu Zimei was condemned for being "immoral," "promiscuous," and "perverse" for announcing her stance on sexual
liberation.[38] Internet users posted humiliating messages on her blog and on
discussion forums, using vulgar and sexually suggestive language. Academics
drew on psychoanalysis and pathology to explain Mu Zimei's behavior, as
exemplified by the article "Sex, Lies, and Mu Zimei" published on *Frontiers*
(*Tianya*), an authoritative literary journal.[39] In an effort to decode Mu Zimei's
personality, this essay derogatively stated that her sexual promiscuity merely
demonstrated her desperate need for attention. It further argued that Mu
Zimei's condescending attitude toward men proved her perversity instead
of signaling true sexual liberation.[40]

As Mu Zimei's candid attitude toward sex clearly touched a nerve with
moral defenders, her portrayal of sexual encounters has become less important. For one, the sexual explicitness of Mu Zimei's blog is only text-based

and, thus, is far surpassed by the websites featuring visual sexual content that are the primary targets of state censors. Moreover, Mu Zimei's blog entries about her sexual experiences do not focus on rendering erotic effects but instead aim at reflecting the alternative lifestyle of an urban, white-collar women. Thus, her style "is belletristic rather than pornographic, focusing more on contexts and feelings than simply bodies in motion."[41] The post that first brought Mu Zimei to the forefront of media attention writes:

> After nagging for a while, I said, "Wang Lei, how about doing it here. Making love is so simple."
>
> On the spot. Right in a dark corner near Sleepers [*Zhenmu*, the bar's name].
>
> He lifted my white skirt. I said, "Wearing a skirt is really convenient!"
>
> He said, "Thrust your hips and bend over at the waist."
>
> Lots of people love to use doggy style. But it's not easy to do it outdoors.
>
> Finished really soon. Wang Lei said the environment wasn't very good. No music.
>
> I said, "Wang Lei, you're also in poor health. Otherwise we could walk together, make love, and never stop."
>
> In 1998, I ran wildly at midnight to Wang Lei's bar, Unplugged Electricity [*Bu chadian*]. But I saw only the "closed" sign.
>
> In 1999, I was listening to Wang Lei's "Everything Starts with Love" and admired him so much.
>
> In 2000, I read an interview of Wang Lei in *Pictorial* . . .
>
> In 2001, I was in Wang Lei's bar, Voltage [*Diewa*], and broke down in tears while listening to his songs . . .
>
> In a promiscuous gathering a few months ago, Wang Lei's score dropped to a 70. After we made love on the spot, it became a 50.[42]

Other than Wang Lei's status as a famous rock star, this post is representative of Mu Zimei's portrayal of her sexual experiences. The one-night stand is usually depicted to express her reflections on the relationship between a self-indulgent woman and various men. Thus, sexual encounters merely serve as a less commonly employed channel for her to identify the truths and lies she has discovered about men: she claims to treat men as objects, so all sexual activities are intended to bring new inspiration to her work. More important, Mu Zimei's status is that of a female, urban, "artistic youth" (*wenyi qingnian*), a term that refers to a "young person of artistic and cultural sensibility, or rather, of quasi-hipster quality."[43] This accounts for the most intriguing aspect of her blog on the one hand, while triggering a screechy wave of moral panic on the other hand. Her portrayal of bars (which became extremely popular afterwards), the night life, sexual adventures, and friends in her circles in Guangzhou satisfies urban readers' cultural imagination about alternatives.

Mu Zimei's style of blogging factors into her failure to elevate her cultural status, as she is stigmatized as a sex symbol who constantly sparked the public's sexual fantasies in popular discourses. This fact piqued the commercial interest of several companies to such an extent that they purchased and registered the trademark "Mu Zimei" to advertise adult products.[44] More important, compared with writing for traditional media outlets and formal publication, a blog showcases a more true-to-life style because of "its overt autobiographical voice and . . . its organization as a diary of prosaic events."[45] This assertion is substantiated by Mu Zimei's initial understanding of the blog as a private diary, which not only enhances the realistic dimension of her entries but also provides for a realistic style of interpretation by visitors. The incorporation of a time-honored genre (the private diary) into a new form (blog) initiated a whole new experience for publishing and reading entries, as well as for interaction among Internet users. As Mu Zimei states, realness is an essential component of her writing style: "I am the kind of person obsessed with reality (*zhenshi*), be it in the past or present. My writing has been rooted in real-life experiences. It is only the format and sentiments that might be subject to change over time."[46] Indeed, the formal characteristics of a blog—in particular its openness, immediacy, and interactivity—are what unexpectedly electrified the media's interest in Mu Zimei. Afterward, Mu Zimei took advantage of the blog as a new medium and responded to the moral charges of the mass media and netizens. Her responses, in the form of blog posts, provided a record of the Mu Zimei controversy from a witness's perspective.

Mu Zimei's self-defense, however, reflects a contradictory perception of truth value and the power of realness. In addition to clarifying the distorted report of *New Express Media*, the newspaper that brought her nationwide notoriety, Mu Zimei began to record interviews she gave to offer readers a different perspective. Meanwhile, she insisted on the authenticity of her writing and asserted her unwillingness to conform to social norms, as noted in this entry:

> I record my life as it is, even if the record is interfered with and destroyed, and even if men feel threatened whenever they talk about me. If this storm, which is a testament of the Chinese people's inferiority, results in the fact that not a single man dares to make love with me, then it only demonstrates how obstinate they are. That said, I probably should sue the mass media for infringing upon my "sex life."[47]

In addition to defending her sexual rights, Mu Zimei's statement conveys a firm belief in the power and legitimacy of her claims for truth. The rationale behind the statement is that since realism is a state-sanctioned artistic style, she has done nothing wrong in recording her life faithfully. Meanwhile, contradicting her own claims, Mu Zimei attempted to become detached from the figures portrayed in her blog entries. While acknowledging that she was seen as a sex symbol in the public mind, she endeavored to distinguish herself from that symbol by emphasizing her real identity as a "person who writes and treats words with awe."[48] Mu Zimei suggested that readers treat her blog entries as a literary work instead of a faithful representation of her personal life. While Mu Zimei's stance swung between recording reality and mediating that reality via blogging, few readers paid attention to how she personally defined her social role. Mu Zimei continues to be stigmatized as an "obscene" and "immoral" sex blogger instead of being seen as a serious writer.

Although Mu Zimei fails to be recognized as a top-notch writer, the repercussions that have arisen out of the Mu Zimei controversy far surpass any possible influence she might have exerted from a literary perspective. In an early interview, Mu Zimei stated: "Sex is never taboo in Chinese society; however, sexual expression is."[49] Even though she did not initially intend to break this taboo, in retrospect, her public disclosure of the ordinarily private topic of sexual experience widened the discursive scope of women's sexual expression. Mu Zimei has inspired many successors, who have not only actively displayed their bodies and uttered sexual expressions in the blogo-sphere but also expanded the discursive scope from what was merely Mu Zimei's private war to a wider collective declaration, by women, against the deep-rooted patriarchal perception of gender norms and social injustice in Chinese society. These women bloggers come from a variety of sociocultural backgrounds, ranging from college students and professors to urban profes-sionals to rural migrants. Their activities exemplify how the society- and state-imposed discursive space are constantly being reshaped, so much so that Mu Zimei's sex diary could hardly create a media buzz today.

Specifically, while Mu Zimei's rebellion lay in her somewhat solitary battles against social norms, Zhuying Qingtong (Bamboo Shoots and Green Pupil) and Liumang Yan (Hooligan Swallow) have furthered Mu Zimei's radical stance by boldly displaying images of their bodies on the Internet. From 2004 to 2005, both figures celebrated the notion of female "corporeal awakening" (*shenti de juexing*) and posted nude pictures of themselves on their personal blogs on Tianya. The writings and pictures of Zhuying Qing-tong and Liumang Yan were intermittently removed by webmasters due to censorship concerns, but this action seemed to only enhance their level of fame. Concurrently, these two names were frequently discussed by major portal websites and print media outlets.

While Zhuying Qingtong and Liumang Yan celebrated the female body, Digua Zhu (Ground Melon Pig), a journalist in Beijing, took to blogging to defend women's reproductive rights. Digua Zhu started a blog devoted to her unborn child in 2006 and used it to call societal attention to single mother-hood. In her blog, titled "Little Sayings from Ground Melon Pig to Piggy," Digua Zhu recorded, in detail, the process of becoming a mother, including the unfair treatment she received as a single pregnant woman, the difficulty of scheduling an appointment with a gynecologist, and the expectations she had for her child, whom she nicknamed "Piggy." Her optimistic attitude, keen observations about daily life, and lyrical writing style inspired her friends, anonymous readers, and other single mothers. Within a month, Digua Zhu's blog had had more than 370,000 visitors,[50] and netizens had left her more than 600,000 messages.[51] Hailed as a "spokeswoman for single mothers," Digua Zhu later established an online group for single mothers at Sina, in which women could share experiences, support one another, and celebrate the sisterhood of single mothers. As in the case of the Mu Zimei phenomenon, commercial Internet portals played an important role in publicizing this issue. Sina played an instrumental role in facilitating online discussions of single motherhood, by setting up a special section and inviting Digua Zhu to chat with netizens online. These activities, among others, have contributed to the diversification of civic discourses and have enhanced the degree of societal tolerance in general.

These examples illustrate the repercussions of the Mu Zimei phenomenon, which celebrated individual choices, alternative lifestyles, and free expression. The nature of blogging, in particular its instantaneity, interactivity, and close affinity with everyday life, facilitated the escalation of the Mu Zimei controversy. The rhetoric of realness not only constituted the root cause of the public fury over Mu Zimei's "manizing" activities but was also employed as Mu Zimei's defense of her sexual rights and right to free speech. When Mu Zimei stepped out of the semi-narcissistic private domain to offer more critical reflections on gender-related issues, her transition did not catch much media attention. In contrast, the transition of Han Han from a youth idol to a serious social critic has been widely hailed.

The Literary Path of a Cultural Icon

As China's first teen literary celebrity, Han Han (b. 1982) experienced a sensational rise as a rebellious youth idol. This meteoric rise speaks volumes about the rapid transformation of the market-driven cultural field of the time. In 1999, while still a high school student in Shanghai, Han Han won first place in the inaugural National New Concepts Composition Competition (*xin gainian zuowen dasai*) hosted by *Mengya* (Sprout), a youth literary magazine aiming to transform itself from a high-end literary journal into a popular one to solve its dire financial situation.[52] The contest capitalized on the ongoing popular debate surrounding language arts education in secondary school. Many believed that rote learning had suffocated creativity and stifled student interest in literature; leading universities in China were experimenting with new models of liberal arts education by setting up honors classes. The contest built on this trend and promoted "new ways of thinking" (*xin siwei*), "new expressions" (*xin biaoda*), and "true experiences" (*zhen tiyan*) in creative writing, winning it acclaim from academia.[53] To increase the contest's authority, the organizers invited renowned literature professors, famous writers, and editors to be judges; among these judges, Wang Meng, then vice president of the Chinese Writers' Association, was the most remarkable. The authority of those who had won recognition from conventional literary organizations, all affiliated with the state, was thus transferred to this newly invented form of literary competition. In addition, prizewinners might be recommended to the seven prestigious Chinese universities, which cosponsored the contest. The fact that winners might bypass onerous college entrance exams had tremendous appeal to high school students and their parents.

Hosting the New Concepts Composition Contest proved to be a landmark event for *Sprout*. The journal not only earned its way out of financial difficulty, but it also successfully transitioned from a purely literary magazine to one that includes other areas of cultural production. The subscription numbers of *Sprout* increased significantly, partially because several award winners from the inaugural contest did go on to enter prestigious universities without taking the college entrance exams. Also, the alliance between the journal and the Writers Publishing House, a previously state-sponsored institution that was undergoing reforms to increase profits, created a marketing miracle in a sluggish book market. The Writers Publishing House bought the publishing rights to the prizewinning essays from the New Concepts Composition Contest, resulting in a collection that was an immediate commercial success, with more than 600,000 copies sold.[54] In the years following the contest, *Sprout* has continued to innovate and to establish itself as a transmedia brand that includes the *Sprout* book series, magazines, literary contests, websites, and a school. At the end of 2010, *Sprout* was officially transformed from a public institution (*shiye danwei*) into a business enterprise (*qiye danwei*), that is, from a quasi-government agency into a commercial organization.[55]

Within this context, Han Han became China's first teen literary celebrity.

Han Han's case was compelling for the popular media on a variety of levels. He missed the competition finals and was given another chance to compose an essay instantaneously in front of *Sprout*'s editors, who were so impressed with his writing that they wanted to ensure that his work was not ghostwritten. This not only created a sense of mystique surrounding youth literary talent in the popular media but also built up the journal's image of cultivating new talent.[56] Shortly after the competition, Han Han published his first novel, *Sanchong men* (*Triple Door*, 2000), which criticized the dark side of China's rote-learning-oriented education system. Moreover, while Han Han's fellow awardees followed the mainstream path and enrolled in college in 1999, he quit school because of poor academic performance. Han Han then turned down an acceptance offer from Fudan University that allowed him to audit courses at the prestigious school, all while *Triple Door* sat for months at the top of the bestseller list in Beijing and Shanghai. Han Han earned a cult following among students who shared his feelings about the repressive school environment,[57] while his case also stimulated much societal discussion about China's "quality education" (*suzhi jiaoyu*). Mainstream coverage of Han Han's story flourished in the publications of municipal and provincial media organizations. These reports framed Han Han as a talented yet rebellious urban youth. His participation in the newly launched talk show *Duihua* (Dialogue), hosted by CCTV, reinforced this image.

Aired on October 25, 2000, the *Dialogue* episode on Han Han invited a wide variety of individuals—two renowned professors, literature professor Chen Xiaoming from the Chinese Academy of Social Sciences and education professor Chen Yongming from Eastern China Normal University, as well as high school teachers, parents, journal editors, and high school and college students—to discuss the Han Han phenomenon. Ironically, despite the show's title, "Dialogue," the sixty-minute program was filled with tension between Han Han and the hostess, the special guests, and the live audience. The episode only seemed to demonstrate the difficulty of engaging in real conversation in such a public forum. Largely because of CCTV's official responsibility to "guide public opinion," *Dialogue* focused on presenting the "deviant" aspect of Han Han, in an effort to minimize the possible "negative" influence he might exert on his peers. The program spared no effort in refuting Han Han's famous statement that "all-around development means all-around mediocrity" and emphasized the benefits of implementing holistic learning. Apart from a few supporters, most participants questioned the durability of Han Han's writing, challenged his defiance of educational institutions, and treated him as an unruly juvenile who had yet to grow up. The paternalistic, condescending, and authoritative stance that the majority of the show's attendees adopted was most evident in the frequent use of "he" and "Han Han" instead of "you" when conversing with Han Han, who was treated like an absent object. On the few occasions when some sort of exchange did take place, participants sought to impose their personal opinions on Han Han instead of learning about his thoughts. The most intense confrontation took place between Han Han and a thirty-year-old female audience member, who rebuked Han Han for his sense of self-importance:

FEMALE AUDIENCE MEMBER: . . . even Wang Shuo,[58] who has so many years of life experiences . . . seldom publishes nowadays and admits a drain of talent. You are only eighteen. That is to say, you only have ten years of life experience since your childhood; how dare you compare yourself to him?

HAN HAN: I never thought of making such a comparison. On a different note, how do you know I don't have much to write about?

FEMALE AUDIENCE MEMBER: Because you lack real life experience.

HAN HAN: Well, how would you know that my life experiences are not as rich as [Wang Shuo's]?

FEMALE AUDIENCE MEMBER: Because you're not as old as him.

HAN HAN: Oh yeah? May I ask how old you are?

FEMALE AUDIENCE MEMBER: I am 30.

HAN HAN: Really . . . but from what you just said, it seems like your life experience is not even as rich as mine.

FEMALE AUDIENCE MEMBER: Seriously? If you want to pursue this matter further, you should talk to my son. We can also chat online, if possible. You also surf the web, right?

HAN HAN: Yes.

FEMALE AUDIENCE MEMBER: Which software do you mainly use to chat?

HAN HAN: I don't use software.

FEMALE AUDIENCE MEMBER: Then, let me be more specific, do you use OICQ, ICQ, or chat rooms?

HAN HAN: Chat rooms.

FEMALE AUDIENCE MEMBER: Oh . . . Then you have not grown up. In other words, what I want to tell you is: if you really want to grow up, you had better use OICQ and ICQ; that's what adults do.

This exchange exemplifies the conversational style of the *Dialogue* episode. Most speakers were condescending toward Han Han and conformed to hierarchies of age, social status, and seniority. The term "adult society," mentioned frequently throughout the program, was used as a way of rejecting Han Han's right to express his opinion because he was a minor. Han Han's attempts to respond were vain: the hostess often ignored him and gave other attendees opportunities to speak, with one scene even showing that a response by Han Han was edited out. When Han Han did speak up, his ingenious plays on words only irritated attendees, some of whom attributed his case to "excessive rebellion" (*guodu panni*) and "lopsided development" (*jixing fazhan*), and concluded that he was "obviously not a role model to imitate and follow." Compared with the live audience and the hostess, the two professors held moderately positive attitudes, although their pedantic scholarly expression failed to elicit any sympathy for Han Han. The discussion finally reached its climax when Chen Yongming suggested that Han Han learn to "coexist with adult society" and Chen Xiaoming awkwardly blurted out that he would rather communicate with Han Han via written letters.

The *Dialogue* program reflected the futility of the interaction between scholars and Han Han, who refused to conform to social norms. More important, it illustrates the lack of power Han Han held in the realm of traditional media. In a setting in which professors were consecrated as academic authorities, parents and teachers executed their "inborn rights" to lecture, the hostess wielded power over who could speak, and television producers edited out unwanted scenes, Han Han was unable to turn the tables in his favor. Interestingly, if *Dialogue* incidentally raised the issue of the relationship between youth culture and new media—as shown by the female audience member's view on the norms for conducting online chats—then Han Han's subsequent rise as an online opinion leader illuminates how the blogosphere has served as a powerful "battlefield" for him and his supporters to upset the established order.

Following his initial success as a teen writer, Han Han published seven novels and has consistently ranked among China's top ten wealthiest writers. In 2003, he became a professional racecar driver and has won seven national championships, enhancing his star persona as a cool urban idol. In addition to writing and rally racing, Han Han has added many new titles to his repertoire: singer; editor-in-chief for a short-lived literary magazine, *Duchang tuan* (Party, 2010); scriptwriter; director; editor-in-chief for a smartphone application, *Yige* (One); and, most important, influential opinion leader. In blogging about current affairs, Han Han transitioned from an urban youth idol into a public intellectual, with a more prominent cultural status. His social critiques focus mostly on hot-button issues, such as corruption, bureaucracy, censorship, inflation, and popular nationalism. On average, each of Han Han's blog entries registers several million visits and generates more than 10,000 responses from a wide audience that includes journalists, general readers, fans, and intellectuals. Because of the influence of his blog, Han Han has gained global attention, which in turn reinforces his iconic status domestically. The British magazine *New Statesman* ranked Han Han among "The World's 50 Most Influential Figures in 2010."[59] *Time* magazine, which lauded him as "China's modern day Mark Twain, rattling his nation's conscience, and ridiculing its political culture through satire and prose," ranked Han Han number two in the 100 most influential people of 2010.[60]

Because Han Han started out as an alternative youth idol who challenged the norms of Chinese society, particularly its educational systems and paternalistic culture, his transition into a distinctive online opinion leader has created much media hype but has generated little critical investigation. Current scholarship analyzes the "Han Han effect" mostly through the lens of youth culture and commercial literature.[61] Han Han's contentious activities are often approached as isolated events rather than as parts of a process. A case in point is how critics of various political and cultural stances hold polarized views of Han Han. The New Left reads Han Han's blog, at best, as "flirting with the system,"[62] while liberal-leaning domestic media outlets hail him as the leading agent for change in Chinese society.[63] Western mainstream media frame Han Han as an anti-state hero who shares the same cause as Liu Xiaobo and Ai Weiwei, two of China's most renowned dissident intellectuals.[64] However, with few exceptions,[65] we learn little about how and why Han Han's blog evokes a wide range of responses or about the political and cultural ramifications of his blog entries.

To address these problems, I engage here in a close reading of Han Han's blog entries, as well as the dynamic responses that the blog provokes. At a macro level, the relative relaxation of the media environment from 2007 to 2012, the indispensable role Sina played in promoting Han Han's reinvented image as a public intellectual, and the digital labor involving netizens, web editors, and media professionals together have paved the way for Han Han's transition into a public spokesperson. Meanwhile, the peculiar style that Han Han employs to get his message across, to interact with readers, and to get around censorship exemplifies how being mindful of the elasticity of discursive parameters is the key to Han Han's simultaneously entertaining and enlightening cultural contention at a micro level.

Tracking Han Han's Style: Literary Debate

Since the beginning of Han Han's writing career, his literary talent has been exemplified by a keen observation of society and ingenuity with wordplay. Han Han's subject matter has gradually shifted from an iconoclastic attack on the educational system and paternalistic culture to a satirical portrayal of society as a whole. His two most recent novels, *Tade guo* (*His Country*, 2009) and *1988: Wo xiang he zhege shijie tantan* (*1988: I Would Like to Have a Chat with This World*, 2010), depart from the adolescent mood of youth rebellion exhibited in his earlier works. These two novels showcase how an emphasis on economic development has caused multifarious social problems, such as pollution, the real estate bubble, complicity between officials and businessmen, and disillusioned youth. At the same time, Han Han's style has remained consistent in all genres he has written in, including fiction, essays, blog entries, and film. He is particularly talented at employing irony, parody, and homophones to create a comic effect. For instance, in *Triple Door*, Han Han plays with the word *cuo*, which is homophonous with a different character, to mock the aimlessness of an official: "The idling away of time (*cuotuo suiyue*) relies on the word '*cuo*.' During the Cultural Revolution, he was sent down to the countryside and made ropes (*cuo masheng*). Later, he got a position as a town mayor and played mahjong (*cuo majiang*) until he got a hunchback. This truly reflects the essence of '*cuotuo*.'"[66] Han Han is also adept at offering innovative interpretations of common words: "Problems of management often occur at the border of two provinces. But usually the issues that two provinces face (*liangge sheng de shi*) cannot be solved easily (*bu shengshi*)."[67]

Another common strategy employed by Han Han is to juxtapose the expected with the unexpected. Han Han's famous statement that "I failed seven subjects; the red lights illuminate my future path" illustrates this logic. Although the first line evokes readers' empathy for the narrator's poor grades, the second immediately negates this predictable reaction and celebrates the new opportunities opened up by the failure. However, Han Han's strong use of satire and wordplay cannot offset one fundamental flaw of his writing in genres such as fiction and film: the lack of sophistication. Concerning the seven novels that Han Han has published, critics generally agree that their narratives often seem to flow randomly at the author's will and that characters remain undeveloped.[68] By the same token, despite the huge commercial success of the road trip comedy *The Continent* (*Hou hui wu qi*), a film written and directed by Han Han, the movie lacks a coherent structure and substance. Loosely organized around three characters' adventures on a road trip to western China, the fragmented Han-style humor (*Hanshi duanzi*), although hilarious, nevertheless fails to tell a well-structured story. Recently, even Han Han has become less defensive about this criticism and openly admitted: "I am not comfortable with composing a story with intricate plots full of ups and downs, nor do I favor this kind of story."[69]

Interestingly, if Han Han's capacity for structuring sophisticated narratives is limited, then this "drawback" turns out to be a blessing when it comes to blogging, which plays by a different set of rules. Han Han's blog entries reflect the essence of Internet communication, which combines "the need for speed" with "the need for entertainment."[70] The strength of Han-style writing—as exemplified by the fragmented narrative, the abundance of witty lines, and a concern with current affairs that is often expressed in the guise of playfulness and mockery—is maximized on blogs. The mixture of styles—his formal and linguistic play, his bold expression of resistance, and his interactivity—constitutes the appeal of Han Han as an online personality and of his blog entries. In this sense, Han Han's blog provides an alternative way for Internet users to consume public affairs.

The significant role that style plays in Han Han's blog entries was first identified in an influential online debate from 2006, called "the Han-Bai controversy" (*Han Bai zhi zheng*), between Han Han and Bai Ye (b. 1952), a well-established literary critic. The births of both figures' blogs were part of the large-scale campaign that Sina launched in 2005 to promote celebrity blogging. As a popular cultural icon, Han Han immediately captured much attention with his blog, where his readers have competed with one another to leave follow-up comments and to interact with their idol in this seemingly intimate space. In contrast, Bai Ye was less well known outside literary circles. The two figures' debate on "pure literature" in relation to the "post-80s" writers elicited multiple parties to join the fray, which lasted more than one month online, finally extending into traditional media outlets and causing quite a stir both within and outside literary circles. Given that this dispute was ideologically nonthreatening, Sina capitalized on the Han-Bai controversy as a golden opportunity to promote its newly launched blogging service. Editors at Sina spared no effort in following the debate and summarizing the key arguments and relationships among those involved. All major commercial portals immediately followed suit, compiling their own special issues and contributing to the Han-Bai controversy that spilled over into conventional media.

The Han-Bai controversy started with Han Han's response to an article that Bai Ye had cross-posted to his newly activated blog in 2006. In this article, titled "The Status Quo and Future of 'Post-80s' Writers," Bai Ye cautions about the tendency of post-80s writers, such as Han Han, to strive for market success.[71] For Bai, these writers "have entered the market and yet have not stepped into the literary circle," because few of them publish in literary magazines; therefore, their works are "amateur writings (*piaoyou xiezuo*) at best."[72] Irritated by Bai Ye's authoritative tone of voice and consecration of the literary circle, Han Han satirically attacked Bai's literary parochialism in an updated post entitled "The literary world is nonsense, no one should be a pretentious prick."[73] Han Han states that his writing fully qualifies as "pure literature" because he never tries to flatter authorities, nor does he curry favor with the market because his books sell anyway. Han Han also plays on the Chinese words *tan* (forum) and *quan* (circle), claiming that "in the end, all forums (*tan*) will become altars (*jitan*); all circles (*quan*) will become funeral wreaths (*huaquan*)." This line was immediately circulated among netizens who indulge in playfully mocking authorities.

For better or worse, Han Han's naming of Bai Ye greatly increased the popularity of Bai's blog, as Han's devoted fans soon flooded Bai's blog space and left angry messages. In reply, Bai Ye targeted the frequent use of obscenities by Han Han and his fans, accused the younger generation of "humiliation" and "personal attacks," and linked the debate on pure literature to such broader issues as Internet legislation, moral education, and online ethics.[74] Bai's presentation of himself as a victim of verbal abuse won sympathy from some renowned figures, who declared a "blog war" on Han Han: literary critic Xie Xizhang; writer Lu Tianming; Lu Tianming's son, film director Lu Chuan; and music producer Gao Xiaosong. Some of their key charges against Han Han are as follows:

> Han Han hates my article mainly because I do not think highly of his works . . . nobody has the right to swear at others . . . Han Han and his followers have to accept the moral law of self-examination and public trial. I hope this incident demonstrates the necessity of strengthening Internet legislation and Internet ethics. (Bai 2006)
>
> If I were Han Han's parents, I would definitely give him a big slap in the face. Someone's got to teach him a lesson. (Xie 2006)
>
> Han Han is too spoiled. Otherwise he would tolerate others' criticism, and would not take pride in swearing publicly. . . . It's not surprising though, since Han Han is just a teenager and is not well educated . . . simply nobody wants to point out to him what good literature is. (Lu Tianming 2006)

These quotations show that Bai Ye's camp relies heavily on seniority and hierarchy in social status to condemn Han Han. All criticisms target the vulgarities that Han Han uses and attribute Han's attitude to his lack of higher education and proper parenting, as well as his failure to achieve recognition from literary authorities. Thus, the older generation's main problem with Han Han is his unruly attitude, while the literary merit of Han's work becomes a secondary issue. This paternalistic tone of voice sounded self-righteous yet turned out to be counterproductive online. Han Han's supporters, including writer Han Dong, critic Wu Liang, publisher Lu Jinbo, and a famous blogger, He Caitou, joined the blog war and accused the older generation of monopolizing cultural resources. Meanwhile, with many more netizens rushing to the blogs of Bai Ye's camp and leaving abusive messages, Bai and his allies were shocked to witness how the norms they expected in social life were overturned in the blogosphere. After weeks of bickering between the two sides, Bai Ye and his supporters—including Lu Chuan, Lu Tianming, and Gao Xiaosong—all closed their blogs, following Gao's closing remarks that the blogosphere was "dirty," "foolish," and "uncivilized." The debate officially concluded with Han Han's blog post "Finally I Marry My First Love: I Beg You, Sue Me Please," published on March 29, 2006.[75] The withdrawal of Bai's camp from the blogosphere symbolized the victory of Han Han's camp on the Internet. Subsequently, Bai Ye and his supporters fell back on traditional media outlets and continued to denounce Han Han.

Because the trigger point of the Han-Bai controversy was pure literature, the virtual fight has been investigated as a power struggle between what Pierre Bourdieu calls "the heretical challenge of new modes of cultural practice" and "the orthodoxy of established traditions" in the literary field.[76] However, for Marco Fumian, both figures' stances actually contradict their practices, as Bai Ye actively promotes popular literature and Han Han has found success in large part due to long established literary institutions.[77] Therefore, despite their contention, there exists a mutualistic symbiosis between the two.[78] In line with this finding, my discussion focuses on how the Han-Bai controversy quickly evolved into a cultural phenomenon and what role the blogosphere played during the process.

One of the major distinctions between traditional literary debates and the Han-Bai controversy is that the former primarily take place in print media, which require a turnaround time that delays the immediate exchange of opinions. Also, in print media, ordinary readers remain largely invisible in the public space, as reader responses are selectively published. By contrast, the dispute between Han Han and Bai Ye took place on a platform accessible to every Internet user. The fact that renowned figures and ordinary netizens had equal rights to publish opinions contributed to the changing nature of this debate. Bai Ye and his supporters, mostly in their fifties and sixties and lacking much experience with the Internet, assumed there to be an automatic conversion of social prestige into the online space. When their authority was questioned on message boards, they did not change their gestures, wording, or tone. The pedantic style that Bai and his supporters employed in blogging was eclipsed by Han Han's inflammatory, colloquial, and humorous responses. Indeed, Han Han's very first charge against Bai Ye concerned his writing style:

> I read the literary critic Bai Ye's work (this guy's article is extremely lengthy and makes me dizzy). After reading a large section of repetitive words, I realized that was only part two. . . . What was even more shocking was that toward the end, when I read the title, I found out the author only intended to offer a simple analysis.[79]

Well aware of how Internet users enjoy reading punch lines, Han Han selected examples that were most favorable to him and made arguments in a catchy manner. He made a fuss about how Bai Ye miswrote the name of his book and questioned Bai's credentials as a literary critic. Lu Tianming's comment that "Han Han is just a teenager" incurred Han's bitter recrimination that Lu fabricated his resume: "Uncle Lu, I am twenty-four now, and I have been out of school for seven years." Both charges inflamed Han Han's fans, who immediately mobilized to defend their idol in his opponents' space. In addition to their playful linguistic style, Han Han's rejoinders emphasized formal and visual elements of style. Because of the involvement of many parties and their various views, Han Han highlighted the statements of his opponents by bolding, underlining, or coloring them. The employment of these formal and visual techniques, thereby, brought Han Han's central statement to the fore.

The significance of the Han-Bai controversy lies not merely in how it exemplifies the animosity between young writers and well-established critics, a common quarrel in literary circles; rather, it illustrates how, for the first time, elements of style are essential for the tech-savvy generation to challenge the literary and cultural establishment in a highly performative space. Bai's moral charge against Han Han sounded pedantic and went against the playful mood that dominates the Chinese Internet, thereby lessening its power to persuade young netizens. As a result, the serious stance that Bai and his camp took was immediately undermined by the banter of Han Han and the quasi-flash-mob performance of his fans. Thus, Bai Ye and his supporters seemed to be fighting a battle they were destined to lose. By contrast, the tech-savvy generation employed a different set of rhetorical, formal, and mobilization styles and stressed the importance of satire and playfulness in their rebellion against cultural authorities. Han Han's particular style of blogging, the nature of the Internet audience, and the implementation of different rules of the game in the technology-mediated online sphere were essential to the "fiasco" of Bai Ye's attack and the younger generation's "virtual" triumph. The Han-Bai controversy heralded Han Han's adoption of a distinctive contentious style that fostered his transition from one of the post-80s writers into a unique opinion leader.

Serious Play, Playful Seriousness: Blogging about Style

Since the Han-Bai controversy, Han Han has broadened the scope of his blog by engaging in sharp criticism of current affairs. Despite occasionally encountering censorship issues, Han Han is one of the few public figures who has vehemently denounced the authorities and yet remains popular. His rise as a social commentator and the uproar that it provoked exposed a lacuna in the contemporary cultural market. Compared with the flourishing of blog content in other professions, particularly in the entertainment sectors, the productivity of professional writers in the blogosphere is rather low. Most writers remain conservative about posting new articles on blogs for a variety of reasons, such as copyright infringement, the prestige they attribute to traditional publishing conduits, and the perceived difficulty in engaging with readers. Writers in their fifties and sixties, such as Chi Li, Xu Kun, Lu Tianming, and Chen Ran, expressed anxiety about interacting with readers online.[80] Some shut down their blogs shortly after starting them. Han Han's fellow post-80s writers, such as Guo Jingming, Zhang Yueran, and Jiang Fangzhou, have embraced the blog as an effective publicity medium, but their blogs contain mostly work-related announcements and content already published elsewhere. As for the Internet writers who rose to fame by amassing recognition on literature websites, represented by Anni Baobei and Tong Hua, they have turned to print media and publish original content less and less frequently online. Therefore, the relative scarcity of original content on writers' blogs offered a space for Han Han to stand out from his fellow writer-bloggers. Also, that Han Han's writings are first published online increases the exclusive value of both his personal blog and Sina, to such an extent that the commercial portal has enthusiastically promoted most of his essays.

Han Han's rise as a "stinky public intellectual" (*chou gongzhi*)—as he called himself in a blog post—differs from other intellectuals, activists, and dissidents who have been actively making use of digital media to promote political and cultural agendas. None of these intellectual websites and blogs attract the same degree of attention that Han Han's does. Despite the varying degree of user engagement, ranging from reading to posting reflective responses to circulating the blog content, these numbers matter in a digital economy that is founded on holding users' attention.[81] The traffic volume that Han Han's blog generates thus bears the potential for both commercial and political influence in society. Han Han's social critiques are based mostly on mainstream media coverage of issues that have already caught the public's attention, such as corruption, bureaucracy, censorship, inflation, and popular nationalism. His analyses of social controversies demonstrate a genuine concern for disadvantaged groups, a yearning for cultural tolerance, and an admirable individuality that does not blindly cater to public sentiment or to authority. Moreover, Han Han's blog entries are concise, incisive, and humorous, providing an alternative interpretation of current events that both entertains and resonates with his audience. Because of the lack of institutionalized channels in China for public comment on current affairs, Han Han's topical blog posts take on more cultural and political significance than they might in the context of a nonauthoritarian regime.

I investigate two examples of blog posts to illustrate the basic pattern that Han Han employs when commenting on public affairs, as well as his shrewd awareness of the conversational parameters. Drawing connections between individual events (e.g., cases of corruption and school attacks) and important national events or discourses (e.g., political conferences, the Shanghai Expo, and state propaganda), Han Han contrasts the powerless (victims) with the powerful (officials and the state). This dichotomy enables Han Han, who sides with the powerless, to channel public frustrations into accusations against a monolithic state power for all issues under discussion. Moreover, Han Han draws a clear distinction between criticizing the Chinese government and criticizing the Chinese Communist Party.[82] Well aware of the risks involved in attacking the Party and the central government, Han Han targets mostly local governments and local officials. In this way, he contributes to the popular myth that those in the top leadership are righteous officials. Han Han's mockery of the Guangxi Tobacco Bureau and criticism of the Taizhou government in Jiangsu, which are discussed in detail below, are cases in point. Further, walking a fine line between what can and cannot be articulated, Han Han's performative style of blogging, his way of engaging the audience, and his playing with censorship rules epitomize a new mode of navigating current affairs. The fact that Han Han can reach out to a mainstream audience and contest the limits of discursive boundaries that are demarcated by official and mainstream forces bespeaks the significance of his cultural contention, which should not be downplayed simply because he does not take an oppositional stance. On the contrary, Han Han's particular style of blogging has contributed to the rise of digital contention in China that does not aim at radically breaking from current social or political systems but seeks to foster microruptures from within hegemonic formations.

Sex Diary, Corruption, and Social Satire:
A Signature Style

The first case demonstrates how Han Han contributed to reshaping public opinion on a sensational Internet incident regarding official corruption and debauchery in China. On November 23, 2009, the diary of a senior government official was leaked on Tianya. The diary consisted of more than 500 entries, which recorded bribes that the official had received, personal hobbies, work-related matters, and—most titillating for readers—his sexual exploits with many mistresses from January 1, 2007, to June 10, 2008. The interweaving of personal sexual activities and the work duties of a Communist Party official made the diary one of the most popular items online at the time. The following entry is typical of the description of the official's daily life:

> I prepared for the "politeness and courtesy" lecture in the morning. At noon, I accompanied Li Dehui, who came from Xiamen, to have lunch and some wine. I stayed in the dormitory in the afternoon. At night, I had dinner with Huang Huiting and others, and I drank quite a lot of wine. Huang and his people are going to Chongqing and Chengdu tomorrow. I will send Su and Tan Shanfang to see them off. At 10ish, Tan Shanfang drove me over to her house. We made love three times. We had one more session early in the morning. I did not ejaculate.[83]

Another entry from December 29, 2007, states:

> 2007 has been a good year. Work is going smoothly. Income is as high as 200,000 yuan [USD 30,000]. Womanizing is on the right track. It's been a lucky year with women. I need to pay attention to my health, with so many sex partners.[84]

The truthful recording of officialdom and the sharing of the mistresses' names stimulated netizens to engage in collective intelligence gathering. They quickly identified the diary's author as Han Feng, director of the sales division at the Guangxi Tobacco Monopoly Bureau. In response, Han Feng claimed that his diary had been altered, rumors spread that his rival had hired hackers to break into his computer, and others conjectured that the distressed husband of one of Han Feng's alleged mistresses had posted the diary online.[85] Soon after Han Feng's exposure, the case was investigated by the local government, followed by the removal of Han Feng from his position and the passing of a sentence, on March 13, 2010, of up to ten years in prison on charges of bribery.

Amid the frenzy that Han Feng's dairy caused in online communities, and shortly before the verdict was released, Han Han offered a different perspective: he listed nine reasons to illustrate that Han Feng had in fact been a good cadre member. Calling the diary a "most valuable piece of social literature," Han Han commented that Han Feng did not abuse his power that much:

> His diary reveals the life of the thriftiest womanizing official in the country. Other officials give their mistresses houses and cars, but his most expensive gifts are mobile phones and MP4 players. By those standards, he is a pretty decent official, and it shows that his women are pretty good too. If we had more men and women like these, imagine how many times the Treasury could save the equivalent of an aircraft carrier. . . .
>
> Even though he had quite a lot of women, he also went out walking with his wife twenty-five times, bought her a mobile phone, and didn't use his position to help relatives gain advantages through back-door deals. . . .
>
> In his diary, there are no hints of a taste for luxury cars, super-expensive real estate, or collections of famous and ultra-valuable literature. He doesn't even think about these things. . . . How great, a Party official who appreciates the simple pleasures of life. . . .
>
> With regard to work, we don't see any evidence of him doing any actual work. But the so-called cadres and cadres, as long as they have sexual relationships with their subordinates, then they have put into practice what this word indicates.[86]

Han Han concludes the essay by suggesting that Han Feng should retain his position because he is easily satisfied, whereas many officials of Han Feng's rank behave much worse. In the end, Han Han created a ballot and invited readers to vote on whether they thought Han Feng should retain his current post. Among 349,709 participants, 96 percent of voters sided with Han Han. He analyzed the ballot result in a follow-up essay:

> Of course, from now on I will set up the voting function more often, in order to compensate for everyone's dismay that no one has seen a ballot but somehow so many representatives in the National People's Congress have

been elected. . . . The result of the vote on Han Feng tells us that we have officially entered the era in which there are almost no cadre who are not corrupt, and the only difference is between good corrupt cadre and bad corrupt cadre. Everyone obviously thinks that Han Feng belongs to the good
corrupt cadre category. . . .

The expectation of cadre by ordinary people in this country is not that
they will serve the people, but that they don't make trouble for people. You
can have your fabulous house, drive your luxurious car, have your mistress;
we will not bother you as long as you do not step over my son, evict me from
my house, or take my girl—then you are a good cadre in the eyes of ordinary
people. If netizens have a problem with this, just delete their posts. If writers
have a problem with it, just harmonize them. If journalists have a problem
with this, just a one-sentence instruction—"do not report negative news."[87]

These two entries about Han Feng's diary exemplify the signature style
of Han Han's social critique. Both entries were published around the time
of the 2010 annual meeting of the National People's Congress (NPC) and
the Chinese People's Political Consultative Conference (CPPCC), thereby
attracting much media attention. The ballot and the follow-up analysis did
not mean to solicit netizens' opinions on the Han Feng incident; instead, the
entries playfully drew parallels between the online poll and the absence of
democracy in Chinese political life. Shortly after Han Han published these
two essays, an unprecedented "backlash of sympathy for the allegedly corrupt
official" occurred on discussion forums online.[88]

This instance illustrates how Han Han capitalizes on his influence as
a cultural icon and directs readers' attention to public affairs. While Han
Han endorses public sentiment against corruption, the style he employs to
convey ideas functions as both a form of "expressing nonconformity" and
a "strategy for entering and leaving the mainstream cultures," to borrow
Annette Wong's words.[89] Han Han's mockery and perspective demonstrate
an individuality that distinguishes him from the digital crowd. However, at
times he also sides with the crowd by setting a clear-cut boundary between
"you" and "we." He uses "you" to address corrupt officials, while categorizing
himself as a member of "we," the ordinary people. This binary construction

of "us" versus "them" enables Han Han to side with "the people," an essential component of Party discourse, and "tell the truth through the safest channel."[90] Moreover, Han Han's stylization of language accords with the performativity of Internet writing that "encourages one-liners, catchphrases and incisiveness, as well as quotability."[91] Han Han's reinterpretation of "cadre" (*ganbu*), a term embedded in Communist discourse, as "having sexual relations with one's subordinates" (*ganle ziji de buxia*) innovatively ridicules the status quo of officialdom. Such witty lines immediately resonate with readers, who widely circulate them online. Thus, while reflecting his perceptive observations, cynical ridicule of officialdom, and strategic analysis, Han Han's style of engaging social commentary is fun to read and easy to understand, making it more approachable for readers than lengthy scholarly discussions of current affairs.

Tragedy, Wordplay, and Resulting Censure

The second example focuses on a spate of school attacks that took place in five Chinese provinces from March to May 2010: the attackers considered themselves mistreated by society and retaliated by murdering innocent children. Published shortly after the attack by a knife-wielding man at a kindergarten in Taizhou, Jiangsu province, Han Han's essay "Children, You're Spoiling Grandpas' Fun" lambasted the local government's control of the media and the fishy official claim of "no injuries" in the aftermath of the tragedy. He also commented on the hypocrisy of official discourse that promoted the "Song of Harmony" at the Shanghai Expo, which was being hosted not far from Taizhou. The text reads, in part, as follows:

> In a society that has no release valve, killing the weakest members of society has become the only release. I would advise deploying the security that is currently protecting all the local governments in the country to protect our nursery schools. A government that can't even keep children safe doesn't need so many people to protect it. . . .
>
> In the Taizhou kindergarten murder case, the news media has been controlled. These children's births were untimely, and their deaths are even more untimely. To those officials in the relevant departments, this incident

comes as unpleasant noise interrupting the festive atmosphere [of the opening of the Shanghai Expo].

. . . When we search for Taizhou online, all that comes up is "The Three Recent Lucky Events in Taizhou," dated April 30.

. . . I just want to tell everybody, right here, that when the story of a person breaking into a kindergarten to slash thirty-two children can't become news, you have all been slashed as well. Not even one paper can report on this because a few hundred kilometers away, a grand meeting is being held, and hundreds of millions of fireworks will be released, while at the same time, in your old hometown of Taizhou, they want to hold the International Tourism Festival, the trade fair, and the OCT opening ceremony—those "three blessed events."

Maybe, in the eyes of all those old farts, you are killjoys, intent on spoiling the big party.

But among all of us poor children, it is you who are poisoned by contaminated milk, it is you who are injured by bad vaccines, it is you who are killed in the earthquakes, it is you who are burned to death. When the adults' rules make problems, it is you against whom those affected will pick up a knife to avenge themselves.

I wish that you had indeed been injured with no deaths, as the Taizhou government says. The elderly are neglecting their duties; I wish that after you grow up, you will not only want to shelter your own children, you will want society to shelter everyone else's children as well.[92]

This post resonated with public sentiment about recent social scandals related to child victims. Largely because of the sensitive timing of the Shanghai Expo, editors at Sina deleted this entry several hours after it was published. To protest, Han Han posted another entry titled "." The main body contained only one line: "Grandpas, Please Enjoy Yourselves."[93] As of October 13, 2013, this one-line blog entry had generated 1,193,485 visits and 24,475 discussion threads.

Han Han's entry and its repercussions in netizen communities demonstrate a high degree of performativity. Although Han Han did not mention a single word about being "harmonized" (*hexie*), a euphemism for censorship, his use of a dot as the post's title stimulated readers' curiosity, and they quickly found out what had happened. Han Han had earlier informed his fans that if he did not feel like blogging on a given day, he would use punctuation marks so that fans would not be kept waiting for updates. Also, Han Han's change in his blog's background song to "Red Weeping Eyes" immediately caught the attention of devoted fans. Originally a love song, the lyrics read: "I thought you were gone; my eyes got red. I thought I cried; my eyes got red. . . . I thought the world was dirty; my eyes got red. I thought the sky turned black; my eyes got red." In this way, Han Han's post caused an uproar in the online community by conglomerating seemingly informal and disparate elements of writing, such as the allusion to reality via a popular song, and the use of a punctuation mark and a one-liner.

Han Han's essay also strayed from his signature playful mockery, a change that readers understood: "This is so not like you [Han Han]. But to tell the truth, there is no way to tease under such circumstances." "My eyes got red while listening to 'Red Weeping Eyes.' [Reality] cannot be more ruthless." Meanwhile, netizens sarcastically reperformed the binary rhetoric Han Han established in this entry: "you" (innocent children) versus "they" (powerful "grandpas").[94] The use of "grandpas" as a metaphor for officials satirized the state's incapacity to protect its own children and the hypocrisy of official ideology. Internet users appropriated the words "grandpas" and "enjoy yourselves" in imagined situations to comment on this incident. Examples include: "Grandmas, watch out for grandpas and do not allow them to overly enjoy themselves"; "Grandpas, let's wait and see how you can enjoy yourselves"; "Let grandpas enjoy themselves. We have shared the essay on Renren [a social networking site]"; "Grandpas are reacting faster and faster."[95] The collective recreation of the terms "grandpas" and "enjoy yourselves" epitomizes the public's reaction to social injustice and media control. In the process, Han Han was hailed as the spokesperson for a public that was frustrated with the censors and that voiced sympathy for disadvantaged groups.

In addition, netizens' responses to the Taizhou tragedy and the removal of Han Han's blog post on the message board involved a high degree of performativity. When Han Han's essay disappeared, Internet users instantly mobilized to search for the post on other sites and then cross-post it on discussion forums and in personal web spaces. The original essay was divided into smaller parts and posted on the message board of Han Han's blog. Many users also volunteered links to forums and blogs that had posted the essay. Netizens proposed that all readers subscribe to an RSS feed or Google Reader and disseminate Han Han's articles as soon as they became available. This collaborative action of publicizing censored text symbolically defended social justice and protested against authority. As a result, the dissemination power of the Internet and the collective agency of Internet users led to the proliferation of Han Han's essay. Some users first read the article elsewhere and then logged in to the message board to support Han Han. Meanwhile, the censors—in particular, the editors of Sina—became the direct target of attack. Readers sarcastically praised the efficiency of web editors at removing sensitive posts and imagined editors' reactions to Han Han's essays: "Maybe they [editors] agreed with what you [Han Han] said but had to delete it to earn their living. Such struggles must have been painful."[96] Some Internet users pointed out the complicity between commercial forces and the state: "They [Sina] are, after all, businessmen. If they offend someone [in a high position], they lose business. Billions of dollars would be gone. So investors of Sina would rather offend us: powerless civilians."[97] These readers' reflections on how editors at Sina mediate the relationship between Internet users and the state illustrate the role that commercial media play in both censoring and propagating writing about controversial issues.

The Rules of the Censorship Game

The two essays written by Han Han also demonstrate how commercial media and individual actors capitalized on the rules of the censorship game to promote Han Han's rise as a spokesperson. The rules of the censorship game require the removal of content deemed sensitive or subversive by Sina's editors and administrators, who enforce strict self-censorship to avoid hot-button issues. But more important, these rules foreground the dialectic logic of deletion and recommendation and illuminate how, under specific circumstances, the removal of online content functions similarly to the recommendation mechanisms web editors employ to attract user attention. On these occasions, multiple actors, including commercial websites, Internet users, and individual agents, jointly promote the censored content. Because the state gives greater leeway to large commercial websites, Sina takes advantage of this unspoken rule to promote articles that are contentious and intriguing to its audience. Web editors sometimes even recommend controversial blog entries on the home page of Sina and then remove the content several hours later. This short span of time allows Internet users to circulate the content elsewhere. Moreover, as the case of the Taizhou school attack demonstrated, deletion serves as "an awesome advertisement"[98] and ironically contributes to the wide reception for these Internet essays. As for contentious online content that remains in line with dominant ideologies, web editors spare no effort in implementing publicity campaigns to promote such content. Many of Han Han's posts have been recommended to either the home page of Sina or the home page of its blog channel. Han Han's post on Han Feng's sex diary, for instance, was recommended on the front page of Sina's blog channel because the post accorded well with the government anticorruption campaign. In either case, post deletion and recommendation boosted web traffic as well as Han Han's popularity. In this way, Sina calculates the rules of a "game" in which the mechanisms of censorship and recommendation are activated at the same time.

Furthermore, while the degree to which Han Han is censored is minimal, he presents himself as both a victim and a beneficiary of censorship. Between 2006 and 2013, Sina removed twenty-two of his Internet essays, and all were widely available elsewhere. However, Han Han strategically participates in the game by retaining traces of censorship in his blog and constantly reminding his readers about censored texts. For essays that are removed, Han Han reposts the title with the main body consisting only of a dot, as in the case of "American Drama in Chongqing" (*Chongqing mei ju*) and "Huang Yibo is a good cadre member" (*Huang Yibo shi ge hao ganbu*). Editors still recommended both entries—with their main bodies missing—on Sina's front page. Thus were many readers lured into looking for full text of the essay. In response to another deleted article, Han Han stated: "I cannot do anything about this. You get it if you are fast. You lose it if you are slow (*shou kuai you, shou man wu*)."[99] Han's insinuation about post deletions factors into publicizing such entries. He also occasionally removes his own essays, a tactic that usually stimulates public sentiment against the censors.

The rules of the censorship game involve a common strategy that commercial portals and individual bloggers adopt to attract user attention under an authoritarian regime. Internet users participate in this game not only to lend moral support to their idol but also to playfully make conjectures about which essays will be removed to test their judgment on where the discursive boundaries are drawn. The interaction of these agents enhances Han Han's cultural cachet. Meanwhile, Han Han exploits his popularity to broaden the parameters of artistic expression. From 2010 to 2012, for example, Han Han increased his direct appeals for the loosening of censorship control. He called for individuals to create a larger discursive space (relatively) autonomous from ideological intervention. Han Han commented on issues such as the governmental ban on "obscene" text messages, self-censorship, propaganda films, copyright infringement, and artistic freedom in an explicit manner. At the end of 2011, Han Han published, as a series, three entries entitled "On Revolution" (*Tan geming*),[100] "On Democracy" (*Shuo minzhu*),[101] and "Wanting Freedom" (*Yao ziyou*),[102] in which he advocated for greater artistic freedom and presented a pragmatic view of democracy and revolution in China. Han's proposition that the government and those in artistic circles reconcile so that both could benefit triggered immediate heated debate in media outlets. Some intellectuals read this three-part series as a sign of Han Han's transition to a mature social commentator, but others read it as reflecting Han Han's abandonment of resistance against the dominance of state power. Despite the diverging interpretations of these texts, it is worth reiterating how Han Han's relative independence from both official and commercial establishments allows him greater autonomy to engage in social critique. As a beneficiary of China's economic reforms, Han Han relies on royalties and rally car racing as his primary sources of income. Financial success and an image of individuality have contributed to Han Han's appeal to contemporary Chinese youths, who tend to evaluate individual success on the basis of material gain.[103] However, Han Han redirects the public's attention from his fame, lifestyle, and youthful rebellion to broader social issues. Han Han's iconic status, which is derived from a combination of fan power, mobilization tactics, Sina's promotional strategies, and his particular style of blogging, allows him to navigate the boundaries for discussing controversial issues.

Conclusion

Using the examples of Mu Zimei and Han Han, this chapter examines how free expression has been significantly redefined via digital media. The heated discussion that Mu Zimei's blog triggered regarding the issues of women's sexual expression and gender norms reflects the collaboration and contestation of varying agents, including new and old media, state-affiliated organizations and commercial media, moral defenders and sexual libertines. Through the clash of these different views, Mu Zimei's sex blog constitutes a productive site fostering cultural diversity. As for Han Han, his return to a cultural public sphere via blogging evidences both his personal inclinations and a strategic move to carve out another niche in the market for himself. Although Mu Zimei and Han Han are perceived differently in Chinese society, denoting the gender biases revolving around their roles in public domains, both have implemented Fang Xingdong's rhetoric of promoting free speech via blogging. These two instances demonstrate the pivotal role the Internet plays in connecting conventional media outlets to discussion of controversial topics. Not only may the same issue be addressed differently via specific media, but the interplay of diverse actors also facilitates the constant redefinition of permissible individual expression.

Since 2012 and the new regime under Xi Jinping, the state has employed increasingly coercive measures and legislation to curb individual expression.[104] Amid this stifling political climate, anonymous Internet users began to side with the state and vehemently defame public intellectuals. Previously, the heavy promotion of liberal-leaning media outlets in China contributed to readers' positive responses to public intellectuals' posts, increasing readers' critical agency and concern for current affairs. But around 2011, it suddenly became trendy to defame or satirize public intellectuals on discussion forums; they were stigmatized as self-centered, opportunistic, inconsistent, and lacking common sense.[105] A heated debate in 2012 between Han Han and Fang Zhouzi, a scientist who is better known for disclosing academic fraud in China, is emblematic of this changed cultural atmosphere. Although Fang Zhouzi's charge against the credibility of Han Han's writing ended up going nowhere, Han Han's defensive strategies backfired this time.[106] Despite Han Han's witty responses and the ample evidence he provided, a large number of

Internet users and Fang Zhouzi's supporters obsessed over the logical flaws and inconsistencies that appeared in some of Han's writings. Consequently, the "Fang-Han Debate" officially marked the end of Han Han's acclaimed image as a public intellectual. Meanwhile, he has ventured into the entertainment industry with his directorial debut, *The Continent* (2014), followed by another two movies, *Duckweed* (*Chengfeng polang*, 2017) and *Pegasus* (*Feichi rensheng*, 2019). Han Han's entry into and his exit from the Chinese blogosphere constituted yet another reinvention, a new self-positioning strategy in response to the drastically changing sociopolitical conditions.

In contrast to Han Han's career path, Mu Zimei has never been recognized as a public intellectual, despite the fact that her writings have played a similar function. In contrast to the nationwide condemnation she experienced around 2003 to 2006, Mu Zimei enjoys a greater degree of popularity today thanks to her Weibo account (active until June 17, 2019) and quality writing. Nevertheless, her quotidian accounts of potentially immoral and disagreeable behavior deconstruct the intellectuality inherent in her writing. Meanwhile, the fact that none of these newer writings and disputes have stimulated the same degree of public sensation, state reaction, and nationwide controversy as occurred ten years prior illustrates the opening up of society, as well as the increased proliferation of entertainment-related attractions.

The gradual exit of Mu Zimei and Han Han from the blogosphere showcases the decline in influence of blogging since around 2013, when many celebrities who joined the blogging bandwagon early on seemed to have lost interest in blogging. Although blogging as a new medium might have lost favor over time, the style of writing on blogs, as a strategy of contention, may nevertheless transfer to newer digital platforms, such as microblogs, WeChat, and other emerging mobile applications. This finding becomes apparent through the evidence presented in the next two chapters.

6 DIGITAL WITNESSING ON WEIBO

AS 2017 NEARED AN END, Liu Zhenyun (b. 1958), a prominent writer in China, incorporated "eating melon" (*chigua*) in the title of his newly released fiction *Look for My Sister-in-Law* (*Chigua shidai de ernü-men*). Liu uses the metaphor, "eating melon" to characterize the reinvigoration of collective spectating in the contemporary era. Liu's fiction refers to the important prototype of "apathetic spectators" (*kanke*) that appear many times in writings of Lu Xun (b. 1881), the godfather of modern Chinese literature. In Lu Xun's renowned works, represented by "Preface to *Call for Arms*" (*Nahan zixu*), "Medicine" (*Yao*), and "The New Year's Sacrifice" (*Zhufu*), there often exist groups of spectators who are extremely indifferent to the sufferings of themselves, others, and their country. Lu Xun attributed the deep-rooted problems of Chinese culture and China's downfall to these apathetic spectators. In what follows, social and literary critics frequently reference these indifferent spectators to condemn the inferiority of the Chinese national character, especially when social scandals occur. As the word "spectator" often refers to those who either ignore or take pleasure in others' suffering, it carries a negative implication in the Chinese context. A century later, however, digital media have invigorated the culture of spectators and the act of spectating, and endowed them with new connotations.

Originating from BBS forums in the early 2000s, the term *"weiguan"* (to crowd around) shares some similarities with the traits of the spectators that Lu Xun described. In a lighthearted manner, netizens use *weiguan* to express their neutral stance on occasion of disputes among BBS users, ranging from entertainment-related gossip to fan wars and trivial matters like personal taste to current affairs. Internet users employ other Internet-based slang terms and emoticons to express similar opinions, such as *"chigua"* (to eat melon), *"luguo"* (to pass by), and *"piaoguo"* (to float by). Moreover, the online culture of *weiguan* has roots in the operational mechanisms of BBS forums, thereby departing from the act of spectating. To encourage user participation, most BBS forums award Internet users with virtual points based on the number of posts they publish. Those who accumulate high numbers of points are endowed with symbolic prestige unavailable to ordinary users. To gain more points, many BBS users post such replies as "to pass by" and "to float by" to indicate they are not really interested in the topics under discussion. Nevertheless, although *weiguan* conveys the message that ongoing events are "none of my business," the attention rule on the Internet enables the act of *weiguan* to demonstrate a minimal level of public participation. Due to the proliferation of online attractions, the fact that netizens take efforts to "surround and watch" certain events instead of others showcases their invested interests and agency. Given the feasibility and relatively low risk of online participation, which requires only a few clicks of the mouse or keystrokes, *weiguan* may easily go viral and bear the potential of exerting pressure on authorities. Therefore, the connotations of *weiguan* have some subtle twists in the contemporary context. Despite the playfulness online *weiguan* conveys, it offers a relatively safe channel for Internet users to project collective attention onto contentious issues. Seen in this light, the apathetic spectators Lu Xun criticized have demonstrated their potential to transform into active onlookers. This revived culture of *weiguan* has played a significant role in revealing public opinions and enacting profound changes in contemporary society.

The popularity of microblogging, primarily promoted by the portal websites Sina, Tencent, Sohu, and NetEase, advances this trend. A special feature that Sina offers, "to pay attention" (*guanzhu*), allows users to click on the button to follow certain users, issues, and institutional accounts. This feature is subsequently adapted by a diverse range of social media platforms, including live broadcasting sites; Zhihu, a Q&A-based website; and public accounts of WeChat. More important, the technological features of microblogging, particularly its networking capacity, make it one of the most phenomenal platforms for web-based incidents. In 2010, the term *weiguan* formally reentered the public realm, only one year after Sina launched its microblogging service. In the article titled "To pay attention is power, onlookers change China," the liberal-leaning newspaper *Southern Weekend* acknowledged the positive role that online *weiguan* played in a wide range of civic engagement activities.[1] As a "networked collective action,"[2] *weiguan* largely factored into the central role Weibo assumed in contentious activities from 2010 to 2013.[3]

Taking digital witnessing (*weiguan*) as my entry point, this chapter spells out the functions of microblogging platform in China. Delving into representative Weibo-based incidents from 2009 to 2018, I examine the role that digital witnessing plays in promoting citizen activism and shaping public culture on the Chinese microblogosphere. These cases exemplify the evolving transition of digital witnessing on Weibo, from an emphasis on responsibilities of spectators to multifarious forms of collective spectating mobilized by a diverse range of social actors. I analyze the role of digital witnessing in three aspects: (1) the flourishing of citizen journalism through eyewitnesses' sharing of firsthand information; (2) the "grassroots surveillance"[4] effort of Internet users to obtain information about truth; and (3) the state's adjusted responses to digital witnessing. Taken together, digital witnessing on Weibo demonstrates how the technological features, business operations, the state, and Internet users have jointly shaped the sociocultural meanings of this platform. Last, I discuss Sina Weibo's evolution into a mainstream media outlet that commodifies digital witnessing through celebrating an interactive consumption of mundaneness, frivolity, and public culture, a result of the corporation's constant negotiation with the state, Sina's competitors, and ever-changing user demographics.

Digital Witnessing: A New Epoch

The importance of witnessing has long been studied in the fields of literature, religion, and law. John Durham Peters argues that the act of witnessing involves three parties: "the agent who bears witness," "the utterance or text itself," and "the audience who witnesses."[5] The process of witnessing consists of dual actions: "the passive one of *seeing* and the active one of *saying*. In passive witnessing an accidental audience observes the events of the world; in active witnessing one is a privileged possessor and *producer* of knowledge in an extraordinary, often forensic, setting in which speech and truth are policed in multiple ways."[6]

To a large degree, "the audience who witnesses," as well as "the passive one of *seeing*," shares similar traits with the apathetic spectators that Lu Xun criticized a century ago. While there are no less passive spectators in the contemporary era, digital media have reshaped the process of witnessing and the connotation of being a witness. Not only is the process of "*saying*" made feasible by the prevalence of smartphones and wireless transmission, the forms of "*saying*" are also diversified, ranging from images to texts to videos, documentaries, and voice messages. Consequently, witnessing in the digital age bears sophisticated connotations compared to earlier times, while the extent to which digital witnessing may enact social changes is a subject of heated debates. Some researchers read digital witnessing as a passive form of seeing. Since Internet users may easily engage in these activities, including clicking, linking, sharing, and tweeting, such simple acts as "clicktivism" and "slacktivism" have demonstrated to have rather limited effects.[7] Other scholars address the ways in which digital witnessing fosters a refashioned understanding of citizen activism. For instance, eyewitnesses' recording and sharing of ongoing events, such as on occasion of war and disasters, break the monopoly of professional journalism and convey a sense of authenticity for their presence on the spot.[8] Yet the extent to which citizen voice may take effect or exert a greater level of influence in society is contingent on whether citizen voice accords with the stance of professional journalists.[9] Scholars also argue for the significance of conceptualizing "bearing witness"[10] as a form of social activism, given that the process of witnessing often entails the sense of agency, responsibility, and performativity among participants. As Sue Tait states, bearing witness "exceeds seeing" because it stresses the importance of "perform[ing] responsibility."[11] Similarly, Kari Andén-Pa-padopoulos analyzes how the use of smartphone enacts the "performative ritual" and fosters the forging of solidarity among those who participate in civic engagement activities.[12]

In authoritarian regimes like that of China, the lack of information transparency and general distrust of official media allocate more weight to the importance of witnesses and the act of "bearing witness." The agency embedded in the process of "bearing witness" is at first exemplified by the independent filmmaking movement since the early 1990s.[13] Filmmakers, representatively Jia Zhangke, Zhang Yuan, and Wu Wenguang, employed the truth claim that "my video camera does not lie" to carve out a niche market and challenge the grand narrative of history in works of their predecessors, fifth-generation directors. This younger generation relied on location shooting and handheld cameras to highlight the importance of personal experiences, individual memories, and family history. If these filmmakers are the intermediaries who, by means of works of art, designate "truth" as a raw material, then digital media allow individuals to formulate this raw material into their own product. Through its technical features, which allow timely dissemination of information, and the promotional strategies of Sina, Weibo enables its preliminary function as a "model of social media witnessing and memory-making"[14] in the early phase.

Drawing on these scholarly findings, the following discussion addresses the evolving forms and content of digital witnessing on Weibo. I argue that the cultural connotations of digital witnessing are defined by particular sociopolitical conditions, technological affordances, Sina's exploration of monetization models, and market dynamics. Early Weibo-based incidents, such as the high-speed rail incident and the Guo Meimei incident, highlight the power of digital witnessing that mobilized netizens to defend social justice, push for information transparency, and expose corruption-related issues. As both cases targeted state authorities, the repercussions were a massive crackdown on Weibo and influential opinion leaders in the years to come. The arrest of Xue Manzi in 2013 landmarks the enhanced control over online space, concurrent with the state media's endeavor to connect with the younger generation of China's Internet audience. The broadcasting of Xue Manzi's confession on China Central Television (CCTV) illustrates how state authorities reclaimed the power of truth by gathering a television audience to watch the media scandal. In contrast, the Leon Dai incident exemplifies how state media capitalize on digital witnessing to ally with the post-1990s and millennial generations. These four cases demonstrate that the sociopolitical meanings of digital witnessing are not stable constructions but are subject to the appropriation of diverse agents. The final two examples analyze the function of digital witnessing that aims at defending consumers' rights, advocating humanism, and exposing institutional problems of Chinese society. While these latter cases were less confrontational to state authorities, they catalyzed netizens' reflections on social norms and advocated an adherence to professionalism in all walks of life. Thus, although the media ecology of Weibo has significantly changed over the years, brought forth by tightened censorship control, enhanced visibility of state actors, and changing business models of Sina Corporation, Weibo still constitutes the premium platform for discussing public issues.

The Wenzhou Train Crash: The Forming of a Digital United Front

In the evening of July 23, 2011, two bullet trains, D301 and D3115, crashed at 20:34 (Beijing Time) on a viaduct in the suburb of Wenzhou, Zhejiang province. Six carriages were derailed; four fell off the viaduct. The incident caused 40 deaths and 192 injuries. Only seven hours after the crash, the Ministry of Railways announced the completion of rescue operations and rushed to bury the derailed carriages. Despite this proclamation, twenty-one hours after the accident, a two-and-a-half-year-old girl Xiang Weiyi (Yiyi), who lost both parents in the accident, was found alive, thanks to the persistence of the local SWAT team. As this case foreshadowed, the attitude of state authorities could principally be described as irresponsible, for within hours of the incident, the Shanghai Railway Bureau hastily concluded that the rear-end collision was caused by lightning. Then, on July 24, Wang Yongping, the spokesperson of the Ministry of Railways, said at the press conference that the wreckage was buried "for the convenience of rescue efforts," followed by another statement that "as to whether you believe [this rationale] or not, I do anyway." Wang also commented that the survival of Yiyi "is a miracle," which immediately sparked outrage among journalists, who rebutted immediately: "this is not a miracle!"[15] Under public pressure, the buried car was unearthed and sent to another site for investigation on July 25. To pacify public anger, the then premier Wen Jiabao visited the crash site on July 28 and held a news conference, promising a thorough overhaul of the accident; on August 16, Wang Yong-ping was dismissed from his position. Following that, the State Council released a detailed report on December 28, 2011, concluding that "design flaws, sloppy management and the mishandling of a lightning strike" were the major causes of the accident.[16] Fifty-four personnel were held account-able. Among them was the former minister of the Ministry of Railways, Liu Zhijun, who was expelled from the Chinese Communist Party on cor-ruption charges in May 2011.

Widely acknowledged as the milestone event for both Weibo and tradi-tional journalism,[17] the "7.23 accident" signifies the forging of a unified pub-lic that brought together Internet users, traditional media channels, digital media, and journalists for a shared cause. Infuriated by state authorities' improper handling of the accident, including the hasty rescue efforts, the lack of information transparency regarding the number of casualties, and the prioritization of economic gain over human lives, all parties mobilized to push for a change. In addition, the factional struggles from within the Party, including the top leadership, the Ministry of Railways, the central and local governments, and the Central Propaganda Department,[18] opened up opportunities for the flourishing of criticisms and in-depth investiga-tion of the accident. Although the Central Propaganda Department issued directives on how to report the accident as early as July 24, these orders were soon leaked online and stimulated more public outrage. The directives read as follows:

> In regard to the Wenzhou high-speed train crash, all media outlets are to promptly report information released from the Ministry of Railways. No journalists should conduct independent interviews. All subsidiaries includ-ing newspaper, magazines and websites are to be well controlled. Do not link reports with articles regarding the development of high-speed trains. Do not conduct reflective reports.
>
> Reporting of the accident is to use "in the face of great tragedy, there's great love" as the major theme. Do not question. Do not elaborate. Do not

associate. No re-posting on micro-blogs will be allowed! Related service information may be provided during news reporting. Music is to be carefully selected![19]

Despite the Party's request that all media should "report information released from the Ministry of Railways," the latter soon became a public target. The accuracy of the information that the Ministry disclosed was severely questioned. Even the state-affiliated CCTV broadcasted several programs that targeted the Ministry of Railways.[20] The State Administration of Work Safety also stated that the accident was not a "natural disaster."[21] Encouraged by these signals, traditional media outlets, ranging from provincial television stations to commercial newspapers and magazines to semi-official media organizations, assumed an active role in engaging in-depth investigation of the accident. Between July 23 and July 29, reports on the accident and online comments flourished in media spaces, until the Central Propaganda Department issued another directive, which designated the "7.23 accident" as a highly censored topic beginning on July 29.[22]

"The 7.23 accident" underscores the crucial role that Weibo played in unifying interest groups, instantaneously disseminating information, and catalyzing citizen activism on a massive scale. The relevance of this accident to millions of train users, the public's distrust of state authorities, and a rising, increasingly rights-conscious middle class all engendered "a networked *weiguan* community."[23] This community not only closely monitored the updates of the accident but also functioned as active agents who questioned state authorities' decisions and affected the ways in which the accident was handled. Within a week of the "7.23 accident," more than 30 million messages on the train crash were posted on Sina Weibo and Tencent Weibo.[24] Between July and October, there were 9.72 million messages related to the accident.[25] The content ranges from speculations about the real causes of the accident to coordination of volunteer activities to update rescue work and search for missing passengers to commemorate the passing of victims. My analysis focuses on the particular function that Weibo played during the "7.23 accident," paying special attention to the process of forming a unifying public voice.

Weibo demonstrated the power of digital witnessing that challenged state authorities from various viewpoints. Reports from witnesses who were on the train, reports from witnesses' family, recollections of volunteers, and journalists' in-depth investigation of the accident altogether provided firsthand information unavailable in state media. As Peters states, "liveness serves as an assurance of access to truth and authenticity."[26] Liveness matters even more on such occasions when information is not transparent. Indeed, shortly before the collision, "Smm_miao," a local resident in Wenzhou, already noticed something went wrong with the high-speed train. At 20:27, he posted a message on Weibo: "After all the wind and storm, what's going on with the high-speed train? It's crawling slower than a snail. I hope nothing happens to it."[27] Twenty-eight minutes later, he uploaded a photo that showed the crash site and rescue work organized by local residents.[28] Passengers on the train also recorded their experiences on Weibo. Just four minutes after the accident, an online ID "Yuan Xiaoyuan" posted a message: "Something has happened to D301 in Wenzhou. There was an emergency shutdown and a strong collision. Twice! The power is out. I am in the last carriage. I'm praying I will be okay."[29] Yuan sent out seven messages in total. Thirteen minutes after the accident, another passenger "yang quan quan yang" tweeted: "Help! The high-speed train D301 has derailed somewhere not far from Wenzhou South Station. Children are crying! There are no staff coming. Come and help us!"[30] This post was retweeted over 100,000 times; the passenger was rescued two hours later.[31] These messages from eyewitnesses offered firsthand information about the accident, while the official Xinhua News Agency did not report on the collision until one hour later.[32]

These witnesses' narratives on the train crash were enriched when more survivors, victims, public intellectuals, celebrities, and journalists participated. They posted insider information, shared updates, and commented on the collision. Among the victims the story of Yang Feng and Xiang Weiyi (Yiyi) attracted most media attention. Yang Feng lost six family members in the crash, among them his fiancée Chen Bi, who was seven months pregnant. Upon learning about the accident, Yang and his cousin rushed to the crash site from Shaoxing, Zhejiang, at 2:00 a.m. on July 24. They found out only that rescue operations were announced to have completed, and police were awaiting orders from higher-ups. In despair, Yang mobilized personal friends and family members to look for Chen Bi. In the afternoon, Yang finally saw his fiancée's remains, which were disfigured. In interviews, Yang requested that the Ministry of Railways answer two questions: (1) whether the early termination of rescue efforts decreased the chances of his fiancée's survival, and (2) what had caused the disfiguring of Chen Bi's remains, the excavator or the collision. Yang pinned his hopes on the power of social media, for which he launched the Weibo account "Yang Feng Chen Bi" to update the progress of his appeal. As to the two-and-a-half-year-old girl Yiyi, not only did her surgery attract nationwide attention but the Weibo accounts of Yiyi's parents also became sites of public commemoration. Yiyi's father, nicknamed "Xianzuo butan yuwen" (Xiang Yu'an) on Weibo, had used this space to record his daily life. Xiang Yu'an had posted a picture of Yiyi when they were on the train, writing, "This is the first time that Yiyi goes on a long journey to Hangzhou by the bullet train. [Post it] as a keepsake." As of August 3, 2018, this post was shared 210,139 times and generated 56,912 comments.[33] Likewise, Yiyi's mother, Shi Lihong, had opened an account on Sina Weibo on May 27, 2011, and titled her space "Memoirs of Yiyi's growth" (*Chengzhang huiyilu*). One hour before the accident, she updated the last post: "Little person, bad-tempered. My baby, when can you grow up and become thoughtful?"[34] Both accounts continue to attract large number of visits for Internet users. On anniversaries and holidays, Internet users return to these sites to memorialize the deceased and wish the best for survivors. In these two stories, Weibo connects the victims, albeit in different ways: Yang Feng's Weibo account is intended to exert public pressure on authorities, while the Weibo accounts of Yiyi's parents have become sites of public memorial.

In addition to witnesses' Weibo accounts, social actors, ranging from local governments to media outlets to journalists, capitalized on Weibo to enlist public support. Of the major commercial portals—in particular Sina, Sohu, Tencent, and NetEase, and video sharing sites like Youku and Tudou—Weibo constituted the primary site for Internet users to share firsthand information, coordinate rescue efforts, question the credibility of official media, and push for information transparency. Web administrators at commercial portals played crucial roles in verifying information, following updates, and compiling special issues dedicated to this accident. Within less than an hour after the train crash, the management team of Sina Weibo set up a page on the accident, a common practice of portal websites for time-sensitive topics. Sina's self-positioning as a news media allocated more weight to the corporation's emphasis on the timeliness of the report, where staff members worked around the clock to update information about injured passengers, posted search notices for missing passengers, and aggregated related posts.[35] Given the hierarchical structure of Weibo, where posts of well-known figures tend to receive greater level of attention from Internet users and Sina,[36] it is crucial for web administrators to identify time-sensitive posts and promote them.[37]

Moreover, the "7.23 accident" demonstrates an unusual case in which institutions and individuals, traditional media, and online media worked together to push for further investigation and to extend moral support to victims. If the online public demonstrated their power by sharing information and commenting on the accident, then influential opinion leaders contributed significantly by steering online discussions. According to Changchang Wu, three types of opinion leaders emerged during the "7.23 accident": (1) "leading headlines on the official blogs of specific media outlets," (2) "journalists from the Southern Newspaper Group and a few Beijing newspapers," and (3) "public intellectuals."[38] Official blogs such as the Weibo accounts of Zhejiang Provincial Health Department and Blood Centre of Zhejiang Province promptly updated the progress of blood donation and rescue efforts. Weibo accounts of dominant and mainstream media, including CCTV, *Chengdu Commercial Newspaper*, *China Economy Press*, 21 *Century Economy Herald*, and *Finance and Economics Magazine* (*Caijing*), all disseminated related information and published commentaries in a timely manner. Journalists, some of whom were also train passengers, courageously disclosed state cover-ups of the train wreckage. Influential individuals, including journalists, celebrities, and online opinion leaders, like Han Han, Li Chengpeng, Yao Chen, He Weifang, and Yuan Tengfei, published commentaries on the accident. The combined efforts of these individuals thus harmonized the voices of the public, giving hope to all and serving as a united front against an inattentive state.

Cultural Response to Official Discourse

Similar to earlier cases of web-based incidents, "the 7.23 accident" sparked cultural creativity that mocks the irresponsibility of state authorities and pretentiousness of official discourses. In the face of tragedy, the cultural responses to the accident highlight the essential role that emotion plays in collective actions. As Guobin Yang has argued, "sympathy" and "play" epitomize two common types of emotional response to Internet incidents, which bear great potential for inspiring collective actions.[39] The flourishing of netizens' reflections about the tragedy and memorial of the death showcases two distinctive, often juxtaposed, styles: the parodic and the sentimental. These writings mock the rigidity of political culture in China, evoke emotional responses from readers, and provoke further reflections on the flaws of existing systems. Some representative examples are "the style of bullet train" (*gaotie ti*), formed as a collective response to Wang Yongping's outrageous statements "as to whether you believe it or not, I do anyway" and "this is a miracle." An Internet user at Tencent Weibo initiated a campaign titled "sentence making contest by using high-speed train style." The original post states: "Make a sentence by using 'XXX, whether you believe it or not, I do anyway.' The winner will win 100,000 Q currency [*Q bi*, virtual currency of QQ], as well as the position of spokesperson of the Ministry of Railways. Whether you believe it or not, I do anyway." More than 7,000 Internet users participated in the competition,[40] which was soon extended to other online forums like Baidu Tieba and Tianya Community. Some of the representative works are as follows:

Case One

Master Tang Seng and his three disciples set out to the West again to acquire Buddhist scriptures. Tang Seng would like to take a shortcut, so he asked Wu Kong what to do. Wu Kong said: "I heard that the airplane is much faster than White Dragon Horse." Ba Jie suggested: "Master, I heard that spaceship of Shenzhou No. 6 is even faster." At this moment, Sha Seng took out four tickets for the bullet train, pointing at Tang Seng, and said: "Master, I heard that this stuff can send you to the West right away. As to whether you believe it or not, I do anyway."[41]

Case Two

When I was little, miracle was a soft baby bottle, with melamine inside, and social conscience outside. When I grew up, miracle was an auditorium in fire. The children were inside, while officials were outside. Later on, miracle was a bus on fire. Inside, were the people; outside, was the life-saving hammer. Now, miracle is a bloody carriage, you are inside, while the forklift is outside.[42]

Case Three

After several rounds of investigations by authoritative departments and experts, they finally reached a conclusion: The only, real direct cause of this incident was Thunder God and Thunder Goddess. China's high-speed rail is indeed safe, and is top-notch worldwide! As to whether you believe it or not, I do anyway![43]

These examples playfully satirize the hypocrisy of official discourses through the conduit of humor, sentimentalism, and parody. Case one appropriates the classical work *Journey to the West* and plays on the double meaning of "going to the west" (*shang xitian*), which could either refer to the acquisition of Buddhist scriptures or simply death. The joke ridicules how quickly the high-speed rail could take people's lives. Case two is a rewrite of the influential poem "Nostalgia" (*xiangchou*) by Yu Guangzhong. While the original work describes the nostalgic sentiments shared among those who were separated by the 1949 divide, the rewrite references the word "miracle" (*qiji*), used by Wang Yongping to describe the survival of Yiyi, to paraphrase social scandals that dismiss the dignity of human lives over the years. As to case three, it emulates the long-winded style of official rhetoric. By stating that "China's high-speed rail is indeed safe," the line lampoons the pretentiousness of state discourses. Interestingly, while these three cases illustrate how the rigidity of official discourses often are subject to public mockery, state media organs learned to appropriate the style of popular discourses in the years to come.

In contrast to the creative works by anonymous Internet users, well-established figures published essays that fostered collective reflections on the drawbacks of Chinese systems. One essay published by the state-affiliated

China Youth Daily, titled "The Train that Never Arrives,"[44] renarrated the story of passengers on the bullet train based on the author's interviews and collection of primary sources, interweaving victims' own records of their experiences on the train into the narrative. The essay begins with two college students' journey out of Beijing: Zhu Ping plans to visit her father who has been hospitalized, while Lu Haitian is eager to start his summer internship at the Wenzhou Television station. While on the train, they both update their status for family and friends on social networking sites and mobile phones. They choose to take the bullet train to arrive at their destination faster—Lu Haitian even changes his ticket to experience the high-speed train. Ironically, this so-called China Speed only ends up taking their lives.

Another representative piece was written by Han Han and published in his blog. Typical of Han Han's style, "The Derailed Country," alternated between the use of "they" and "you" and "they" and "we" to distinguish between authorities and ordinary citizens. Han Han's essay analyzed the accident from the perspectives of both authorities and victims.[45] Journalist Tong Dahuan also published a widely circulated post. His writing questioned the accelerated pace of economic development in China and called for the respect of human dignity: "China, please slow your soaring steps forward. . . . Wait for your people. . . . [W]ait for your conscience! We don't want derailed trains, or collapsing bridges, or roads that slide into pits. We don't want our homes to become death traps. Move more slowly. Let every life have freedom and dignity."[46]

As "the largest 'online mass incident'"[47] in China, the "7.23 accident" unmasks how web administrators, Internet users, journalists, witnesses, and dominant and mainstream media outlets formed a unifying voice and collectively enriched narratives revolving around the accident. Weibo not only demonstrated the power of digital witnessing that transformed seemingly passive spectators into active agents, but it also functioned as the pivotal "organizing agents,"[48] the center of citizen activism. A defining moment of Weibo, the "7.23 accident" alerted the state about the power of microblogging and showcased the urgency for the state to reinvent its propaganda strategies when facing China's Internet public.

The Guo Meimei Incident:
Battles for Truth and Authority

Ranked as one of the most sensational web-based incidents in 2011, the Guo Meimei incident refracts the multifaceted syndromes of contemporary society, ranging from moral crisis to corruption of officialdom to incivility of online sphere and problems regarding charity work. Born in Yiyang, Hunan province, Guo Meimei (Guo Meiling, b. 1991) grew up with her mother and studied performance at Beijing Film Academy in 2008–9. Afterwards, she stayed in Beijing and took minor roles in the media industry. Internet users first noticed Guo Meimei for her display of luxurious handbags and sports cars on Weibo. One of Guo's posts stated: "It is challenging to learn to be a manager for the Red Cross." She identified her title as the general manager of Red Cross Society of Commerce of China, and next to her title was a symbol "v," indicating that Sina had verified her identity.

On June 21, 2011, an Internet user nicknamed "maihaozi" first picked up Guo's post and shared her Weibo address on the entertainment and gossip forum of Tianya. The discussion thread has a long title: "Another new finding on Weibo: The twenty-year old, 'general manager of the Red Cross Society of Commerce,' shows off wealth in various ways; gather online immediately!" This Internet user also commented on Guo's posts, which soon resonated with fellow posters: "The Red Cross is outrageously rich! From now on, whoever donates to the Red Cross is a fool! This woman seems to be sitting around every day, apart from showing off wealth and driving luxurious cars! Looks like she is from a wealthy family, and her mom seems to be a rich lady too!"[49] Within three days, this post generated 1,565,448 visits and 9,440 comments. In line with the "gossiping" convention of Tianya, Internet users were immediately mobilized to conduct searches to discover the true identity of Guo Meimei, her mother, and their connections with the Red Cross. They searched all available social media accounts of Guo Meimei, including QQ, QQ space, NetEase album, Kaixin, Xiaonei, and Sina Weibo; shared their findings; and pieced together Guo's story by analyzing her posts and the friends with whom she socialized.[50] A keyword search of Guo Meimei yielded 9 million results on the Weibo accounts of Sina, Tencent, Sohu, and NetEase.[51] The thorough investigation by Tianya users soon alerted Guo Meimei's acquaintances. Several of them left her messages on Weibo to inform her about Internet users' searches of her. In turn, these interpersonal conversations between Guo Meimei and her friends triggered more responses from Tianya users. Meanwhile, celebrities like Yang Lan, Hong Huang, and Lüqiu Luwei all expressed their concern about this issue. The information flow between Tianya and Weibo, two of the most influential platforms, amplified the networked effects of the Guo Meimei incident. At the same time, largely due to the lack of trustworthy news resources, rumors abounded about Guo Meimei and her connections with the Red Cross.[52]

One of the major concerns of Internet users was whether Guo Meimei had abused public donations to the Red Cross, given the massive amount of wealth the twenty-year-old seemed to have amassed. Moreover, a popular belief in the rigorous verification procedure Sina conducts, along with the prestige that the "v" symbolizes, reinforced the conjecture that Guo Meimei was somehow related to the Red Cross. In Guo's response, she at first defended her lifestyle and then explained the function of the Red Cross Commerce of China. Subsequently, Guo clarified that she was not affiliated with the Red Cross and that she changed her profession from "actor" to the general manager of the Red Cross Commerce of China simply "for fun." Then, Guo revealed that her wealth drew from her "foster father" (*gandie*) Wang Jun in Shenzhen, who at that time ran a business that partnered with the Red Cross Commerce of China, a subsidiary of the Red Cross.[53] These contradictory responses drew even more suspicions from netizens, while Sina made a public apology for not carefully verifying Guo's profession before approving her status change. The Red Cross Society of China announced on June 22, 2011, that Guo Meimei did not work for the organization and hosted a press conference on June 28 to clarify the issue.[54] On July 7, "Pingan Beijing," the official Weibo account of Beijing Municipal Public Security Bureau, publicized the investigation result and supported the statement of the Red Cross.

Dominant and mainstream media outlets did not respond to the incident until several days later. Reports from CCTV, Xinhua News Agency, and *Beijing News* endeavored to sever the tie between Guo Meimei and the Red Cross Society of China, dismissed some of netizens' conjectures as rumors, and framed the Red Cross as a victim.[55] One week after the incident, CCTV broadcasted an episode of *Oriental Horizon* (*Dongfang shikong*). Although this program claimed to "disclose the truth about the Guo Meimei incident," the protagonist was absent. Citing the collective findings of Internet users, *Oriental Horizon* interviewed personnel related to the Red Cross Society of China and Tianlue Corporation, which collaborated with the Red Cross Commerce of China.[56] Despite these employees' testimony that Guo Meimei worked for neither organization, Internet users were not convinced. They questioned instead who was the secret supporter of Guo Meimei. Overnight the Red Cross Society of China suffered from a severe credibility crisis. Between June and August 2011, donations to the Red Cross Society of China dropped 80 percent, according to the Ministry of Civil Affairs's statistics.[57] The repercussion of the Guo Meimei incident lasted for quite some time. In 2013, an earthquake occurred in Ya'an, Sichuan province. When the Red Cross posted its rescue effort on Weibo, it received repetitive responses like "go away" (*gun*) and such emoticons as "thumbs down" in the comments section.[58]

The Guo Meimei incident not only triggered the credibility crisis of the state-backed charity organizations, but it also demystified the authority of "v" that Sina tried to promote. Further, this incident exemplified the ways in which collective witnessing mobilized netizens to uncover the truth and to verify statements from all parties, including the Red Cross, Guo Meimei, her friends, celebrities, and official media. Ironically, "truth," the keyword that motivated Internet users to conduct comprehensive searches about Guo Meimei, was not unveiled until years later. Although a committee was established to supervise the Red Cross Society of China in 2012, the committee's proposal to fully investigate the Guo Meimei incident was never approved.[59] Between 2011 and 2014, Guo remained a mysterious figure in the public domain, so that notoriety revolving around her was being turned into business opportunities. Because of the scandal, Guo Meimei's followers on Weibo increased drastically. As Guo recalled in an interview, originally she had only about a hundred followers on Weibo. Most of them were her friends. When the incident first caught the public's attention, the number of followers increased by tens of thousands per day.[60] By June 27, 2011, the number of Guo's followers increased to 700,000.[61] The huge number of followers paved the way for Guo Meimei to make inroads into the entertainment industry. Two months after the incident, Guo started her own work studio, issued several solo songs on Weibo, and invested and starred in a movie *I am Guo Meimei* in 2013. She also opened a store on Taobao, one of the most popular e-commerce sites in China. News about Guo Meimei continued to appear in media spaces, such as her owing a huge amount of debts to a casino in Macau.[62] It later turned out that these news items were fabricated to boost the visibility of Guo Meimei as well as the casino.

Dramatically, the Red Cross Society of China had barely recovered from this scandal when Guo Meimei made national headlines again. In July 2014, Guo was charged with illegal betting on the World Cup in March, June, and July 2013 with about 2.14 million RMB (330,000 USD) at stake. On August 3, 2014, CCTV broadcasted the investigation of the case and concluded that Guo Meimei paid for her luxurious lifestyle by profiting from the sex trade. On September 10, 2015, Guo was sentenced to five years in jail and fined 50,000 RMB (7,757 USD) for running an illegal casino.[63] CCTV broadcasted the trial live on its legal channel, while Sina News offered technical support for live broadcasts online.[64] The title of the program, "Courtroom Scene Live" (*Tingshen xianchang*), emphasizes the importance of witnessing on the scene and indicates the sense of authenticity and authority conveyed through the legal setting. In this trial, Guo appeared barefaced, with her jail clothes and glasses, so gone was the glorified image of Guo Meimei on Weibo. She talked about the gambling activities she and her boyfriend organized and admitted her involvement with sex transactions. Guo Meimei's public confession and formal apologies to the Red Cross thereby reached every household through the joint channel of television and Internet in China. Further, Guo's ex-boyfriend Wang Jun, the "foster father" Guo Meimei referred to in 2011, disclosed the truth about Guo Meimei and demonized her. Wang commented that "I have never seen someone who is so vain," and that "she is like a ghost, and whoever sees her will have bad luck."[65] To this end, official media restored the authority regarding the report of Guo Meimei. The framing of Guo as a professional mistress who violated the law took effect. As a consequence of the comprehensive digital witnessing of the first phase of the Guo Meimei incident, even CCTV relied on netizens' findings to report this case. The latter phase ushered in a period of authority reclamation by official media by resorting to the power of the court, legal witnesses, and formal interviews.

In so doing, the issue of immorality revolving around mistresses and illegal gambling diluted the credibility crisis that the Red Cross had been coping with over the years. In this respect, CCTV's broadcasts continued to capitalize on moral issues in the report of Xue Manzi incident in 2013.

Public Confession, Populist Turn

The Xue Manzi incident signified a major turning point for Weibo. A Chinese American entrepreneur and investor, Xue Manzi (Xue Biqun, b. 1953), has attracted more than 11 million followers on Sina Weibo as of June 29, 2020. Xue assumed an active role in publishing incisive comments on current affairs and promoting civic engagement activities, including charity work and campaigns against child trafficking. On August 20, 2013, Xue Manzi was arrested in Beijing under the charge of "soliciting a prostitute."[66] Soon after, footage that recorded his arrest in Anhui Beili of Beijing, alongside interviews of prostitutes, was released.[67] Xue made an appearance on the news channel of CCTV, during which he confessed about this misconduct and extended his unequivocal support of governmental actions.[68] Ironically, just two days before Xue Manzi's detainment, CCTV aired an episode of *Dialogue* that featured him and several other well-known figures, including Pan Shiyi, a real estate guru; Zhou Xiaoping, a controversial commentator; and Chen Tong, the then editor-in-chief of Sina Corporation.[69] In this program, Xue Manzi discussed the responsibilities of "Big Vs" and endorsed the seven baselines that the program proposed for Internet celebrities to adhere to. The airing of these two programs just two days apart seemed to indicate the inconsistency of online opinion leaders in terms of their speech and actions. By labeling Xue Manzi as being "morally degenerate," state media conflated Xue's public engagement activities with his private sexual behavior. The issue of immorality thereby functions to invalidate Xue Manzi's contribution to the public domain.

The Guo Meimei incident and the case of Xue Manzi converge in the sense that the state capitalizes on morality issues and legal measures to fulfill its political agenda. In the case of Guo Meimei, morality is an effective means for state media to elicit public condemnation of her, meanwhile diverting audience attention from the fundamental problems of the Red Cross. By contrast, state media delegitimize Xue Manzi's civic engagement initiatives by emphasizing his immoral behaviors. CCTV's broadcasting of these two cases uses footage, interviews, court settings, and legal measures to convey the sense of authenticity and authority when delivering information. In other words, state media quickly learn to use "*xianchang*," being on the scene, to reverse the connotation of digital witnessing as showcased in the "7.23 accident." Now state actors are the ones who have access to information and truth, and by disseminating knowledge about truth, the state reclaims its power in news reports.

The arrest of Xue Manzi heralded massive crackdowns on Weibo, focusing particularly on public intellectuals and online opinion leaders. These moves that constrain online expressions illustrate "the return of ideology" on the Chinese Internet, often implemented in the name of morality charges, anti-rumor campaigns, cyber sovereignty, and "rule of law."[70] In the aftermath of the National Propaganda and Ideology Work Conference in August 2013, the Ministry of Public Security launched anti-rumor campaigns. Soon after, Qin Huohuo (Qin Zhihui) and Lier chaisi (Yang Xiuyu), two influential people working for Internet public relations industry, were arrested for "spreading rumors."[71] Then, on September 8, 2013, the Chinese Supreme People's Court and Supreme People's Procuratorate issued a judicial interpretation. The new rule stipulated that individuals who post false information online may face up to three years in prison if the post is viewed more than 5,000 times or retweeted 500 times.[72] In the following years, a series of new measures were implemented at both the institutional and policy levels to strengthen state control over the Internet. Some examples include Xi's launching of Central Leading Group for Cyberspace Affairs, the comprehensive implementation of real-name registration systems, and state media's enhanced visibility in the microblogosphere to reinvent propaganda work and modes of governance.[73]

Amid this backdrop, influential opinion leaders became extremely cautious about what to post on Weibo. Also gone was the glory that public intellectuals enjoyed in the age of blogging and the early phase of Weibo. Various parties have actively participated in the campaign to mock public intellectuals, including the state-employed "fifty-cents army," the "voluntary fifty-cents army" (*ziganwu*) who side with the state, nationalists, and some state-affiliated media organizations. Among these actors, the rise of "Little Pinks" (*Xiao fenhong*) on Weibo in 2016 is most phenomenal. Originating from the literature website Jinjiang Literature City, the term "Little Pinks" was first used to refer to romance readers who also engaged in discussing political issues on that site. In 2016, the term suddenly gained prominence on social media platforms and has been widely used since to define young patriotic netizens.[74] These Internet users allied with state media to participate in populist movements that attack cultural elites and arouse nationalistic sentiments. The state's enhanced visibility online, the younger generation's confidence about the country, and the decline in influence of public intellectuals are all contributing factors.

Reinventing Propaganda: Little Pinks and State Media

During the "7.23 accident," Wang Yongping's famous statement that "whether you believe it or not, I do anyway" immediately triggered public outrage as Wang's wording depicted the condescending attitude of state officials and their lack of sympathy toward victims. The uproar that this statement evoked, as illustrated by the viral dissemination of Internet memes and jokes as well as offline mobilizations, alerted the Chinese state to the urgency of reinventing its governance and propaganda models. The eruption of the Leon Dai incident in 2016, triggered jointly by patriotic netizens and official media, hallmarks the effectiveness of the state media's experimentalist measures, particularly the emerging form of soft propaganda that began to appropriate the offerings of popular culture and capitalize on collective sentiments. A renowned Taiwanese actor and director, Leon Dai was replaced as a cast member in Zhao Wei's new film *No Other Love* (*Mei-you biede ai*) because of his alleged pro-Taiwanese independence stance, among other charges. The state media, as represented by the Weibo account of Communist Youth League of China (CYL), played a crucial role in appropriating digital populism to resonate with a domestic audience. Taking a departure from the "artificiality of the official language,"[75] the CYL adopts a discursive style that is more accessible to the younger generation. This changed rhetorical style, along with the new tactics that the CYL employs to engage its audience, selectively resonates with public sentiments to rejuvenate propaganda work. It thereby differs from the implementation of the top-down propaganda policies of earlier times.

The web-based Leon Dai incident, like the Chou Tzu-yu incident and Diba Expedition, occurred amid the rising tide of nationalism in 2016 and revolved around China's relationship with Taiwan and the US. These incidents illustrate the increasing convergence of entertainment and politics, as well as its resultant effect on expressions of nationalism. The Chou Tzu-yu incident began on January 15, 2016, when Taiwanese singer Chou Tzu-yu, a member of the South Korean pop idol group TWICE, made a video apology to the public for holding the flag of the Republic of China on South Korean Television in November 2015. However, the real cause of this incident was that JYP Entertainment, Chou's employer, was perceived as being arrogant toward Chinese fans of TWICE.[76] These Chinese fans reacted to the condescending behavior and began to take issue with Chou's political stance. Since Chou's apology video was released the day before Taiwan's presidential election, her statement that she was "proud of being Chinese" immediately sparked outrage among the Taiwanese. Many who were previously uninterested in participating in the election voted for Tsai Ing-wen, the leader of the Democratic Progressive Party and an advocate of Taiwanese independence from China. Tsai's election win subsequently inspired the online Diba Expedition in mainland China, in which users on Diba (Emperor Bar), a subforum of Baidu Tieba, organized troll-like activities. In a mass online action on January 20, 2016, Internet users in China circumvented the Great Firewall and left tens of thousands of messages opposing Taiwanese independence on Tsai Ing-wen's Facebook page and several media websites in Taiwan, including SET News Channel, *Apple Daily*, and *Liberation News*. These netizens' use of massive images, emojis, and playful promotions of mainland China constituted the highlight of this event.

What distinguishes the Leon Dai incident from the aforementioned cases of cyber nationalism is the active role that the state media played in online mobilization. Three months after the Diba Expedition, actress-director Zhao Wei announced the names of the leading actors in her new movie *No Other Love* on Weibo. Among them was Leon Dai; some Internet users suspected Dai of supporting Taiwanese independence. They also requested that Zhao

Wei remove Kiko Mizuhara, a model and actress, who is said to have made derogatory comments about China. Initially, the movie studio did not respond to these requests. Upon the completion of shooting *No Other Love*, Zhao Wei posted a group picture with Leon Dai on June 27, 2016, inadvertently stirring up another round of controversy. On June 30, the official Weibo account of *No Other Love* issued a statement that the studio would sue anyone who disseminated false information about Leon Dai. This was followed by Dai's denial of the charges against him as a "backer of Taiwanese independence" (*Tai du*) on his Weibo account.

From April to June 2016, online bickering revolving around Leon Dai's political stance occurred from time to time, but it was quite scattered. The tipping point happened when the CYL published essays on July 6 that questioned the political stances of Leon Dai and Zhao Wei. Meanwhile, the territorial disputes between China and its neighboring countries were escalating. On July 12, the Hague-based Permanent Court of Arbitration announced the United Nations tribunal, which ruled that China's "sovereignty claims over the South China Sea, and its aggressive attempts to enforce them" were invalid.[77] The Foreign Ministry of China denounced this rule; official media outlets began a series of publicity campaigns to maintain regime legitimacy. The viral circulation of the poster "Only this can be China, and not one bit less" (*Zhongguo yidian dou buneng shao*), created by the *People's Daily's* Weibo account, is one example. Against this backdrop, the movie studio announced the removal of Dai from *No Other Love* on July 15, just nine days after the CYL published the initial post. This was followed by the public apologies from Zhao Wei and Leon Dai on their Weibo accounts.

The CYL's direct involvement with the Leon Dai incident began on July 6, when it reposted an essay written by Zhao Liangchen.[78] Zhao's essay first summarized the controversy *No Other Love* had provoked since April and cited netizens' comments to demonstrate that Leon Dai's political stance was questionable. Then, the essay listed ten points to imply that Leon Dai supported Taiwanese independence. Photos, news reports, interviews, and screenshots of online comments were used to support each point. In particular, Dai's involvement in the Sunflower Movement in Taiwan, his support of the Umbrella Movement in Hong Kong, and his comments on the performance of the Falun Gong group made up the majority of the evidence against him. More important, the essay quoted the opinions of "the majority of netizens" to demonstrate strength in numbers. A frequently repeated statement was that "commentaries that win over 500 likes all are those that question, resist against, and condemn" Leon Dai, Zhao Wei, and Guan Hu (the director who extended support to Leon Dai). At the end, in a statement directed at Zhao Wei, the author suggested that "it is OK to make a mistake, but it is important to realize the mistake and fix it. Be mindful about the mistake you have made when you were young and the words you said then." This line referred to an incident in 2001, when Zhao Wei had to make multiple public apologies for wearing a dress that looked like a Japanese military flag. This incident led Zhao to hit a roadblock in her career, and it took quite a few years for her to become popular again.

The style of this post resembles many online disputes that make full use of one-liners and visual sources to demonstrate a simplistic point that may easily arouse public sentiment. Even more dramatic was Sina's removal of the post at 17:55 p.m., ten minutes after it first appeared on the CYL's Weibo. After the CYL publicized this post removal, Sina soon responded that the post deletion was an "accident." Because the post contained such sensitive words as "Falong Gong," a religious group in exile, it was automatically filtered and censored by the system.[79] Although the post was recovered at 18:15 p.m., twenty minutes after its removal, the CYL's self-positioning as a victim of censorship, implemented by a commercial website, immediately created a nationwide sensation. Furthermore, the reactions of several of the CYL's allies amplified the effect caused by the "accidental" censorship. For instance, the Weibo account of *Ziguangge* (The hall of purple light), the core journal of the Chinese Communist Party, shared the original post and added a line: "[I am doing this] in case your post is deleted again." On July 14, the official Weibo account of *People's Daily* reposted the commentary by *China National Defense News*, which stated that Zhao Wei's deeds "have challenged the baseline of the masses." Thus, the networked effects activated by the allies of the CYL, including its local branches, other official mouthpieces, and patriotic netizens, enhanced the visibility of official media as represented by the CYL.

Two days after the announcement of the South China Sea Verdict, the CYL published an original post that started with a statement on the changing connotation of "people" in the age of consumerism:

> Against the backdrop of media commercialization and industrialization, "people" become media consumers who are exploited by the few to generate big profits.
>
> Media are manipulated by capitalistic corporations to self-promote and to maintain their own interests. Under the manipulation of capital, news reports entertain the audience in order to create high ratings and distribution, instead of satisfying the real needs of the people.[80]

The post further argued that capitalist operation, as represented by all kinds of elites and commercial corporations, played a vital role in "manipulating" people's opinions. Evoking socialist rhetoric about the evils of "capitalism," the CYL made the "winners" of the capitalist economy, such as powerful corporations like Sina and individuals like Ma Yun and Zhao Wei, the target of the public. The CYL framed these entrepreneurs as "evil capitalists" who conspire with commercial sites like Sina to remove unfavorable posts and manipulate public opinion. This simplistic rationale immediately resonated with the disadvantaged groups who already felt indignant about the expanding gap between the rich and the poor in contemporary society. Additionally, in line with the state-sponsored attempts to blemish public intellectuals, the post framed public opinion leaders as those "elites" who "control media resources and discursive power." According to the post, these elites act as the spokespeople of "capital" and possess a greater degree of mobilizing power than do official media outlets. Moreover, because of the infiltration of capital into official media organizations, and into their websites and Weibo accounts, those media organizations that advocate "socialism with Chinese characteristics" are marginalized in the microblogosphere. Consequently, "different voices are repressed."[81] In siding with the "people," a loaded term that has roots in socialist legacies, the CYL positioned itself as a victim of "capital." By dichotomizing *us*, the people, and *them*, the "elites" and "capitalists," the CYL echoed contemporary outrage at the ever-growing disparity between social classes. In the comments section of the post, slogans such as "capital controls public opinions," "capital monopolizes the state," and "capital manipulates politics" were frequently quoted and paraphrased. Since the publication of this post, the public target has shifted from Leon Dai and his political stance to Zhao Wei and Ma Yun, capitalists who are seen as "public enemies" and "traitors" of China. By contrast, the CYL is perceived as the "hero" that defended the national interest for Chinese citizens. In this regard, the populist stance taken by the CYL, reinforced by the rhetoric revolving around class, capital, and media, effectively steered public discussion.

Following Zhao Wei's and Leon Dai's apologies and the studio's decision to remove Dai from *No Other Love*, the nationalistic fervor seemed to spin out of control as protestors took to the streets to boycott foreign brands. In line with Party-mouthpiece Xinhua News Agency's statement that "getting oneself worked up is not patriotism," the CYL posted two essays four days apart that discussed patriotic behavior.[82] In both essays, the CYL acted as the spokesperson of the younger generations, in particular the post-90s and the millennial generations who participated heavily in these collective actions. The CYL argued that the use of memes (*biaoqing bao*) characterized the "ritual of patriotism" (*aiguo yishi*) for the younger generation. According to the CYL, this ritual was "serious [in terms of goals] yet frivolous [in terms of style]" (*yansu er bu zhuangzhong*). Those who adopted this ritual, it argued, differed from the extremists who took to the streets and worried only that the "world is not chaotic enough." In addition, the CYL sided with the younger generation in calling those born in the 1950s and 1960s "weird uncles" (*guai shushu*), an Internet-based slang term, and went on to categorize two types of "weird uncles." The first consisted of ordinary Internet users who were inconsistent in terms of speech and actions. By comparing these individuals' Weibo posts published before and after the South China Sea verdict, the CYL concluded that those discontented with their quality of life and the existing system would call for extremist actions. By contrast, the second type of "weird uncles" was comprised of well-known cultural celebrities who criticized patriotic netizens, as represented by Zhang Ming, Lian Yue, and Wuyue Sanren. In its first essay, the CYL quoted the posts of Lian Yue and Zhang Ming:

Only two kinds of people talk about patriotism. The first kind are clever liars, usually politicians; the second kind are fools who get excited easily. These two kinds are a perfect match: the former is in charge of harvesting the fruits, and the latter is responsible for participating in all events. I wish them a happy marriage for hundreds of years. (Lian Yue)

In this land, loving one's country is often indivisible from labeling traitors. Assuming there are no apparent traitors, you still have to identify some. You love your country, but you do not love the people living in the country. You randomly label anyone a "traitor" and impose violence on them in terms of language and actions. For some people, the nicest thing about loving one's country is to impose violence on one's compatriots. And these people are only capable of imposing violence on one's countrymen. (Zhang Ming)

By selecting the posts of these famous critics as public targets, the CYL spoke on behalf of the younger generation: "Could you [Lian Yue] not impose such silly labels on us? If you have to impose one, we are the 'gang of memes' (*biaoqingbao dang*), OK?" The CYL's reply to Zhang Ming demonstrated a similar logic: "Teacher, we love our country, but we do not identify traitors. It is your generation's hobby to identify traitors. What we really love is 'memes,' understand?" By sarcastically addressing well-established intellectuals as "teachers" and "your generation," referring to the generation that grew up during the Cultural Revolution, the CYL cleaved the representations of "you" and "us" in two—the old critical intellectuals versus young patriotic netizens. According to the CYL, those in the "you" category seemed to possess authority and yet were hypocritical in that they distorted the intention of patriotic netizens. For the younger generation, playing with memes was of the utmost importance, thereby differing significantly from the Red Guard generation that took action on the streets. Noticeably, in this post, the CYL employed two sets of linguistic constructs to enhance its persuasive appeal. The first discursive system appropriated the socialist rhetoric of "people," "capital," and class. As my analysis of the post "scholarly observations" demonstrates, the CYL employed this oft-used style of official rhetoric to criticize the collaboration between capitalist corporations and the media, including some official media outlets. By contrast, the second discursive system was informal and largely drew on Internet-based slang terms, as exemplified by the CYL's posts on patriotism. In this respect, the CYL defended the Little Pinks and attacked public intellectuals who criticized patriotic netizens.

The second essay, titled "The right way to love one's country," exemplified the CYL's continuous experiment to incorporate popular discourse into the interpretation of patriotism.[83] In this post, the CYL used popular slang terms such as "rich second generation" and "the master of studying" to interpret stories of well-known patriotic figures such as Fang Zhimin and Qian Xuesen. Then the essay listed contemporary figures, ranging from patriotic cartoonists to ordinary, hard-working youth, to illustrate various ways of loving one's country. The article concluded, "There are so many patriots in this country. There are so many proper ways of loving one's country. Why would you have to believe in the silliest one?" This rhetorical question reiterated the CYL's earlier assertion that while playing with memes is a perfect example of patriotism, substantial political actions offline are "silly" and that embracing a dedicated work ethic would be a more productive way to love one's country.

Between July 6 and July 20, the eruption of the Leon Dai incident—due in large part to the active role of the CYL—led to a surge of nationalistic sentiments that were soon transferred to offline actions and subsequently cooled down by the state. The Leon Dai incident speaks volumes about the intertwined relationship between entertainment and politics, as well as the increasingly blurred boundary between playfulness and seriousness in collective actions. If patriotic netizens demonstrate their devotion to "serious play" in these incidents by creating Internet memes and paraphrasing official ideologies, then the CYL's strategies illustrate a case of "playful seriousness,"[84] where official media outlets try hard to sustain the legitimacy of the regime and to test its mobilization power, in an approachable manner. The CYL's capitalization on digital populism and popular culture has played a prominent role during this process. Acting as the defender of Little Pinks, the organization deliberately allied with the post-90s and millennial generations, in the name of the "people." Together, they rebelled against public opinion leaders and incorporated popular rhetoric into the paraphrasing of official discourses. Admittedly, in the comments section, posters' opinions diverged greatly, ranging from support of the CYL or support of Leon Dai and Zhao Wei, to questioning of the CYL's possible manipulation. Nevertheless, the majority of posters identified with the rationale of the CYL and soon marginalized any dissenting voices. In this way, the CYL's adoption of populist strategies and an anti-elitist stance quickly took root among young netizens. More important, the strategies adopted by the CYL showcase the crucial transition of an official culture that reinvents its language and sociality to resonate with popular sentiments. Seen in this light, microblogging accounts such as those belonging to the CYL, *People's Daily*, *China Daily*, and *Voice of China* (*Zhongguo zhisheng*) exemplify the significance of conceptualizing official microblogging accounts as a new form of state propaganda.[85]

Weibo Complaints:
Consumer Activism on the Rise

In addition to the proactive role that state actors assumed to ally with patriotic netizens, new developments in Weibo-based incidents gave way to a focus on everyday civic issues. Instead of directly challenging state authorities, microbloggers turned to issues related to consumers' rights, environments, marginalized class, and so on. In contrast to early Weibo-based incidents, these cases are less sensational in nature, due to the increasingly conservative stance Sina takes, the weakened role of editorial teams, and the decline of investigative journalism. Nevertheless, these seemingly ordinary cases demonstrate how the "politics of mundanity"[86] contribute to raising citizens' awareness about their rights and advocating professionalism in all walks of life. Here I analyze two cases, in which Internet users defended their rights and stimulated in-depth discussions about institutional flaws on Weibo.

Calling for Humane Treatment

On November 9, 2015, Zhang Yang, a journalist based in Liaoning province, went on a business trip to Beijing and boarded the airplane CZ6101 in Shenyang, Liaoning. Shortly after the plane took off, Zhang felt sick and asked a flight attendant of China Southern Airlines to reserve an ambulance for him. However, after the airplane landed, it took fifty minutes before the gate was open. What was even worse, instead of helping Zhang Yang get off the plane, flight attendants and medical staff spent quite some time arguing which party should be responsible for this action. Zhang ended up crawling off the plane by himself. Subsequently, Zhang was sent to Beijing Capital Hospital and then transferred to Beijing Red Cross Emergency Rescue Center, also known as Beijing 999. In both places, Zhang underwent various physical examinations, while the real cause of his pain was not identified. Moreover, medical staff members were quite indifferent to Zhang's suffering, and a doctor repeatedly asked whether Zhang was a drug user. Finally, Zhang's colleagues arrived and took him to Peking University People's Hospital for a surgery. It turned out that Zhang contracted ileus, and by this time, fifteen hours had already passed since he landed in Beijing.

After he recuperated from surgery, Zhang Yang recorded his experience on Weibo under the alias "a somewhat idealistic journalist" (*yige youdian lixiang de jizhe*).[87] Zhang's essay questioned the improper treatment of him by various parties. Thanks to his background in journalism and good writing skills, within a day this essay received more than 7 million visits. Subsequently, Zhang published another two essays that targeted the medical emergency team Beijing 999 and coordination procedures at airports during emergencies.[88] These essays were widely circulated online, and dominant mainstream media, such as *People's Daily* and *China Youth Daily*, expressed their concerns about this issue.[89] The China Southern Airlines immediately responded, visited Zhang in Shenyang, and put the case under investigation. Beijing Red Cross Emergency Rescue Center, however, did not respond to the incident until November 30, when the National Health and Family Planning Commission requested its Beijing division to investigate the case because of the complaint Zhang filed. The response from the Emergency Rescue Center was rather arrogant: "If Zhang Yang is discontent with how he was treated by Beijing 999, he should resort to legal measures to resolve the conflicts between patients and doctors . . . instead of misleading the public and exacerbating the problems."[90] The Center also clarified that Zhang was brought to Beijing Emergency Medical Center, the hospital affiliated with Beijing 999, via a detour because of a "traffic jam and long waitlists in other hospitals." Zhang Yang's point-by-point rebuttal to the Center's statement won massive support from netizens.[91] The hashtags "who will get me off this plane" (*shei lai tai wo xia feiji*) and "Beijing 999" (*jijiu men*) elicited a large number of responses on Weibo. In addition, medical experts contributed to disseminating information about emergency care and pinpointing flaws in existing systems.[92] On December 6, 2015, and under public pressure, the Center finally apologized to Zhang Yang for the improper handling of his medical emergency.

Between November 20 and December 9, 2015, Zhang Yang posted forty-six tweets and five essays related to this incident, updating followers about the progress of his appeal. On the day he received the Center's apology, Zhang wrote a wrap-up essay titled "Tolerance is also powerful." In it, he requested an overhaul of the existing system to improve medical services on three levels: (1) permission of patients to select hospitals based on medical condition, (2) acceleration of information exchange between major hospitals, and (3) communication and bedside manner toward severely ill patients.[93] Zhang forwent compensation packages offered from the parties involved and instead insisted that more attention be devoted to the fundamental issues of emergency care, coordination efforts, and patient-doctor relations. While Zhang Yang's essay series evoked public sympathy toward his suffering and elicited anger toward the unprofessionalism of all parties involved, his writings ultimately are significant because they foreground pragmatic, rational solutions to real-world problems.

Defending Consumers' Rights

If commenting on current affairs involves high stakes, then defending consumers' rights falls into a safer zone of contention. The advent of Weibo in China opens new avenues for consumers to file complaints since users may easily direct their messages to CEOs of commercial companies. The public sharing of individual complaints eases the process of collective supervision, which urges businesses to be more responsive to customers' needs. Well-known figures, including television host Meng Fei, writers Liu Liu and Jiang Fangzhou, and publisher Hong Huang, are all outspoken about defending their rights as consumers. They share with fans the frustrations they experience when dealing with customer service. These publicized experiences help resolve matters immediately because of these figures' established fame. More important, they function as spokespersons of ordinary people and call for merchants to adhere to professional ethics. A case in point is how Liu Liu, a well-known writer, wrote and reflected about her experience of dealing with the customer service at Jingdong (JD), an influential e-commerce company, and Tiantian Orchard, fruit supplier of Jingdong. On July 11, 2015, Liu Liu posted pictures of rotten mangosteens she purchased from Jingdong on her Weibo. She had requested Jingdong to refund her, yet after a lengthy process of dealing with the customer service, her request was rejected. Ironically, right after Liu Liu publicized her experience, she received an apology phone call from Tiantian Orchard. Within half an hour the customer service of Jingdong called and promised a full refund. Liu Liu posted her reply on Weibo: "I have tried to communicate with you [Tiantian Orchard] so many times. I did whatever you asked and uploaded pictures. I talked with the customer service at Jingdong as well. All were futile. Once I publicized this matter on Weibo, you promised a refund right away. Are you here just to cheat ordinary customers? Forget about the money."[94] Many Internet users responded to this post and shared their unpleasant experiences of dealing with Jingdong in the comments section. Liu Liu published an essay titled "All I Want Is Fairness" to make a formal request to her readers. Portions of the essay read as follows:[95]

> If you do a key word search "complaints" on my Weibo, you will see all kinds of follow-up comments, ranging from hundreds to thousands. All these posters had similar experiences, yet they appealed over and over again, to no avail. If you live in China, with no fame, power, or money, you cannot live a normal life. You devote most of your energy to matters that have nothing to do with work, creativity, and happiness.
>
> For the sake of our children and the future of our nation, I hope that everyone, from now on, may treat others politely and with respect. If you do so, you will reduce your chance of experiencing frustrations in your own life.

Similar to the case of Zhang Yang, Liu Liu pointed out some of the fundamental problems of contemporary Chinese society: (1) the lack of integrity of business corporations, and (2) the conditional implementation of rules, worshipping the powerful while neglecting the ordinary. The complaints that Hong Huang and Jiang Fangzhou published on Weibo reflected similar logic. On November 30, 2017, Hong Huang filed a complaint to Geli, the domestic electronic service provider, on her Weibo: "As environmentalists, we purchased your floor heating system last year. For two winters, room temperature was so low that we took turns catching colds. The system breaks down easily and customer service is terrible. You agreed to visit us the day before yesterday; still nobody has dropped by as of today."[96] The customer service then quickly responded, and Hong replied: "Thank you. But I seriously hope you don't make me be a bitch each time. Only when I complain in front of netizens do you actually take care of things. We've been calling for three days. You either run out of parts or you don't have time. Or you schedule a visit but then bail on us." By the same token, Jiang Fangzhou's complaints about dishonest sales tricks of Ctrip, a travel service provider, on December 5, 2015, received more than 3,000 follow-up posts.[97] Jiang also wrote a long tweet to summarize all the tricks she figured out and warned others to learn from her lessons.[98]

These Weibo-based complaints pertaining to consumers' experiences, particularly from well-known figures, shifted the power of digital witnessing into public supervision, thereby pushing service providers to improve the status quo. When formal channels of supervision failed, Internet users, influential figures, and their fans assumed the role. Together, these scattered incidents challenged the monopoly and arrogance of business corporations, urged business enterprises to adhere to professionalism, and focused on catalyzing lasting changes, one step at a time.

Conclusion

This chapter probes Weibo-based incidents through the analytical lens of digital witnessing and its evolving trajectories since 2009. The forging of "Weibo publics," albeit "flashy,"[99] illustrates how social elites, ordinary users, traditional media, and commercial portals each take up different positions, enjoy different degrees of visibility, and fulfill their roles as all take stock of current happenings online. Seen in this light, the Chinese microblogosphere best exemplifies the mutually adaptive process between the state, media, and society. In the case of the high-speed rail crash and the Guo Meimei incident, digital witnessing initiated by eyewitnesses, journalists, and local residents in Wenzhou challenged the credibility of state authorities and pushed for information transparency. Traditional journalism also played an important role in incorporating online findings into journalistic reports, thereby carrying out the mission to uncover the truth. Digital witnessing, thus, not only fostered the dissemination of valuable firsthand information from witnesses' viewpoints, but it also celebrated the sense of solidarity among citizens who shared grievances and anger, and fought against social injustice. By contrast, the confessions of Guo Meimei and Xue Manzi illustrate how the state turned to traditional means of witnessing to restore authority. Appropriating legal terms such as "court trial" and "on the scene," the release of court footage, alongside witnesses' testimonies, underscored the credibility of these information. Moreover, by highlighting the moral dimension of both cases, state media diverted public attention from issues related to public domain, like corruption and charity work, to topics about private lives, like sexual transactions. By these means, state media reduce the extent to which these incidents elicit more in-depth discussions pertaining to public issues. Further, the Leon Dai incident paints a picture of how state media sectors learn to manipulate collective witnessing for their own benefits. Amid the rising tide of cyber nationalism in 2016, patriotic netizens were mobilized to ally with the Communist Youth League of China to continue on campaigns against cultural elites. Therefore, digital witnessing on Weibo not only transforms passive spectators into active agents who challenge state authorities, but it is also subject to the manipulation of official media in their own interests.

Furthermore, the functions of digital witnessing on Weibo are constantly shaped by technological affordances, sociopolitical circumstances, adjustment of corporate strategies, and the veritable tide of demographic changes in Weibo users. Early cases of digital witnessing highlighted the essential role of Weibo in the timely dissemination of information and mobilization of collective actions. Sina's then self-positioning as a "news and information platform" facilitated this process, thanks in large part to editorial teams'

role in setting up special topic pages and collecting all related information on time-sensitive issues.[100] Since around 2013, following the changing
sociopolitical circumstances, content of digital witnessing has shied away
from head-to-head confrontation against the Chinese state. Recent cases
of digital witnessing focused on issues pertaining to everyday life, such as
healthcare, medical emergency, and defense of consumers' rights. Moreover,
Weibo's enhanced collaboration with traditional media outlets, alongside
Sina's expansion of its user base into third- and fourth-tier cities in China,
consolidates Weibo's status as a mainstream media outlet. Newer initiatives
to commodify Weibo, as exemplified by the predominance of live broadcasts,
monetization of original content, and increasing number of social influencers, accentuate the transition of Weibo from its early emphasis on news
media into a "platformatized corporation" (*pingtai xing gongsi*) that aims at
bridging content producers and consumers.[101] Some of the examples include
establishing connections between online retailers and their customers, writers and their readers, short-form video producers and their audiences, film
critics and their followers, and celebrities and their fans. These endeavors to
commodify original content not only factor into a changing connotation of
digital witnessing but also herald the advent of monetizing user-generated
content through networks of fan labor in the age of mobile applications.
As the next chapter will make clear, this trajectory would not bode well for
traditional media.

7 WECHAT

An Inflorescence of Content Production

IN 2011, Tencent released a video to advertise its QQ platform,[1] an instant communication software that also provides games, music, shopping, blog and microblog hosting, and movies. QQ began in 1999 as a messaging software that imitated the functions of AOL-owned ICQ. The two-minute promotional video reminds netizens of the beginnings of their lives online and shows them how QQ has changed the ways in which people connect with family and friends. The clip's narrative involves a Chinese family whose son experiences hardship while studying and working in the US. On the eve of the Lunar New Year, the son video-chats with his parents via QQ and tries to hide a broken arm, suffered during an accident while on his way to deliver Chinese food. Through the computer screen he sees freshly prepared dumplings, the traditional Chinese food served to celebrate the Lunar New Year. Food back home, which indicates love, cultural tradition, and family bonds, is contrasted with food in America, which is the means by which the male protagonist makes a living, in a life abroad full of difficulties and loneliness. These different connotations of food, seen across geographical boundaries, foreground the value of family bonds, while QQ, the communicative tool, fosters mutual understanding among family members. The last line of the commercial, "twelve years of companionship, Tencent," underscores the fact this Internet company has grown along with China's first generation of Internet users, both young and old.

Tencent's companionship of Chinese netizens soon reached another milestone with the launch of QQ's successor, WeChat, in 2011. Although these two products share many similar features—including group chat, file sharing, and location-based search—the birth of WeChat symbolized the new age of mobile Internet and reaffirmed the leading role of Tencent in the global market. A multifunctional platform, WeChat enables a host of users' daily activities, ranging from ordering food and booking movie tickets to sharing personal experiences to seeking information and socializing with friends, family, and coworkers. As the app that accounts for the largest share of data consumption within China, WeChat promotes a lifestyle that is popular among Chinese users, foreigners living in China, and users in overseas markets.[2] On average, a user spends sixty-six minutes per day on WeChat,[3] and the international version of WeChat has more than 100 million users residing in over 200 countries.[4]

The enormous popularity of WeChat has stimulated strong interest among researchers. In addition to addressing the democratic implications of this platform,[5] existing scholarship has examined the role that WeChat has played in catalyzing new forms of social events[6] and civic engagement activities, like microphilanthropy,[7] and promoting ethnic cultures.[8] Scholars have also investigated the use of WeChat by specific groups, such as senior citizens and college students,[9] and have studied the factors that motivate users to share articles in their "moments" section.[10] Although these studies have contributed to our understanding of user behaviors and the functions of WeChat, the ways in which WeChat has revolutionized the commodification, dissemination, and production of original content have received little critical attention. Nevertheless, the extent to which public accounts, also known as "official accounts" and hailed as the most innovative feature of WeChat,[11] stimulate the flourishing of self-media (*zi meiti*) is unprecedented in China's Internet history. Moreover, the integration of two functions, content publishing and content commodification, into one platform has exerted tremendous influence on the media industry.[12]

This chapter makes inroads into this uncharted territory, working to demystify the immense popularity of WeChat public accounts. I first delineate the evolution of self-publishing, from the age of Bulletin Board Systems

(BBSs) to the emergence of public accounts, and analyze how public accounts have reshaped the modes of reading, writing, publishing, and circulating essays on small screens. Then, I engage in a close reading of Mi Meng's essays, taken from one of the most controversial WeChat public accounts. I argue that Mi Meng's transition from a journalist to a digital influencer illustrates her responses to the changing ethos of the wider media environment. In particular, I examine Mi Meng's timely capitalization on the predominant social sentiment of feeling like a failure in the face of the increasing income gap and sense of social precariousness, and chart how this capitalization paved the way for her sensational rise. Paradoxically, this era of precarity accounted for the sudden downfall of Mi Meng's commercial empire in early 2019. Last, I address how the involvement of fan labor, personal branding, and networking capacity characterizes content production and its monetization in the age of WeChat.

From BBSs to Public Accounts

By involving a large number of players, including individuals, institutions, enterprises, and governments, WeChat public accounts have significantly advanced the trend of self-publishing that has appeared in the years since the Internet was introduced to China. BBSs have cultivated the rise of a variety of amateur attention agents, ranging from online opinion leaders to the first generation of Internet writers, many of whom soon signed contracts with publishing houses. Collective intelligence featured in reading and commenting on online content is essential to the productivity of discussions emerging on BBS, but in contrast to self-publishing in the form of installments on BBS, blog entries tend to feature longer essays and highlight individual authorship. As the Chinese translation of the word "blogger" (*bozhu*) shows, a blogger is considered the "host" of a blog, while visitors are viewed as guests or friends (*boyou*) whom the host gradually gets to know. In addition to the numerous celebrities who began to blog, a large number of grassroots bloggers emerged, writing about food, travel, fashion, and photography. Some of these bloggers have since transitioned into writing professionally and have built their cult followings. The advent of microblogging, with Weibo, reinvented the feature of self-publishing,

transforming it into self-broadcasting, since Weibo enables the instanta-
neous dissemination of information in the case of time-sensitive events.
Moreover, Weibo invented the "long tweet" (*chang weibo*) feature to incorporate the function of blogging into the microblogging platform, incentiv-
izing this in 2014 through the integration of a payment function. Readers
could "tip" (*dashang*) the writers they liked, while the "paid content" (*fufei
yuedu*) feature required readers to either make payment before accessing
the full text of a post or to pay a subscription fee on a weekly, monthly, or
yearly basis. These moves adapted the common practices of pay-per-read
originating from literary websites and monetized user-generated content
on a massive scale.

WeChat public accounts advanced these earlier forms of self-publishing
in several important aspects. To begin with, public accounts may be perceived as an upgraded version of RSS feeds, in that users select the accounts
they want to follow or un-follow at any time. However, the blending of e-
commerce capabilities into the WeChat platform and the prevalent use of
smartphones have galvanized aspiring individuals, media and cultural institutions, private enterprises and small business owners, and governments to
use public accounts in heretofore unknown ways. E-commerce offers flexible
models of commodifying original content on WeChat, ranging from the
production of sponsored content to the marketing of personal brands or the
offering of monetary rewards for content contributors. By connecting content
generators with content consumers via public accounts, Tencent functions as
a content censor that complies with state rules and protects the copyright of
original content contributors.[13] Therefore, unlike Sina with its editorial teams,
Tencent plays a minimal role in promoting content on public accounts. The
corporation grants individual account operators the liberty and responsibility to engage their audience and sustain their interest. Consequently, it
is vital that account operators maintain an intimate relationship with their
followers to ensure the survival of their public accounts in the competitive
mobile sphere. Most public accounts regularly solicit reader submissions,
rewarding the authors of selected submissions, and screen reader comments
to identify their preferences and determine possible content topics. In addition, the interface of mobile screens offers a more intimate space for social

influencers to engage fans. Thus, WeChat public accounts promote a different kind of celebrity culture, one that emphasizes the ordinariness of content contributors instead of celebrating extraordinariness, as seen in the case of celebrity blogging.

Second, public accounts decentralize the process of content production and information dissemination. Given that public accounts may update only once daily, this rule limits the scope of coverage for each account and diversifies content offerings in a marketplace that covers topics as diverse as education and entertainment, art and history, fashion and comics, film reviews and relationship counseling. An account's popularity depends entirely on readers' willingness to share the content in their "friend's circle" (*pengyou quan*) and groups. Given that each reader's social circles vary, this circulation chain is quietly powerful. Relatedly, the number of visits to a public account an essay generates is not always visible to viewers. If an essay creates fewer than 100,000 page views, the number of visits is displayed at the bottom of the page. Essays that generate more than 100,000 visits carry only a symbol "100,000+" (10*wan jia*) at the bottom, indicating the popularity of the content, while the specific number of page views is not disclosed. The total number of subscribers to an account is also invisible to the public.

Third, as the content published on public accounts is designed to accommodate reading on small screens, the style and design of WeChat essays differ from articles published on websites and in print media. Typically, an account promotes one headline essay each day, along with one to four secondary essays. Since WeChat users need to first click on the title before accessing the content, titles are designed to create suspense or sensation. One common practice is to establish a connection between the content of an essay and some breaking news items or entertainment gossip. For instance, an essay published on an account specializing in comics and photography was titled: "If you are bitten by a fierce dog, there might be a vaccination. However, if you are bitten by evil people, there are no solutions."[14] This title comments on the social scandal that ensued from hundreds of thousands of Chinese children being injected with faulty vaccines.[15] The established connection between the social scandal about faulty vaccines and the author's response drives the reader to open the page. Another title of an essay published on a fashion-related account stated: "Everyone's praising Gao Yuanyuan's new hairstyle. But do you know about her past hair faux pas?"[16] As these two examples show, account holders tend to use titles to tell a miniature narrative in one sentence, to play on suspense and sensation, and to appeal emotionally to readers. Thus, titles of WeChat essays tend to be longer than those of traditional media articles and of articles found on websites. On average, the title of a WeChat essay consists of 25.1 characters, while the average number of characters for print media and websites-hosted articles is 16.1.[17] The more characters a title has, the more information the title is likely to offer, thereby increasing the probability that readers will click on the essay. Additionally, the layout of WeChat essays differs from BBS posts, tweets, and blog entries. Because of the shorter attention span for users of smartphones and tablets, essays on public accounts often intermit text with images, emoticons, and short-form videos to sustain user interest. In most cases, essays on public accounts average between 900 and 1,500 characters, which translates to a three- to five-minute read time. Key points are often highlighted to make it convenient for readers to skim.

The production, consumption, and publication of original content on public accounts offer a whole new experience of reading essays, interacting with writers, and sustaining writing as a business. As of September 2017, there were 20 million registered WeChat official accounts.[18] Among these accounts, the massive growth of personal media accounts is the most phenomenal, due in large part to the drastic decrease in interest in print media, especially newspapers, since the second decade of the new millennium. This sharp decline in print media provided the perfect timing for media professionals and institutions to explore alternative opportunities. Hoping for a career breakthrough, a large number of media professionals, particularly those in the fields of news and entertainment, resigned from their previous positions and created their own media platforms on WeChat.[19] Some of the well-known examples are Wang Xiaolei, Huang Tongtong, Fang Yimin, Ma Ling, Meng Jing, Huang Zhangjin, and Cheng Yan. These individuals previously worked for a variety of influential institutions, ranging from the official Xinhua News Agency to the commercial mainstream media outlet *Sanlian Newsweek* and the liberal-leaning newspaper *Southern Metropolis*

Daily. These professionals' training in journalism, their sensitivity to current events, their established media connections, and their existing fan bases prepared their rise to national prominence in the age of WeChat. Indeed, these figures host some of the most influential public accounts, which showcase a diversification of the specialized content market. For instance, "Liushen Lei Lei Reads Jin Yong" (*Liushen Leilei du Jin Yong*) integrates the writer's reading of the work of martial arts fiction writer Jin Yong into a discussion of contemporary issues, such as food and festivals. "Master Gu" (*Gu ye*) offers innovative interpretations of famous literary or artistic works, particularly paintings, and establishes connections between these works and aspects of readers' everyday lives, like the struggle with procrastination or a fondness for popular dramas. Fashion-related accounts, such as "Becky's Fantasy" (*Li Beika de yixiang shijie*), "Yu Xiaoge," and "Shiliupo's Report" (*Shiliupo baogao*), teach readers about name brands and share tips for matching clothes and doing makeup. The enormous popularity of these accounts delivers the promise of content entrepreneurship in the age of WeChat, while creating a buffer zone from social tensions.

Chicken Soup for the Soul, Chinese Style

The year 2012 witnessed the formal debut of "the Chinese dream" as the new propaganda slogan that endeavored to redefine China's position in the global world order. If this vision of "national rejuvenation" speaks of a confidence about hope for a bright future, then the emergence of the most popular Internet meme in the same year, "*diaosi*," offers an alternative interpretation of "hope." As a gendered term, "*diao*" refers to male genitals, while "*si*" means "hair" or "string." Originating from a forum on Baidu Tieba frequented by fans of Li Yi, a mediocre soccer player, the term became a synonym for a less desirable kind of man characterized by the words "short, ugly, and poor" (*ai cuo qiong*), in contrast to the idealized type of man characterized by the description "tall, rich, and handsome" (*gao fu shuai*).[20] Some of the prominent traits of "*diaosi*" are their lack of self-esteem, their habit of taking pleasure in small victories, and their seeking of satisfaction from those who seem to be more miserable than they are.[21] Between 2012 and 2015, the release of two influential web-based video series,

Diors Man (*Diaosi nanshi*, 2012–15) and *Never Expect* (*Wanwan meixiang-dao*, 2013–15), furthered the popularity of *diaosi* culture. These mini-series displayed hilarious scenarios in which disadvantaged men enjoyed taking advantage of others and celebrated vulgarity in every aspect of life.[22] Very soon, the scope of "*diaosi*" was extended to women. The term "short, fat, and round" (*ai fei yuan*) came to be synonymous with female "losers" who are poor and lack physical attractiveness, while desirable women are summarized as being "white, rich, and pretty" (*bai fu mei*).

Alongside the prevalence of official narratives about China's rising economic and military power, the popularity of *diaosi*-related discourses speaks volumes about the sense of disillusionment shared by individuals in contemporary society.[23] The ambiguous relationship between hope and disillusionment, between confidence and self-abasement, characterizes the zeitgeist of the era. In her insightful analysis of the memes relating to "losers," Marcella Szablewicz argues that urban youth have embraced the expression "*diaosi*" to challenge mainstream society's narrowly defined, materialistic model of success.[24] These self-proclaimed "losers" rely on the use of vulgarity and self-deprecation to celebrate their alternative identities. Moreover, these shared linguistic practices react against the rigid style of official discourse and foster the process of self-identification and community building among underprivileged groups.[25] The culture of losers, however, is "amorphous" and "contradictory"[26] in the sense that, when granted the opportunity, this same group of youths also tends to assimilate into mainstream society.

The connotations of *diaosi* quickly moved beyond the realm of youth subculture and the focus on new categories of femininities and masculinities. Indeed, the term is now widely employed to convey the prevalent feeling of precariousness that is shared by the majority of society, including such seemingly disparate groups as young college students, migrant workers, and members of the upper and middle classes. In 2013, around 500 million Chinese self-identified as *diaosi*.[27] In 2014, a survey of residents in fifty Chinese cities revealed that 62.2 percent of those aged between twenty-one and thirty identified themselves as *diaosi*.[28] In the face of a narrowing window for upward mobility, the *diaosi* mentality illustrates a shared social sentiment among urban dwellers who feel a lack of control over many aspects of their lives. By calling themselves "losers," they convey their sense of cynicism in the face of skyrocketing housing prices, environmental problems, food safety concerns, burdensome medical expenses, unequal distribution of resources, and a general decline of social trust. Read in this light, the enormous popularity of inspirational stories on WeChat public accounts may be perceived as a search for an antidote to the prevalent *diaosi* mentality, in an effort to provide hope, however ephemeral, for those who are struggling to cope with difficulties in their everyday lives.

In 2016, the Kantar Group released a report on the fifty most popular public accounts on WeChat. The findings revealed an explosive growth of official accounts dealing with relationship issues. In 2014, three out of the top fifty accounts fell into this category, while in 2016, nineteen out of the top fifty accounts were about relationship issues, with a particular focus on inspirational stories.[29] The inundation of the category with motivational stories formed a symbiotic relationship with the predominant culture of "losers" online. In the face of declining opportunities for social advancement for young people, even official media outlets, as represented by the WeChat account of *People's Daily*, began to send out motivational speeches on a daily basis. Personal media accounts, on topics ranging from relationship counseling to fashion, and entertainment gossip to art appreciation, complemented these official channels and functioned as a more effective buffer for social tensions. My analysis of Mi Meng, operator of one of the most phenomenal public accounts, demonstrates how her timely resonance with this popular sentiment accounted for her rapid rise to popularity.

The Rise of Mi Meng: Major Controversies

The rise of Mi Meng to national prominence exemplifies the strategic capitalization on the predominant *diaosi* sentiment, while her career trajectory inspires those who are struggling to climb the social ladder, as she, a girl from a small Sichuanese city, worked her way up from career journalism to senior editor-in-chief of the renowned *Southern Metropolis Daily*. Originally named Ma Ling (b. 1976), Mi Meng obtained a master's degree in classical literature from Shandong University. In 2002, Mi Meng joined the renowned *Southern Metropolis Daily* in Shenzhen and began her career as a journalist for the Supplement Department. She worked her way up to senior editor-in-chief and authored several books and essay collections. In 2014, because of the drastic decline in print media, Mi Meng resigned from her position and started her own film and television production company. Within ten months, she had spent her entire investment of 4 million RMB (640,000 USD) in vain. Hoping to build more effective networks, Mi Meng brought her core team to Beijing and started over.

The public accounts of WeChat offered an accidental opportunity for Mi Meng to recover from her past failure. Prior to her WeChat fame, Mi Meng occasionally wrote about history, entertainment gossip, and film and television drama reviews online as a hobby, but she did not seriously consider managing a public account until the failure of her media startup. In September 2015, Mi Meng formally launched her public account and updated it with essays on a daily basis. Very soon, her fourth essay, titled "Why you care about appearances," garnered more than 100,000 visits,[30] a number that many account operators yearned to reach. In the days that followed, Mi Meng's film reviews of *Chronicles of the Ghostly Tribe* (*Jiuceng yaota*), *Lost in Hong Kong* (*Gang jiong*), and *Goodbye Mr. Loser* (*Xialuote fannao*) attracted an increase in followers by the tens of thousands. Within two months, Mi Meng's following had increased to 400,000 fans. As of January 2018, Mi Meng had more than 8 million followers; it took over three years for "Luoji Siwei," another well-known WeChat account, to achieve the same level of popularity.[31] Female readers constituted 85 percent of Mi Meng's fan base, most of whom were college students, white-collar workers, or housewives. Each day, Mi Meng promoted two essays: a headline article and a secondary essay. On average, each headline article received 2 million views, while the secondary essay typically generated more than 1 million reads.[32] Mi Meng's large fan base ensured the advertising value of her account, as it was reported that Mi Meng charged 680,000 RMB (107,969 USD) for a headline essay with embedded advertisement, while a secondary advertising cost 250,000 RMB (39,694 USD).[33]

Mi Meng's meteoric rise to prominence in 2016 surprised some media observers, who had predicted an end to the fast growth of public accounts. On the one hand, Mi Meng is an example of those media professionals who successfully make the transition to being content entrepreneurs. Thus, her story justifies the excessive promotion of inspirational stories on her account, since she made her own name as one of the most influential microcelebrities in the age of WeChat, with no illustrious family background or strong financial backing to guarantee her success. On the other hand, Mi Meng's new start ushered in a staggering change to her writing style and the value system represented in her essays. As a result, her former colleagues and readers bemoaned the disappearance of her talent and trademark incisive analysis of cultural phenomena. In July 2016, Mi Meng wrote an essay on patriotism that provoked drastic backlash among elite groups, to the extent that quite a few media professionals blacklisted her on their WeChat accounts. Titled "My country, forever shall I love you and forever shall I be in tears,"[34] this essay resonated with the high tide of popular nationalism against the backdrop of the United Nations tribunal's 2016 ruling that China's claims of sovereignty over the South China Sea were invalid. The essay began by showing an image of the poster "Only this can be China, and not one bit less," created by the *People's Daily*'s Weibo account. Then, Mi Meng showed screenshots of a conversation she had with a friend and explained that she had blocked this friend because of their differing stances on patriotism. She did not regret blocking this person, but only wished she had done it sooner. She wrote:

Okay, let me tell you why I love China.

Our great China has gourmet food! Delicious! Yum! What is the best patriotic education? Go abroad! Every time you go abroad, it is a reinforcement and baptism of patriotism. It is fine to occasionally eat foreign food, but you will collapse if you end up doing so every day.

The most patriotic part of my body is my stomach. Small-town food in China could easily beat the food in quite a few foreign countries.

Life in our great country is: Super! Convenient! I went to Macy's in the United States with a few friends. We wanted to take a taxi to get back to the hotel, but the Macy's was in a suburb in the middle of nowhere. We waited for more than an hour by the highway and still couldn't hail a taxi. Later, some American friends helped us flag one down. When the driver finally arrived, I almost burst into tears.[35]

As in the QQ promotional video described at the beginning of this chapter, the inconvenience and difficulty of living abroad is emphasized here, to highlight the appeal of the homeland. The promotional video focuses on an individual's experience to celebrate the power of communication technologies that transcend geographic boundaries. In contrast, Mi Meng's essay establishes causality between personal preferences and lifestyles and the urge to love one's motherland, criticizing those who raise doubts about patriotism.

Mi Meng's rationale and actions accord with those of such patriotic netizens as the Little Pinks. They organized the Diba Expedition, in January 2016, to playfully protest the pro-Taiwanese independence stance, using the emoticons evoked by gourmet food and beautiful scenery. Because of the similarities in their ideologies, Mi Meng's writing offended many liberal-leaning media professionals who were critical of the Little Pinks. Mi Meng's former colleagues argued that she sold her audience core values that she would not even believe herself.[36] Sun Xuyang, a former journalist for *Southern Metropolis Daily*, commented that Mi Meng's essay demonstrated opportunism. Jiang Yingshuang, also a former journalist for *Southern Metropolis Daily*, argued against the essay's logic, which deliberately conflated such disparate concepts as the nation, ruling powers, and gourmet food: "If she really is a senior media professional, it is ridiculous to me that she wrote such stuff."[37] In addition to these criticisms, netizens retrieved Mi Meng's earlier Weibo posts on similar issues to demonstrate the inconsistency of her positions. Back in 2011, in reference to the issue of food safety, Mi Meng sarcastically wrote two commentaries:

> Even sweet potato vermicelli could be mixed with ink and paraffin wax . . . finally there is hope for the internalization of Chinese cuisine. When we have western food, they often ask, "How would you like your [steak] cooked?" Now, we can ask, "How much poison would you like in your food: twenty percent, fifty percent, or seventy percent?"[38]
>
> With the exception of your honorable country (*gui guo*), where else could you see such miracles?[39]

In another post on contemporary Chinese films, she satirized patriotism:

I forgot to mention that although I dislike the core values of *American Dreams in China*, it is still better than *So Young*. . . . One line in *So Young* claims: "Love a person, just the way you love the motherland." That is simply too terrifying (I repeat, patriotism is not unrequited love, but incest).[40]

As these examples show, instead of feverishly praising the greatness of Chinese food, the first two posts criticize the issue of food safety in China. Mi Meng uses the word "miracle" to satirize the official comment on the survival of the two-and-a-half-year-old girl Yiyi as a "miracle" during the Wenzhou high-speed rail incident in 2011, and criticizes the state's inept handling of important matters pertaining to citizens' everyday lives. While Mi Meng distances herself from the nation by employing the term "your honorable country" (*gui guo*), her WeChat essay used "our great China" (*women da Zhongguo*) to evoke a sense of belonging and national pride among readers. As for the third Weibo post, by calling patriotism "paraphilia," Mi Meng draws a distinction between mutual affection between people and the act of loving the nation. Because of Mi Meng's strikingly inconsistent stances on these issues, she was criticized for blindly catering to audience tastes and, moreover, was charged with creating a media sensation through her use of profanity. Nevertheless, in Mi Meng's defense, public accounts exemplify an emerging mobile screen culture that is fragmented, entertainment-oriented, and forthright.[41] Therefore, Mi Meng's change of writing style and subject only illustrates her strategy of adjustment to fit into the changing technologically mediated media sphere.

Performed "Losers" Win

Mi Meng's experience as a senior editor-in-chief prepared her well for her transition into the role of operator of a public account. Knowing well the kind of content and topics that attract readers, Mi Meng mostly wrote about relationship issues, career tips, parenting, current events, and entertainment news. Her opinions were given in a straightforward manner, and stories were based on personal experiences, readers' inquiries, interviews, and current affairs. These essays resonated with the sense of social precariousness prevalent among her readers—a group that ranged from college students to young professionals to members of the middle class—albeit for different reasons. Consequently, Mi Meng's essays offered a channel for her reading public to quickly vent their frustrations by the means of indecency and self-mockery. While echoing the self-proclaimed "losers" who mock the societal obsession with material success, Mi Meng's rags-to-riches stories convinced her fans to follow her advice to achieve their own future material success, effectively functioning as motivational speeches for the younger generation.

As we have begun to see, Mi Meng's essays illustrate a thorough capitalization on the "loser" mentality to carve out her own market niche. Mi Meng presented herself as a loser, her writings focusing on her traumatic childhood experiences, her humble family background, and the career setbacks she suffered. She explored her father's boastful extramarital affairs, her mother's subsequent bullying by one of her father's mistresses, and her parents' divorce and subsequent tense remarriage. She writes, "The meal I often had when I was little was rice with tears (*yanlei ban fan*). Salty. Not too bad."[42] The line thereby sentimentalized this latter tension and foreshadowed later writings that illustrated her status as a "loser"—a result of her early family problems. By the same token, her essay series on the failure of her first startup company employed a self-mocking tone to ridicule the many rookie mistakes she made.[43] In contrast to these miserable past experiences, a happy present, achieved through marriage and a career breakthrough, demonstrated the possibility of transcending one's "loser" status. Mi Meng presented her marriage life as ideal, with a loyal husband and lovely son, right up until her acknowledgment of her divorce in September 2018. Her record of personal experiences easily struck a chord with readers who suffered from bad parental or marital relationships, meanwhile inspiring them not to give up their pursuit of happiness.

If these lyrical essays fit into the conventional category of "chicken soup for the soul," then a more typical style of Mi Meng's essays is marked by the creation of suspense, the frequent use of curse words to create sensational effects, the adoption of a self-deprecating tone, and the use of clickbait titles to intrigue readers. As Mi Meng's signature line stated, "I am a hooligan woman (*nü liumang*). Please do not take advantage of me." As with the rough tone taken in this signature, Mi Meng's frequent use of curse words in her essays formed a strong contrast between her background as a well-educated, middle-class woman and her performed identity as a rebellious "loser." In the face of the increasing income inequality in Chinese society, Mi Meng drew a line between herself and the privileged class. Additionally, Mi Meng's self-portrayal accorded with the common perception of female losers: short, fat, and round. She emphasized a lack of confidence about her appearance that she has felt since she was little, and asserted that her media appearances have been photoshopped to such an extent that these images no longer look like her. She constantly employed self-mockery to highlight her unattractive appearance and emphasized her lack of cosmopolitan experiences. For example, Mi Meng recorded the moment when she bumped into one of her employees at an airport. Noticing that the employee was walking to the business lounge, she stopped him, only to find out that her employee was indeed flying business class, while she, the boss, was flying economy.[44] Another example of performing the role of "losers" is as follows:

> The day before yesterday, I had a business meeting with a friend in an upscale hotel. I ordered a glass of orange juice, 98 RMB [15 USD]. So expensive. I drank it right away and looked around. All the rich people were sipping elegantly. I had to lick my lips. Sigh. It's such a hassle to be a rich person. Let me be myself.
>   Then the waiter asked me, "Would you like another cup?"
>   My brain screamed, "Do you think I'm a fool? 98 RMB a cup, who the hell would order another one?!"
>   After we got out, my assistant asked me: "Since you can get a free refill, how come you didn't want another cup?"
>   What? I *am* an idiot. Can I go back and get my refill?[45]

In Mi Meng's self-portrayal, a "loser" is one who lacks refined manners, takes pleasure in a small gain, and does not have a cosmopolitan outlook. Additionally, Mi Meng's frequent use of vulgarity and profanity constitutes a signature style that intended to mark her status as a "loser." Notably, Mi Meng's Weibo posts from 2010 to 2015 exhibited traces of vulgar linguistic choices. In these cases, the targets of this vulgarity were the state authorities and government. In the age of WeChat, however, the purpose of Mi Meng's curse words and profanity was to highlight the "loser" mentality to resonate with popular sentiments. As a well-educated woman, who majored in Chinese literature, Mi Meng easily created a sensation with her use of profanity. A quick search of her essay titles highlights the frequent appearance of such words as slut (*jianren*), cunt (*bi*), sucker (*shabi*), and aphrodisiac (*chunyao*). Some examples include: "WTF! My son is out of school" (*Mengbile! Wode erzi shixuele*), and "Life is not just about poetry and faraway places. It is also full of stupid cunts" (*Shenghuo bu zhiyou shi he yuanfang, haiyou shabi jiafang*). Indeed, the first essay that brought Mi Meng to the attention of Internet users was titled "To that low bitch: Why the hell should I help you?" (*Zhi jianren: Wo weishenme yao bang ni*). In this essay, Mi Meng denounced those who assume that others are obliged to do them a favor: "You are incapable. Why the hell do you have such a strong sense of entitlement? You wasted more than an hour of my time, and you still feel superior to me? If you run a start-up, you need to have good products. It is so stupid to sell your misery to evoke sympathy, do you not realize that?"[46] Writings like these helped readers to vent frustrations that otherwise would have had no outlet in ordinary social situations.

Furthermore, despite Mi Meng's status as a wealthy businesswoman, she portrays herself in her WeChat essays as a country bumpkin and offers her readers a voyeuristic glimpse into the lifestyle of the upper class in Chinese society. These writings shy away from addressing the root causes of social inequality, but instead teach readers to be content with the status quo. On November 18, 2017, a tragic fire in Beijing led to the brutal eviction of migrant workers from the city.[47] One month after the fire, Mi Meng published an essay that portrayed the living conditions of these "floaters in Beijing" (*beipiao*). Mi Meng grouped her interviewees based on their economic conditions. Notably, this essay emphasized that the poor lived a happy life, while the rich felt anxious and were at times confused. A twenty-two-year-old salesgirl, living in a communal apartment with twenty-five other people, stated: "I am happy. I only regret that I did not come to Beijing earlier." The girl, who paid 3,400 RMB (600 USD) in monthly rent, stressed the importance of living a quality life: "Even though I do not own an apartment, I enjoy making my living space a cozy home." In contrast, an actress with a wealthy family who paid 24,000 RMB (4,000 USD) per month for her rent, was confused about her life. The last interviewee, a twenty-seven-year-old man from an illustrious business family, lived in a 1.6 billion RMB (231 million USD) mansion but yearned for family dinners. He also worried about the potential failure of his startup business.[48] The essay concluded:

> We feel that some people are born to be rich while others are born to fall behind. It's really sad. However, those born in wealthy families have their own worries and also face brutal competition.
>
> During our interview, we asked those who were worried about paying their rent: "Since life is so hard, why do you still stay in Beijing?"
>
> One person said, "I know I had a late start. The probability of my dream coming true is low, like 0.0001."
>
> I was about to comfort her.
>
> Then, she went on and said, "however, that 0.0001 is still bigger than 0."[49]

While this post seemed to reference the eviction of the migrant workers from Beijing that had occurred one month earlier, Mi Meng did not comment on this matter. Instead, her strategic presentation of the lives of the rich and the poor seemed to proffer only a false hope for those who are struggling and soothed readers who would never have access to luxurious lifestyles.

If these wealthy singles have worries about their future, then women who marry wealthy men face a different range of challenges. In an essay titled "The difficult life of rich housewives," Mi Meng first exaggerated her shock about the amount of wealth these families possess: "By the way, how many zeros do I need to count to 10 billion?" Then, she listed various challenges these housewives encounter, to convince readers that it is good to be ordinary. Mi Meng presented upper class marriages as a job, since housewives in these marriages need to be prepared for all potential dangers, particularly from mistresses. Mi Meng quoted one interviewee's statement: "You need to make your husband feel that you are smart, but not too smart. If you are not smart, he will be bored; if you are too smart, he will be on guard." Of the job of the housewife, Mi Meng commented, "The most important agenda is to ensure that her husband is highly dependent on her. She needs to play the role of partner, housekeeper, family, friend, lover, and so on. The higher the cost of substituting her, the safer she is."[50] The family life of upper-class housewives differed significantly from that of Mi Meng's own marriage, which, according to her, was based on true love. By showcasing the challenges wealthy singles and couples encounter, Mi Meng's writing endeavored to foster readers' identification with the wealthy, by either explicating their anxieties or applauding their work ethic. Thus, essays on this topic not only satisfied her readers' voyeuristic curiosity about the lives of the upper class but also contributed to consolidating the established social order by making readers feel better about their ordinary lives.

By presenting herself as a "loser," albeit a performed identity, Mi Meng established emotional connections with her fans as she discussed a wide variety of topics, ranging from relationship issues to workplace politics to tips for upward mobility. Segments of her personal experiences, like her family background and career setbacks, were fully appropriated to associate herself with a loser identity. Mi Meng's career turn, on the other hand, exemplified how a "loser" may transition into a "winner" through the magic power of individual effort, a major selling point of her WeChat essays.

Cultivating Affective Ties

An oft-occurring narrative in Mi Meng's essays is her fervent celebration of individual effort, as if personal endeavor were the single determining factor in social advancement. Stories are widely circulated about how she works eighteen hours per day on average. Photos of her typing on the computer while having intravenous therapy inspire fans to copy her strong work ethic. Consequently, Mi Meng's public persona as a hardworking, independent woman, alongside her self-proclaimed feminist stance, has consolidated her role as a mentor among fans. The majority of Mi Meng's fans are female, aged between eighteen and twenty-eight, and residing in metropolitan areas, particularly Guangdong, Shanghai, and Beijing.[51] Central to Mi Meng's philosophy is the importance of financial independence for women; in the case of housewives, a woman must take good care of herself and ensure that her husband is willing to support her. For Mi Meng, a woman, no matter how her situation is, deserves a good quality of life. She believes that economic gain is the basis for this quality of life. In contrast, a man deserves condemnation if he fails to be any of the following: loyal, caring, hard-working, and demonstrating potential for promotion. This line of reasoning easily wins approval from her millions of followers, who are eager to adopt Mi Meng's advice on gender relations and career tips.

Acting as the spokesperson for her female fans, Mi Meng defends women unequivocally, as exemplified by her comments on scandalous celebrity affairs pertaining to gender-related issues. In response to the extramarital affairs of Lin Dan, a renowned badminton player, during his wife Xie Xingfang's pregnancy, Mi Meng published three consecutive essays criticizing disloyal men. The first essay summarized Mi Meng's reflections on her in-depth interviews with two men who had extramarital affairs. Calling the role of the housewife a "high stakes occupation," Mi Meng warned her female readers to think twice before making this life choice. More important, she argued, housewives should protect their financial rights and take good care of themselves. Mi Meng used her own cousin as an example to explain what it means to be a successful housewife. This cousin is the sole owner of two houses purchased by her husband, and she is quite disciplined in her efforts to maintain her physical attractiveness.[52] Since being a housewife is a lifelong career, Mi Meng suggested: "Do not give up on your appearance. Be pretty, even if just for your own sake. . . . We need to love ourselves first and be selfish. Don't make unlimited sacrifices for your husband, or try to save money for him. Because if your husband does not appreciate that, he will be blind to all your efforts."[53] This extract rationalized the mission of housewives—trade beauty and youth for financial wealth—while husbands who violate this rule were ruthlessly called "scumbags" (zha nan) and "trash" (laji). Mi Meng's third essay on the topic responded to Xie Xingfang's defense of her husband and criticized women for tolerating men's wrongdoings:

> That this man dared to have extramarital affairs during his wife's pregnancy proves that he loves only himself. You and your child are not as important as his sexual desire.
>
> It is women's complicity that encourages these men to act unscrupulously.

Our society really endorses double standards.

Disloyal men are always forgiven. Yet if women do the same things, they are bitches.

Frankly speaking, after reading today's news I feel quite hopeless.

Not just because of what Lin Dan and Xie Xingfang said, but also because of others' responses.

People left messages in the comments section of Xie Xingfang's Weibo, and applauded her for taking the big picture into consideration. . . .

Our society seems to be moving backwards.[54]

Morally appealing and emotionally arousing as these writings are, they nevertheless attempt to address complex relationship problems with a simplistic prescription that disloyal husbands should be ostracized, while housewives need to manage their marriage like a business to reduce potential risks. Quite ironically, when Mi Meng reminded housewives to protect their rights and economic freedom, she exhibited little compassion to economically disadvantaged men. For Mi Meng, in addition to disloyalty, another intolerable "sin" men commit is to be content with living in poverty. In an essay titled "Why the Hell Do You Enjoy Living in Poverty," Mi Meng told a story about divorce. Although the husband was a good person, he spent a lot of time playing computer games and did not care about career advancement. The wife was ambitious but could not cope with the pressure of shouldering the financial responsibility for the family alone. Ultimately, the wife asked for a divorce and soon remarried. Mi Meng's story ended with the ex-husband's reflections four years after the divorce: a confession that loving someone meant empowering oneself to manage risks together.[55] However, since Mi Meng's definition of "empowerment" was solely based on a man's economic power, richer women apparently had the automatic right to divorce their less wealthy husbands. Another essay about a breakup conveyed a similar logic, with Mi Meng once again complaining about unambitious men:

A friend of mine said that her boyfriend had been eating ramen for three months to save money. Then, he bought her a designer bag. So, she broke up with him.

They had been dating for 8 years, since they were 21.

She said if he had done this at 21, she would have been moved to tears.

But now they were close to 30 and he still could not afford a 2,000 RMB (300 USD) designer bag. She felt quite desperate.

In the past 8 years she had been promoted four times, while her boy-friend still earned a monthly wage of 2,700 RMB (450 USD).

Even more ridiculously, when women complain about their lack of earning power, men get defensive and ask women: How come you're so materialistic?!!

"Materialistic," fuck that.

Sounds as if she dated you when you were rich.

You have been in poverty for years. She is still with you, simply because she is not "materialistic."

Such is the opinion of many men.

They don't have a sense of family responsibility, they have no sense of urgency, they don't care about the future, and they don't worry about their children.

If they can't afford to buy a house, they say renting a house is not bad.

If they can't afford to raise children in big cities, they say it's not a big deal to send children back to their hometown [to live with grandparents].

When they're middle-aged and still don't have a career, they say ordinariness is the essence of life.

Indeed, they could quite happily live an uneventful life. However, they pass on responsibility, risk, and anxiety to the women around them.

They are indeed carefree, while the women around them are working their asses off.

Pardon my French. Unambitious men are assholes.[56]

These essays reflect the anxiety of most young people in metropolitan cities, amid astronomical housing costs, declining social mobility, and un-equal distribution of resources. Because of these challenging circumstances, committed relationships require teamwork and progress from both sides of the couple to improve their living situation. However, instead of analyzing the root cause of the social inequality that creates "winners" and "losers,"

Mi Meng attributed the success of female winners to their individual effort, as demonstrated by conditions ranging from overwork and constant self-improvement to taking meticulous care of their bodies. In contrast, men's lack of motivation at work was seen to account for their failure in intimate relations, insomuch as they would not be capable of taking care of their spouses. This line of reasoning exaggerated the role of individual effort in securing both career and relationship success in contemporary society. Mi Meng's denouncement of economically disadvantaged men as "irresponsible" reinforces mainstream ideals of masculinity that disproportionately focus on men's economic status. By playing on female readers' intense feelings against male "losers," Mi Meng succeeded in cultivating affective ties with her many female fans.

The Bond between Idol and Idolizer: Fan Labor

In January 2017, a commercial video was released to advertise Mi Meng's brand. Titled "Do not brownnose the world; please yourselves only," the commercial's narrative sets up a binary opposition between "the world" and the self, or "I."[57] "The world" defines women's role as wives and mothers, and accordingly, advocates that women should strive to live stable lives. However, the video suggests that "I," a woman among many, should not really care about what "the world" says, but just listen to her inner voice. This commercial summarizes well the positioning of Mi Meng's WeChat account in the marketplace—a force to fight against conservative societal expectations of women and to encourage them to pursue their passions. Intriguing as this narrative is, it risks reducing the complexity of any social problems to a simplistic statement that "the entire world is wrong," so "you should go your own way." Nevertheless, this inflammatory celebration of individualism among women, devoid of any substantial content, is what connects Mi Meng with her followers. While Mi Meng has incurred some significant criticism for these pro-feminist views, these external disagreements have only forged more cohesive bonding between her and her fans. Whenever controversies arise, Mi Meng publishes essays to defend her fans and shows that she cares about their feelings. In response to some critics' comments that they would not consider marrying Mi Meng's fans, Mi Meng stated:

Sorry, I have to tell the truth.

It doesn't matter whether you want to marry my fans or not, but rather whether they want to marry you.

You really think you have a choice?

To the misogynists: you are not even worthy of picking up my fans' shoes. Go away. The farther, the better.

P.S. Special thanks to my male fans. Although I have said this before, let me say it again.

I often speak from a female standpoint because our society is too male-centered. I want to offer new possibilities.

It's really awesome that you accept that.

Thank you for your understanding and respect.[58]

In another Weibo post, Mi Meng wrote: "To those who attack me, let me tell you this in four characters: It does not matter as long as you are happy (*kaixin jiu hao*). To those who attack my fans, let me also send you four characters: Go to hell (*qu ni ma de*)."[59] When discussing potentially depressing topics, Mi Meng showed concern for her fans' feelings, as this line indicates: "Today's essay must have made you feel depressed. Sorry, I'm just telling the truth. Cheer up. Let me comfort you with movie tickets, OK? . . . I will give two tickets to each fan. This offer applies to the first 50 participants!"[60] All these deeds and expressions aim to make her fans feel good about their loyalty, as their concerns are responded to on a daily basis.

In an effort to maintain and increase bonding with fans, influential public accounts often acknowledge the value of fan labor and raise its visibility in the mobile sphere. In the case of Mi Meng, she regularly solicited fans' submissions about potential essay topics. Some examples have been: "Your most successful dating experience," "Your experience of dealing with horrible kids," and "The secret you would take to the grave."[61] Selected submissions were published, and readers were encouraged to vote for their favorite piece. The winner was awarded 2,000 RMB (350 USD). These selected submissions were often in short form and fun to read. To encourage fans to post comments, from time to time Mi Meng sent out small gifts, like lipstick, to reward the first ten commenters.[62] Devoted fans also got involved in the process of content production. Oftentimes, if Mi Meng's team could not decide on a title prior to the publication of an essay, they invited fans to vote between several titles in closed fan groups.

In contrast to entertainment celebrities, Mi Meng, as a social influencer, is more approachable to her fans because of the everyday engagement she fosters with them, as well as her emphasis on the ordinariness embedded in her public persona. Consequently, Mi Meng's devoted fan base has paved the way for her to make more ambitious career moves. In addition to writing scripts, Mi Meng has expanded her public account into a streamlined production suite. In 2017, Mi Meng's team launched the first New Media Creation Contest to recruit and cultivate talents in writing. This title was in reference to the influential New Concepts Composition Contest launched by the state-sponsored magazine *Sprout* in 1998.[63] The launches of these two contests, about twenty years apart, form an interesting parallel, as both events occurred at a crucial moment for print media. In the late 1990s, the New Concepts Composition Contest was invented to resolve the dire financial situation of *Sprout*. The contest was an explorative move for the magazine to experiment with the market logic of the time. Twenty years later, print media are increasingly marginalized in the face of the digital revolution. If the New Concepts Contest symbolized the beginning of literary commercialization, by cultivating the first generation of popular youth writers like Guo Jingming, Han Han, and Zhang Yueran, then the first New Media Creation Contest thoroughly deconstructed the seriousness of literature and writing. A quick look at the judges invited by both contests illustrates this point. Renowned writers and literature professors were the judges for the New Concepts Contest, while bestselling authors and popular singers, like Zhang Jiajia and Xue Zhiqian, were invited by Mi Meng to identify market tastes. While the New Concepts Contest marked the crucial transformation of print media at the early stage of media commercialization, the design of the New Media Contest symbolized another important juncture of content production driven by digital technologies.

The year 2018 witnessed a full-scale expansion of Mi Meng's WeChat account. The management of Mi Meng's account foregrounded a changing mode of writing, from an author-centered model to one of team production that involved core writers, an editorial team, and fan labor. Mi Meng mentored quite a few writers and coauthored with them on her flagship WeChat account.[64] Subsequently, these core writers created subaccounts (*xiao hao*) that specialized in fashion, e-commerce, retail, and inspirational stories,[65] most representatively "Talent Limited Youth" (*Caihua youxian qingnian*), "I Stay at Home for Another Day" (*Wo you zhai le yi tian*), and "Hong Pangpang." These subaccounts were operated independently and capitalized on Mi Meng's existing resources to conduct extensive market surveys that aimed to understand issues of interests to fans. In turn, these accounts had grown rapidly by proffering content that precisely addressed fans' needs.[66] For instance, "Hong Pangpang," a fashion account launched in April 2018, gathered 400,000 followers within two months.[67] Fans of this account took pleasure in participating in market surveys, expressed excitement when their suggestions were adopted, and felt proud that they were contributing to the popularity of the account.[68] Clearly, maintaining affective ties with fans is crucial in expanding and managing public accounts. While the essence of all personal media accounts is to sell sponsored content to subscribers, the establishment of affective ties with audiences tones down the apparent commercial logic behind the operation of these accounts. Seen in this light, the case of Mi Meng epitomizes the operation methods of influential accounts that capitalize on fan economy, affective labor, and individual pleasure.

Writing in the Age of Social Precarity

As promising as it may have seemed, the rapid expansion of Mi Meng's subaccounts was riddled with controversy. While the public accounts that dealt with fashion and e-commerce were less controversial, subaccounts that published original essays about contemporary issues had to be careful to strike a balance between maintaining Mi Meng's signature style and offering something new to readers. The downfall of Mi Meng in early 2019 not only showcases the problems brought forth by this model of team production but also illustrates the condition of precarity in which every individual is situated—and which, ironically, was one of the major contributing factors in Mi Meng's rise to popularity.

Mi Meng's downfall began with an article published by Talent Limited

Youth—one of Mi Meng's subaccounts—on January 29, 2019, just before the Lunar New Year. Launched on April 1, 2017, Talent Limited Youth targeted readers born after 1995; it gathered 500,000 fans within eight months of its launch.[69] The article, titled "The Death of a Star Student from a Humble Background" (*Yi ge hanmen zhuangyuan zhi si*), dealt with several elements that were commonly featured in Mi Meng's writing in a sensational way: class difference (*hanmen*), academic overachievers (*zhuangyuan*), and tragic death. The essay recorded the life struggle of a young man, Zhou Youze, from a humble family. Zhou enrolled in a top university in China and worked hard to support his parents and younger sister from that point on. He was also a man with integrity, who refused opportunities to make quick money that might harm others. Sadly, Zhou died of cancer at the age of twenty-four and had only 3700.6 RMB (610 USD) in his bank account upon his death. Detailing her interactions with Zhou Youze since their high school years, the narrator of the essay reflected upon the privileges she enjoyed and upon her own comparative lack of integrity.[70] The essay immediately went viral and moved millions of readers. Very soon, however, the piece sparked a controversy that, alongside the intervention of state media, led to WeChat's decision to remove it from the site.

The controversy arose out of the production team's labeling of the essay as "nonfiction" (*fei xugou xiezuo*). To enhance the realism of the writing, the team coupled the text with images that showcased the high school that Zhou Youze attended, the book that the author bequeathed to Zhou Youze, and the upscale neighborhood where the author lived. At the bottom of each photo was a note of when the photo was taken. Additionally, the author made several truth claims at the end of the essay. For example, the author admitted to using a pseudonym for the main character, to protect the privacy of the Zhou family. The choice of "Youze" indicated the author's hope that Zhou would have better options in his next life. The author also urged insiders not to disclose details about the family to the public. In a move that was even more sentimentally appealing, the author announced that she would cover the four-year college tuition for Zhou Youze's younger sister.[71] These narrative choices effectively enhanced the authenticity of this story. However, readers soon discovered that the article contained many factual errors and logical fallacies.[72] The unrealistic portrayal of business meetings with investors—perhaps intended to form a contrast to the simple personality traits of Zhou Youze—made many businesspeople question the credibility of the story.[73] Talent Limited Youth defended the essay's authenticity and claimed to have changed some details to protect the family's privacy. This response ended up backfiring. On the same day, the Weibo account of *People's Daily* criticized the essay's flaws and warned that self-media account operators should be mindful about their role in society.[74] On February 1, 2019, Mi Meng issued a public apology on her WeChat account: "As an influential We Media source, we must shoulder our social responsibility and pass on positive energy and values."[75] She also announced that her Weibo account would be closed permanently and that she would shut down her flagship WeChat account for two months. However, this gesture was deemed "insincere" by *People's Daily*, which judged that:

> Mi Meng's apology letter dodges the real problems and reveals her usual tendency to play on boundaries. It is fine to write for profit . . . but it's not okay to always over-sensationalize things or resort to sappy stories, and even circulate pornography. It is particularly shameful to manipulate public sentiment. If [you] do not establish a healthy value system, these kinds of apologies simply shy away from real problems and [your claim to] "take social responsibility" is meaningless.[76]

Other official media outlets soon followed suit in criticizing Mi Meng. Two months after the initial allegations were made, Mi Meng announced the dissolution of her media company. In her WeChat "moments" update, Mi Meng posted pictures of the graduation ceremony she hosted for her employees, celebrating the fact that she successfully got her second startup company shut down. Playful as this event may seem, Mi Meng's sudden rise in popularity and her dramatic downfall, in the span of three and a half years, speaks volumes about the promises and perils of content entrepreneurship in the current era of precarity.

Most ironically, the factors that contributed to Mi Meng's rise equally accounted for her downfall. Mi Meng's writings avoided probing into the root causes of societal problems and glamorized the power of individual effort. While her own "rags-to-riches" story justified this position, she also created a distance between herself and the wealthy class, to forge an alliance with ordinary readers and project a voyeuristic gaze at the well off. Mi Meng's "disciples," however, departed from this formula. In the essay, the unnamed narrator belonged to the privileged class that differed drastically from Zhou Youze's social standing. In the eyes of the narrator, Zhou was a noble character: responsible (he supported his parents and younger sister), smart (he was a star student), hard-working, and with high moral standards. Despite all these qualities, Zhou Youze was unable to transcend his class status and had very little to show for his hard work and decency at his death. In contrast to Zhou Youze's failure, the narrator and her classmates belong to the group of individuals who moved up the career ladder, despite their self-proclaimed loss of integrity. The narrator, just two years out of college, can afford to live in the business district of Beijing. She attributed this rapid improvement of her financial situation to her capacity to adapt to the work environment: she had learned to be calculating, observing, and accommodating to the requests of different clients, to the extent that she behaved, according to her grandmother, like a sly, middle-aged person. The narrator's classmates, similarly, were all on track to either get promoted or receive important opportunities for career enhancement. Although the narrator bemoaned their loss of youthful innocence, her social group contained people who could easily figure out ways to achieve upward mobility. In other words, individual effort seems to produce rewards only for those from already privileged backgrounds.

Read in this light, the moral of the essay takes an ironic turn. Initially, the narrator's reflection on how "corrupted" her group had become and her offer to cover the four-year college tuition for Zhou Youze's sister were the most touching aspects of the story. The portrayal of the sufferings of Zhou Youze and his family functioned similarly to Mi Meng's own writing, in the sense that by reminding readers—most of whom were in much better situations than Zhou—to remain appreciative of what they have, the essay contributed to consolidating the existing social order. However, this tear-jerking sentimentality was soon negated by the readers' discovery of the factual and logical errors in the essay. Subsequently, rereading the article with the fictional aspects of the story in mind, the fabricated tale touches on one of the most serious problems of contemporary society. If even a college-educated, outstanding student could not transcend his class status and humble origins, what hope could there be for the millions of urban migrant workers and their children who have no access to basic education? When the essay failed to offer a solution or even hope for these strugglers, it not only challenged the fundamentals of Mi Meng's writings but also irritated the state media. Resonating with voices that were already strongly against Mi Meng, the Weibo account of *People's Daily* chose to pick on this most influential public account and, in doing so, issued warnings to all account holders and reasserted the authority of official media in the online sphere.

Conclusion

The rapid collapse of Mi Meng's commercial empire could easily be used as another example to demonstrate the state's enhanced control over the online sphere. At the peak time of her popularity, Mi Meng had 13 million fans on WeChat and 2.6 million followers on Weibo. And yet, with the publication of just a few Weibo posts by *People's Daily*, Mi Meng closed down her media company. This reading, however, does not address the broader sociocultural implications for understanding the new wave of the mobile revolution in China. Mi Meng's career breakthrough represents similar transitions from media professional to content entrepreneur in the age of WeChat. Mi Meng's sensational rise is inseparable from her well-performed role as a "loser," the dominant identity on the Chinese Internet since 2012. Meanwhile, Mi Meng's personal experience convinced her readers of the possibility of transcending one's "loser" status and reinforced the value of the inspirational stories shared on her account. By acting as a spokesperson for women, Mi Meng qualified her role as a mentor who offered advice to the younger generation of followers. At the same time, the tremendous influence of Mi Meng's public account brought forth its own vulnerability. Just as Mi Meng achieved near-instant fame in the latter half of 2015, it took only two months from her disciples' publication of the controversial essay to the formal dissolution of Mi Meng's media company. While the age of social precarity in China cultivated the rise of Mi Meng in the first place, as her inspirational stories struck a chord with an insecure public, this social condition similarly accounted for her downfall.

In the wake of the crisis in print media that began in 2012, the rise of WeChat public accounts has significantly altered media ecosystems and promoted the ascent of a mobile screen culture. For those making a living by writing, official accounts offer unprecedentedly ample opportunities to commodify original content, ranging from selling sponsored content and developing retail stores to teaching online courses. Essential to these means of profit making is the ability to cultivate and maintain affective ties with account followers. Despite the disappearance of Mi Meng from public sight, her case well represents the ascent of a different logic for managing public accounts that fully capitalize on the power of networked publicity through fans' private connections. Differing from traditional celebrities, who receive attention simply because of who they are, digital influencers need to constantly demonstrate their care of and attention to fans' feelings. The relationships they create with their fans, in turn, help these microcelebrities identify market needs and generate targeted content. Thus, the involvement of fan labor, personal branding, and networking capacity are the key measures that characterize effective content production and its monetization on WeChat public accounts. Consequently, this trend has significantly reshaped content marketing, celebrity culture, and digital ecosystems in the age of mobile apps.

8 AMBIVALENT REVOLUTION

MORE THAN TWENTY YEARS after the Internet was first introduced to China, the country's sociopolitical, economic, and cultural landscapes have been drastically revolutionized. Starting out as an alternative space accessible to only a few techno elites in the mid-1990s, the Chinese Internet today constitutes a dominant, mainstream social space that congregates users of diverging ideological stances, exhibits variegated cultural formations, and incubates innovative business models. Despite these sophisticated digital ecosystems, revolutionary narratives on Internet studies in China have tended to prioritize outcome (i.e., the democratization of China via digital media) over process (i.e., the ways in which Chinese society is being transformed). This book, instead, follows China's digital revolution from the perspective of cultural innovations. The analytical lens of "network of visibility" adds much-needed nuance to these narratives by investigating the mechanisms behind the vibrancy of digital culture. What is made visible online results from networked effects, enacted by the respective agendas of users, commercial corporations, media outlets, and state actors. These diverse players' competition for discursive legitimacy, defined by the two parameters of market popularity and content authority, constitutes the network of visibility that explains the dynamics of the online sphere.

By approaching China's digital revolution as a process of networked cultural innovations, this book traces the emergence and maturation of digital culture in China through four major technological platforms that have marked trends in Internet use over the past two decades: the bulletin board system, the blog, the microblog, and WeChat. This evolving trajectory of the Chinese Internet embodies a shift from the age of youthful innocence that celebrated idealism, egalitarianism, and community effects to an era of commerce, openly commodifying original content and exploring the business potential that new technologies bring forth. During this process, digital platforms have fostered the creative visibility of user-generated content, cultivated technological innovation, and mediated the formulation of social relations online.

My analysis further sheds light on how the Internet, commercialized traditional media, and state sectors together nurture the rise of China's digital publics across a variety of media platforms. The relationship between commercial media outlets and public deliberation about societal issues has long been debated. Habermas and his supporters, for example, lament that media commercialization exacerbates a decline of the bourgeois public sphere that gathers individuals to rationally debate societal issues.[1] Critics of this Habermasian notion of the public sphere, in contrast, challenge the assumption of a universal public sphere that dismisses differences of gender, race, class, and ethnicity.[2] They also question the prioritization of rationality as the basis of liberal democracy. Consequently, scholars argue for the significance of emotion (*qing*), as well as the existence of commercial media, in catalyzing the formation of critical publics.[3] Paradoxically, nurtured by consumer culture, these modern publics also are susceptible to manipulation by commercial forces and higher authorities.[4]

The advent of the Internet has complicated the implications commercial media outlets bear for the forging of critical publics. For one thing, the fluid nature of the web furthers the need to reconceptualize such ideas as the public, publicness, and publicity. Peter Dahlgren, for example, calls for studying the online public sphere in plural forms and stresses the importance of approaching the mundane aspects of political practices in civic lives.[5] Weiyu Zhang focuses on the study of "public" as a noun, defining it as a "relational concept" that "illustrates the network logic (in contrast to the hierarchy logic) of connecting individuals and building visibility."[6] In his analysis of the cross-Strait tension between netizens from mainland China and Taiwan, Shi-Diing Liu reveals how Internet chat rooms constitute an "'affective space' of a terrain of contestation,"[7] which in many ways is incompatible with the normative image of a consensual public sphere. The display of emotional intensity and the creation of the space of contestation are far more important than reaching a consensus.[8] Similarly, in many cases of web-based incidents, the creation of emotional appeal within digital publics has shown great potential to incite collective action.[9] The web-based incidents covered in this book demonstrate the symbiotic relationship that has developed between entertainment culture and micropolitics, and that is embedded in netizens' everyday engagement with the Internet. They reveal how microcontention in the online sphere, although often deemed trivial, contributes to the forging of politically minded citizens, thereby bearing significant implications for democratic practices. In this sense, I conceptualize digital publics as a fluid construction, which is subject to constant reconfiguration due to changing user demographics, emerging taste preferences, new technological affordances, and shifting socioeconomic conditions. In examining the roles of various actors, we begin to understand the working mechanism behind the forging of digital publics across the four digital platforms, as well as the ways in which dominant and mainstream ideologies have nourished digital publics since the late 1990s.

The period of governance under President Xi Jinping has been interpreted as an era of radical change for China, particularly in the areas of foreign policy, economic planning, legislation, and media policies.[10] Most significant, the national legislature amended the Constitution and abolished the two-term limit on the presidency in 2018. This amendment changed the stipulation of the 1982 Constitution that ended the lifelong rule of state leaders. This political event, together with an enhanced control over media outlets, has naturally led to a shared sense of disillusionment among China observers that the Internet no longer contributes to a democratic revolution in an authoritarian regime—in fact, that it seems to be helping to strengthen authoritarian control. While this observation has validity, it cannot account for how and why the productivity of the online sphere and the vibrancy of the digital economy can flourish in an authoritarian regime that endeavors to enhance its authoritative voice online. After all, a number of Internet memes appeared overnight after the announcement of the abolition of the two-term limit. They were soon censored, but two memes enjoyed a brief flurry of popularity. The first, titled "the wisdom of Winnie the Pooh," showed this cute character clinging to a pot of honey. A line next to the image explained: "Find the thing you love and stick with it."[11] The second showed the flag and emblem of the Communist Party, with an embedded note that swore loyalty to the Party (*yongyuan gen dang zou*). The text above this image read: "My mom said I have to get married before Xi Dada's term in office ends. Now I can breathe a long sigh of relief."[12] The first meme illustrates the power of global popular culture, while the second plays on traditional expectations about marriage in Chinese society. Emblematic of the vitality of the online space, these two memes illustrate the dialectical relationship between playfulness and political commentary, as well as the cultural mechanisms behind these memes.

In his analysis of contemporary Chinese politics, Cheng Li pinpoints the many "paradoxical policy moves and ambiguous ideological stances" that characterize the Xi Jinping regime.[13] The furthering of economic liberalization, exemplified by moves that support private sectors and the creative economy, conflicts with the endorsement of state-owned enterprises and propagation of national brands.[14] The implementation of judicial reforms contradicts the brutal persecution of human rights lawyers and legal professionals.[15] The tightened control over the media, along with the alienation of intellectuals, conflicts with the launch of aggressive initiatives to recruit foreign-educated returnees for think-tanks and for work in the fields of education and research.[16]

Cheng Li argues that these contradictions should be read within the context of Xi's endeavor "to strike a delicate balance between various constituencies and socioeconomic forces."[17] Li makes the appeal that "analysts of Chinese leadership politics must learn to live with complexity, tolerate ambiguity, and expect uncertainty."[18] Li's statement equally applies to Chinese Internet studies, in which a focus on China's political system (i.e., its status as a nondemocratic country) tends to dismiss the many intricacies of the Chinese context. The significance of studying the ambivalence regarding the Chinese Internet is even more explicitly articulated in Guobin Yang's forceful statement: "Ambivalence is a way of resisting binary thinking, that tendency to see only black or white and not grey in a world of complexity. An approach that welcomes ambivalence and rejects binarism, together with a sensitivity to history, culture, and the integration of media and society, may help to avoid the kind of sterile debates that have been waged on questions like whether the internet will lead to democratization in China."[19]

To this end, I hope this book spells out some of the ambivalence, nuances, and paradoxes revolving around the Chinese Internet over a span of two decades. The development of the four platforms traced in this book demonstrates, in microcosm, how emerging new applications constantly alter the market, as well as how older applications must continuously reinvent themselves to remain competitive. Indeed, this constantly shifting dynamic between new and old players in the content industry largely accounts for the vibrancy of online culture in China. From the mid-2010s onward, the digital industry has witnessed the emergence of competitive players, as represented by live streaming platforms YY and YiZhibo, mobile applications Douyin and Kuaishou, and on-demand service platforms. It remains exciting to explore how creative practices of Internet users continue to flourish in the commercially dominated online sphere while also problematizing existing sociopolitical conditions and endowing new meaning on digital technologies in China.

NOTES

Chapter 1

1. See, e.g., *Merriam-Webster Dictionary*, s.v. "revolution," https://www.merriam-webster.com/dictionary/revolution (accessed May 10, 2018) ("revolution" refers to "a sudden, radical, or complete change;" "a fundamental change in political organization;" an "activity or movement designed to effect fundamental changes in the socioeconomic situation;" "a fundamental change in the way of thinking about or visualizing something;" and "a changeover in use or preference especially in technology").

2. Chase, *You've Got Dissent!*; Esarey, and Xiao, "Political Expression in the Chinese Blogosphere"; Leibold, "Blogging Alone"; Sullivan, "China's Weibo."

3. Tsui, "Panopticon"; Zittrain and Edelman, "Internet Filtering in China"; Shie, "Tangled Web"; Wacker, "Resistance is Futile"; Qiu, "Virtual Censorship in China."

4. Marvin, "When Old Technologies Were New"; Williams, "The Technology and the Society."

5. Jeffreys, *Sex and Sexuality in China*, 4.

6. Jeffreys, *Sex and Sexuality in China*, 4.

7. Jeffreys, *Sex and Sexuality in China*, 9.

8. X. Tang, *Visual Culture in Contemporary China*, 7.

9. X. Zhang, *Transformation of Political Communication*, 192.

10. Stockmann, *Media Commercialization and Authoritarian Rule*.

11. X. Zhang, *Transformation of Political Communication*, 28–29.

12. Haiqing Yu, *Media and Cultural Transformation*, 150; Lagerkvist, *After the Internet, Before Democracy*, 33.

13. Balla, "Government Consultation and Political Participation"; Esarey, "Winning Hearts and Minds?"; Schlæger, and Jiang, "Official Microblogging and Social Management."

14. Yu Hong, *Networking China*.

15. Rongbin Han, *Contesting Cyberspace in China*; Roberts, *Censored*; Y. Lei, *Contentious Public Sphere*.

16. Feng, *Romancing the Internet*; Hockx, *Internet Literature in China*; Inwood, *Verse Going Viral*; H. Gong and Yang, *Reconfiguring Class*; W. Zhang, *Internet and New Social Media Formation*.

17. Hockx, *Internet Literature in China*.

18. Inwood, *Verse Going Viral*.

19. Feng, *Romancing the Internet.*
20. H. Gong and Yang, *Reconfiguring Class.*
21. Williams, *Long Revolution,* 47.
22. Lister, Giddings, and Dovey, *New Media,* 220.
23. McDougall, *Mao Zedong's "Talks."*
24. Link, *Roses and Thorns,* 8.
25. Clark, *Chinese Cultural Revolution,* 2–3.
26. J. Wang, "Culture as Leisure."
27. Xinhua News Agency, "Full Text."
28. X. Zhang, *Transformation of Political Communication,* 52.
29. Jiao, "Culture a Key Priority."
30. Jiao, "Culture a Key Priority."
31. "13th Five-Year Plan."
32. J. Wang, "State Question," 37.
33. Bourdieu, *Field of Cultural Production.*
34. Y. Zhu, *Chinese Cinema.*
35. Y. Zhu, *Chinese Cinema,* 78.
36. S. Cai, *State Propaganda.*
37. Huang and Zhou, *Zhongguo chuanmei shichang da bianju,* 67.
38. Keane, *Chinese Television Industry.*
39. Kong, *Consuming Literature,* 14.
40. Kong, *Consuming Literature,* 31.
41. Herrmann and Knight, "Mechanisms of Human Attention"; Thorngate, "Professional Issues."
42. Simon, "Designing Organizations."
43. Davenport and Beck, *Attention Economy,* 20.
44. Goldhaber, "Value of Openness."
45. Franck, "Economy of Attention."
46. Thompson, "New Visibility," 32.
47. Thompson, "New Visibility."
48. Thompson, "New Visibility."
49. Stockmann, *Media Commercialization and Authoritarian Rule,* 4.
50. Hassid, "China's Contentious Journalists."
51. L. Peng, *Zhongguo wangluo meiti de diyige shinian,* 86.
52. Chen and Zeng, *Xinlang zhidao,* 36–38.
53. K. Liu, *Globalization and Cultural Trends,* 134.
54. Haichao Zhang, *Yanqiu weiwang,* 51–52.
55. Haichao Zhang, *Yanqiu weiwang,* 58–59.
56. X. Wu, *Cao Guowei.*
57. X. Wu, *Cao Guowei.*
58. Chen and Zeng, *Xinlang zhidao,* 229.
59. Chen and Zeng, *Xinlang zhidao,* 229.
60. K. Liu, *Globalization and Cultural Trends,* 131.

61. X. Fan, *Communications and Information in China*, 20.

62. L. Peng, *Zhongguo wangluo meiti de di yige shinian*, 68.

63. L. Peng, *Zhongguo wangluo meiti de di yige shinian*, 75.

64. L. Peng, *Zhongguo wangluo meiti de di yige shinian*, 80.

65. B. Cai, "2015 nian zhongguo baozhi chanye."

66. B. Cai, "2015 nian zhongguo baozhi chanye."

67. Cui, *Zhongguo chuanmei chanye fazhan baogao.*

68. C. Huang, "China's State-Run Tabloids."

69. Y. Zhao, *Media, Market, and Democracy.*

70. Y. Zhao, *Media, Market, and Democracy*, 76–77, 92.

71. Jiazhou chengzi, "Yinian shifen baozhi xiukan."

72. W. Liu, "Stop Press."

73. Wang and Sparks, "Chinese Newspaper Groups."

74. Creemers, "Cyber China."

75. Esarey, "Winning Hearts and Minds?"; Schlæger and Jiang, "Official Microblogging and Social Management."

76. Steinberg, "Genesis of the Platform Concept," 188.

77. Kenney and Zysman, "Rise of the Platform Economy," 64.

78. Steinberg, "Genesis of the Platform Concept."

79. Gillespie, "Politics of 'Platforms.'"

80. Kelkar, "Engineering a Platform."

81. Lamarre, "Platformativity," 285.

82. Lin Zhang, "When Platform Capitalism Meets Petty Capitalism."

83. J. Chen, "Thrown under the Bus."

84. Cunningham, Craig, and Lv, "China's Livestreaming Industry."

85. Srnicek, *Platform Capitalism*; Dijck, Poell, and Waal, *Platform Society.*

86. Steinberg, *Platform Economy.*

87. Gillespie, *Custodians of the Internet.*

88. Steinberg, *Platform Economy*, 92.

89. Hall, "Cultural Identity and Diaspora."

Chapter 2

1. Wong and Nah, *China's Emerging New Economy*, 8.

2. Barboza, "China Surpasses U.S."

3. "China Builds World's Largest Internet Infrastructure."

4. China Internet Network Information Center (CNNIC), "Di sishiwuci zhongguo hulianwangluo fazhan zhuangkuang."

5. CNNIC, "Di sishiwuci zhongguo hulianwangluo fazhan zhuangkuang."

6. Office of Cyberspace Administration of China, "Di sishiyici zhongguo hulianwangluo fazhan zhuangkuang."

7. CNNIC, "Di sishisici zhongguo hulianwangluo fazhan zhuangkuang."

8. CNNIC, "Di sishisici zhongguo hulianwangluo fazhan zhuangkuang."

9. X. Fan, *Communications and Information in China.*

10. L. Peng, *Zhongguo wangluo meiti de diyige shinian*, 16.

11. Negro, *Internet in China*, 40.

12. Negro, *Internet in China*, 40.

13. F. Liu, *Urban Youth in China*, 36–37.

14. Y. Zhou, *Historicizing Online Politics*, 137.

15. Tai, *Internet in China*, 129.

16. L. Peng, *Zhongguo wangluo meiti de diyige shinian*, 19–20.

17. Tai, *Internet in China*, 127–28.

18. Yu and Si, "China Leads World in Internet Market."

19. "China Builds World's Largest Internet Infrastructure."

20. Xinhuawang, "China Pushing to Build."

21. L. Peng, *Zhongguo wangluo meiti de diyige shinian*, 23–33.

22. L. Peng, *Zhongguo wangluo meiti de diyige shinian*, 45.

23. Junhua Zhang, "China's 'Government Online.'"

24. Ma, Chung, and Thorson, "E-government in China."

25. One of the most successful cases is "The First Blog of Public Security" (*Zhongguo gongan diyi boke*), hosted by the News Center at the Department of Public Security in Hebei, China. Created by Hao Chao, one of the News Center staff members, this blog has attracted a large number of visitors for its timeliness in disseminating information and interacting with netizens. "The First Blog of Public Security" was also the first governmental organization to have a blogging account in China. The blog remains active to this day.

26. Senft, "Bulletin-Board Systems," 45.

27. Senft, "Bulletin-Board Systems," 47.

28. Senft, "Bulletin-Board Systems," 47.

29. Senft, "Bulletin-Board Systems," 45–47.

30. W. He, *Networked Public*, 215.

31. Ji, "BBS wangshi."

32. Ji, "BBS wangshi."

33. G. Yang and Wu, "Remembering Disappeared Websites," 2115.

34. S. Li, "Online Public Space," 67.

35. Tai, *Internet in China*, xiii–xix.

36. Renminwang, "Zhongyang."

37. Tkacik, "China's Orwellian Internet."

38. "Shuimu BBS tiaozheng."

39. W. He, *Networked Public*, 217–42.

40. W. He, *Networked Public*, 217–42.

41. W. He, *Networked Public*, 217–42.

42. X. Fang and J. Wang, *Boke*, 101.

43. Jia Zhang, "'Boke zhifu' Fang Xingdong," 51.

44. J. Wang and X. Fang, *Boke*, 169.

45. J. Wang and X. Fang, *Boke*, 170.

46. J. Wang and X. Fang, *Boke*, 178–79.

47. The four articles are: X. Fang and J. Sun, "Blog"; X. Fang, "Guanyu blog weilai"; X. Fang, "Blog zhiwang"; H. Lu, "Wei shouquan de boke."

48. W. Jiang, "Zai boke shijie fenxiang."

49. According to statistics from Blogchina, there were 20,000 visits to the website in October 2002. In June 2003, the number of visits reached 20,000 every three days. X. Fang and J. Wang, *Boke*, 173–75, 191 .

50. Xue, "Fang Xingdong."

51. Jian, "Fang Xingdong," 78.

52. Du, *Boke chutan*, 53.

53. D. Chen, *Bite zhijing*, 221–30.

54. The only exceptions are Tianya and NetEase. Both sites began providing blogging services before 2005.

55. Du, *Boke chutan*, 179.

56. SimilarWeb.

57. Sina, "Business Overview."

58. Sina, "Business Overview."

59. Alexa, "Top Sites in China," https://www.alexa.com/topsites/countries/CN (accessed June 24, 2018); Alexa, "The Top 500 Sites on the Web," https://www.alexa.com/topsites (accessed June 24, 2018).

60. Lijie Zhang, "Piaoliang de tuoer men."

61. Fang Xue, "Chen Tong," 81.

62. Chen and Zeng, *Xinlang zhidao*, 229.

63. Personal interviews with web editors.

64. Chen and Zeng, *Xinlang zhidao*, 13-25.

65. Dong and Li, *Yu wushiwei wangzhan zhubian mianduimian.*

66. G. Yang, "Chinese Internet Literature."

67. Lazzarato, "Immaterial Labour."

68. Chen and Zeng, *Xinlang zhidao*, 87–92.

69. Personal interviews with web editors.

70. L. Hu, "Mingren boke."

71. Personal interviews with web editors.

72. Personal interviews with web editors.

73. Personal interviews with web editors.

74. Lagerkvist, "In the Crossfire of Demands."

75. Personal interviews with web editors.

76. See, for example, http://blog.sina.com.cn/lm/huati/news/20100113/1155198.html (accessed July 12, 2012).

77. Lijie Zhang, "Piaoliang de tuoer men," 21.

78. Personal interviews with web editors.

79. Personal interviews with web editors.

80. Personal interviews with web editors.

81. Ying Li, "Wo bishi xinlang mingren boke"; Zeng, "Jingying yu caogen zhibian."

82. Y. Li, Wu, and Zhang, "Niubo wangshi."

83. Personal interviews with web editors.

84. Rong, "Jiaoxun gongxiang."

85. Kuang, "Guochan weibo xingshuai shi."

86. BBC, "Xinjiang Arrests."

87. CNNIC, "Di sishisici zhongguo hulianwangluo fazhan zhuangkuang."

88. "White Paper on Year One."

89. "White Paper on Year One."

90. Personal conversations with web editors at Sina.

91. Kuang, "Guochan weibo shengshuai shi."

92. Xia, *Weibo kongjian de shengchan shijian*, 64.

93. On August 13, 2007, Tencent launched its microblogging website Taotao. Yet, due to concerns about operational issues, the corporation merged Taotao into Qzone, a pre-existing personal webpage for Tencent's QQ users, on January 26, 2010. Then, on April 1, 2010, Tencent launched another microblogging service called "wei boke," and invited renowned celebrities, including the Olympic champion Liu Xiang, celebrity Xu Jinglei, and controversial figure Fang Zhouzi, to set up microblog accounts on this platform. On July 23, 2014, Tencent closed its microblog division, and put all its effort into developing and promoting WeChat.

94. X. Wu, *Tengxun zhuan*, 769–70.

95. J. Lu, *Weibo wenzheng*, 11.

96. "Report on the Development of Microblog," 3; Xinlang weibo shuju zhongxin, "2013 xinlang meiti weibo baogao," 3.

97. "White Paper on Year One."

98. Xinlangwang, "2012 nian xinlang zhengwu weibo"; Renminwang, "2017 nian san jidu wangluo yulun shengtai."

99. Xinlangwang, "Zhongguo weibo yuannian."

100. Renminwang, "2013 nian zhongguo huliangwang yuqing."

101. W. Zhang, *Internet and New Social Formation*, 119.

102. Svensson, "Voice, Power and Connectivity."

103. Personal interviews with web editors at Sina.

104. Buckley, "Formal Arrest of Advocate"; C. Huang and Zhai, "Xi Jinping Rallies Party."

105. Personal conversations with management personnel at Sina.

106. Schiavenza, "China's Weibo Losing Users."

107. "Xinlang weibo fuzongcai Cao Zenghui."

108. "Xinlang weibo fuzongcai Cao Zenghui."

109. H. Gao, "Lianxu qige jidu yingli."

110. H. Gao, "Lianxu qige jidu yingli."

111. X. Yang, Sun, and Lee, "Micro-Innovation Strategy."

112. J. Huang, "Weixin."

113. X. Wu, *Tengxun zhuan*, 794.

114. https://mp.weixin.qq.com/s/K5uGwPreMx-iMbVToy3tnw (accessed May 10, 2018).

115. https://www.digitaling.com/articles/41203.html (accessed May 10, 2018).

116. Y. Hu, "Fenlie de 'weixin zhifu."

117. Graziani, "WeChat Impact Report 2018."

118. Harwit, "WeChat."

119. "Weixin gongzhong zhanghao chaoxi"; Xinhuawang, "Xinhua Insight."

120. Graziani, "WeChat Impact Report 2018."

Chapter 3

1. L. Tang, "Nonsensical Speech," 1.

2. R. Zhang, "Top 10 Chinese Films in 2013."

3. H. Gong and Yang, "Digitized Parody"; Haiqing Yu, "After the 'Steamed Bun'"; Hongmei Li, "Parody and Resistance"; G. Yang and Jiang, "Networked Practice"; B. Meng, "Regulating Online Spoofs"; B. Meng, "From Steamed Bun to Grass Mud Horse"; Rea, "Spoofing (E'gao) Culture."

4. J. Wang, *High Culture Fever.*

5. Williams, *Marxism and Literature.*

6. Williams, *Marxism and Literature,* 84.

7. Williams, *Marxism and Literature,* 131.

8. Williams, *Marxism and Literature,* 132.

9. G. Cheng, "Qinghua daxue de wangshang 'xuni shenghuo.'"

10. Yi, "Liu Zhenwei," 73.

11. Lixian Zhang, *Dahua xiyou baodian,* 91.

12. Plumblade, "Wo lai shuoshuo weishenme."

13. *Bible of A Chinese Odyssey* consists of four parts: the *dahua* novel; a collection of journal articles and online discussions of the film; a collection of *dahua* stories created by netizens; and an analysis of Stephen Chow's other films. According to Zhang Lixian, the book was primarily compiled for university students. Zhang planned to release the book before the Class of 2000 graduated. Lixian Zhang, *Dahua xiyou baodian.*

14. Yao, "'Dahua' wenhua," 76.

15. Yau, "Introduction," 23.

16. Hongshu Zhang, "Dahua xiyou de chuanbo," 83.

17. L. Peng, *Zhongguo wangluo meiti de di yige shinian,* 38.

18. "Movie ban jinghua gongbulan."

19. Lixian Zhang, "Dahua xiyou de chuanbo," 83.

20. Z. Lu, "Dahua xiyou zhilu."

21. Yi, "Liu Zhenwei," 73.

22. Hongrui Li, "Online Literature Readers."

23. Z. Zhou, "Huigu yu pingpan."

24. M. Jin, "Wenxue wangluo shidai."

25. Dun, "Luelun Cai Zhiheng."

26. Yan, "Xin meiti zhongde qingchun xiezuo."

27. *Tsinghua yehua.*

28. J. Zhao, "Zhao Jianzhou."

29. J. Wan, "Dangdai xiaoyuan qingchun."

30. G. Cheng, "Qinghua daxue de wangshang 'xuni shenghuo.'"

31. Furong Jiejie, *Huobingker de Blog.*

32. Eimer, "China Cracks Down."

33. "Furong Jiejie wei yan shanzha pai xiezhen."

34. Furong Jiejie, *Furong Jiejie's Microblog*, March 1, 2018.

35. Furong Jiejie, "Beida."

36. Xudong Hu, "Furong Jiejie yu xiju baoli."

37. Huanpei dingdang, "Furong jiao rumen."

38. Luo, "Zilian shidai de zilian yanchu."

39. H. Xiao, "Ziwo chuyan, gexing jingji."

40. dachy, "Zheli haoxiang meiren baba Furong Jiejie"; dachy, "Furong jiao di'ertan"; Huanpei dingdang, "Furong jiao rumen."

41. Furong Jiejie, "Qinai de oufen"; Furong Jiejie, "Pandian Furong Jiejie de 2006."

42. Bakhtin, *Problems of Dostoevsky's Poetics*, 7.

43. Bakhtin, *Problems of Dostoevsky's Poetics*, 7.

44. Hills, "Virtually Out There," 154.

45. Hills, *Fan Cultures.*

46. G. Yang, *Power of the Internet in China*, 173–74.

47. Huanpei dingdang, "Furong jiao rumen."

48. dachy, June 14, 2005.

49. dachy, June 14, 2005.

50. Gray, "New Audiences, New Textualities"; Gray, "Antifandom and the Moral Text," 841.

51. Fiske, "Cultural Economy of Fandom."

52. Fiske, "Cultural Economy of Fandom."

53. "Furong Jiejie wei yan shanzha pai xiezhen."

54. Xudong Hu, "Furong Jiejie yu xiju baoli."

55. Y. Li and Zhang, "Chen Mo," 43.

56. M. Liu and Chen, "Furong Jiejie." The batch of photos on Tianya is available at http://forum.yorkbbs.ca/showtopic-910942-1.aspx (accessed July 5, 2012).

57. M. Liu and Chen, "Furong Jiejie."

58. Y. Li and Zhang, "Chen Mo," 43.

59. Yunzhongyuyizi, "Qianwanli zhuixun."

60. For example, Zhu Dake, a cultural critic, states that Furong Jiejie and other Internet celebrities like Mu Zimei and Juhua Meimei all exhibit different degrees of mental illness, including narcissism, melancholia, mild schizophrenia, and so on. D. Zhu, *Liumang de shengyan*, 366.

61. Yinhe Li, "Furong Jiejie dale yanlun ziyou de cabianqiu."

62. Furong Jiejie, "Furong Jiejie zhende shi zhaoyao jing."

63. Furong Jiejie, "Bukan huishou (10)."

64. Furong Jiejie, *Furong Jiejie's Microblog*, June 6, 2010; Furong Jiejie, *Furong Jiejie's Microblog*, June 16, 2010.

65. Furong Jiejie, "Furong Jiejie de shouzhi geren danqu."

66. Huiyu Zhang, "'Furong Jiejie' de misi."

67. Wuyishanxia, November 17, 2010.

68. Tyler and Bennett, "'Celebrity Chav,'" 379.

69. Tyler and Bennett, "'Celebrity Chav,'" 379.

70. Tyler and Bennett, "'Celebrity Chav,'" 379.

71. Papi Jiang, "Papi de dapei zhi."

72. Z. Bai, "Wanghong Papi Jiang."

73. Papi Jiang, *Nizai shenghuo zhong yiding ye tingdao guo.*

74. Papi Jiang, *Dangdai ren bibei shouce*; Papi Jiang, *Yici kanwan shanghaihua jia yingyu.*

75. Jie Zhang, "Papi Jiang."

76. "'Wangluo hongren' cuisheng 'wanghong jingji.'"

77. J. Wu and Yun, "From Modernization to Neoliberalism?," 18.

Chapter 4

1. Rea, "Entering the Cultural Entrepreneur," 10.

2. Y. Zhao, *Media, Market, and Democracy*, 109.

3. Dickson, "China's Cooperative Capitalists"; Davies, "China's Celebrity Entrepreneurs."

4. Inwood, *Verse Going Viral*, 150.

5. Y. Zhao, *Media, Market, and Democracy*, 219–35.

6. Osburg, *Anxious Wealth.*

7. Marks, "Xu Jing Lei."

8. A. King, "China's Pop Fiction."

9. A. King, "China's Pop Fiction."

10. S. Cai, *Contemporary Chinese Films*, 42.

11. Liang and Shen, "Fan Economy."

12. "Guo Jingming: Wode chenggong tianjing diyi."

13. Jia, "Guo Jingming."

14. Jia, "Guo Jingming."

15. Shen and Zhang, "Zhuanfang Guo Jingming."

16. T. Chen, "Shangren Guo Jingming," 74.

17. Chenchen Chen, "Guo Jingming tuandui wenxue," 45.

18. Jenkins, *Convergence Culture*, 97–98.

19. Jenkins, *Convergence Culture*, 97–98.

20. Jenkins, *Convergence Culture*, 2.

21. J. Jacobs, "Communication Overexposure," 1.

22. Readers' comments on Yang Lan's blog are all retrieved from Lan Yang, *Yang Lan de boke.*

23. Lan Yang, *Yang Lan de boke.*

24. Lister, Giddings, and Dovey, *New Media*, 23.

25. Lister, Giddings, and Dovey, *New Media*, 23.

26. Jinglei Xu, *Lao Xu de boke.*

27. Hong, "Shanghai riji er."
28. Hong, "Zhao xieshou."
29. Jenkins, *Fans, Bloggers, and Gamers*, 147.
30. Terranova, "Free Labor."
31. Lan Yang, interview, February 27, 2008.
32. Andrejevic, "Watching Television without Pity," 24.
33. Andrejevic, "Watching Television without Pity," 24.
34. Andrejevic, "Watching Television without Pity," 25.
35. Terranova, "Free Labor," 33–34.
36. Lan Yang, "Zhenxi ta, jiuxiang zhenxi ziji."
37. Lan Yang, "Zhenxi ta, jiuxiang zhenxi ziji."
38. Warrior, November 25, 2008; Shizi, December 18, 2005.
39. Xiaoyu Lei, "Yang Lan."
40. Kong, *Consuming Literature*, 74.
41. CNN, interview of Yang Lan.
42. Lan Yang, "Nüxing de jiefang."
43. Lan Yang, "Nüxing de jiefang."
44. Lan Yang, "Nüxing de jiefang."
45. Lan Yang, "Nüxing de jiefang."
46. Lan Yang, "Zhou Jielun de 'gangqin ke.'"
47. Gledhill, "Pleasurable Negotiations," 239.
48. "Popular Young Writer."
49. Henningsen, *Copyright Matters*.
50. Henningsen, *Copyright Matters*.
51. Kunze, "Cross-Media, Cross-Promotion."
52. Saipo Zhao, "Fensi, diaosi, yu hulianwang shangye moshi."
53. Jung, "Shared Imagination of Bishōnen."
54. Louie, "Popular Culture and Masculinity Ideals."
55. Fumian, "Social Construction of a Myth."
56. J. Guo, "Wo he Luo Luo zuole shenme nie"; J. Guo, "Xiao Si da jiangtang."
57. Balaji and Hughson, "(Re)producing Borders and Bodies," 208.
58. Y. Wang, "Guo Jingming: Ouxiang de zhizao he huimie."
59. Lim, "Pop Idol Writer."
60. J. Guo, "Rende jixian shi neng tuchu zise wanyi'er?!"
61. J. Guo, "Rende jixian shi neng tuchu zise wanyi'er?!"
62. J. Guo, "Jintian Xiaoshidai 3.0 shangshi le."
63. "Guo Jingming zhuanfang."
64. E. Chen, "Neoliberal Self-Governance," 270–71.

Chapter 5

1. Han Han, "Erlingyiling nian shiyue bari."
2. K. Liu, "'Dinner Party of Discourse Owners,'" 125.
3. Singhal and Greiner, "Performance Activism and Civic Engagement," 50.

4. R. Huang and Yip, "Internet and Activism in Urban China"; Hung, "Politics of China's Wei-Quan Movement"; G. Yang, *Power of the Internet in China*.

5. X. Zhang, *Transformation of Political Communication*.

6. G. Yang, *Power of the Internet in China*.

7. N. Zhang, "Web-based Backpacking Communities," 277.

8. Gleiss, "Speaking Up."

9. Macgilchrist and Böhmig, "Blogs, Genes and Immigration," 97.

10. Logan, "Presence and Absence," 1.

11. Link, *Roses and Thorns*.

12. Barmé, *In the Red*; X. Zhang, *Transformation of Political Communication*.

13. Pugsley and Gao, "Emerging Powers of Influence"; Haiqing Yu, "Beyond Gatekeeping."

14. King, Pan, and Roberts, "Censorship in China."

15. Stern and O'Brien, "Politics at the Boundary," 177.

16. Fengle and QY, "Mu Zimei fangtan."

17. Y. Chen, "Mu Zimei wunian hou xiaotan xingai riji."

18. Farrer, "China's Women Sex Bloggers."

19. Farrer, "China's Women Sex Bloggers."

20. Q. Zhou, "Nü xieshou yong shenti xiezuo."

21. Watts, "Now China Joins"; Y. Lu, "Cong Mu Zimei shijian kan wangluo chuanbo."

22. Yardley, "Internet Sex Column Thrills."

23. Mu Zimei's writings quoted are retrieved from http://muzimei.51da.com/ (accessed June 25, 2012).

24. Xin, "Xinwen pinglun."

25. Xin, "Xinwen pinglun."

26. X. Wan, "Mu Zimei fabiao xin riji."

27. X. Sun, "Cong xinlang shizu kan wangzhan."

28. J. Cai, "Columnist's Online Diary."

29. I. Wang, "Sex Diary Banned."

30. Berg, "Consuming Secrets," 324.

31. McDonald, "China's Web Censors Struggle."

32. McDonald, "China's Web Censors Struggle."

33. Beech, "Sex, Please."

34. Kong, *Consuming Literature*.

35. Kong, *Consuming Literature*.

36. Mu Zimei, "Da Shengbaoluoye bao wen."

37. Mu Zimei, "Dengshi jiaohuan."

38. Y. Liao, "'Mu Zimei xianxiang'"; Xiaomei Hu, "Xing huangyan Mu Zimei."

39. Xiaomei Hu, "Xing huangyan Mu Zimei."

40. Xiaomei Hu, "Xing huangyan Mu Zimei."

41. Farrer, "China's Women Sex Bloggers," 11.

42. Mu Zimei, *Yiqingshu*.

43. Chiafu Chen, "Ordinary."

44. Shan, "Zhan Mu Zimei de pianyi."

45. Farrer, "China's Women Sex Bloggers," 21.

46. Mu Zimei, "Preface to *Rongqi*."

47. Mu Zimei, "Wugu."

48. Mu Zimei, "Preface to *Rongqi*."

49. Mu Zimei, "Da Shengbaoluoye bao wen."

50. "Mingbo fangtan disi qi."

51. "Single Mother Issue in Spotlight."

52. C. Zhao, "Cong mengya zazhi wushi nian lishi tanqi."

53. C. Zhao, "Cong mengya zazhi wushi nian lishi tanqi," 151.

54. C. Zhao, "Cong mengya zazhi wushi nian lishi tanqi," 151.

55. L. Li, "Chun wenxue zazhi zoudao le shizi lukou?"

56. Hu Weishi, the editor of *Sprout*, recalled her impression when reading the two writing samples that Han Han submitted. According to her, writers Fang Fang, Tie Ning, and Ye Zhaoyan, as well as Chen Sihe, the renowned literature professor at Fudan University, were all impressed. Yet, because of miscommunication, Han Han did not receive the official notice to attend the finals. Hu managed to persuade the committee to give Han Han another opportunity to compose an essay after the finals ended. Renjun Han, *Erzi Han Han*, 44–50.

57. Renjun Han, *Erzi Han Han*, 105–32.

58. Wang Shuo (b. 1958) rose to prominence in the late 1980s for his "hooligan" style of writing that mocks the pretentiousness of intellectuals and ridicules official ideology. Wang Shuo and Han Han represent different stages of China's literary commercialization process: Wang was China's first bestselling author; Han Han was China's first teen literary celebrity. Both writers stand out for their distinctive style and antiestablishment stances and assume diverse roles in the cultural realm. Guoqing Zheng has offered a detailed analysis of how the shared aesthetic style of Wang Shuo and Han Han, marked by a juxtaposition of irony, parody, and sentimentalism, is an integral component of the new commercial mainstream. For an extensive discussion of Wang Shuo's role as a literary entrepreneur and of his literary style, see Barmé, *In the Red*; Kong, "Literary Celebrity in China"; and G. Zheng, *Meixue de weizhi*, 17–30.

59. "50 People Who Matter 2010."

60. "2010 *Time* 100 Poll."

61. Fumian, "Temple and the Market"; Clark, *Youth Culture in China*; Coderre, "Meaningful Mobility."

62. Q. Yang, "Dikang de 'jiamian,'" 87.

63. Lijun Yang, "Han Han and the Public."

64. CNN, "Han Han"; Krotoski, "Internet's Cyber Radicals."

65. Strafella and Berg, "Making of an Online Celebrity."

66. Han Han, *Sanchong men*, 18.

67. Han Han, *Guangrong ri*, 1.

68. Y. Guo, "Han Han."

69. L. Sun, "Han Han."

70. A. Wong, "Cyberself," 281.

71. Y. Bai, "'Balinghou' de xianzhuang yu weilai."

72. Y. Bai, "'Balinghou' de xianzhuang yu weilai."

73. Han Han, "Wentan shige pi."

74. Y. Bai, "Wode shengming."

75. Han Han, "Wo zhongyu qudao le chulian duixiang."

76. Bourdieu, *Field of Cultural Production*, 16.

77. Fumian, "Temple and the Market."

78. Fumian, "Temple and the Market," 154.

79. Han Han, "Wentan shige pi."

80. Shu, "Shu zuojia bukan qifan"; S. Peng, "Cong mingren 'guan bo re' kan baoye de qiantu."

81. S. Guo, "Ruled by Attention."

82. Lijun Yang, "Han Han and the Public."

83. K. Jacobs, *People's Pornography*, 80.

84. Han Zhang, "Sexy Diarist Nabbed."

85. Han Zhang, "Sexy Diarist Nabbed."

86. Han Han, "Han Feng shige hao ganbu."

87. Han Han, "Wo qu nali zhao."

88. Han Zhang, "Sexy Diarist Nabbed."

89. A. Wong, "Cyberself," 267.

90. B. Xu, "Meiguo ren kan budong Han Han."

91. A. Wong, "Cyberself," 281.

92. Han Han, "Haizi men, nimen saole yeye de xing."

93. Han Han, "Yeyemen, nimen qing jinxing."

94. Han Han, "Yeyemen, nimen qing jinxing."

95. Han Han, "Yeyemen, nimen qing jinxing."

96. Han Han, "Yeyemen, nimen qing jinxing."

97. Han Han, "Yeyemen, nimen qing jinxing."

98. Han Han, "Yeyemen, nimen qing jinxing."

99. Han Han, "Erlingyiyi nian shiyi yue sanri."

100. Han Han, "Tan geming."

101. Han Han, "Shuo minzhu."

102. Han Han, "Yao ziyou."

103. F. Liu, *Urban Youth in China*.

104. Phillips, "Publishers under Pressure."

105. Rongbin Han, "Withering Gongzhi."

106. For comprehensive information about this debate and the online "Down with Han Han movement," see *Dao Han yundong*.

Chapter 6

1. S. Xiao, "Guanzhu jiushi liliang."

2. Jian Xu, *Media Events in Web 2.0 China*, 86.

3. S. Wu and Liu, "Politics of Naming."

4. J. Lu and Zeng, "Microblogging and Grassroots Surveillance."

5. Peters, "Witnessing," 709.

6. Peters, "Witnessing," 709.

7. Morozov, *Net Delusion*.

8. Chouliaraki, "Digital Witnessing."

9. Chouliaraki, "Digital Witnessing."

10. Ristovska, "Strategic Witnessing."

11. Tait, "Bearing Witness."

12. Andén-Papadopoulos, "Citizen Camera-Witnessing."

13. Z. Zhang, "Introduction"; Edwards and Svensson, "Show Us Life."

14. E. Han, *Micro-Blogging Memories*, 202.

15. "Wenzhou dongche xinwen fabuhui."

16. "Design Flaws and Poor Management."

17. G. Qian, "Dongche shigu zhong de baodao"; Y. Chen, "Zhongguo chuanmei de shehui yundong."

18. Y. Zheng, "Zhongguo dongche shigu de zhidu fansi."

19. "Directives from the Ministry of Truth."

20. For instance, *Jingji banxiaoshi* [Economy time] at CCTV broadcasted an interview with Liu Tiemin, a member of the emergency management expert group of the State Council, on July 27. Upon hearing that the train wreckage was at first buried and later unearthed for investigation, Liu was shocked: "Unbelievable. I could not believe it. This is ridiculous." China Central Television, *Jingji banxiaoshi*.

21. "Anjian zongju."

22. Explanations for the seven-day-freedom of media vary. Some argue that the delay in official response was due to the need to figure out who the real target is, and how to make adjustment accordingly, while some argue that factional struggles from within the top leadership was a major factor. According to Michael Anti, an independent journalist based in Beijing, those from the top leadership would like to get rid of Liu Zhijun and his kingdom. Therefore, they allowed public criticism of the Ministry of Railways for quite a few days to capitalize on public sentiments as a political weapon. For details, see E. Han, *Micro-Blogging Memories*, 31; Anti, "Behind the Great Firewall."

23. Jian Xu, *Media Events in Web 2.0 China*, 104.

24. R. Yu, "Micro Blogs."

25. S. Yang, "2011 nian di san jidu wangluo yuqing," 310.

26. Peters, "Witnessing," 719.

27. Wines and LaFraniere, "Baring Facts."

28. X. Xu, "Internet Facilitated Civic Engagement."

29. A. Li, "China's Micro-Blogs."

30. A. Li, "China's Micro-Blogs."

31. A. Li, "China's Micro-Blogs."

32. E. Han, *Micro-Blogging Memories*, 29.

33. Weibo account of "Xianzuo butan yuwen."

34. L. Shi, "Chengzhang huiyilu."

35. E. Han, *Micro-Blogging Memories*; R. Yu, "Micro Blogs."

36. G. Han and Wang, "Mapping User Relationships."

37. According to Eileen Le Han, Sina only promotes tweets that received 10,000 reposts or were forwarded 10,000 times. Therefore, it is much easier for well-established figures to receive attention from Internet users. By contrast, ordinary users would have to count on the function of well-known people if they want to attract large Internet traffic. E. Han, *Micro-Blogging Memories*, 32.

38. C. Wu, "Micro-Blog and the Speech Act," 47.

39. G. Yang, "Beiqing yu xixue."

40. "Tiedaobu fayanren 'fanzheng wo xinle.'"

41. Tiantanglu chalukou, "Gaotie ti huole!"

42. Tiantanglu chalukou, "Gaotie ti huole!"

43. S. Lin, "'×××, zhiyu ni xin bu xin, wo fanzheng xinle.'"

44. H. Zhao, "Yongbu dida de lieche."

45. Han Han, "Tuojie de guodu."

46. D. Tong, "Zhongguo ni manxie zou."

47. Bondes and Schucher, "Derailed Emotions," 45.

48. Bondes and Schucher, "Derailed Emotions," 61.

49. Maihaozi, "Weibo you you xin faxian."

50. For a detailed summary of Tianya users' findings, see http://blog.sina.com.cn/s/blog_56fc0caa0100uvif.html (accessed May 28, 2018).

51. L. Tong, *Weibo fazhan yanjiu baogao.*

52. Q. Liao, and Shi, "She Gets a Sports Car."

53. Sohu's interview of Guo Meimei, *Wangluo hongren.*

54. "Zhongguo shangye xitong hongshizihui."

55. Q. Wang, "Shuttling between Politics and Entertainment"; Y. Cheng, "Social Media Keep Buzzing!"

56. China Central Television, "Gongyi yu sili."

57. Moore, "Chinese Charity Donations Fall."

58. Hou and Tsai, "Weibo shidai zhongguo wangluo shequn chuanbo."

59. Y. Cheng, "Social Media Keep Buzzing!"

60. "Souhu shipin dashiye."

61. Q. Liao and Shi, "She Gets a Sports Car."

62. "Guo Meimei: Huai mingsheng yeshi mingsheng."

63. China Central Television, "Guo Meimei kaishe duchang an."

64. Ren, "China's Most Despised Woman."

65. "Qidi 'wangluo hongren' Guo Meimei."

66. Buckley, "Crackdown on Bloggers."

67. "Shexian juzhong yinluan."

68. "Xue Manzi miandai weixiao huiguo."

69. China Central Television, "Wangluo mingren shehui zeren luntan."

70. G. Yang, "Return of Ideology."

71. M. Wu, "China's Crackdowns."

72. Kaiman, "China Cracks Down on Social Media."

73. Creemers, "Pivot in Chinese Cybergovernance."

74. X. Shi, "Zhi Xiaofenhong."

75. Link, *Anatomy of Chinese*, 237.

76. H. Wang, Li, and Wu, "Cong 'mimei' dao 'xiao fenhong.'"

77. Perlez, "Tribunal Rejects Beijing's Claims."

78. L. Zhao, "Zhao Wei."

79. There has also been speculation that the removal of this post was not "accidental." Some China observers argue that the central leadership disagreed with how the CYL handled this matter and requested that the post be removed. However, the CYL failed to understand the message from the top leadership and sensationalized the deletion of the post. Since this kind of speculation is difficult to verify unless reliable insider information is provided, I focus on analyzing the discourses that are visible in the public domain. Voice of America, "Focus Dialogue."

80. X. Li, "Xueshu guancha."

81. X. Li, "Xueshu guancha."

82. Xiying Lei, "Youxi rensheng de biaoqingbao yu dangdai qingnian bei 'guai shushu' bangjia de 'aiguo,'" July 14, 2016; Xiying Lei, "Youxi rensheng de biaoqingbao yu dangdai qingnian 'aiguo yishi' de xuanze," July 16, 2016.

83. Jinjidexiongbaba, "Guanyu aiguo."

84. S. Guo, "Appeal of Style."

85. Esarey, "Winning Hearts and Minds?," 71.

86. J. Liu, "'Moments of Madness.'"

87. Y. Zhang, "Nanhang CZ6101."

88. Y. Zhang, "Shifeijian"; Y. Zhang, "999 jijiu."

89. K. Zhou, "Nanhang."

90. M. Gong and Zhang, "999 shoudu huiying."

91. Y. Zhang, "Wo dui 999 jijiu huiying de xiangguan shengming."

92. Bighammer_wong, "Shengsi shisu xia."

93. Y. Zhang, "Kuanrong, ye shi yizhong liliang."

94. L. Liu, *Liu Liu de Weibo.*

95. L. Liu, "Wo yaode zhishi gongping."

96. Hong, *Hong Huang de Weibo.*

97. F. Jiang, *Jiang Fangzhou de Weibo.*

98. F. Jiang, "Wo zai he xiecheng de jiufen zhong xuedao de."

99. W. Zhang, *Internet and New Social Formation*, 119.

100. E. Han, *Micro-Blogging Memories*, 2.

101. Q. Ma, "Cao Guowei."

Chapter 7

1. https://www.youtube.com/watch?v=CeAJXGVThAQ (accessed May 10, 2018).

2. Xinhuawang, "WeChat Publishes Report."

3. Brennan, "2017 WeChat Data Report."

4. X. Wu, *Tengxun zhuan*, 802–3.

5. Holmes, Balnaves, and Wang, "Red Bags and WeChat"; DeLuca, Brunner, and Sun, "Constructing Public Space."

6. Y. Chen, Mao, and Qiu, *Super-Sticky WeChat*.

7. Haiqing Yu, "Philanthropy on the Move."

8. Xinru Sun, "Self-Narration and Double Articulation."

9. C. Lin, Fang, and Jin, "You Are What You Post"; Lei Guo, "WeChat."

10. Wei, Huang, and Zheng, "Use of Mobile Social Apps"; L. Guo, Zhang, Kang, and Hu, "Transforming Followers into Fans."

11. X. Wu, *Tengxun zhuan*, 796.

12. X. Wu, *Tengxun zhuan*, 796.

13. Xinhuawang, "Nearly 500 Public WeChat Accounts"; Ng, "Politics, Rumors, and Ambiguity"; W. Gao, "Perils of Making New Media."

14. D. Lin, "Bei egou yaole you yimiao."

15. Hernández, "In China, Vaccine Scandal."

16. B. Li, "Doukua Gao Yuanyuan de xin faxing."

17. L. He, Hu, Li, and Zhang, "'Biaotidang' yu 'funengliang.'"

18. Graziani, "WeChat Impact Report 2018."

19. "Fang Yimin (Li Beika)."

20. Z. Wang, "'Diaosi' de kuanghuan yu luomo."

21. Z. Wang, "'Diaosi' de kuanghuan yu luomo."

22. Y. Shen, "Wangluo zizhiju."

23. Sum, "Makings of Subaltern Subjects."

24. Szablewicz, "'Losers' of China's Internet."

25. P. Yang, Tang, and Wang, "*Diaosi* as Infrapolitics."

26. Szablewicz, "'Losers' of China's Internet," 260.

27. Sum, "Makings of Subaltern Subjects."

28. Fauna, "Diaosi."

29. W. Qian, Wang, and Yang, "Zhongguoshi jitang jianzhi."

30. Mi Meng, "Ni weishenme shi waimao xiehui."

31. Jin Jin, "Mi Meng: Yinian xiechu babai wan fensi," 42.

32. Tao, "Want Fame and Fortune?"

33. Tao, "Want Fame and Fortune?"

34. Mi Meng, "Yongyuan aiguo."

35. Mi Meng, "Yongyuan aiguo."

36. W. Wang, "Mi Meng chongxin faming le yizhong nüren"; G. Yu, "Mi Meng weishenme hui 'yongyuan aiguo?'"; Y. Tang, "Yongyuan aiguo."

37. Jin Jin, "Mi Meng: Wanghong, bingren."

38. Mi Meng, *Mi Meng de Weibo*, April 22, 2011.

39. Mi Meng, *Mi Meng de Weibo*, April 22, 2011.

40. Mi Meng, *Mi Meng de Weibo*, April 22, 2011.

41. Jin Jin, "Mi Meng: Yinian xiechu babai wan fensi."

42. Mi Meng, "Wode baba."

43. Mi Meng, "Wo shi ruhe chenggong de."

44. Mi Meng, "Diyi ci zuo toutengcang."

45. Mi Meng, "Wo yigeren huode haohao de."

46. Mi Meng, "Zhi jianren"; Mi Meng, "Beipiao zui pa tingdao de sige zi."

47. C. Gao, "Beijing."

48. Mi Meng, "Beipiao zui pa tingdao de sige zi."

49. Mi Meng, "Beipiao zui pa tingdao de sige zi."

50. Mi Meng, "Youqian kuotai de jiannan shenghuo."

51. Shushengwanyou, "Mi Meng pingshenme."

52. Mi Meng, "Women nanren chugui."

53. Mi Meng, "Women nanren chugui."

54. Mi Meng, "Shuwo zhiyan"; Mi Meng, "Xie Xingfang."

55. Mi Meng, "Ni pingshenme qiongde xinan lide."

56. Mi Meng, "Zhi nanyou."

57. Shushengwanyou, "Mi Meng pingshenme."

58. Mi Meng, "Mi Meng fensi buneng qu?"

59. Mi Meng, *Mi Meng de Weibo*, December 6, 2017.

60. Mi Meng, "Youqian ren zhongcheng juanshu."

61. Mi Meng, "Women de mudi shi."

62. http://chuansong.me/n/921248551045 (accessed May 11, 2018).

63. Mi Meng, "Ta nazou le xinmeiti."

64. Siqiang Zhao, "'Caihua youxian qingnian.'"

65. Jessie, "Mi Meng."

66. "Zuowei Mi Meng de xiaohao."

67. "Zuowei Mi Meng de xiaohao."

68. "Zuowei Mi Meng de xiaohao."

69. Lanjing hunshui, "Mi Meng jiuwu hou tuandui."

70. Caihua Youxian Qingnian, "Yige hanmen zhuangyuan zhi si."

71. Caihua Youxian Qingnian, "Yige hanmen zhuangyuan zhi si."

72. "'Hanmen zhuangyuan zhisi.'"

73. Weifeng fudong, "Weishenme shuo."

74. Weibo account of *People's Daily*, January 30, 2019.

75. Verberg, and Koetse, "Mi Meng and 'Self-Media.'"

76. Weibo account of *People's Daily*, February 1, 2019.

Chapter 8

1. Habermas, *Structural Transformation*.

2. Negt and Kluge, *Public Sphere and Experience*; Fraser, "Rethink the Public Sphere"; Garnham, "Media and the Public Sphere."

3. Lean, "Making of a Public."

4. Lean, "Making of a Public."

5. Dahlgren, "Internet," 148–49.

6. W. Zhang, *Internet and New Social Media Formation*, 3.

7. S. Liu, "Undomesticated Hostilities," 438.

8. S. Liu, "Undomesticated Hostilities," 438.

9. G. Yang, "Beiqing yu xixue."

10. Economy, "China's New Revolution."

11. "Amazing Memes."

12. "Amazing Memes."

13. C. Li, *Chinese Politics*, 354.

14. C. Li, *Chinese Politics*, 354–57.

15. C. Li, *Chinese Politics*, 354–57.

16. C. Li, *Chinese Politics*, 354–57.

17. C. Li, *Chinese Politics*, 354–57.

18. C. Li, *Chinese Politics*, 357.

19. G. Yang, "Lightness, Wildness, and Ambivalence," 178.

BIBLIOGRAPHY

Alexa. "Top Sites in China." https://www.alexa.com/topsites/countries/CN (accessed June 24, 2018).

———. "The Top 500 Sites on the Web." https://www.alexa.com/topsites (accessed June 24, 2018).

"The Amazing Memes Showing How China's Internet Has Reacted to Xi as Perpetual President." Shanghaiist.com. February 26, 2018. https://medium.com/shanghaiist/the-amazing-memes-showing-how-chinas-internet-has-reacted-to-xi-as-perpetual-president-9e8a3a069a6a (accessed February 26, 2018).

Andén-Papadopoulos, Kari. "Citizen Camera-Witnessing: Embodied Political Dissent in the Age of 'Mediated Mass Self-Communication.'" *New Media & Society* 16, no. 5 (2014): 753–69.

Andrejevic, Mark. "Watching Television without Pity: The Productivity of Online Fans." *Television & New Media* 9, no. 1 (2008): 24–46.

"Anjian zongju: '7.23' dongche zhuiwei shigu bushi tianzai" [State Administration of Work Safety: The rear-end collision on July 23 was not a natural disaster]. August 8, 2011. *Zhongguo xinwenwang.* http://www.chinanews.com/gn/2011/08-04/3235166.shtml (accessed May 28, 2018).

Anti, Michael. "Behind the Great Firewall of China." Ted Talk. July 30, 2012. https://www.youtube.com/watch?v=yrcaHGqTqHk (accessed May 28, 2018).

Bai, Ye. "'Balinghou' de xianzhuang yu weilai" [The status quo and future of "post-80s" writers]. *Changcheng* [The Great Wall] 6 (2005): 217–24.

———. "Wode shengming—huiying Han Han" [My statement: In response to Han Han]. March 4, 2006. http://www.docin.com/p-47772878.html (accessed June 19, 2011).

Bai, Zong. "Wanghong Papi Jiang chengzhang shi" [A recollection of how Papi Jiang becomes an Internet celebrity]. *Mingren zhuanji (caifu renwu)* [VIP of fortune], no. 5 (2016): 35.

Bakhtin, Mikhail. *Problems of Dostoevsky's Poetics.* Minneapolis: University of Minnesota Press, 1984.

Balaji, Murali, and Khadeem Hughson. "(Re)producing Borders and Bodies: Masculinity and Nationalism in Indian Cultural Texts." *Asian Journal of Communication* 24, no. 3 (2014): 207–21.

Balla, Steven J. "Government Consultation and Political Participation on the Chinese Internet." In *China's Contested Internet*, edited by Guobin Yang, 75–107. Copenhagen: NAIS Press, 2015.

Barboza, David. "China Surpasses U.S. in Number of Internet Users." *New York Times*, July 26, 2008. https://www.nytimes.com/2008/07/26/business/worldbusiness/26internet.html (accessed March 14, 2020).

Barmé, Geremie. *In the Red: On Contemporary Chinese Culture*. New York: Columbia University Press, 1999.

BBC. "Xinjiang Arrests 'Now over 1,500.'" August 3, 2009. http://news.bbc.co.uk/2/hi/asia-pacific/8181563.stm (accessed May 27, 2018).

Beech, Hanna. "Sex, Please—We're Young and Chinese." *Time*, January 15, 2006. http://www.time.com/time/magazine/article/0,9171,1149406,00.html (accessed May 12, 2010).

Berg, Daria. "Consuming Secrets: China's New Print Culture at the Turn of the Twenty-First Century." In *From Woodblocks to the Internet: Chinese Publishing and Print Culture in Transition, Circa 1800 to 2008*, edited by Cynthia Brokaw and Christopher A. Reed, 315–32. Leiden: Brill, 2012.

Bighammer_wong. "Shengsi shisu xia sheizai tuo houtui—yige xiao daifu dui yige jizhe de jishu fenxi" [When push comes to shove, who's dragging their feet? Technical analysis from a junior doctor in response to the journalist's report]. December 2, 2015. https://weibo.com/p/1001643914007051411098?containerid=1001643914007051411098&fullscreen=true&showurl=http%3A%2F%2Fweibo.com%2Fp%2F1001643914007051411098&url_open_direct=1&luicode=10000011&lfid=100808d6e79d77d24f035cc7b913648309dccd&ep=D6gg35FQA%2C1291471320%2CD6gg35FQA%2C1291471320 (accessed May 28, 2018).

Bondes, Maria, and Günter Schucher. "Derailed Emotions: The Transformation of Claims and Targets during the Wenzhou Online Incident." *Information, Communication & Society* 17, no. 1 (2014): 45–65.

Bourdieu, Pierre. *The Field of Cultural Production: Essays on Art and Literature*. New York: Columbia University Press, 1993.

Brennan, Matthew. "The 2017 WeChat Data Report." November 9, 2017. http://blog.wechat.com/2017/11/09/the-2017-wechat-data-report/ (accessed April 22, 2018).

Buckley, Chris. "Crackdown on Bloggers Is Mounted by China." *New York Times*, September 10, 2013. http://www.nytimes.com/2013/09/11/world/asia/china-cracks-down-on-online-opinion-makers.html?_r=0 (accessed July 8, 2016).

——. "Formal Arrest of Advocate Is Approved by China." *New York Times*, August 23, 2013. http://www.nytimes.com/2013/08/24/world/asia/chinese-rights-advocate-is-formally-arrested.html (accessed August 2, 2015).

Cai, Bin. "2015 nian zhongguo baozhi chanye fazhan baogao" [A 2015 report on the development of China's newspaper industry]. March 1, 2017. http://guoqing.china.com.cn/2017-03/01/content_40382829.htm (accessed July 14, 2018).

Cai, Jane. "Columnist's Online Diary Opens a New Chapter in Sexual Revolution." *South China Morning Post*, November 18, 2003, 1.

Cai, Shenshen. *Contemporary Chinese Films and Celebrity Directors*. New York: Palgrave Macmillan, 2017.

———.*State Propaganda in China's Entertainment Industry*. New York: Routledge, 2016.

Caihua Youxian Qingnian [Talent Limited Youth]. "Yige hanmen zhuangyuan zhi si" [The death of a star student from a humble background]. January 29, 2019. https://www.wolege.com/1442.htm (accessed May 11, 2019).

Chase, Michael. *You've Got Dissent! Chinese Dissident Use of the Internet and Beijing's Counter-Strategies*. Santa Monica: Rand, 2002.

Chen, Chenchen. "Guo Jingming tuandui wenxue de kua meiti chuanbo yanjiu" [A study of cross-media dissemination of literature by Guo Jingming's work team]. Unpublished master's thesis, China West Normal University, 2016.

Chen, Chiafu. "The Ordinary, the Artistic and the Idiotic (Putong, Wenyi and Erbi)—The Hottest Internet Meme Happening Now in China." November 2, 2011. http://www.ministryoftofu.com/2011/11/wu-wen-er-the-ordinary-the-artistic-and-the-idiotic-the-hottes-chinese-internet-meme-happening-now/ (accessed January 4, 2016).

Chen, Dingjia. *Bite zhijing: Wangluo shidai de wenxue shengchan yanjiu* [Bit boundary: A study of literary production in the Internet age]. Beijing: Zhongguo shehui kexue chubanshe, 2011.

Chen, Eva Yin-i. "Neoliberal Self-Governance and Popular Postfeminism in Contemporary Anglo-American Chick Lit." *Concentric: Literary and Cultural Studies* 36, no. 1 (2010): 243–75.

Chen, Julie Yujie. "Thrown under the Bus and Outrunning it! The Logic of Didi and Taxi Drivers' Labour and Activism in the On-Demand Economy." *New Media & Society* 20, no. 8 (2018): 2691–711.

Chen, Tao. "Shangren Guo Jingming" [The businessman Guo Jingming]. *Zhongguo xinwen zhoukan* [China newsweek], no. 23 (2013): 72–74.

Chen, Tong, and Xiangxue Zeng. *Xinlang zhidao: Menhu wangzhan xinwen pindao de yunying* [The Dao of Sina: Management of portal website's news channe]. Fuzhou: Fujian renmin chubanshe, 2005.

Chen, Yang. "Mu Zimei wunian hou xiaotan xingai riji, cheng xing bu zhishi yundong" [Mu Zimei talks about her sex diary five years later: Sex is not just a workout]. *Xinkuaibao* [New Express], March 28, 2008. http://blog.sina.com.cn/s/blog_513ed669010093da.html (accessed June 19, 2010).

Chen, Yu. "Zhongguo chuanmei de shehui yundong qingxiang: Yi Wenzhou dongche zhuiwei shigu weili" [The trend of media activism in China: A case study on the Wenzhou high-speed train crash]. *Conference Proceedings of the 2012 Annual Convention for the Chinese Communication Society*, 2012.

Chen, Yujie, Zhifei Mao, and Jack Linchuan Qiu. *Super-Sticky WeChat and Chinese Society*. Bingley, UK: Emerald, 2018.

Cheng, Gang. "Qinghua daxue de wangshang 'xuni shenghuo:' Huozai jiujing" [Virtual life of Tsinghua university students: Life in *Jiujing*]. *Zhongguo qingnian bao* [China Youth Daily], May 5, 2000. http://www.xys.org/xys/netters/others/net/qinghua.txt (accessed March 24, 2011).

Cheng, Yang. "Social Media Keep Buzzing! A Test of the Contingency Theory in China's Red Cross Credibility Crisis." *International Journal of Communication* 10 (2016): 3241–60.

"China Builds World's Largest Internet Infrastructure." *People's Daily Online*, November 3, 2009. http://en.people.cn/90001/90778/90860/6802372.html (accessed July 4, 2018).

China Central Television (CCTV). *Duihua* [Dialogue], October 25, 2000. http://www.tudou.com/programs/view/yvQ5Q9YKdzs/ (accessed June 2, 2010).

———. "Gongyi yu sili: 'Guo Meimei shijian' zhenxiang diaocha" [Public welfare and personal gains: A factual investigation of "Guo Mei Mei Incident"]. *Dongfang shikong* [Oriental horizon], June 30, 2011. https://v.qq.com/x/page/7ua2cRhS2wr.html? (accessed May 28, 2017).

———. "Guo Meimei kaishe duchang an tingshen zhiji" [Court trial of Guo Meimei's hosting of gambling activities]. *Tingshen xianchang* [Courtroom scene live], September 12, 2015. CCTV's Legal Channel. https://www.youtube.com/watch?v=N9UMMFl1KH0 (accessed June 5, 2018).

———. *Jingji banxiaoshi* [Economy time], July 27, 2011. https://www.youtube.com/watch?v=LFzaNx7m6X8 (accessed May 28, 2018).

———. "Wangluo mingren shehui zeren luntan" [Symposium on the social responsibilities of Internet celebrities]. *Duihua* [Dialogue], August 18, 2013. https://www.youtube.com/watch?v=_AavzbWD09c (accessed July 8, 2016).

China Internet Network Information Center (CNNIC). "2006 nian zhongguo boke diaocha baogao" [Survey results of Chinese blogs in 2006]. 2006. http://www.cnnic.cn/uploadfiles/pdf/2006/9/28/182836.pdf (accessed August 2, 2012).

———. "Di sishisan ci zhongguo hulian wangluo fazhan zhuangkuang tongji baogao" [The 43rd statistical report on Internet development in China]. February 28, 2019. http://www.cac.gov.cn/wxb_pdf/0228043.pdf (accessed March 1, 2019).

———. "Di sishisici zhongguo hulian wangluo fazhan zhuangkuang tongji baogao" [The 44th statistical report on Internet development in China]. August 2019. http://www.cnnic.cn/hlwfzyj/hlwxzbg/hlwtjbg/201908/P020190830356787490958.pdf (accessed January 1, 2020).

———. "Di sishiwuci zhongguo hulianwangluo fazhan zhuangkuang tongji baogao" [The 45th statistical report on Internet development in China]. March 2020. http://www.cac.gov.cn/2020-04/27/c_1589535470378587.htm (accessed April 1, 2020).

———. "Zhongguo hulianwangluo fazhan zhuangkuang tongji baogao" [Survey results of the Internet development in China]. 2007–12. http://www.cnnic.cn/research/zx/qwfb/ (accessed July 1, 2012).

Chouliaraki, Lilie. "Digital Witnessing in War Journalism: The Case of Post-Arab Spring Conflicts." *Popular Communication* 13, no. 2 (2015): 105–19.

Clark, Paul. *The Chinese Cultural Revolution: A History*. Cambridge: Cambridge University Press, 2008.

———. *Youth Culture in China: From Red Guards to Netizens*. Cambridge: Cambridge University Press, 2012.

CNN. "Han Han: China's Rebel Blogger." 2010. http://articles.cnn.com/2010-06-03/tech/

han.han.china_1_chinese-govern-ment-han-han-china?_s=PM:TECH (accessed December 20, 2013).

———.Interview of Yang Lan. *Talk Asia*, October 14, 2007. http://edition.cnn.com/2007/WORLD/asiapcf/08/22/talkasia.yanglan/index.html (accessed July 15, 2012).

Coderre, Laurence. "Meaningful Mobility and the Ties That Bind: 1988 as Postsocialist Road Story." *Modern Chinese Literature and Culture* 26, no. 2 (2014): 1–37.

Creemers, Rogier. "Cyber China: Updating Propaganda, Public Opinion Work and Social Management for the Twenty-First Century." *Journal of Contemporary China* 26, no. 103 (2017): 85–100.

———."The Pivot in Chinese Cybergovernance: Integrating Internet Control in Xi Jinping's China." *China Perspectives*, no. 4 (2015): 5–13.

Cui, Baoguo. *Zhongguo chuanmei chanye fazhan baogao* [Report on the development of traditional media market]. Beijing: Shehui kexue wenxian chubanshe, 2018. http://www.sohu.com/a/237156451_654813 (accessed July 14, 2018).

Cunningham, Stuart, David Craig, and Junyi Lv. "China's Livestreaming Industry: Platforms, Politics, and Precarity." *International Journal of Cultural Studies* 22, no. 6 (2019): 719–36.

dachy. "Zheli haoxiang meiren baba Furong Jiejie" [How come nobody gossips about Furong Jiejie]. May 24, 2005. http://www.tianya.cn/publicforum/content/funinfo/1/41700.shtml (accessed July 11, 2011).

———."Furong jiao di'ertan: Furong Jiejie dazhan Furong gege" [The second article on the Furong Cult: Sister Furong fights with Brother Furong]. May 25, 2005. http://www.tianya.cn/publicforum/content/funinfo/1/41956.shtml (accessed July 11, 2011).

———.June 14, 2005. http://cache.tianya.cn/publicforum/content/funinfo/1/42481.shtml (accessed July 11, 2011).

Dahlgren, Peter. "The Internet, Public Spheres, and Political Communication: Dispersion and Deliberation." *Political Communication* 22, no. 2 (2005): 147–62.

Dao Han yundong [Down with Han Han movement]. http://www.daohan.org/ebook/cn/# (accessed December 23, 2015).

Davenport, Thomas H., and John C. Beck. *The Attention Economy: Understanding the New Currency of Business*. Boston: Harvard Business School Press, 2001.

Davies, David J. "China's Celebrity Entrepreneurs: Business Models for 'Success.'" In *Celebrity in China*, edited by Louise Edwards and Elaine Jeffreys, 193–216. Hong Kong: Hong Kong University Press, 2010.

DeLuca, Kevin Michael, Elizabeth Brunner, and Ye Sun. "Constructing Public Space: Weibo, WeChat, and the Transformative Events of Environmental Activism in China." *International Journal of Communication* 10 (2016): 321–39.

"Design Flaws and Poor Management Caused Wenzhou Collision, Report Confirms." January 8, 2012, *Railway Gazette International*. http://www.railwaygazette.com/news/policy/single-view/view/design-flaws-and-poor-management-caused-wenzhou-collision-report-confirms.html (accessed October 18, 2017).

Dickson, Bruce J. "China's Cooperative Capitalists: The Business End of the Middle Class." In *China's Emerging Middle Class: Beyond Economic Transformation*, edited by Cheng Li, 291–309. Washington, DC: Brookings Institution Press, 2010.

Dijck, José van, Thomas Poell, and Martijn de Waal. *The Platform Society: Public Values in a Connective Society*. New York: Oxford University Press, 2018.

Dong, Jiangyong, and Boming Li. *Yu wushiwei wangzhan zhubian mianduimian—BiaNews wangbian xunlianying xilie jiangzuo* [Face to face conversations with fifty editors-in-chief: Lecture series on training web editors]. Beijing: Tsinghua University Press, 2010.

Du, Qingjie. *Boke chutan* [A preliminary study of blog]. Hefei: Anhui jiaoyu chubanshe, 2008.

Dun, Yulin. "Luelun Cai Zhiheng wangluo xiaoshuo de youmo fengge" [A preliminary analysis of the humorous style of Cai Zhiheng's Internet novel]. *Shijie huawen wenxue luntan* [Forum of Global Chinese Literature] 4 (2003): 44–48.

Economy, Elizabeth C. "China's New Revolution: The Reign of Xi Jinping." *Foreign Affairs* (May/June 2018): 60–74.

Edwards, Dan, and Marina Svensson. "Show Us Life and Make Us Think: Engagement, Witnessing and Activism in Independent Chinese Documentary Today." *Studies in Documentary Film* 11, no. 3 (2017): 161–69.

Eimer, David. "China Cracks Down on the Sex Bloggers." *Independent*, July 17, 2005. https://www.independent.co.uk/news/world/asia/china-cracks-down-on-the-sex-bloggers-299629.html (accessed August 2, 2012).

Esarey, Ashley. "Winning Hearts and Minds? Cadres as Microbloggers in China." *Journal of Current Chinese Affairs* 44, no. 2 (2015): 69–103.

Esarey, Ashley, and Qiang Xiao. "Political Expression in the Chinese Blogosphere: Below the Radar." *Asian Survey* 48, no. 5 (2008): 752–72.

Fan, Xing. *Communications and Information in China: Regulatory Issues, Strategic Implications*. New York: University Press of America, 2001.

Fang, Xingdong. "Blog zhiwang: Maite delaji" [The king of blog: Matt Drudge]. *Nanfang zhoumo* [Southern Weekend], September 5, 2002, 31.

———."Guanyu blog weilai de 1000 yuan duzhu" [Bet 1,000 RMB on the future of blog]. *Nanfang zhoumo* [Southern Weekend], September 5, 2002, 31.

Fang, Xingdong, and Jianhua Sun. "Blog: Geren riji tiaozhan chuanmei jutou" [Blog: Personal diary challenges traditional media giant]. *Nanfang zhoumo* [Southern Weekend], September 5, 2002, 31.

Fang, Xingdong, and Junxiu Wang. *Boke: E shidai de daohuozhe* [Blog: Prometheus of the E era]. Beijing: Zhongguo fangzheng chubanshe, 2003.

"Fang Yimin (Li Beika): Wode zhuanxing zhilu" [Fang Yimin (Li Beika): My change of career path]. October 14, 2016. https://read01.com/5gzyjQ.html (accessed May 10, 2018).

Farrer, James. "China's Women Sex Bloggers and Dialogic Sexual Politics on the Chinese Internet." *China Aktuell: Journal of Current Chinese Affairs* 36, no. 4 (2007): 1–36.

Fauna, "Diaosi: Peking University Releases Report on China's 'Losers.'" December 3, 2014. https://www.chinasmack.com/diaosi-peking-university-releases-report-on-chinas-losers (accessed July 29, 2018).

Feng, Jin. *Romancing the Internet: Consuming and Producing Chinese Web Romance*. Leiden: Brill, 2013.

Fengle and QY. "Mu Zimei fangtan: Dui wo laishuo boke shi yizhong zilian" [Interview of Mu Zimei: Blog represents a kind of narcissism for me]. November 23, 2003. http://life.bokee.com/78/2003-11-22/9249.html (accessed August 11, 2011).

"50 People Who Matter 2010." *New Statesman*, September 27, 2010. https://www.newstatesman.com/2010/09/global-influence-world-2 (accessed March 19, 2018).

Fiske, John. "The Cultural Economy of Fandom." In *The Adoring Audience: Fan Culture and Popular Media*, edited by Lisa A. Lewis, 30–49. New York: Routledge, 1992.

Franck, Georg. "The Economy of Attention." *Telepolis*, translated by Silvia Plaza, December 7, 1999. http://www.heise.de/tp/artikel/5/5567/1.html (accessed July 15, 2012).

Fraser, Nancy. "Rethink the Public Sphere: A Contribution to the Critique of Actually Existing Democracy." In *Habermas and the Public Sphere*, edited by Craig Calhoun, 109–42. Cambridge, MA: MIT Press, 1992.

Fumian, Marco. "The Social Construction of a Myth: An Interpretation of Guo Jingming's Parable." *Oriental Archive* 78 (2010): 397–419.

——. "The Temple and the Market: Controversial Positions in the Literary Field with Chinese Characteristics." *Modern Chinese Literature and Culture* 21, no. 2 (2009): 126–66.

Furong Jiejie. "Beida, ni shi wo qianshi zui shen zui mei de tong" [Peking University, You are the most traumatic and beautiful sadness of my past life]. September 2002. http://www.frjj.cc/thread-3353-1-1.html (accessed June 15, 2011).

——. "Bukan huishou (10)" [Unbearable memories: 10]. *Official Blog of Furong Jiejie*. June 16, 2005. http://frjj.blog.sohu.com/18415716.html (accessed June 29, 2010).

——. "Furong Jiejie de shouzhi geren danqu" [The first single of Furong Jiejie]. March 24, 2006. http://www.newsmth.net/pc/pcarch.php?userid=huobingker&y=2006&m=3 (accessed July 2, 2010).

——. *Furong Jiejie's Microblog*. June 6, 2010. http://www.weibo.com/frjj (accessed August 2, 2012).

——. *Furong Jiejie's Microblog*. June 16, 2010. http://www.weibo.com/frjj (accessed August 2, 2012).

——. *Furong Jiejie's Microblog*. March 1, 2018. https://weibo.com/frjj?refer_flag=1001030101_&is_all=1#_rnd1520617975361 (accessed August 2, 2018).

——. "Furong Jiejie zhende shi zhaoyao jing" [Furong Jiejie is indeed a demon-spotting mirror]. *Official Blog of Furong Jiejie*. July 30, 2005. http://blog.sina.com.cn/s/blog_4b674096010005v1.html (accessed June 29, 2010).

——. *Huobingker de Blog* [Blog of huobingker]. http://www.newsmth.net/pc/pccon.php?id=5280&nid=155536&s=all (accessed August 2, 2012).

——. "Pandian Furong Jiejie de 2006, chongman yanlei he chiru, puman xianhua he mengxiang de yangguang dadao, zhitong shijie" [A summary of Furong Jiejie's 2006: Full of tears and humiliation; got connected to the world through the avenue of sunshine covered with flowers and dreams]. January 1, 2007. http://www.tianya.cn/publicforum/content/funinfo/1/283410.shtml (accessed June 29, 2010).

——. "Qinai de oufen, rang Furong Jiejie na shenme lai henhen ai si nimen" [My dear fans, what should I do to reciprocate your love]. September 24, 2006. http://www.tianya.cn/publicforum/content/funinfo/1/246108.shtml (accessed June 29, 2010).

"Furong Jiejie wei yan shanzha pai xiezhen" [Furong Jiejie took glamour shots to auction a role in *Under the Hawthorn Tree*]. http://news.xinhuanet.com/photo/2010-04/13/c (accessed October 10, 2010).

Gao, Charlotte. "Beijing: How Does a Tragic Fire Turn into the Mass Eviction of Migrant Workers?" *Diplomat*, November 27, 2017. https://thediplomat.com/2017/11/beijing-how-does-a-tragic-fire-turn-into-the-mass-eviction-of-migrant-workers/ (accessed May 25, 2018).

Gao, Honghao. "Lianxu qige jidu yingli, Weibo jiujing kaoshenme shixianle lianxu zengzhang?" [Generating profits for seven quarters in a row: What's the secret of Weibo]. *Caijing* [Finance and Economics], August 10, 2016. http://www.caijingmobile.com/wxshare/282672.html?from=timeline&isappinstalled=0 (accessed June 5, 2018).

Gao, Wei. "The Perils of Making New Media the Philosopher King: A Case Study from Tencent's Weixin." *Peking University Law Journal* 4, no. 2 (2016): 267–89.

Garnham, Nicholas. "The Media and the Public Sphere." In *Habermas and the Public Sphere*, edited by Craig Calhoun, 359–76. Cambridge, MA: MIT Press, 1992.

Gillespie, Tarleton. *Custodians of the Internet: Platforms, Content Moderation, and the Hidden Decisions that Shape Social Media*. New Haven, CT: Yale University Press, 2018.

———. "The Politics of 'Platforms.'" *New Media & Society* 12, no. 3 (2010): 347–64.

Gledhill, Christine. "Pleasurable Negotiations." In *Cultural Theory and Popular Culture: A Reader*, edited by John Storey, 236–49. Essex: Pearson Education, 1994.

Gleiss, Marielle Stigum. "Speaking Up for the Suffering (Br)other: Weibo Activism, Discursive Struggles, and Minimal Politics in China." *Media, Culture & Society* 37, no. 4 (2015): 513–29.

Goldhaber, Michael H. "The Value of Openness in an Attention Economy." *First Monday*, June 5, 2006. http://firstmonday.org/htbin/cgiwrap/bin/ojs/index.php/fm/article/view/1334/1254 (accessed May 18, 2012).

Gong, Haomin, and Xin Yang. "Digitized Parody: The Politics of *Egao* in Contemporary China." *China Information* 24, no. 1 (2010): 3–26.

———. *Reconfiguring Class, Gender, Ethnicity and Ethics in Chinese Internet Culture*. New York: Routledge, 2017.

Gong, Mian, and Heng Zhang. "999 shoudu huiying Nanhang jijiu: Qiangjiu guocheng fuhe zhenliao guifan" [Beijing 999 responds to the China Southern Airlines debacle for the first time: Rescue procedure accords with treatment norms]. *Jinghua shibao* [Jinghua Times], December 1, 2015. http://news.xinhuanet.com/local/2015-12/01/c_128485017.htm (accessed May 28, 2018).

Gray, Jonathan. "Antifandom and the Moral Text: Television without Pity and Textual Dislike." *American Behavioral Scientist* 48, no. 7 (2005): 840–58.

———. "New Audiences, New Textualities: Anti-fans and Non-fans." *International Journal of Cultural Studies* 6, no. 1 (2003): 64–81.

Graziani, Thomas. "WeChat Impact Report 2018: All the Latest WeChat Data." July 4, 2018. WALKTHECHAT. https://walkthechat.com/wechat-impact-report-2016/ (accessed July 13, 2018).

Guo, Jingming. "Jintian Xiaoshidai 3.0 cijin shidai shangshi le, xiangyao dui nimen shuode hua" [*Tiny Times 3.0* is released today: What I would like to tell you]. *Guo Jingming de boke* [Guo Jingming's blog]. December 8, 2011. http://blog.sina.com. cn/s/blog_46d7df020102dvyl.html (accessed May 7, 2018).

———. "Rende jixian shi neng tuchu zise wanyi'er?!" [The upper limit of a human being is to throw up something purple]. *Guo Jingming de boke* [Guo Jingming's blog]. September 9, 2008. http://blog.sina.com.cn/s/blog_46d7df020100a907.html (accessed May 5, 2018).

———. "Wo he Luo Luo zuole shenme nie" [The karma that Luo Luo and I received]. *Guo Jingming de boke* [Guo Jingming's blog]. January 12, 2006. http://blog.sina.com.cn/s/ blog_46d7df02010001t1.html (accessed May 30, 2018).

———. "Xiao Si da jiangtang" [Lecture of Little Four]. *Guo Jingming de boke* [Guo Jingming's blog]. October 23, 2005. http://blog.sina.com.cn/s/blog_46d7df020100009h. htm (accessed May 30, 2018).

Guo, Lei. "WeChat as a Semipublic Alternative Sphere: Exploring the Use of WeChat among Chinese Older Adults." *International Journal of Communication* 11 (2017): 408–28.

Guo, Lingyun, Mingli Zhang, Kai Kang, and Mu Hu. "Transforming Followers into Fans: A Study of Chinese Users of the WeChat Official Account." *Online Information Review* 41, no. 7 (2017): 1029–45.

Guo, Shaohua. "The Appeal of Style: Han Han and Microcultural Contention in Digital China." *Modern Chinese Literature and Culture* 28, no. 2 (2016): 90–138.

———. "'Occupying' the Internet: State Media and the Reinvention of Official Culture Online." *Communication and the Public* 3, no. 1 (2018): 19–33.

———. "Ruled by Attention: A Case Study of Professional Digital Attention Agents at Sina.com and the Chinese Blogosphere." *International Journal of Cultural Studies* 19, no. 4 (2016): 407–23.

Guo, Yun. "Han Han: Xianghe shijie tan shenme" [What does Han Han want to say to the world]. *Zhongguo tushu pinglun* [China Book Review] 4 (2011): 86–88.

"Guo Jingming: Wode chenggong tianjing diyi" [Guo Jingming: My success is fated]. *Wangyi xinwen lingyimian* [The Other Side], no. 32, 2010. http://news.163.com/special/00014029/guojingming.html (accessed May 12, 2018).

"Guo Jingming zhuanfang" [An interview with Guo Jingming]. Official Channel of SMG Shanghai TV. April 22, 2014. https://www.youtube.com/watch?v=pIpv6ZYnENM (accessed May 7, 2018).

"Guo Meimei: Huaimingsheng yeshi mingsheng" [Guo Meimei: Notoriety is also fame]. *Jinghua shibao* [Jinghua Times], August 4, 2014. http://money.163.com/14/0804/03/ A2PAR2TN00253B0H.html (accessed May 28, 2017).

Habermas, Jürgen. *The Structural Transformation of the Public Sphere: An Inquiry into a Category of Bourgeois Society*. Cambridge, MA: MIT Press, 1989.

Hall, Stuart. "Cultural Identity and Diaspora." In *Colonial Discourse and Post-Colonial Theory: A Reader*, edited by Patrick Williams and Laura Chrisman, 392–403. New York: Columbia University Press, 1994.

Han, Eileen Le. *Micro-blogging Memories: Weibo and Collective Remembering in Contemporary China*. New York: Palgrave Macmillan, 2016.

Han, Gang Kevin, and Wen Wang. "Mapping User Relationships for Health Information Diffusion on Microblogging in China: A Social Network Analysis of Sina Weibo." *Asian Journal of Communication* 25, no. 1 (2015): 65–83.

Han, Han. "Erlingyiling nian shiyue bari" [October 8, 2010]. *Han Han de boke* [Han Han's blog]. October 9, 2010. http://blog.sina.com/cn/s/blog_470128obo100lvjb. html (accessed December 29, 2013).

———. "Erlingyiyi nian shiyi yue sanri" [November 3, 2011]. *Han Han de boke* [Han Han's blog]. November 3, 2011. http://blog.sina.com.cn/s/blog_470128obo102dwxv.html (accessed June 12, 2012).

———. *Guangrong ri* [Glory days]. Beijing: Ershiyi shiji chubanshe, 2007.

———. "Haizi men, nimen saole yeye de xing" [Children, you're spoiling grandpas' fun]. *Han Han de boke* [Han Han's blog]. May 2, 2010. Translated by Jennifer Grace Smith. May 3, 2010. http://chinaelectionsblog.net/?p=4611 (accessed June 11, 2012).

———. "Han Feng shige hao ganbu" [Han Feng is a good party official]. *Han Han de boke* [Han Han's blog]. March 4, 2010. http://blog.sina.com.cn/s/blog_470128obo100h7b2. html (accessed June 12, 2012).

———. *Sanchong men* [Triple door]. Beijing: Zuojia chubanshe, 2000.

———. "Shuo minzhu" [On democracy]. *Han Han de boke* [Han Han's blog]. December 24, 2011. http://blog.sina.com.cn/s/blog_470128obo102dz84.html (accessed December 12, 2013).

———. "Tan geming" [On revolution]. *Han Han de boke* [Han Han's blog]. December 23, 2011. http://blog.sina.com.cn/s/blog_470128obo102dz5s.html (accessed December 12, 2013).

———. "Tuojie de guodu" [Derailed nation]. Translated by *China Digital Times*. July 27, 2011. http://chinadigitaltimes.net/2011/07/han-han-"the-derailed-country"/ (accessed May 23, 2012).

———. "Wentan shige pi, shei dou bie zhuangbi" [The literary world is nonsense; no one should be a pretentious prick]. March 2, 2006. *Han Han de boke* [Han Han's blog]. http://www.bullogger.com/blogs/twocold/archives/11927.aspx (accessed June 28, 2012).

———. "Wo qu nali zhao, xiang ni name hao" [Where can I find someone as good as you are]. *Han Han de boke* [Han Han's blog]. March 14, 2010. http://blog.sina.com. cn/s/blog_470128obo100hcf6.html. Translated and posted by Qiang Xiao, "210,000 Netizens Vote on Han Han's Blog." March 13, 2010. http://chinadigitaltimes. net/2010/03/210000-netizens-vote-on-han-hans-blog (accessed June 12, 2012).

———. "Wo zhongyu qudaole chulian duixiang: Qiuqiu ni, kuai gaowo" [Finally I marry my first love: I beg you, sue me please]. *Han Han de boke* [Han Han's blog]. March 29, 2006. http://www.bullogger.com/blogs/ twocold/archives/11927.aspx (accessed June 28, 2012).

———. "Yao ziyou" [Want freedom]. *Han Han de boke* [Han Han's blog]. December 26,

2011. http://blog.sina.com.cn/s/blog_470128ob0102dz9f.html (accessed December 12, 2013).

———. "Yeyemen, nimen qing jinxing" [Grandpas, please enjoy yourselves]. *Han Han de boke* [Han Han's blog]. May 2, 2010. http://blog.sina.com.cn/s/blog_470128ob0100ic2e.html (accessed June 11, 2012).

Han, Renjun. *Erzi Han Han* [My son Han Han]. Shanghai: Shanghai renmin chubanshe, 2008.

Han, Rongbin. *Contesting Cyberspace in China: Online Expression and Authoritarian Resilience*. New York: Columbia University Press, 2018.

———. "Withering Gongzhi: Cyber Criticism of Chinese Public Intellectuals." *International Journal of Communication* 12 (2018): 1966–87.

"'Hanmen zhuangyuan zhisi' baowen zao qunchao; Mi Meng huiying: juedui zhenshi" [The popular essay "The death of a star student from a humble background" receives public mockery; Mi Meng defended the essay's authenticity]. January 31, 2019. *Caijing*. https://tech.sina.com.cn/i/2019-01-31/doc-ihqfskcp1908249.shtml (accessed May 11, 2019).

Harwit, Eric. "WeChat: Social and Political Development of China's Dominant Messaging App." *Chinese Journal of Communication* 10, no. 3 (2017): 312–27.

Hassid, Jonathan. "China's Contentious Journalists: Reconceptualising the Media." *Problems of Post-Communism* 55, no. 4 (2008): 52–61.

He, Lingnan, Lingshu Hu, Wei Li, and Zhian Zhang. "'Biaotidang' yu 'funengliang'— Meitilei weixin gongzhonghao de yuyan fengge fenxi" ["Headline party" and "negative energies": An analysis of linguistic style of public accounts of media genres]. *Xinwen zhanxian* [The Press], no. 7 (2016). http://paper.people.com.cn/xwzx/html/2016-07/01/content_1702728.htm (accessed May 10, 2018).

He, Wei. *Networked Public: Social Media and Social Change in Contemporary China*. Heidelberg: Springer, 2017.

Henningsen, Lena. *Copyright Matters: Imitation, Creativity and Authenticity in Contemporary Chinese Literature*. Berlin: Berliner Wissenschafts-Verlag, 2010.

Hernández, Javier C. "In China, Vaccine Scandal Infuriates Parents and Tests Government." *New York Times*, July 23, 2018. https://www.nytimes.com/2018/07/23/world/asia/china-vaccines-scandal-investigation.html (accessed July 23, 2018).

Herrmann, Christoph S., and Robert T. Knight. "Mechanisms of Human Attention: Event-Related Potentials and Oscillations." *Neuroscience and Biobehavioral Reviews* 25, no. 6 (2001): 465–76.

Hills, Matthew. *Fan Cultures*. London: Routledge, 2002.

———. "Virtually Out There: Strategies, Tactics and Affective Spaces in On-line Fandom." In *Technospaces: Inside the New Media*, edited by Sally R. Munt, 147–60. London: Continuum, 2001.

Hockx, Michel. *Internet Literature in China*. New York: Columbia University Press, 2015.

Holmes, Kyle, Mark Balnaves, and Yini Wang. "Red Bags and WeChat (Wēixìn): Online Collectivism during Massive Chinese Cultural Events." *Global Media Journal* 9, no. 1 (2015): 15–26.

Hong, Huang. *Hong Huang de Weibo* [Weibo account of Hong Huang]. https://weibo.com/honghuang?from=myfollow_no-group&is_all=1 (accessed May 28, 2018).

———. "Shanghai riji er, Zhang Dachuan shuo" [Shanghai diary II: Words of Zhang Dachuan]. *Hong Huang de boke* [Hong Huang's blog]. May 28, 2007. http://blog.sina.com.cn/s/blog_476bdd0a010008uf.html (accessed February 21, 2010).

———. "Zhao xieshou" [Looking for writers]. *Hong Huang de boke* [Hong Huang's blog]. March 21, 2007. http://blog.sina.com.cn/s/blog_476bdd0a010007t3.html (accessed July 15, 2012).

Hong, Yu. *Networking China: The Digital Transformation of the Chinese Economy.* Chicago: University of Illinois Press, 2017.

Hou, Cheng-nan, and Tzung-je Tsai. "Weibo shidai zhongguo wanglu shequn chuanbo zhong xianghu jiankong zhuangtai zhi fenxi: Yi Guo Meimei shijian weili" [An exploration of surveillance of online community in the age of microblogs: The case of Guo Meimei]. *Yuanjing jijinhui jikan* [Prospect Quarterly] 17, no. 2 (2016): 65–111.

Hu, Lisha. "Mingren boke: Wangluo de you yichang yule" [The celebrity blog: Another round of Internet entertainment]. *Wangluo chuanbo* [Network Dissemination] 4 (2006): 48.

Hu, Xiaomei. "Xing huangyan Mu Zimei" [Sex, lies, Mu Zimei]. *Tianya* [Frontiers] 3 (2005): 29–43.

Hu, Xudong. "Furong Jiejie yu xiju baoli" [Furong Jiejie and comedic violence]. *Xin jingbao* [Beijing News], June 10, 2005. http://gb.cri.cn/3821/2005/06/10/762@578468.htm (accessed June 13, 2011).

Hu, Yong. "Fenlie de 'weixin zhifu' Zhang Xiaolong: Chanpin zhexue xiangzuo, shiyi yonghu xiangyou" [Zhang Xiaolong, the father of WeChat, has a foot in both camps: Between product philosophy and one billion users]. January 23, 2018. http://tech.163.com/18/0123/10/D8R2E14R00097U7R.html (accessed May 10, 2018).

Huang, Cary, and Keith Zhai. "Xi Jinping Rallies Party for Propaganda War on Internet." *South China Morning Post*, September 4, 2013. http://www.scmp.com/news/china/article/1302857/president-xi-jinping-rallies-party-propaganda-war-internet (accessed August 2, 2017).

Huang, Chengju. "China's State-Run Tabloids: The Rise of 'City Newspapers.'" *International Communication Gazette* 63, no. 5 (2001): 435–50.

Huang, Jinping. "Weixin shi ruhe feiqilai de" [How did WeChat become popular]. *Nanfang zhoumo* [Southern Weekends], February 4, 2012. http://www.newhua.com/2012/0204/143932.shtml (accessed July 20, 2018).

Huang, Ronggui, and Ngai-ming Yip. "Internet and Activism in Urban China: A Case Study of Protests in Xiamen and Panyu." *Journal of Comparative Asian Development* 11, no. 2 (2012): 201–23.

Huang, Shengmin, and Yan Zhou. *Zhongguo chuanmei shichang dabianju* [A new century for China's media market]. Beijing: Zhongxin chubanshe, 2003.

Huanpei dingdang. "Furong jiao rumen zhi chuji saomang shouce" [Basic literacy manuals for disciples of the Furong Cult]. May 27, 2005. http://tieba.baidu.com/f?kz=115575462 (accessed June 29, 2010).

Hung, Chin-fu. "The Politics of China's Wei-Quan Movement in the Internet Age." *International Journal of China Studies* 1, no. 2 (2010): 331–49.

Inwood, Heather. *Verse Going Viral: China's New Media Scenes*. Seattle: University of Washington Press, 2014.

Jacobs, Joanne. "Communication Overexposure: The Rise of Blogs as a Product of Cybervoyeurism." *The 2003 Annual Conference of the Australia and New Zealand Communication Association*, 1–23.

Jacobs, Katrien. *People's Pornography: Sex and Surveillance on the Chinese Internet*. Bristol, UK: Intellect, 2012.

Jeffreys, Elaine. *Sex and Sexuality in China*. London: Routledge, 2006.

Jenkins, Henry. *Convergence Culture: Where Old and New Media Collide*. New York: New York University Press, 2006.

———.*Fans, Bloggers, and Gamers: Exploring Participatory Culture*. New York: New York University Press, 2006.

Jessie. "Mi Meng: Yiqianwan fenhou, wo neng ganshenme" [Mi Meng: What's next after having ten million fans]. April 13, 2017. *Yizhao*. http://www.1zhao.com/2017/04/13/2739/ (accessed May 11, 2018).

Ji, Tianqin. "BBS wangshi" [Recollections of BBS]. *Nandu zhoukan* [Southern Metropolis Weekly] 201, no. 20. https://www.toutiao.com/i6259687306064560642/ (accessed July 11, 2018).

Jia, Mei. "Guo Jingming on His Latest Best Seller." *China Daily*, March 1, 2012. http://www.chinadaily.com.cn/life/2012-03/01/content_14730726.htm (accessed May 2, 2018).

Jian, Ping. "Fang Xingdong: Boke zhe shenghuo" [Fang Xingdong: Blogging about life]. *Women of China* 11 (2005): 76–78.

Jiang, Fangzhou. *Jiang Fangzhou de Weibo* [Weibo account of Jiang Fangzhou]. https://weibo.com/1049198655/D6YOUpnwO?type=comment (accessed May 28, 2018).

———. "Wo zai he xiecheng de jiufen zhong xuedao de ding jipiao changshi" [Some common knowledge about ticket reservations I learned when dealing with Ctrip]. December 6, 2015. https://weibo.com/1049198655/D7awnCHHd?type=comment#_rnd1516390045650 (accessed May 28, 2018).

Jiang, Weiwei. "Zai boke shijie fenxiang he jiaoliu" [Share and communicate in the world of blogs]. *Zhongguo qingnianbao* [China Youth Daily], September 25, 2002. http://www.china.com.cn/chinese/feature/203384.htm (accessed April 19, 2012).

Jiao, Priscilla. "Culture a Key Priority in Five-Year Plan." *South China Morning Post*, March 28, 2011. http://www.scmp.com/article/742247/culture-key-priority-five-year-plan (accessed June 9, 2018).

Jiazhou chengzi. "Yinian shifen baozhi xiukan: 2018 nian zhimei gai zenmeban" [Ten newspapers end publication within a year: What should print media do in 2018]. *Chuanmei toutiao* [Headlines of Traditional Media], December 17, 2017. http://www.sohu.com/a/211077385_570250 (accessed July 14, 2018).

Jin, Jin. "Mi Meng: Wanghong, bingren, chaoshui de yizhong fangxiang" [Mi Meng: Internet celebrity, patient, and a direction of the tide]. March 14, 2017. https://www.digitaling.com/articles/35675.html (accessed May 11, 2018).

———. "Mi Meng: Yinian xiechu babai wan fensi" [Mi Meng: Get 8 million fans within a year]. *Xiandai qingnian: Xijie* [Modern Youth: Details], no. 4 (2017): 42–45.

Jin, Meijie. "Wenxue wangluo shidai de kuanghuan—Cai Zhiheng Diyici de qinmijie-chu yu wangluo wenxue de xingsheng" [Carnival in the age of literary Internet: The flourishing of Internet literature and *The First Intimate Contact*]. *Beifang wenxue* [Northern Literature] 7 (2016): 75–76.

Jinjidexiongbaba. "Guanyu aiguo de zhengque dakai fangshi" [The right way to love one's country]. Weibo Account of the Communist Youth League. July 20, 2016. https://weibo.com/ttarticle/p/show?id=2309403999380288997740 (accessed June 5, 2018).

Jung, Sun. "The Shared Imagination of Bishōnen, Pan-East Asian Soft Masculinity: Reading DBSK, Youtube.com and Transcultural New Media Consumption." *Intersections: Gender and Sexuality in Asia and the Pacific*, no. 20 (2009). http://intersections.anu.edu.au/issue20/jung.htm (accessed May 6, 2018).

Kaiman, Jonathan. "China Cracks Down on Social Media with Threat of Jail for 'Online Rumours.'" *Guardian*, September 10, 2013. http://www.theguardian.com/world/2013/sep/10/china-social-media-jail-rumours (accessed November 24, 2015).

Keane, Michael. *The Chinese Television Industry*. London: BFI/Palgrave Macmillan, 2015.

Kelkar, Shreeharsh. "Engineering a Platform: The Construction of Interfaces, Users, Organizational Roles, and the Division of Labor." *New Media & Society* 20, no. 7 (2018): 2629–46.

Kenney, Martin, and John Zysman. "The Rise of the Platform Economy." *Issues in Science and Technology* 32, no. 3 (2016): 61–69.

King, Aventurina. "China's Pop Fiction." *New York Times*, May 4, 2008. http://www.nytimes.com/2008/05/04/books/review/King-t.html?pagewanted=all (accessed May 2, 2018).

King, Gary, Jennifer Pan, and Margaret E. Roberts. "How Censorship in China Allows Government Criticism but Silences Collective Expression." *American Political Science Review* 107, no. 2 (2013): 1–18.

Kong, Shuyu. *Consuming Literature: Best Sellers and the Commercialization of Literary Production in Contemporary China*. Stanford, CA: Stanford University Press, 2005.

———. "Literary Celebrity in China: From Reformers to Rebels." In *Celebrity in China*, edited by Louise Edwards and Elaine Jeffreys, 125–43. Hong Kong: Hong Kong University Press, 2010.

Krotoski, Aleks. "The Internet's Cyber Radicals: Heroes of the Web Changing the World." *Guardian*, November 27, 2010. http://www.theguardian.com/technology/2010/nov/28/internet-radicals-world-wide-web (accessed May 23, 2011).

Kuang, Xinhua. "Guochan weibo xingshuai shi" [The rise and fall of domestic microblogs]. *Xin zhoukan* [News Week], April 9, 2010, 36.

Kunze, Rui. "Cross-Media, Cross-Promotion: Intermediality and Cultural Entrepreneurism in Postsocialist China." *Concentric: Literacy & Cultural Studies* 43, no. 2 (2017): 133–61.

Lagerkvist, Johan. *After the Internet, Before Democracy: Competing Norms in Chinese Media and Society*. New York: Peter Lang, 2010.

——. "In the Crossfire of Demands: Chinese News Portals between Propaganda and the Public." In *Chinese Cyberspaces: Technological Changes and Political Effects*, edited by Jens Damm and Simona Thomas, 38–56. Abingdon, UK: Routledge, 2006.

Lamarre, Thomas. "Platformativity: Media Studies, Area Studies." *Asiascape: Digital Asia* 4, no. 3 (2017): 285–305.

Lanjing hunshui. "Mi Meng jiuwu hou tuandui: Women buzhi shi yuexin wuwan de dasi shixisheng" [Mi Meng's post-1995 team members: We are not just seniors in college, nor just interns with a monthly income of 50,000 RMB]. January 22, 2018. http://view.inews.qq.com/a/20180122B0VLSI00 (accessed May 11, 2019).

Lazzarato, Maurizio. "Immaterial Labour." Generation Online. 1996. http://www.generation-online.org/c/fcimmateriallabour3.htm (accessed January 15, 2015).

Lean, Eugenia. "The Making of a Public: Emotions and Media Sensation in 1930s China." *Twentieth-Century China* 29, no. 2 (2004): 39–61.

Lei, Xiaoyu. "Yang Lan: Wosuo jingli de jianxin yu shibai" [Yang Lan: Difficulties and failures I experienced]. *Yang Lan de boke* [Yang Lan's blog]. March 8, 2011. http://money.163.com/11/0308/09/6UK60AL800253G87.html (accessed July 15, 2012).

Lei, Xiying. "Youxi rensheng de biaoqingbao yu dangdai qingnian 'aiguo yishi' de xuanze" [Playful emojis and the choice of "patriotic rituals" by contemporary youth]. Weibo Account of the Communist Youth League. July 14, 2016. http://weibo.com/ttarticle/p/show?id=2309403997192900768824 (accessed August 4, 2018).

——. "Youxi rensheng de biaoqingbao yu dangdai qingnian bei 'guai shushu' bangjia de 'aiguo'" [Playful emojis and the blemishing of contemporary youth by "weird uncles"]. Weibo Account of the Communist Youth League. July 16, 2016. http://weibo.com/ttarticle/p/show?id=2309403997890828716695 (accessed August 4, 2018).

Lei, Ya-Wen. *The Contentious Public Sphere: Law, Media, and Authoritarian Rule in China*. Princeton, NJ: Princeton University Press, 2018.

Leibold, James. "Blogging Alone: China, the Internet, and the Democratic Illusion?" *Journal of Asian Studies* 70, no. 4 (2011): 1023–41.

Li, Amy. "China's Micro-blogs Break the Ban." Doha Centre for Media Freedom. August 16, 2011. http://www.dc4mf.org/en/node/412 (accessed June 5, 2018).

Li, Beika. "Doukua Gao Yuanyuan de xin faxing haokan, keni zhidao ta caiguo duoshao lei?" [Everyone's praising Gao Yuanyuan's new hairstyle. But do you know about her past hair faux pas?] *Li Beika de yixiang shijie* [Becky's Fantasy]. July 10, 2018. https://www.sohu.com/a/240476296_110497 (accessed June 5, 2019).

Li, Cheng. *Chinese Politics in the Xi Jinping Era: Reassessing Collective Leadership*. Washington, DC: Brookings Institution Press, 2016.

Li, Hongmei. "Parody and Resistance on the Chinese Internet." In *Online Society in China: Creating, Celebrating, and Instrumentalising the Online Carnival*, edited by David Kurt Herold and Peter Merolt, 71–88. London: Routledge, 2011.

Li, Hongrui. "Online Literature Readers Number 350 Million in China." Chinaculture.org. October 24, 2017. http://www.chinadaily.com.cn/culture/2017-10/24/content_33649952.htm (accessed May 29, 2018).

Li, Liang. "Chun wenxue zazhi zoudaole shizi lukou? Cong mengya zazhishe zhuanzhi shuokaiqu" [The crossroad of pure literary magazines: The institutional reform of *Sprout*]. *Xi'an wanbao* [Xi'an Evening News], January 21, 2011, 17.

Li, Shubo. "The Online Public Space and Popular Ethos in China." *Media, Culture & Society* 32, no. 1 (2010): 63–83.

Li, Xiguang. "Xueshu guancha: Shou ziben kongzhi, bufen zhuliu meiti renge fenlie" [Scholarly observations: The schizophrenia of some mainstream media under the manipulation of capital]. Weibo account of the Communist Youth League. July 14, 2016. http://weibo.com/ttarticle/p/show?id=2309403997274060493474 (accessed June 5, 2018).

Li, Yan, Da Wu, and Wenyu Zhang. "Niubo wangshi, yizhong qinghuai de bofa yu daijin" [The history of Bullog: The expression and disappearance of an attitude]. *Boke tianxia* [Blog globally], August 5, 2013. http://admin.wechat.com/mp/appmsg/show?__biz=MTA3NDI5ODU0MQ==&appmsgid=10000750&itemidx=1&sign=b3d843023ee3ec95ca75fd8b6fc8ff79 (accessed July 11, 2018).

Li, Ying. "Wo bishi xinlang mingren boke de badao, xuwei" [I look down upon the aggressiveness and hypocrisy of Sina's celebrity blog]. *Sanyue feng* [Wind in March] 1 (2006): 19–20.

Li, Ying, and Lijie Zhang. "Chen Mo: Yongsu hua de wangluo hunzi" [Chen Mo: A philistine Internet hooligan]. *San Yuefeng* [Wind in March] 10 (2006): 42–43.

Li, Yinhe. "Furong Jiejie dale yanlun ziyou de cabianqiu" [Furong Jiejie maneuvers the boundary of free speech]. *Xin Jingbao* [Beijing News], July 10, 2005. http://news.hsw.cn/gb/news/2005-07/10/content_2035589.htm (accessed June 14, 2011).

Liang, Yilu, and Wanqi Shen. "Fan Economy in the Chinese Media and Entertainment Industry: How Feedback from Super Fans Can Propel Creative Industries' Revenue." *Global Media and China* 1, no. 4 (2016): 331–49.

Liao, Qinying, and Lei Shi. "She Gets a Sports Car from Our Donation: Rumor Transmission in a Chinese Microblogging Community." *Proceedings of the 2013 Conference on Computer Supported Cooperative Work*, 587–98.

Liao, Yan. "'Mu Zimei xianxiang' yu wangluo chuanbo de xinren weiji" [The Mu Zimei phenomenon and the credibility crisis online]. *Shengping shijie* [Voice and Screen World] 3 (2004): 15–16.

Lim, Louisa. "A Pop Idol Writer for China's New Generation." *Morning Edition*, NPR, May 28, 2009. http://www.npr.org/templates/story/story.php?storyId=104569352 (accessed May 5, 2018).

Lin, Chenglong, Wei Fang, and Jianbin Jin. "You Are What You Post in 'Circle of Friends' of WeChat: Self-Presentation and Identity Production from a Personality Perspective." *Global Media and China* 2, no. 2 (2017): 138–52.

Lin, Dihuan. "Bei egou yaole you yimiao, bei eren yaole mei yimiao" [If you are bitten by a fierce dog, there might be vaccines. However, if you are bitten by evil people, there are no solutions]. *Xiao Lin* [Little Lin]. July 22, 2018. https://www.wxwenku.com/d/108109408 (accessed June 14, 2019).

Link, Perry. *An Anatomy of Chinese: Rhythm, Metaphor, Politics*. Cambridge, MA: Harvard University Press, 2013.

———. *Roses and Thorns: The Second Blooming of the Hundred Flowers in Chinese Fiction, 1979–80*. Berkeley: University of California Press, 1984.

Lister, Martin, Seth Giddings, and Jon Dovey. *New Media: A Critical Introduction*. New York: Routledge, 2003.

Liu, Fengshu. *Urban Youth in China: Modernity, the Internet and the Self*. New York: Routledge, 2011.

Liu, Jun. "From 'Moments of Madness' to 'the Politics of Mundanity'—Researching Digital Media and Contentious Collective Actions in China." *Social Movement Studies* 16, no. 4 (2017): 418–32.

Liu, Kang. "'Dinner Party of Discourse Owners:' China's Intellectual Scene Today." *Minnesota Review* 12, no. 79 (2012): 113–36.

———. *Globalization and Cultural Trends in China*. Honolulu: University of Hawai'i Press, 2004.

Liu, Liu. *Liu Liu de Weibo* [Microblog of Liu Liu]. July 11, 2015. https://weibo.com/1706987705/CqBLwD1jC?from=page_1003061706987705_profile&wvr=6&mod=weibotime&type=comment (accessed May 28, 2018).

———. "Wo yaode zhishi gongping" [All I want is fairness]. *Liu Liu de Weibo* [Microblog of Liu Liu]. July 13, 2015. https://weibo.com/p/1001603864111611018706 (accessed May 28, 2018).

Liu, Muyang, and Mo Chen. "Furong Jiejie: Wuliao wenhua xianfeng" [Furong Jiejie: Pioneers of nonsense culture]. *Waitan huabao* [Shanghai Bund Pictorial], June 23, 2005, 6.

Liu, Shi-Diing. "Undomesticated Hostilities: The Affective Space of Internet Chat Rooms across the Taiwan Strait." *Positions* 16, no. 2 (2008): 435–55.

Liu, Wentao. "Stop Press: The Rapid Demise of China's Newspapers." *Sixth Tone*, February 4, 2018. http://www.sixthtone.com/news/1001645/stop-press-the-rapid-demise-of-chinas-newspapers (accessed July 15, 2018).

Lin, Shuang. "'×××, zhiyu ni xin bu xin, wo fanzheng xinle' gaotie ti zaoju" [Sentence making by using ". . . whether you believe it or not, I do anyway"]. Tianya Forum. July 27, 2011. http://bbs.tianya.cn/post-free-2226331-1.shtml (accessed June 5, 2018).

Logan, Christie. "Presence and Absence in Online Performance: Configurations in the Problematic of Access." *American Communication Journal* 6, no. 3 (2003): 1–8.

Louie, Kam. "Popular Culture and Masculinity Ideals in East Asia, with Special Reference to China." *Journal of Asian Studies* 71, no. 4 (2012): 929–43.

Lu, Hongbing. "Wei shouquan de boke" [Unauthorized blog]. *Nanfang zhoumo* [Southern Weekend], September 5, 2002, 31.

Lu, Jia, and Fanxu Zeng. "Microblogging and Grassroots Surveillance in China." *China: An International Journal* 12, no. 3 (2014): 55–71.

Lu, Jinzhu. *Weibo wenzheng* [Microblog intervenes in governance]. Beijing: Dongfang chubanshe, 2012.

Lu, Yan. "Cong Mu Zimei shijian kan wangluo chuanbo zhong de baguanren" [The role of gatekeepers in new media through the lens of the Mu Zimei incident]. June 29,

2007. http://www.66wen.com/05wx/xinwen/xinwen/20070629/52526_2.html (accessed June 24, 2012).

Lu, Zhong. "Dahua xiyou zhilu" [Journey of *A Chinese Odyssey*]. In *Dahua xiyou baodian* [Bible of *A Chinese Odyssey*], edited by Lixian Zhang, 96–97. Beijing: Xiandai chubanshe, 2000.

Luo, Huilin. "Zilian shidai de zilian yanchu: Cong Furong Jiejie xianxiang kan xiaofei shehui de xinli tezheng" [Narcissistic performance in an era of narcissism: An analysis of psychological traits of a consumerist society through the lens of the Furong phenomenon]. *Zhongguo zhaobiao* [China Tendering] 9 (2005): 58–59.

Ma, Lianjie, Jongpil Chung, and Stuart Thorson. "E-government in China: Bringing Economic Development through Administrative Reform." *Government Information Quarterly* 22 (2005): 20–37.

Ma, Qian. "Cao Guowei: Weibo pingtai xing gongsi de diwei gengjia wengu" [Cao Guowei: Weibo consolidates its position as a platformatized corporation]. December 1, 2017. http://www.sohu.com/a/207855878_460436 (accessed May 28, 2018).

Macgilchrist, Felicitas, and Inse Böhmig. "Blogs, Genes and Immigration: Online Media and Minimal Politics." *Media, Culture & Society* 34, no. 1 (2012): 83–100.

Maihaozi. "Weibo youyou xin faxian, 20 sui 'Hongshizihui shangye zongjingli,' gezhong xuanfu! Huosu weiguan!!" [Another new finding on Weibo: The twenty-year-old is the general manager of the Red Cross Society of Commerce; she shows off wealth in various ways; gather online immediately]. June 21, 2011. http://bbs.tianya.cn/post-funinfo-2691682-1.shtml (accessed May 28, 2012).

Marks, Kevin. "Xu Jing Lei Tops the Technorati 100." May 4, 2006. http://technorati.com/weblog/2006/05/103.html (accessed February 2, 2007).

Marvin, Carolyn. *When Old Technologies Were New: Thinking about Electric Communications in Late Nineteenth Century*. Oxford: Oxford University Press, 1988.

McDonald, Hamish. "China's Web Censors Struggle to Muzzle Free-Spirited Bloggers." *Sydney Morning Herald*, December 23, 2005, 11.

McDougall, Bonnie S. *Mao Zedong's "Talks at the Yan'an Conference on Literature and Art": A Translation of the 1943 Text with Commentary*. Ann Arbor: University of Michigan Press, 1980.

Meng, Bingchun. "From Steamed Bun to Grass Mud Horse: E'gao as Alternative Political Discourse on the Chinese Internet." *Global Media and Communication* 7, no. 1 (2011): 33–51.

———. "Regulating Online Spoofs: Futile Efforts of Recentralization?" In *China's Information and Communications Technology Revolution: Social Changes and State Responses*, edited by Xiaoling Zhang and Yongnian Zheng, 52–67. London: Routledge, 2009.

Mi Meng. "Beipiao zui pa tingdao de sige zi: Yayi fusan" [The four characters floaters in Beijing are most afraid of hearing: "One month's deposit and three months' rent"]. December 12, 2017. http://chuansong.me/n/2080693251215 (accessed May 11, 2018).

———. "Diyi ci zuo toudengcang, ruhe youya de zhuangbi?" [How to show off elegantly: Fly business class for the first time]. October 24, 2016. https://baike.baidu.com/

tashuo/browse/content?id=feb217783edf34baa353be3d (accessed September 23, 2017).

——. *Mi Meng de weibo* [Microblog of Mi Meng]. April 22, 2011. https://www.weibo.com/abcdecup?refer_flag=1001030101_&is_all=1 (accessed July 24, 2018).

——. *Mi Meng de weibo* [Microblog of Mi Meng]. May 22, 2013. https://www.weibo.com/abcdecup?refer_flag=1001030101_&is_all=1 (accessed July 24, 2018).

——. *Mi Meng de weibo* [Microblog of Mi Meng]. December 6, 2017. https://www.weibo.com/abcdecup?refer_flag=1001030101_&is_all=1 (accessed July 24, 2018).

——. "Mi Meng fensi buneng qu? Hehe, shi ni qubuqi" [You cannot marry Mi Meng's fans? Hehe. You could never measure up]. November 23, 2016. http://chuansong.me/n/1151448051048 (accessed May 11, 2018).

——. "Ni pingshenme qiongde xinan lide" [Why the hell do you enjoy living in poverty]. November 8, 2016. http://chuansong.me/n/1079878351633 (accessed May 11, 2018).

——. "Ni weishenme shi waimao xiehui" [Why you care about appearances]. September 23, 2015. http://chuansong.me/n/1871098 (accessed July 19, 2018).

——. "Shuwo zhiyan, yunqi chugui de doushi laji" [Let me put it this way: Those who have extramarital affairs during their wives' pregnancy are all trash]. November 17, 2016. http://chuansong.me/n/1123088851945 (accessed May 11, 2018).

——. "Ta nazou le xinmeiti chuangzuo dasai wushi wan jiangjin, ping shenme?" [New Media Composition Contest awarded her a bonus as high as 500,000, why's that]. September 14, 2017. http://www.sohu.com/a/192035401_597687 (accessed May 11, 2018).

——. "Wode baba, yao jiehun le" [My father will be getting married]. March 28, 2012. http://blog.sina.com.cn/s/blog_60f286c90102e036.html (accessed September 23, 2017).

——. "Women de mudi shi, bu fangguo yige xionghaizi!" [Our goal is: Not to let go of a single terrible kid]. January 24, 2017. http://chuansong.me/n/1510459351816 (accessed May 11, 2018).

——. "Women nanren chugui, bushi weile xing" [We, men, do not betray marriage for sex]. November 16, 2016. http://chuansong.me/n/1119295751142 (accessed May 11, 2018).

——. "Wo shi ruhe chenggong de ba yijia gongsi kaikua de" [How did I manage to get my company bankrupt]. December 28, 2015. http://chuansong.me/n/2097398 (accessed September 23, 2017).

——. "Wo yigeren huode haohao de, weishenme yao jiehun" [I live well by myself. Why the hell should I get married]. April 28, 2016. http://www.anyv.net/index.php/article-359738, (accessed September 23, 2017).

——. "Xie Xingfang kua Lin Dan you dandang? Hehe" [Xie Xingfang praises Lin Dan as a responsible man? Hehe]. November 18, 2016. http://chuansong.me/n/1128867451239 (accessed May 11, 2018).

——. "Yongyuan aiguo, yongyuan relei yingkuang" [My country, forever shall I love

you and forever shall I be in tears]. July 13, 2016. https://baike.baidu.com/tashuo/
browse/content?id=69510a16151f361b68c4ec33 (accessed May 11, 2018).

———. "Youqian kuotai de jiannan shenghuo" [The difficult life of rich housewives].
March 22, 2017. http://chuansong.me/n/1696500151909 (accessed May 11, 2018).

———. "Youqian ren zhongcheng juanshu" [Ultimately, rich people marry each other].
March 29, 2017. http://chuansong.me/n/1723311751107 (accessed May 11, 2018).

———. "Zhi jianren: Wo weishenme yao bang ni" [To that low bitch: Why the hell should I
help you]. December 12, 2015. http://chuansong.me/n/2031311 (accessed May 11, 2018).

———. "Zhi nanyou: Ni keyi qiong, danshi buneng shinian ru yiri de qiong" [To my boyfriend: You may be poor, but you should not stay in poverty for ten years]. January
18, 2018. http://chuansong.me/n/2148396551820 (accessed May 11, 2018).

"Mingbo fangtan disiqi: Diguazhu—shengxia haizi bushi yishi chongdong" [The fourth
issue of interviewing with famous bloggers: Ground Melon Pig—I did not randomly
decide to have a child]. Sina.com. September 29, 2006. http://blog.sina.com.cn/
lm/8/2006/0929/8568.html (accessed June 19, 2010).

Moore, Malcolm. "Chinese Charity Donations Fall 80 Per cent." *Telegraph*, December
8, 2011. http://www.telegraph.co.uk/news/worldnews/asia/china/8943224/Chinese-
charity-donations-fall-80-per-cent.html (accessed May 28, 2017).

Morozov, Evgeny. *The Net Delusion: The Dark Side of Internet Freedom*. Philadelphia,
PA: Public Affairs, 2011.

"Movie ban jinghua gongbulan dahua xiyou" [Movie forum: Main collections of *A Chinese Odyssey*]. December 11, 1999—February 1, 2009. https://www.newsmth.net/
bbsoan.php?path=%2Fgroups%2Frec.faq%2FMovie%2Fnew2%2Freview%2Fchines
e%2FD%2F17 (accessed June 24, 2020).

Mu Zimei. "Da Shengbaoluoye bao wen" [An interview with Folha de S.Paulo]. August
4, 2008. http://muzimei.blogchina.com/583830.html (accessed May 11, 2019).

———. "Dengshi jiaohuan" [Exchange based on time span]. August 21, 2003. http://www.
qxswk.com/yuedu/8/8931/320594.html (accessed May 11, 2010).

———. *Mu Zimei de weibo* [Mu Zimei's microblog]. https://weibo.com/
u/1496913734?refer_flag=1001030101_&is_all=1 (accessed May 12, 2018).

———. Mu Zimei's blog entries. http://muzimei.51da.com/ (accessed June 25, 2012).

———. "Preface to *Rongqi* [Container]." 2007. https://www.books.com.tw/products/00102
81370 (accessed June 10, 2018).

———. "Wugu" [Innocence]. November 16, 2003. http://www.klawen.com/45/45203/1070
8274.html (accessed June 26, 2012).

———. *Yiqingshu* [Ashes of love]. 2003. https://www.linlins.com/bookshelt/muzimei/
(accessed June 28, 2019).

Negro, Gianluigi. *The Internet in China: From Infrastructure to a Nascent Civil Society*.
New York: Palgrave Macmillan, 2017.

Negt, Oscar, and Alexander Kluge. *Public Sphere and Experience: Towards an Analysis of
the Bourgeois and Proletarian Public Sphere*. Minneapolis: University of Minnesota
Press, 1993.

Ng, Jason Q. "Politics, Rumors, and Ambiguity: Tracking Censorship on WeChat's

Public Accounts Platform." Citizen Lab. July 20, 2015. https://citizenlab.ca/2015/07/tracking-censorship-on-wechat-public-accounts-platform/ (accessed July 15, 2018).

Office of Cyberspace Administration of China. "Di sishiyici zhongguo hulianwangluo fazhan zhuangkuang tongji baogao" [The 41st statistical report on Internet development in China]. January 31, 2018. http://www.cac.gov.cn/2018-01/31/c_1122347026.htm (accessed August 1, 2018).

Osburg, John. *Anxious Wealth: Money and Morality among China's New Rich*. Stanford, CA: Stanford University Press, 2013.

Papi Jiang. *Dangdairen bibei shouce zhi yingyu yu zhongwen de hunda bafa* [The must-have manual for modern people: Eight ways of mixing English and Chinese]. August 22, 2016. https://www.youtube.com/watch?v=OyI_E4EzohA (accessed May 30, 2018).

———.*Nizai shenghuo zhong yiding ye tingdao guo zhexie hua* [You must have heard these lines in your life]. March 11, 2016. https://www.youtube.com/watch?v=IDBehD9f4r8 (accessed May 30, 2018).

———. "Papi de dapei zhi" [Records of Papi's way of matching clothes]. November 20, 2013. http://bbs.tianya.cn/post-tianyamyself-195247-1.shtml (accessed August 2, 2017).

———.*Yici kanwan shanghaihua jia yingyu xilie* [The series of mixing Shanghainese and English]. September 9, 2017. https://www.youtube.com/watch?v=RCwkpwJEbsE((accessed May 30, 2018).

Peng, Lan. *Zhongguo wangluo meiti de diyige shinian* [The first ten years of Internet media in China]. Beijing: Tsinghua University Press, 2005.

Peng, Sen. "Cong mingren 'guan bo re' kan baoye de qiantu—ye tan xin meiti dui baoye de tiaozhan" [The future of news media from the perspectives of celebrities who close their blogs: New media's challenge of print news media]. *Xinwen zhishi* [Knowledge of News] 7 (2007): 44–46.

Perlez, Jane. "Tribunal Rejects Beijing's Claims in South China Sea." *New York Times*, July 12, 2016. https://www.nytimes.com/2016/07/13/world/asia/south-china-sea-hague-ruling-philippines.html?_r=1 (accessed June 5, 2018).

Peters, John Durham. "Witnessing." *Media, Culture & Society* 23, no. 6 (2001): 707–23.

Phillips, Tom. "Publishers under Pressure as China's Censors Reach for Red Pen." *Guardian*, November 13, 2015. http://www.theguardian.com/world/2015/nov/13/china-censorship-xi-jinping-authors-publishers (accessed January 1, 2016).

Plumblade. "Wo lai shuoshuo weishenme *dahua xiyou* hui yinqi zhemeda de fanxiang ba" [Let me discuss why *A Chinese Odyssey* is so influential]. March 25, 2009. http://www.newsmth.net/bbsanc.php?path=%2Fgroups%2Fliteral.faq%2FNostalgia%2FFriends%2FDiscussion%2FM.1237962895.Co (accessed June 21, 2011).

"Popular Young Writer Loses Plagiarism Lawsuit." *China Daily*, December 8, 2004. http://www.chinadaily.com.cn/english/doc/2004-12/08/content_398255.htm (accessed May 5, 2018).

Pugsley, Peter C., and Jia Gao. "Emerging Powers of Influence: The Rise of the Anchor in Chinese Television." *International Communication Gazette* 69, no. 5 (2007): 451–66.

Qian, Gang. "Dongche shigu zhong de baodao yu zhongguo chuanmei de tupo" [Reports on the high-speed rail accident and the breakthrough of traditional media in China]. *Chuanmei toushi* [Media Digest] 8 (2011): 2–3. http://gbcode.rthk.hk/TuniS/app3.rthk.hk/mediadigest/content.php?aid=1174 (accessed June 30, 2020).

Qian, Wei, Shan Wang, and Zhijie Yang. "Zhongguoshi jitang jianshi" [A brief history of Chinese-style inspirational stories]. *Zhongguo xinwen zhoukan* [China Newsweek], November 26, 2016. http://www.jiemian.com/article/979488.html (accessed May 10, 2018).

"Qidi 'wangluo hongren' Guo Meimei" [Truth about Internet celebrity Guo Meimei]. *Fazhi zaixian* [Law online], August 4, 2014. https://www.youtube.com/watch?v=3DzP_EPfgQ (accessed June 5, 2018).

Qiu, Jack Linchuan. "Virtual Censorship in China: Keeping the Gate between the Cyberspaces." *International Journal of Communications: Law and Policy* 4 (Winter 1999/2000): 1–25.

Rea, Christopher. "Enter the Cultural Entrepreneur." In *The Business of Culture: Cultural Entrepreneurs in China and Southeast Asia, 1900–65*, edited by Christopher Rea and Nicolai Volland, 9–34. Vancouver: University of British Columbia Press, 2015.

———. "Spoofing (E'gao) Culture on the Chinese Internet." In *Humour in Chinese Life and Culture: Resistance and Control in Modern Times*, edited by Jocelyn Chey Valerie and Jessica Milner Davis, 149–72. Hong Kong: Hong Kong University Press.

Ren, Yuan. "China's Most Despised Woman: The Professional Mistress Who Refused to Keep Quiet." *Telegraph*, September 25, 2015. http://www.telegraph.co.uk/women/womens-life/11869331/China-Mistress-Guo-Meimei-who-refused-to-keep-quiet.html (accessed June 5, 2018).

Renminwang. "2013 nian zhongguo huliangwang yuqing fenxi baogao" [Report on public opinion of Internet in China in 2013]. March 18, 2014. http://yuqing.people.com.cn/GB/371947/373066/ (accessed June 5, 2018).

———. "2017 nian san jidu wangluo yulun shengtai zhishu fabu—Wangluo yulun shengtai pingwen tisheng, xilie zhuti chuanbo shuaping hulianwang" [A report on Internet public opinion in the third quarter of 2017: The ecology of network public opinion has been steadily improved; a series of theme-based content are widely disseminated on the Internet]. October 17, 2017. http://media.people.com.cn/n1/2017/1017/c14677-29592005.html (accessed June 5, 2018).

———. "Zhongyang, Guowuyuan fa jiaqiang gaijin daxuesheng sixiang zhengzhi jiaoyu de yijian" [The Central Committee of the Chinese Communist Party and the State Council issued a proposition to improve and enhance political education for college students]. October 14, 2004. http://www.people.com.cn/GB/jiaoyu/1055/2920198.html (accessed July 11, 2018).

"Report on the Development of Microblog in 2012–2013" [2012–2013 nian Weibo fazhan yanjiu baogao]. Internet Lab & Zhejiang Media College Internet and Society Institute. June 2013. http://video.zj.com/cns/20122013weibo.pdf (accessed August 2, 2014).

Ristovska, Sandra. "Strategic Witnessing in an Age of Video Activism." *Media, Culture & Society* 38, no. 7 (2016): 1034–47.

Roberts, Margaret E. *Censored: Distraction and Diversion Inside China's Great Firewall.* Princeton, NJ: Princeton University Press, 2018.

Rong, Zhenhuan. "Jiaoxun gongxiang: Weibo bizu Fanfou weihe cheng xianlie?" [Lessons to share: Why Fanfou, the pioneer of microblog, dies]. *Jingliren* [Manager], September 26, 2013. http://finance.sina.com.cn/leadership/mroll/20130926/153516860499. shtml (accessed May 27, 2018).

Schiavenza, Matt. "China's Weibo Losing Users." *Daily Beast*, January 25, 2014. https://www.thedailybeast.com/chinas-weibo-losing-users (accessed August 2, 2017).

Schlæger, Jesper, and Min Jiang. "Official Microblogging and Social Management by Local Governments in China." *China Information* 28, no. 2 (2014): 189–213.

Senft, Theresa M. "Bulletin-Board Systems." In *Encyclopedia of New Media: An Essential Reference to Communication and Technology*, edited by Steve Jones, 45–48. Thousand Oaks, CA: Sage, 2003.

Severdia, Sandra. "Directives from the Ministry of Truth: Wenzhou High-Speed Train Crash." *China Digital Times*, July 25, 2011. http://chinadigitaltimes.net/2011/07/directives-from-the-ministry-of-truth-wenzhou-high-speed-train-crash/ (accessed May 28, 2018).

Shan, Lei. "Zhan Mu Zimei de pianyi—Qianxi zhengyi renwu de shangye yingyong anli" [Take advantage of Mu Zimei: A discussion of capitalizing on controversial figures for commercial purposes]. *Shichang guancha guanggaozhu* [Market Observer] 3 (2007): 30–33.

Shen, Yayuan. "Wangluo zizhiju zhong diaosi xingxiang wenhua piping, yi Diaosi nan-shi weili" [A cultural critique of the image of *diaosi* in a web-based series: A case study of *Diors Man*]. *Jiangxi qingnian zhiye xueyuan xuebao* [Journal of Jiangxi Youth Vocational College] 24, no. 6 (2014): 14–21.

Shen, Yin, and Mei Zhang. "Zhuanfang Guo Jingming: Cong zuoshi dao zuoju" [Interview with Guo Jingming: From getting things done to network at a broader scale]. *Waitan* [The Bund], July 14, 2015. http://bundpic.com/posts/post/55a4b69bf032a0e68c981e23 (accessed May 12, 2018).

"Shexian juzhong yinluan; Xue Manzi qianse jiaoyi liuchang" [Suspected of promiscuity; Xue Manzi exchanges money for sex]. *Redian bobao* [Breaking News], August 29, 2013. https://www.youtube.com/watch?v=7KFj3WWGTy4 (accessed July 8, 2016).

Shi, Lihong. "Chengzhang huiyilu" [Memoirs of Yiyi's growth]. July 23, 2011. https://weibo.com/u/2074537511?is_all=1&noscale_head=1#1516049236244 (accessed June 5, 2018).

Shi, Xiangpu. "Zhi Xiaofenhong: Haiyou shenme bi 'aiguo' geng rongyi?" [To Little Pinks: What else is easier than "patriotism"]. July 18, 2016. http://culture.ifeng.com/a/20160717/49369480_0.shtml (accessed May 27, 2017).

Shie, Tamara Renee. "The Tangled Web: Does the Internet Offer Promise or Peril for the Chinese Communist Party?" *Journal of Contemporary China* 13, no. 40 (2004): 523–40.

Shizi. December 18, 2005. http://blog.sina.com.cn/s/blog_47761464010000qp.html (accessed November 10, 2009).

Shu, Jinyu. "Shu zuojia bukan qifan guanbi boke" [Several writers were fed up with their blogs and shut them down]. *Zhonghua dushubao* [China Readings], July 26, 2006. http://www.chinawriter.com.cn/2006/2006-07-31/19820.html (accessed January 1, 2020).

"Shuimu BBS tiaozheng wei xiaoneixing" [Shuimu BBS has been modified to campus networks only]. *Jinghua shibao* [Beijing Times], March 19, 2005. http://fatduck.org/images/smth/jinghuashibao20050319_04.pdf (accessed July 11, 2018).

Shushengwanyou. "Mi Meng pingshenme xiechu name huo de wenzhang" [Why are Mi Meng's essays so popular]. *Zhanzhang zhijia* [China Webmaster], November 13, 2017. https://www.chinaz.com/web/2017/1113/827487.shtml (accessed May 11, 2018).

SimilarWeb. https://www.similarweb.com/website/sina.com.cn (accessed June 24, 2018).

Simon, Herbert A. "Designing Organizations for an Information-Rich World." In *Computers, Communications and the Public Interest*, edited by Martin Greenberger, 40–41. Baltimore: Johns Hopkins University Press, 1971.

Sina. "Business Overview." http://ir.sina.com/phoenix.zhtml?c=121288&p=irol-homeprofile (accessed June 24, 2018).

Singhal, Arvind, and Karen Greiner. "Performance Activism and Civic Engagement through Symbolic and Playful Actions." *Journal of Development Communication* 19, no. 2 (2008): 43–53.

"Single Mother Issue in Spotlight Thanks to Blog." *China Daily*, October 17, 2006. http://www.china.org.cn/english/Life/184436.htm (accessed October 17, 2006).

"Souhu shipin dashiye: Wangluo hongren di erji: @ Guo Meimei baby" [Sohu video: Internet celebrity Guo Meimei]. *Wangluo hongren* [Internet Celebrity], episode 2. March 18, 2013. https://www.youtube.com/watch?v=WLxbpPo9hT0 (accessed August 4, 2018).

Srnicek, Nick. *Platform Capitalism*. Cambridge: Polity Press, 2016.

Steinberg, Marc. "A Genesis of the Platform Concept: i-mode and Platform Theory in Japan." *Asiascape: Digital Asia* 4, no. 3 (2017): 184–208.

———. *The Platform Economy: How Japan Transformed the Consumer Internet*. Minneapolis: University of Minnesota Press, 2019.

Stern, Rachel E., and Kevin J. O'Brien. "Politics at the Boundary: Mixed Signals and the Chinese State." *Modern China* 38, no. 2 (2012): 174–98.

Stockmann, Daniela. *Media Commercialization and Authoritarian Rule in China*. Cambridge: Cambridge University Press, 2013.

Strafella, Giorgio, and Daria Berg. "The Making of an Online Celebrity: A Critical Analysis of Han Han's Blog." *China Information* 29, no. 3 (2015): 352–76.

Sullivan, Jonathan. "China's Weibo: Is Faster Different?" *New Media & Society* 16, no. 1 (2014): 24–37.

Sum, Ngai-Ling. "The Makings of Subaltern Subjects: Embodiment, Contradictory Consciousness, and Re-hegemonization of the Diaosi in China." *Globalizations* 14, no. 2 (2017): 298–312.

Sun, Linlin. "Han Han: Pai dianying shi xianzai zui xiangzuo de shi" [Han Han: Making movies is what I would like to do the most now]. *Xinjingbao* [Beijing News], April 18, 2014. http://www.bjnews.com.cn/ent/2014/04/18/313480.html (accessed January 1, 2016).

Sun, Xiaoning. "Cong xinlang shizu kan wangzhan de shehui zeren" [Social responsibility of websites: The mistake of Sina]. *Beijing wanbao* [Beijing Evening News], November 16, 2003. http://news.sohu.com/2003/11/16/90/news215659015.shtml (accessed June 24, 2012).

Sun, Xinru. "Self-Narration and Double Articulation: A Study of a WeChat Group of Pumi Villagers." *Communication and the Public* 1, no. 4 (2016): 500–503.

Svensson, Marina. "Voice, Power and Connectivity in China's Microblogosphere: Digital Divides on Sina Weibo." *China Information* 28, no. 2 (2014): 168–88.

Szablewicz, Marcella. "The 'Losers' of China's Internet: Memes as 'Structures of Feeling' for Disillusioned Young Netizens." *China Information* 28, no. 2 (2014): 259–75.

Tai, Zixue. *The Internet in China: Cyberspace and Civil Society*. New York: Routledge, 2006.

Tait, Sue. "Bearing Witness, Journalism, and Moral Responsibility." *Media, Culture & Society* 33, no. 8 (2011): 1220–35.

Tang, Lihong. "Nonsensical Speech: Speech Acts in Postsocialist Chinese Culture." PhD diss., University of Washington, 2008.

Tang, Xiaobing. *Visual Culture in Contemporary China: Paradigms and Shifts*. Cambridge: Cambridge University Press, 2015.

Tang, Yinghong. "Yongyuan aiguo, yongyuan relei yingkuang" [My country, forever shall I love you and forever shall I be in tears]. *China Digital Times*, June 10, 2017. https://chinadigitaltimes.net/chinese/2017/06/晒爱思psyeyes-唐映红: 永远爱国, 永远热泪盈眶/ (accessed October 6, 2018).

Tao, Li. "Want Fame and Fortune? China's Internet Celebrity Business Offers Both." *South China Morning Post*, June 9, 2017. http://www.scmp.com/business/china-business/article/2097688/want-fame-and-fortune-chinas-internet-celebrity-business (accessed September 23, 2017).

Tencent's promotional video of QQ. YouTube. February 2, 2011. https://www.youtube.com/watch?v=CeAJXGVThAQ (accessed May 10, 2018).

Terranova, Tiziana. "Free Labor: Producing Culture for the Digital Economy." *Social Text* 18, no. 2 (2000): 33–58.

"The 13th Five-Year Plan for Economic and Social Development of the People's Republic of China (2016–2020)." Translation Compilation and Translation Bureau, Central Committee of the Communist Party of China. March 15, 2016. http://en.ndrc.gov.cn/newsrelease/201612/P020161207645765233498.pdf (accessed May 16, 2018).

Thompson, John B. "The New Visibility." *Theory, Culture & Society* 22, no. 6 (2005): 31–51.

Thorngate, Warren. "Professional Issues: The Economy of Attention and the Development of Psychology." *Canadian Psychology* 31, no. 3 (1990): 262–71.

Tiantanglu chalukou. "Gaotie ti huole! Zui jingdian zaoju" [The high-speed train style goes viral! The most classical sentences]. *Tiexuewang*. July 28, 2011. http://bbs.tiexue. net/post2_5225203_1.html (accessed June 5, 2018).

"Tiedaobu fayanren 'fanzheng wo xinle' yulu cheng wangluo liuxingyu" ["I do anyway" by the spokesperson of the Ministry of Railways becomes popular online slang]. *Xiandai kuaibao* [Modern Express], July 27, 2011. http://news.ifeng.com/mainland/ special/wzdongchetuogui/content-3/detail_2011_07/27/7965107_0.shtml (accessed June 5, 2018).

Tkacik, John. "China's Orwellian Internet." *Backgrounder*, October 8, 2004. https:// www.heritage.org/asia/report/chinas-orwellian-internet (accessed July 11, 2018).

Tong, Dahuan. "Zhongguo ni manxie zou, dengyideng nide linghun" [China, please slow down—Wait for your soul]. July 26, 2011. Translated by David Bandurski. "China's High-Speed Politics." *New York Times*, July 28, 2011. http://www.nytimes. com/2011/07/29/opinion/29iht-edbandurski29.html (accessed May 23, 2012).

Tong, Liqiang. *Weibo fazhan yanjiu baogao* 2011 [Research reports on the development of Weibo]. Beijing: Renmin chubanshe, 2011.

Tsinghua yehua [Night talks at Tsinghua]. December 31, 2001. http://www.tudou.com/ programs/view/SYnIX5dRq2Q/ (accessed May 10, 2011).

Tsui, Lokman. "The Panopticon as the Antithesis of a Space of Freedom: Control and Regulation of the Internet in China." *China Information* 17, no. 2. (2003): 65–82.

"The 2010 *Time* 100 Poll." April 1, 2010. http://content.time.com/time/specials/packages/ article/0,28804,1972075_1972078_1972568,00.html (accessed March 14, 2018).

Tyler, Imogen, and Bruce Bennett. "'Celebrity Chav': Fame, Femininity and Social Class." *European Journal of Cultural Studies* 13, no. 3 (2010): 375–93.

Verberg, Gabi, and Manya Koetse. "Mimeng and 'Self-Media' under Attack for Promoting Fake News Stories to Chinese Readers." *What's on Weibo*. February 6, 2019. https://www.whatsonweibo.com/mimeng-and-self-media-under-attack-for-promoting-fake-news-stories-to-chinese-readers/ (accessed May 11, 2019).

Voice of America. "Focus Dialogue: Is the Battle between the Youth League and Zhao Wei a Disservice to Xi Jinping?" July 22, 2016. https://www.voachinese.com/a/pro-and-con-wei-zhao-jinping-xi-20160722/3430415.html (accessed June 5, 2018).

Wacker, Gudrun. "Resistance Is Futile: Control and Censorship of the Internet in China." In *From Woodblocks to the Internet: Chinese Publishing and Print Culture in Transition, circa 1800 to 2008*, edited by Cynthia Brokaw and Christopher A. Reed, 353–82. Leiden: Brill, 2010.

Wan, Jingbo. "Dangdai xiaoyuan qingchun de yici dianli" [A ceremony on contemporary youth culture]. *Nanfang zhoumo* [Southern Weekend], April 18, 2002. http:// www.southcn.com/weekend/tempdir/200204180038.htm (accessed June 30, 2011).

Wan, Xingya. "Mu Zimei fabiao xin riji: Cheng 'shibei quanguo zhouma de zhuming nüren'" [Mu Zimei published a new diary entry and called herself "that infamous woman condemned by the whole nation"]. *Zhongguo qingnianbao* [China Youth Daily], November 17, 2003. http://www.qzwb.com/gb/content/2003-11/17/content_1054068.htm (accessed June 29, 2012).

Wang, Haiyan, and Colin Sparks. "Chinese Newspaper Groups in the Digital Era: The Resurgence of the Party Press." *Journal of Communication* 69, no. 1 (2019): 94–119.

Wang, Hongzhe, Simin Li, and Jing Wu. "Cong 'mimei' dao 'xiao fenhong:' Xin meijie shangye wenhua huanjing xia de guozu shenfen shengchan he dongyuan jizhi yanjiu [From "fangirls" to "Little Pinks": An investigation of national identities and mobilization mechanisms under the circumstances of new media and commercial culture]. *Guoji Xinwenjie* [Journal of International Communication] 38, no. 11 (2017): 33–53.

Wang, Irene. "Sex Diary Banned a Day after Hitting Shelves; But Sales of Pirated Version of Racy Weblog Are Set to Boom." *South China Morning Post*, November 29, 2003, 6.

Wang, Jing. "Culture as Leisure and Culture as Capital." *Positions* 9, no. 1 (2001): 69–104.

———. *High Culture Fever: Politics, Aesthetics, and Ideology in Deng's China*. Berkeley: University of California Press, 1996.

———. "The State Question in Chinese Popular Cultural Studies." *Inter-Asia Cultural Studies* 2, no. 1 (2001): 35–52.

Wang, Junxiu, and Xingdong Fang. *Boke: E shidai de daohuozhe* [Blog: Prometheus of the E era]. Beijing: Zhongguo fangzheng chubanshe, 2003.

Wang, Qun. "Shuttling between Politics and Entertainment: Interplay between the Media and Media Users during China's Red Cross Scandal." *Journal of International Communication* 21, no. 2 (2015): 241–56.

Wang, Wusi. "Mi Meng chongxin faming le yizhong nüren: Aiguobiao" [Mi Meng reinvents a kind of woman: Patriotic bitch]. July 15, 2016. https://wangwusiwj.blogspot.com/2016/09/blog-post_53.html (accessed July 24, 2018).

Wang, Ye. "Guo Jingming: Ouxiang de zhizao he huimie" [Guo Jingming: The production and destruction of an idol]. *Haoyun·Money* [Luck and Money], April 3, 2012. http://www.xinli001.com/info/100002448 (accessed May 2, 2018).

Wang, Zheng. "'Diaosi' de kuanghuan yu luomo" [The carnival and loneliness of losers]. *Wenhua chuangxin yu bijiao yanjiu* [Comparative Study of Cultural Innovation], no. 5 (2017): 7–12.

"'Wangluo hongren' cuisheng 'wanghong jingji:' 'Wanghong' men ruhe zhuanqian?" [Internet celebrities boost Internet celebrity economy: How do social influencers make money]. *Yangzi wanbao* [Yangzi Evening News], October 26, 2015. http://education.news.cn/2015-10/26/c_128356818.htm (accessed May 30, 2018).

Warrior. November 25, 2008. http://blog.sina.com.cn/s/blog_477614640100bh02.html (accessed November 14, 2009).

Watts, Jonathan. "Now China Joins the Sexual Revolution." *Guardian*, December 28, 2003, 15.

Wei, Ran, Jinghua Huang, and Pei Zheng. "Use of Mobile Social Apps for Public Communication in China: Gratifications as Antecedents of Reposting Articles from WeChat Public Accounts." *Mobile Media & Communication* 6, no. 1 (2018): 108–26.

Weibo account of *People's Daily*. January 30, 2019. https://www.weibo.com/rmrb?is_all=1&stat_date=201902&page=21#feedtop (accessed May 11, 2019).

Weibo account of *People's Daily*. February 1, 2019. https://www.weibo.com/rmrb?is_all=1&stat_date=201902&page=21#feedtop (accessed May 11, 2019).

Weibo account of "Xianzuo butan yuwen." http://weibo.com/u/2157486862?is_all=1&stat_date=201107#feedtop (accessed August 3, 2018).

Weifeng fudong. "Weishenme shuo Yige chushen hanmen de zhuangyuan zhisi de zuozhe rangwo henbu shufu" [Why I feel uncomfortable about reading "The death of a star student from a humble background"]. Zhihu. January 30, 2019. https://zhuanlan.zhihu.com/p/56044119 (accessed May 11, 2019).

"Weixin gongzhong zhanghao chaoxi xianxiang pinfa: Weiquan kunnan" [Cases of plagiarism as frequent occurrences on WeChat's public accounts: Difficulty in defending writers' rights]. Sina. February 23, 2014. http://tech.sina.com.cn/i/2014-02-23/07309183934.shtml (accessed March 31, 2016).

"Wenzhou dongche xinwen fabuhui wanzheng ban" [A complete version of the Press Conference for Wenzhou High Speed Rail Crash]. July 24, 2011. https://www.youtube.com/watch?v=pNZypM9jr70 (accessed October 18, 2017).

"White Paper on Year One of China's Microblog Market" [Zhongguo Weibo yuannian shichang baipishu]. Sina. September 2010. https://www.slideshare.net/lxm19871231/ss-5245420 (accessed August 2, 2012).

Williams, Raymond. *The Long Revolution*. Harmondsworth: Penguin, 1965.

———.*Marxism and Literature*. Oxford: Oxford University Press, 1977.

———. "The Technology and the Society." In *Electronic Media and Technoculture*, edited by John Thornton Coldwell, 35–50. New Brunswick, NJ: Rutgers University Press, 2000.

Wines, Michael, and Sharon LaFraniere. "In Baring Facts of Train Crash, Blogs Erode China Censorship." *New York Times*, July 28, 2011. http://www.nytimes.com/2011/07/29/world/asia/29china.html (accessed June 5, 2018).

Wong, Annette. "Cyberself: Identity, Language, and Stylisation on the Internet." In *Cyberlines 2.0: Languages and Cultures of the Internet*, edited by Kerri-Lee Krause and Donna Gibbs, 259–86. Albert Park, Australia: James Nicholas, 2006.

Wong, John, and Seok Ling Nah. *China's Emerging New Economy: The Internet and E-Commerce*. Singapore: Singapore University Press, 2001.

Wu, Changchang (rewritten from Chinese by Yuezhi Zhao). "Micro-Blog and the Speech Act of China's Middle Class: The 7.23 Train Accident Case." *Javnost-the Public* 19, no. 2 (2012): 43–62.

Wu, Jing, and Guoqiang Yun. "From Modernization to Neoliberalism? How IT Opinion Leaders Imagine the Information Society." *International Communication Gazette* 80, no. 1 (2018): 7–29.

Wu, Mei. "China's Crackdowns on 'Internet Rumours' and 'Illegal' Internet Publicity Activities." In *Governing Society in Contemporary China*, edited by Lijun Yang and Wei Shan, 41–56. Hackensack, NJ: World Scientific, 2016.

Wu, Shiwen, and Stephanie Na Liu. "The Politics of Naming and Ranking New Media Events in China." *Communication and the Public* 3, no. 2 (2018): 81–96.

Wu, Xiaobo. *Cao Guowei: Shinian ershi ren* [Cao Guowei: Twenty people within ten years]. September 4, 2018. https://www.youtube.com/watch?v=RQabF1zmgOM (accessed August 2, 2019).

———. *Tengxun zhuan 1998–2016: Zhongguo hulianwang gongsi jinhualun* [A biography of Tencent 1998–2016: The evolving history of Chinese Internet companies]. Hangzhou: Zhejiang daxue chubanshe, 2017.

Wuyishanxia. November 17, 2010. http://www.tianya.cn/publicforum/content/funinfo/1/2348114.shtml (accessed August 2, 2012).

Xia, Yuhe. *Weibo kongjian de shengchan shijian: Lilun jiangou yu shizheng yanjiu* [Productive practices in the microblogosphere: Theoretical intervention and empirical studies]. Beijing: Zhongguo shehui kexue chubanshe, 2013.

Xiao, Hui. "Ziwo chuyan, gexing jingji: Jiedu quanqiuhua yujingxia de 'Chaoji Nüsheng' he 'Furong Jiejie' xianxiang [Performative self, individualized economy: Interpret *Super Girl* and "Furong Jiejie" phenomenon against the backdrop of globalization]. In *Quanqiuhua yu "zhongguoxing:" Dangdai wenhua de houzhimin jiedu* [Globalization and "Chineseness:" Postcolonial Readings of Contemporary Culture], edited by Geng Song, 213–32. Hong Kong: Hong Kong University Press, 2006.

Xiao, Shu. "Guanzhu jiushi liliang, weiguan gaibian zhongguo" [To pay attention is power; onlookers change China]. *Nanfang zhoumo* [Southern Weekend], January 14, 2010. http://www.infzm.com/content/40097 (accessed July 15, 2012).

Xin, Xin. "Xinwen pinglun: Mu Zimei shi wangluo yingsu?" [News comment: Is Mu Zimei an Internet poppy]. *Qingdao wanbao* [Qingdao Evening News], November 18, 2003. http://news.sina.com.cn/s/2003-11-18/10032158458.shtml (accessed June 24, 2012).

Xinhua News Agency. "Full Text of Jiang Zemin's Report at the 16th Party Congress." November 17, 2002. http://china.org.cn/english/2002/Nov/49107.htm#6 (accessed July 16, 2012).

Xinhuawang. "China Pushing to Build Internet Infrastructure for Belt and Road Initiatives." November 19, 2016. http://www.chinadaily.com.cn/business/3rdWuzhenWorldInternetConference/2016-11/19/content_27428755.htm (accessed July 4, 2018).

———. "Nearly 500 Public WeChat Accounts Punished over Plagiarism." April 29, 2015. http://www.chinadaily.com.cn/business/tech/2015-04/29/content_20574761.htm (accessed July 15, 2018).

———. "WeChat Publishes Report on Foreign Users' Behavior." May 17, 2017. http://www.chinadaily.com.cn/business/2017-05/17/content_29385933.htm (accessed July 18, 2018).

———. "Xinhua Insight: China Regulates Instant Messengers." August 7, 2014. http://news.xinhuanet.com/ english/indepth/2014-08/07/c_133540435.htm (accessed March 5, 2016).

Xinlangwang. "2012 nian xinlang zhengwu weibo baogao fabu" [A report on the official microblogging accounts at Sina in 2012]. http://news.sina.com.cn/z/2012sinazwwbbg/ (accessed June 5, 2018).

———. "Zhongguo weibo yuannian shichang baipishu" [White paper on the first year of microblogging in China]. September 2010. https://www.slideshare.net/lxm19871231/ss-5245420 (accessed June 5, 2018).

"Xinlang weibo fuzongcai Cao Zenghui: Xinlang Weibo erci jueqi de wuda yunying xinde" [Cao Zenghui, Vice President of Sina Weibo: Five key points on the revival of Sina Weibo]. August 8, 2017. http://t.cj.sina.com.cn/articles/view/5617169084/14ecf3 2bc019001apw (accessed May 27, 2018).

Xinlang weibo shuju zhongxin [Data center of Sina Weibo]. "2013 Xinlang meiti Weibo baogao" [Report on Sina Weibo in 2013]. January 1, 2014. http://data.weibo.com/ report/reportDetail?id=159 (accessed August 2, 2014).

Xu, Ben. "Meiguo ren kan budong Han Han" [Americans don't understand Han Han]. *Nanfang dushibao* [Southern Metropolis Daily], April 15, 2010. http://news.sina. com.cn/pl/2010-04-15/080620078218.shtml (accessed August 1, 2012).

Xu, Jian. *Media Events in Web 2.0 China: Interventions of Online Activism*. Chicago: Sussex Academic Press, 2016.

Xu, Jinglei. *Lao Xu de boke* [Lao Xu's blog]. http://blog.sina.com.cn/xujinglei (accessed July 15, 2012).

Xu, Xiaowen. "Internet Facilitated Civic Engagement in China's Context: A Case Study of the Internet Event of Wenzhou High-Speed Train Accident." Unpublished master's thesis, 2011, Columbia University.

Xue, Fang. "Chen Tong: Xinwen bi dapian geng xiyin ren" [Chen Tong: News is more attractive than blockbusters]. *Nanfang renwu zhoukan* [Southern People Weekly] 5 (2011): 79–81.

——. "Fang Xingdong: Yuanqu de boke jianghu" [Fang Xingdong: The world of the blog fades away]. *Mingren zhuanji* [Biographies of Famous People] 8 (2011): 57–60.

"Xue Manzi miandai weixiao huiguo; Cheng bugan xiang ruhe miandui furen" [Xue Manzi confessed with a smile, and claimed he could not imagine how to face his wife]. https://www.youtube.com/watch?v=aqSyUsiAzNc (accessed July 8, 2016).

Yan, Feng. "Xinmeiti zhong de qingchun xiezuo" [Write about youth on the Internet]. *Wenyi zhengming* [Debates on Arts] 7 (2010): 16–19.

Yang, Guobin. "Beiqing yu xixue: Wangluo shijian zhongde qinggan dongyuan" [Of sympathy and play: Emotional mobilization in online collective action]. *Chinese Journal of Communication and Society* 9 (2009): 39–66.

——. "Chinese Internet Literature and the Changing Field of Print Culture." In *From Woodblocks to the Internet: Chinese Publishing and Print Culture in Transition, circa 1800 to 2008*, edited by Cynthia Brokaw and Christopher A. Reed, 333–52. Leiden: Brill, 2012.

——. "Lightness, Wildness, and Ambivalence: China and New Media Studies." *New Media & Society* 14, no. 1 (2011): 170–79.

——. *The Power of the Internet in China: Citizen Activism Online*. New York: Columbia University Press, 2009.

——. "The Return of Ideology and the Future of Chinese Internet Policy." *Critical Studies in Media Communication* 31, no. 2 (2014): 109–13.

Yang, Guobin, and Min Jiang. "The Networked Practice of Online Political Satire in China: Between Ritual and Resistance." *International Communication Gazette* 77, no. 3 (2015): 215–31.

Yang, Guobin, and Shiwen Wu. "Remembering Disappeared Websites in China: Passion, Community, and Youth." *New Media & Society* 20, no. 6 (2018): 2107–24.

Yang, Lan. "Nüxing de jiefang" [Women's liberation]. *Yang Lan de boke* [Yang Lan's blog]. November 26, 2007. http://blog.sina.com.cn/s/blog_477614640100b0o.html (accessed July 15, 2012).

———. *Yang Lan de boke* [Yang Lan's blog]. December 12, 2005. http://blog.sina.com.cn/s/indexlist_1198920804_67.html (accessed July 12, 2011).

———. "Zhenxi ta, jiuxiang zhenxi ziji" [You treasure it, just like we treasure us]. *Yang Lan de boke* [Yang Lan's blog]. April 15, 2008. http://blog.sina.com.cn/s/blog_47761464010092mj.html (accessed December 29, 2009).

———. "Zhou Jielun de 'gangqin ke'" [The "piano lesson" of Zhou Jielun]. *Yang Lan de boke* [Yang Lan's blog]. December 20, 2005. http://blog.sina.com.cn/s/blog_4776146401000ove.html (accessed July 15, 2012).

Yang Lan's interview with the IESE Business School at the University of Nevada. February 27, 2008. http://www.iese.edu/Aplicaciones/News/videos/view.asp?id=1370&lang=en (accessed July 15, 2012).

Yang, Lijun. "Han Han and the Public." In *Restless China*, edited by Perry Link, Richard P. Madsen, and Paul G. Pickowicz, 109–28. Lanham: Rowman & Littlefield, 2013.

Yang, Peidong, Lijun Tang, and Xuan Wang. "*Diaosi* as Infrapolitics: Scatological Tropes, Identity-Making and Cultural Intimacy on China's Internet." *Media, Culture & Society* 37, no. 2 (2015): 197–214.

Yang, Qingxiang. "Dikang de 'jiamian'—guanyu Han Han de yixie sikao" [Fake resistance: Some thoughts on Han Han]. *Dongwu xueshu* [Soochow Academic] 3 (2011): 86–91.

Yang, Shen. "2011 nian disan jidu wangluo yuqing baogao" [The third quarter online public opinion report of 2011]. Quoted in Jia Lu, and Yunxi Qiu, "Microblogging and Social Change in China," *Asian Perspective* 37, no. 3 (2013): 305–31.

Yang, Xiaoming, Sunny Li Sun, and Ruby P. Lee. "Micro-Innovation Strategy: The Case of WeChat." *Asian Case Research Journal* 20, no. 2 (2016): 401–27.

Yao, Aibin. "'Dahua' wenhua yu qingnian yawenhua ziben—dui dahuaxiyou xianxiang de yixiang shehuixue kaocha" ["Dahua" culture and youth subcultural capital: A sociological investigation of the dahua phenomenon]. *Wenyi lilun yu piping* [Art Theory and Criticism] 3 (2005): 73–77.

Yardley, Jim. "Internet Sex Column Thrills, and Inflames, China." *New York Times*, November 30, 2003, 3.

Yau, Esther C. M. "Introduction: Hong Kong Cinema in a Borderless World." In *At Full Speed: Hong Kong Cinema in a Borderless World*, edited by Ching-Mei Esther Yau, 1–28. Minneapolis: University of Minnesota Press, 2001.

Yi, Lijing. "Liu Zhenwei: Yige meiyou zhangda de laorenjia" [Liu Zhenwei: A senior citizen who has yet to grow up]. *Nanfang renwu zhoukan* [Southern People Weekly] 24 (2010): 72–75.

Yu, Cheng, and Si Ma. "China Leads World in Internet Market." *China Daily*, September

15, 2017. http://www.chinadaily.com.cn/business/tech/2017-09/15/content_32019523. htm (accessed July 5, 2018).

Yu, Ge. "Mi Meng weishenme hui 'yongyuan aiguo?'" [How could Mi Meng "love the country" forever]. *China Digital Times*, July 15, 2016. https://chinadigitaltimes.net/chinese/2016/07/咪蒙为什么会永远爱国/ (accessed October 6, 2018).

Yu, Haiqing. "After the 'Streamed Bun': *E'gao* and Its Postsocialist Politics." *Chinese Literature Today* 5, no. 1 (2015): 55–64.

——. "Beyond Gatekeeping: J-blogging in China." *Journalism* 12, no. 4 (2011): 379–93.

——. *Media and Cultural Transformation in China*. Abingdon, UK: Routledge, 2009.

——. "Philanthropy on the Move: Mobile Communication and Neoliberal Citizenship in China." *Communication and the Public* 2, no. 1 (2017): 35–49.

Yu, Ran. "Micro Blogs Find Their Time Is Now." *China Daily*, August 1, 2011. http://usa.chinadaily.com.cn/china/2011-08/01/content_13020081.htm (accessed May 28, 2018).

Yunzhongyuyizi. "Qianwanli zhuixun, 80hou ta ta ta ta bude bushuo de gushi: Frjj yuyong xieshou Han Xiaoxie xianchang zhuanfang" [Stories that the post-80s generation feels the urge to tell: Live interviews with Han Xiaoxie, the designated writer of Furong Jiejie]. June 21, 2005. http://www.tianya.cn/new/Publicforum/Content.asp?strItem=funinfo&idArticle=50014 (accessed May 25, 2011).

Zeng, Jun. "Jingying yu caogen zhibian: Boke shijie zhong huayuquan de yanzhong shiheng—Dui Xinlang boke de fenxi" [Distinguishing elites and grassroots: The severe imbalance of discursive power in the blogosphere—an analysis of Sina's blog]. *Dongyue luncong* [Dongyue Tribune] 1 (2010): 134–37.

Zhang, Haichao. *Yanqiu weiwang: Zhongguo dianshi de shuzihua chanyehua shengcun* [King of the Eyeball: The digitalization and industrialization of Chinese television]. Beijing: Huaxia chubanshe, 2005.

Zhang, Han. "Sexy Diarist Nabbed for Corruption." *Global Times*, March 14, 2010. http://www.globaltimes.cn/content/512887.shtml (accessed June 14, 2020).

Zhang, Hongshu. "Dahua xiyou de chuanbo yu wangluo xiantan—Shouzhong fenxiang shidai 'jiji de guanzhong' de qianghua" [Distribution and online phenomenon revolving around *A Chinese Odyssey*: The reinforcement of "active audience" in the age of sharing]. *Shandong wenxue* [Shandong Literature] 12 (2007): 82–84.

Zhang, Huiyu. "'Furong Jiejie' de misi" [The myth of Furong Jiejie]. http://intermargins.net/intermargins/TCulturalWorkshop/culturestudy/mainland/04.htm (accessed August 2, 2012).

Zhang, Jia. "'Boke zhifu' Fang Xingdong" [Fang Xingdong: Godfather of blogs]. *Huanqiu renwu* [Global People] 17 (2006): 51.

Zhang, Jie. "Papi Jiang: Self-, Para-, Meta-, and We-Medias in China." Conference paper for the Association of Asian Studies Annual Convention, 2018.

Zhang, Junhua. "China's 'Government Online' and Attempts to Gain Technical Legitimacy." *Asien* 80 (2001): 93–115.

Zhang, Lijie. "Piaoliang de tuoer men" [Beautiful cheaters]. *Sanyue feng* [Wind in March] 1 (2006): 21.

Zhang, Lin. "When Platform Capitalism Meets Petty Capitalism in China: Alibaba and an Integrated Approach to Platformization." *International Journal of Communication* 14 (2020): 114–34.

Zhang, Lixian, ed. *Dahua xiyou baodian* [Bible of *A Chinese Odyssey*]. Beijing: Xiandai chubanshe, 2000.

———. "Dahua xiyou de chuanbo yu wangluo xiantan" [The dissemination and online phenomenon regarding *A Chinese Odyssey*]. In *Dahua xiyou baodian* [Bible of *A Chinese Odyssey*], edited by Lixian Zhang, 83. Beijing: Xiandai chubanshe, 2000.

Zhang, Ning. "Web-Based Backpacking Communities and Online Activism in China: Movement without Marching." *China Information* 28, no. 2 (2014): 276–96.

Zhang, Rui. "Top 10 Chinese Films in 2013." China.org.cn. January 31, 2014. http://www.china.org.cn/top10/2014-01/31/content_31351777_6.htm (accessed May 28, 2018).

Zhang, Weiyu. *The Internet and New Social Formation in China: Fandom Publics in the Making*. New York: Routledge, 2016.

Zhang, Xiaoling. *The Transformation of Political Communication in China: From Propaganda to Hegemony*. Hackensack, NJ: World Scientific, 2011.

Zhang, Yang. "Kuanrong, yeshi yizhong liliang" [Tolerance is also powerful]. December 6, 2015. https://weibo.com/p/1001603916969144372465 (accessed May 28, 2018).

———. "Nanhang CZ6101—Shengsijian, yige jizhe youhua xiang dui nimenshuo" [China Southern Airlines CZ6101: Between life and death, a journalist has something to say]. November 22, 2015. https://weibo.com/p/1001603911940245211603 (accessed June 5, 2018).

———. "999 jijiu—Yige bu xidu de jizhe xiang dui nimen shuode hua" [Beijing 999: What a journalist, with no drug addiction, wants to tell you]. November 25, 2015. https://weibo.com/p/1001603913025663937897 (accessed May 28, 2018).

———. "Shifeijian—Yige jizhe xiang zai dui nanhang shuode hua" [Between right and wrong—What a journalist wants to say to China Southern Airlines again]. November 24, 2015. https://weibo.com/p/1001603912641289580623?pids=Pl_Official_CardMixFeedv6__4&feed_filter=2&page=4 (accessed June 5, 2018).

———. "Wo dui 999 jijiu huiying de xiangguan shengming" [My response to statements of Beijing 999]. November 30, 2015. https://weibo.com/p/1001603915025453592352 (accessed May 28, 2018).

Zhang, Zhen. "Introduction: Bearing Witness: Chinese Urban Cinema in the Era of 'Transformation.'" In *The Urban Generation: Chinese Cinema and Society at the Turn of the Twenty-First Century*, edited by Zhen Zhang, 1–45. Durham, NC: Duke University Press, 2007.

Zhao, Changtian. "Cong Mengya zazhi wushi nian lishi tanqi" [Speaking of the fifty-year history of *Sprout*]. *Wenyi zhengming* [Literary Debate] 4 (2007): 149–52.

Zhao, Hanmo. "Yongbu dida de lieche" [The train that never arrives]. *Zhongguo qingnianbao* [China Youth Daily], July 27, 2011. http://zqb.cyol.com/html/2011-07/27/nw.D110000zgqnb_20110727_1-12.htm (accessed June 23, 2020).

Zhao, Jianzhou. "Zhao Jianzhou: Chuangzuo shouji" [Notes on creating the script]. In

Tsinghua yehua: Chuan baise lianyiqun de nühai [*Tsinghua yehua*: The girl in the white dress], edited by Ke Jiao, 217. Beijing: Xinshijie chubanshe, 2002.

Zhao, Liangchen. "Zhao Wei, Dai Liren ji Meiyou biedeai weishenme zao wangyou pubian qianze dizhi" [Why Zhao Wei, Leon Dai, and *No Other Love* are widely boycotted and denounced by netizens]. Weibo account of the Chinese Communist Youth League, July 6, 2016. https://media.weibo.cn/article?id=2309403994300454153797&s udaref=www.google.com&display=0&retcode=6102 (accessed June 5, 2018).

Zhao, Saipo. "Fensi, diaosi, yu hulianwang shangye moshi" [Fans, losers, and business models of the Internet]. *Wenhua zongheng* [Beijing Cultural Review], no. 10 (2013): 76–80.

Zhao, Siqiang. "'Caihua youxian qingnian' Yang Yueduo: Wo bu juede shisu de chenggong neng rangwo geng kuaile" [Yang Yueduo at "Talent Limited Youth:" I do not think I am happier by achieving the so-called material success]. *Ciwei gongshe*, October 25, 2018. http://www.sohu.com/a/271135060_141927 (accessed April 25, 2019).

Zhao, Yuezhi. *Media, Market, and Democracy in China: Between the Party Line and the Bottom Line.* Urbana: University of Illinois Press, 1998.

Zheng, Guoqing. *Meixue de weizhi: Wenxue yu dangdai zhongguo* [The aesthetic positions: Literature and contemporary China]. Fuzhou: Haixia wenyi chubanshe, 2016.

Zheng, Yongnian. "Zhongguo dongche shigu de zhidu fansi" [Reflection upon the systems revolving around the high-speed rail crash in China]. August 12, 2011. http://www.aisixiang.com/data/42911.html (accessed December 25, 2011).

Zhongguo gongan diyi boke [The first blog of Public Security in China]. http://blog.sina.com.cn/gongan (accessed April 30, 2018).

"Zhongguo shangye xitong hongshizihui jiang zanting huodong; Jieshou shenji diaocha" [The Red Cross Commerce of China will suspend activities temporarily; it will be audited]. *Zhongguo xinwenwang*, July 1, 2011. http://www.chinanews.com/sh/2011/07-01/3152107.shtml (accessed May 28, 2015).

Zhou, Kuanwei. "Nanhang 'huanbing wuren taixia feiji ziji pashang jiuhuche' dangshi chengke: Fangqi peichang" [The passenger of China Southern Airlines who got on the ambulance by himself gave up compensation]. *Pengpai xinwen* [The Paper], November 23, 2015. http://www.thepaper.cn/newsDetail_forward_1400288 (accessed May 28, 2018).

Zhou, Qiong. "Nü xieshou yong shenti xiezuo, Mu Zimei xingai riji fangwen liang jizeng" [A female writer adopts the style of body writing; Mu Zimei's sex diary has led to an increasing number of visits]. November 11, 2003. http://news.sina.com.cn/s/2003-11-11/02312109068.shtml (accessed June 24, 2012).

Zhou, Yongming. *Historicizing Online Politics: Telegraphy, the Internet, and Political Participation in China.* Stanford, CA: Stanford University Press, 2006.

Zhou, Zhixiong. "Huigu yu pingpan: Diyici de qinmi jiechu yu wangluo wenxue de fazhan" [An overview and criticism: *The First Intimate Contact* and the development of Internet literature]. *Shijie huawen wenxue luntan* [Forum for Chinese Literature of the World] 3 (2008): 76–80.

Zhu, Dake. *Liumang de shengyan: Dangdai zhongguo de liumang xushi* [The festival of hooligans: The hooligan narratives in contemporary China]. Beijing: Xinxing chubanshe, 2006.

Zhu, Ying. *Chinese Cinema during the Era of Reform: The Ingenuity of the System*. Westport, CT: Praeger, 2003.

Zittrain, Jonathan, and Benjamin Edelman. "Internet Filtering in China." *IEEE Computer Society* 7, no. 2 (2003): 70–77.

"Zuowei Mi Meng de xiaohao, ta shi zenme 'pang' qilaide?" [How did a subaccount of Mi Meng grow so fast]. *Yijieliaozimei*, April 27, 2018. https://kuaibao.qq.com/s/20180427A0FDP000?refer=spider (accessed May 11, 2018).

INDEX

Lightning Source UK Ltd.
Milton Keynes UK
UKHW010110061120
372905UK00001B/26

9 781503 613775